Women and Trade Unions

Sheila Lewenhak

Women and Trade Unions

An Outline History of Women in the British Trade Union Movement

Ernest Benn Limited
London and Tonbridge

First published 1977 by Ernest Benn Limited
25 New Street Square, Fleet Street, London, EC4A 3JA
& Sovereign Way, Tonbridge, Kent, TN9 1RW

Distributed in Canada by
The General Publishing Company Limited, Toronto
© Sheila Lewenhak 1977

Printed in Great Britain

I S B N 0 510-00007-X

*'Come to the Union sisters old and young, rich and poor,
if you love liberty, study to deserve it. Let us set our wits
to work, 'tis right against might. Children yet unborn must
have to remember, there was woman as well
as man in the Union'.*

P.A.S., a Straw-Bonnet Maker, in
The Pioneer, 3 May 1834

Contents

List of Illustrations   viii

Foreword and Acknowledgements   ix

1 The Beginnings   1

2 Women in the Trade Union and Labour
   Movement Before 1815   13

3 General Union and Segregation   29

4 Pegging Away or 'Pay Up, Lasses!'   45

5 The Women's Trade Union League   67

6 The Mass Organization of Women Begins   83

7 Margaret Irwin and the Scottish TUC   101

8 'Our Mary' and Sweated Labour   114

9 Unity is Strength   128

10 The First World War   144

11 The End of the Women's Trade Union League
    and the National Federation of Women
    Workers   164

12 The Fight to Hold Membership   177

13 The Depression, 1927-34   199

14 The Mid-'Thirties Turning-Point   221

15 Women Versus the Trade Union Establishment   244

16 Revaluation   271

    Bibliography   296

    Index   302

List of Illustrations

Women bell founders, York Minster, early fourteenth century 7
Page from 1795 Rule Book of Friendly Associated Cotton
    Spinners 19
Ellen Richey's trade union membership card, March 1833 33
Women trade unionists' poems, *Pioneer,* November 1833 34
'How to deal with Female Chartists', 1849 46-7
Blackburn Weavers' Banner, *c.* 1890 58
Women trade union leaders and supporters, nineteenth
    and early twentieth centuries 66
Strike Committee of the Dewsbury and Batley Heavy
    Woollen Weavers, 1875 87
Emblem of the Amalgamated Association of Card and
    Blowing Room Operatives, *c.* 1890 90
Woman chain-maker at work, 1910 123
Banner of the London Trousers-Makers' Society, early
    twentieth century 129
Women trade union leaders, 1906-21 150-1
Mary Macarthur addressing a crowd of unemployed,
    November 1918 165
Women trade unionists' pressure-group, 1924 190
Women's contingent of Hunger March, October 1932 201
Mill workers coming out on More Looms Strike, 1932 202
The First Two Trade Union Dames and other women
    officers 222
National Union of Women Teachers' Valentine, 1949 248
Public Service Unions' Equal Pay Demonstration, 1954 254
Some women trade union builders, post-1945 260-1
Woolworth's strike poster, 1961 273
National Union of Agricultural Workers' Tolpuddle
    Demonstration, early 1960s 274
Ford women machinists' strike for equal pay for work
    of equal value, 1968 284

Foreword

There has been so very little written about women's trade unionism, in fact only one major work all told, that the contents of this book may come as something of a shock to many readers. Even economic and social historians and specialist Labour historians have tended to treat women as 'also-rans' when dealing with labour struggles and organization.

The book is intended not only as a contribution to filling this gap, but also for general readers with an interest in the history of women and their struggles for equality. But with a warning: Abandon many of your preconceived ideas. People coming to the subject with open minds are more likely to get something out of the book than those with rigid beliefs in a course of history disseminated not only by historians, but also by press, radio, and television. For the news media what mattered was news. Decisions on what to print or to show were subjective and highly selective according to what owners and editors thought would win readers or spectators. Consequently many aspects of women's trade union history have received scant attention. For instance, after the Second World War, an immense struggle was carried on by women in the unions which was virtually ignored by the mass media until it erupted in 1968 and became a part of Women's Lib.

The book is not a catalogue of details about each and every women's union or union of which they were members. Rather it seeks to show why trade unionism has been less developed among women than men. It traces the fluctuations in the strength of women's trade unionism and the reasons for these.

Readers should be warned that statistics relating to numbers employed cannot be regarded as absolutely accurate, whatever the source, and are merely some guide as to how both numbers employed and numbers in unions rose and fell. The Census of Occupations includes employers, a small category among women, self-employed part-time workers like charladies, and family workers mainly in shops, written off since 1964 as unorganizable. On these counts, the Trades Union Congress prefers government statistics. These, however, tended to be underestimates. For example, between the wars they excluded those not covered by national unemployment insurance schemes. As a result until 1948 large categories of workers were ignored, the main group of women being private, indoor domestic servants. Since then, married women employees on part-time work have not necessarily been included. Therefore statistics should not be taken too literally, but rather regarded as indications of the ebb and flow of the numbers in trades and in unions.

With so vast a subject, no more than an outline could be attempted in an ordinary-sized book. The author freely and gratefully acknowledges her debts to many historians, both medievalists and those concerned with modern history. The debt lessens from Chapter 2 onwards.

Some longstanding assumptions on the history of women in trade unions have been called into question, notably that women played practically no part in trade union organization before the middle-class Women's Trade Union League began to encourage them in the mid-1870s: that women showed little initiative in setting up unions both when the League was in its heyday and earlier: and that the presence of women in an occupation automatically increased the difficulties of organization.

In spite of growing interest on the part of Labour historians there is a great deal of material as yet unconsidered in union branch offices and in local libraries. All those who want to know more, are urged to go and look for themselves. However, I hope that this outline may be accepted as a modest tribute to the women and men trade unionists who actually lived and created these events.

I should like to thank many of those living in present times for making this book possible, in particular, Miss Ethel Chipchase, MBE, Secretary of the TUC Women's Advisory Committee; Mr T.W. Cynog Jones, OBE and the staff that worked with him at the Research Department of the Union of Shop, Distributive, and Allied Workers in Malet Street in London, the TUC Library, and Scottish TUC Research Department; and other members of unions too numerous to mention. Thanks are also due to the Reference Libraries of Birmingham, Manchester, Leeds, Nottingham, the Mitchell Library in Glasgow, the British Museum, the University of London, the Ministry of Labour (as it then was) Statistical Department, the Office of Wages Councils, the Northern Ireland Government Agency in London, and to many Local History Librarians throughout the length and breadth of the country. In the early stages of the research which gave rise to the book, the University of London Research Department and the Houblon-Norman Fund gave grants towards the expense of travelling for which I am grateful. I should also like to thank Professor A. H. John of the Economic History Department of the London School of Economics for his patient encouragement of that part of the work which formed a Ph.D thesis; Dr P. S. Bagwell of the Society for the Study of Labour History; Mrs Rose Pockney of the Rachel Macmillan College of Education; and Miss Ethel Chipchase for reading drafts; but most of all my husband, H.K. Lewenhak, B.Comm., almost a lifelong member of the Association of Cine and Television Technicians, whose generosity and patience, though sorely tried over many years, never failed.

I am most grateful to various authors and copyright-holders, newspapers and journals, trade unions and other institutions for putting material at my disposal. All sources are given in the Notes and Bibliography. I am grateful to the families of the late Arthur Smith and Mary Agnes Hamilton for their help.

Glasgow
November 1976   S.L.

Acknowledgements for Illustrations
(numbers refer to text pages)

The Dean and Chapter, York Minster (photo D. O'Connor): 7; Manchester Public Libraries: 19; Scottish Labour History Society (photo Robert Nicholson): 33; Trustees of the British Museum (photo J.R. Freeman): 34; *Punch:* 46-7; Borough of Blackburn, Museums and Art Galleries: 58; Mr Harold Goldman (*Illustrated Mail,* 1 April 1905): 66(1); Radio Times Hulton Picture Library: 66(3), 66(4), 254; Labour Party Library: 66(5), 66(7), 150(1), 151(6), 222(2), 222(3), 222(4), 222(6); George Outram and Co. Ltd: 66(6); Mr Ben Turner's family and National Union of Dyers, Bleachers and Textile Workers: 87; Amalgamated Textile Workers' Union, NUTAW Division (photo R.B. Fleming): 90; the *Graphic* (3 September 1910): 123; National Union of Tailors and Garment Workers (photo R.B. Fleming): 129; 260(7); Irish Transport and General Workers Union: 150(2), 150(3); R.M. Fox, *Louie Bennett: her Life and Times* (photo Lafayette, Dublin): 151(4); Union of Shop, Distributive and Allied Workers: 151(5), 273; General and Municipal Workers' Union: 151(7), 151(8), 165; TUC: 190, 202, 222(1); Fox Photos Ltd: 201; Associated Newspapers Ltd: 222(5); National Union of Women Teachers (photo Bryan and Shears): 248; National Union of Bank Employees: 260(1); Bolton and District Weavers' and Winders' Association: 260(2), 260(3); Tobacco Workers' Union: 260(4); Amalgamated Engineering Union: 261(5); Civil Service Union: 261(6); Union of Jute, Flax and Kindred Textile Operatives (photo *Dundee Courier):* 261(8); Mrs Liddell: 261(9); Scottish TUC: 261(10); Agricultural Workers' Union (photo Evan Jones): 274; *Morning Star:* 284

WOMEN DISCUSS PAY AND TAX

Co-operative News
30 March 1973

FEMININE PLATFORM SPARED

Daily Telegraph
3 September 1974

WOMEN'S WORK-IN GAINING STRENGTH

Morning Star
27 April 1972

HOW THE SHOP FLOOR HAS BETRAYED WOMEN

Sunday Times
28 November 1972

THREAT OF A PETTICOAT REVOLT

The Times
17 June 1968

1   The Beginnings

This random selection of newspaper headlines in the late 1960s and 1970s on topics of work and trade union organization depends for catching the reader's eye neither on work nor trade union organization, but on references to the female sex. It seems strange that the mass media still regard women workers and trade unionists as news, when they have worked and organized for as long as men.

Women workers did not become important to Britain's economy because of Women's Lib, or the earlier Women's Emancipation movement; nor because of two world wars, although in both the range of work open to them widened. Nor were they brought into the labour force and the unions by the growth of the factory system and coalmining. They were there before unions existed. They shared in labour history from its earliest beginnings. The strangeness, the exoticism almost, of the idea of women as part of the labour movement and as trade unionists is due to their loss of standing as persons before the law.

The misapprehension that women have only recently and suddenly come into the labour force arose largely because so much historical writing has been by and about the upper and middle classes. Attention was first concentrated on aristocratic ladies, then on middle-class women aspiring to emulate them. In order to do so, they stopped productive and remunerative work.

For the mass of the female population, however, as for the mass of men, life meant work. Women's lower status as citizens left them with a low status as workers and held back their trade union organization. But throughout British history they have, to some extent, been involved in organizations of workpeople and played some part in the labour and trade union movement.

In early Anglo-Saxon times, a definite economic value was placed on everyone, male or female, and stated in laws laying down fines to be paid by those who injured or murdered others. The economic value placed on a wife was also stated in laws on divorce and the apportionment of family property on the death of a husband or in case of a divorce. The Jutish King Aethelbert of Kent, who died in AD 616, promulgated the earliest English law of this sort; 'If a woman bears a living child she shall have half the goods left by her husband if he dies first'. If she wanted to leave him and took her children with her, she was entitled to 'half the goods'. But if the husband kept the children, she only had 'a share of the goods equal to a child's'.[1]

King Ine of Wessex in the 690s issued a similar series of laws[2] and two hundred years later a legal treatise, 'Concerning the Marriage of a Woman', gave a similar customary value.[3] The amount to which a wife was entitled varied; the principle did not.

Most people in Anglo-Saxon England, men and women alike, worked in the country growing food and rearing poultry and animals. Country women's wages were explicitly stated in an anonymous Estate Book written about AD 1000, two generations before the Norman Conquest, *The Rights and Duties of All Persons*. The wages paid a specialist cheese-maker who was always a woman consisted of a hundred cheeses and all the buttermilk except a share paid to the herdsman. A non-specialist unfree woman who did general work was paid a basic 8lb. of corn plus a sheep in winter or 3*d*., whey in summer or 1*d*., and some beans yearly during Lent.[4]

After the Norman Conquest, feudal law was much more sharply defined and applied more strictly. Women were relegated to an inferior status. Early in the thirteenth century, Henry de Bracton, a famous lawyer who produced the definitive statement of feudal law, stated flatly in his law book: 'Women differ from men in many respects for their condition is inferior to that of men'.[5] Another great medieval law book, *The Decretum* by Gratian, gives a husband absolute rights over all those in his household, including his wife. But women had not lost all legal rights. While inheritance went by prior right to men, women retained the right to inherit property. Once married, however, it passed to their husbands.

Not so often as men, women are therefore to be found as landlords and tenants in the web of feudal tenures that enmeshed the whole country. They paid the same rents in cash, in kind, or in work as men. They might be high-ranking like Robert de Hastings's daughter, Alice, who in 1278 had the Abbot of Biddlesdon as one of her tenants on her estates in Thornborough.[6] Or they might be peasants like Isabel Pecoc, who in 1306-07 paid 2*s*. 6*d*. at each Michaelmas and Martinmas for her smallholding of strips in the common fields on the Royal Manor of Havering in Essex.[7]

Many of the population, women and men, were unfree bondservants. Among them legal differences and rights of inheritance between the sexes mattered less than the similarities of their servile status and their poverty. Bartholomew Anglicus (fl. 1250-70) wrote in his *De Proprietatibus Rerum* (printed about 1472) a description of the life of a servant woman. She was 'bought and sold like a beast', fed on 'gross meat and simple', placed under the authority of the wife in the household where she served, and beaten with rods. She was kept in subjection not merely by strict compulsion, but also by 'divers and contrary charges' so that she was trapped into displeasing someone or other. She toiled 'among wretchedness and woe'.[8]

We see the reality in prosecutions in manorial courts. On 12 December 1358, at the Court of the Manor of Bradford, Agnes Childyonge, a bondwoman, was fined 12d. for having had an illegitimate child. Isabel Childyong and Alice Gepson were fined for marrying free men which enabled them to escape from their bondage.[9]

But by the mid-fourteenth century feudalism was on the wane. The whole of west Europe was plunged into turmoil caused by wave after wave of bubonic plague, the Black Death. Over the next fifty years population in England dropped by between a third and a half. This huge death toll created an enormous labour shortage. Men and women in bondage and serfdom took the opportunity to flee from the estates to which they were tied, to seek work that would give them the status of free men and women. At first they were often brought back. Landlords could not run their estates without them. Alice Childyong along with Alice daughter of John atte Yate (in Selby) and four men were sentenced at that same court in Bradford on 12 December 1358 to fines for running away.[10]

Governments recognized women as a part of the servile labour force intent on finding freedom, even if succeeding generations and historians have overlooked the fact. In reaction to the first bout of plague in 1348, Edward III's Ordinance of Labourers in the following year declared:

> ... we have thought fit to ordain that every man *and woman* of our realm of England, of whatsoever condition, free or servile, able-bodied and under the age of sixty years, not living by trade nor exercising a certain craft, nor having of his own whereof he (*or she*) shall be able to live, shall be bound to serve him who shall require him ... and if such a man *or woman* so required to serve, refuse to do so ... he shall be taken forthwith ... and sent to the nearest gaol, there to stay in strait keeping until he find security to serve in the form aforesaid ... [11]

The Ordinance failed. Encouraged by their success in flouting the government, in 1381 country people and urban artisans took part in the popular uprising, the Peasants' Revolt. The chief slogan of the rebels also acknowledged women as workers:

> When Adam delved and Eve span,
> Who was then the gentleman? [or lady?]

The revolt was quelled. But the flight of servile peasants from landlords went on. In 1388 Richard II's Statute of Labourers decreed 'that no servant or labourer, be it man or woman' could leave his or her district at the end of a term of employment 'to serve or dwell elsewhere'.[12]

The government laid down national wage rates for agricultural workers in the 1388 Statute. Women labourers and dairymaids were to receive 6s. a year; all the rest—carters, shepherds, oxherds, cowherds, ploughmen—were to receive more. The idea of a special lower 'woman's wage' was established.

It was reaffirmed sixty years later in one of Henry VI's parliaments. Although wage rates in general had risen, the Commons proposed in a Bill of 1444-45 that a woman farm servant, even a skilled dairymaid, should have 10s. a year 'and price of clothing 4s. with meat and drink'. A 'common servant of husbandry', the lowest of the categories of men, by contrast, was to be paid 15s. with clothing worth 40d. or 3s. 4d. Specialist men workers, carters and shepherds, were to have 20s. and clothing worth 4s. with meat and drink. Only children under fourteen years, the Commons thought, should be paid less than women—6s. a year and clothing to the value of 3s. They also suggested that specialist harvest workers paid by the day, that is, mowers, reapers, and carters, should receive higher pay than women and other non-specialist labourers. The women were to have the same as day labourers.[13]

More than five centuries later, in the early 1970s, semi-skilled women in engineering trades were similarly paid less than un-skilled labourers. If anything, during those five hundred years, their economic status had declined.

The 1388 Statute of Labourers referred to people working for 'terms'. Therefore they were no longer tied to one landlord in perpetuity. The Commons in 1445 dealing with this arrangement hoped for some way of making farm servants give due notice of their intention to leave at the end of their terms of employment, instead of going off suddenly and leaving their employers in the lurch. The system of hiring men and women to work on farms for fixed terms was in force by the fifteenth century. It persisted in parts of Britain well into the present century. Hirings took place at Michaelmas in October and at Martinmas in May, these occasions being known as 'hiring fairs'. The system was later applied to non-agricultural work.

Those who ran away tried to make for towns where there was

more freedom. There they could beg, or they might find better conditions of service, and with the drastic and increasing labour shortage, they might raise their earnings. The government decrees forbade urban artisans and craft workers to take more than the existing rates and imposed fines on employees and employers alike who disobeyed. The disobedient workers included women as well as men. In 1351 at the town of Layer de la Hay fines for taking excessive wages were imposed, including the following:

From Alice Smyth for the same	6*d*.
From John Smart for the same	12*d*.
From Margaret Everard for the same	12*d*.
From Alice Gerlond for the same	12*d*.
From Alice Weper for the same	6*d*.
From Agnes Heyward for the same	12*d*.
From John Craw for the same	6*d*
From Christina Bostis for the same	6*d*.[14]

Wages of craft workers in towns, however, were not the subject of detailed legislation. It was left to Justices of the Peace and customers to see that they were reasonable.

From the twelfth century onwards, craft workers were forming gilds. Their purpose was to provide social security, to wrest concessions from feudal lords of towns to enable them to escape from their servile status. Craft gilds also limited competition, and kept up prices for their wares and services by price-fixing and by restricting the number of entrants into their trades.

Manufacture and trade were not specialized separate occupations. A man or woman craft worker sold what he or she made on a market stall or direct from the workroom. Those who wanted the right to trade had first to become freemen or freewomen of their city or town. Rolls of free persons for the chief towns include names of women traders, like the 1318 roll from the borough of Leicester or the roll of 1438-39 for the borough of York. Sometimes the names show the kinds of trades practised, like Matilda le Lorimer (a maker of small metal objects for horseriding such as bits and spurs); Christiana le Mustarder (mustard-maker); Agnes the Breuster (brewer) in Leicester;[15] or Agnes Acclom and Alicia Alison, both semesters (seamstresses), of York.[16]

The gild regulations encompass women as well as men, like the early fifteenth-century Ordinances of the York woollen-weavers' and capmakers' gilds or the Bristol dyers which specified that women, like men, should be fined for bad workmanship.[17] The 1490 Ordinances of the York Ironmongers' gild forbade anyone working in that artifice, 'whether it be man or woman', to open their shops and sell goods on Sundays.[18] In 1541-42, the Tanners' Gild of Gloucester enacted

> that no brother or *sister* of the said craft do entice or procure any Servant of any brother or sister of the said fraternity and craft by means whereof he doth depart from their Service in pain of forfeiture of 5s. ...[19]

There is scarcely a gild occupation in the later Middle Ages whose regulations do not make clear that somewhere women as well as men were members of the craft or mistery. Women were barber-surgeons, bell-founders, tanners, or ironmongers as well as workers in crafts more conventionally associated with their sex such as cooking, fishmongering, glove-making, and the various cloth-making trades. Women engaged in the crafts of the silk industry were given the special privilege of government encouragement and protection. An Act of Henry VI's reign in 1455, for example, excluded foreign imports in order to help them.[20]

One reason women craft workers have been overlooked is that the legal inferiority of women caused writers of gild documents to use masculine nouns and pronouns for both sexes. A merely cursory glance therefore may not reveal that women were members, and generally on the same footing as men.

Women's status in gilds varied, just like that of men. There were women right at the top of their trades, like Christiana who in 1303-04 was a Bell-founder of Gloucester.[21] Or Mariona Kent who was a member of the 'commonaltie' or council of the York Merchant Adventurers' gild in 1474-75.[22] There was little in common between such able and independent women and the uncontrolled, wild women wool-packers of Southampton, for instance. So unruly were they that the mayor, Thomas Dymok, together with his council compulsorily formed them into an all-female gild in 1503 and made them abide by the rules.[23]

The gulf made by wealth and upbringing still produced entirely different sets of priorities in the minds of different categories of women workers in the mid-twentieth century.

Women's work, even when it constituted the primary trade which supported all the rest of a craft, was sometimes relegated to a lower status. Like men, they were sometimes employees of fellow-workers, of journeymen, as in the case of the Coventry capmakers in 1520 who employed women spinners and knitters.[24] A similar subcontracting system grew up in coal mines. In the nineteenth century it appeared in mule-spinning. In the twentieth century it continued in the small metal and jewellery trades in Sheffield and in the Savile Row tailoring workshops. There tailors employed

Women bell founders, York Minster, early fourteenth century

women assistants, both being members of the same trade union.

The employment of women in spinning fetched low pay first because almost all women could spin. Secondly it was an occupation which had been carried on in people's homes for centuries. The women spinners and knitters employed by the Coventry journeymen capmakers, for example, worked in their own homes, helping to make ends meet, just as wives and mothers still do today in a widening range of occupations.

Women and children as well as men and boys had paid labour rent and rent in kind to the manor as part of the price of the family smallholding. So in urban homes, as well as in the rural cottage, all the members of a family contributed to their own maintenance by working for payment of some kind as soon as they were able to do so. Sometimes they all worked in a family business; sometimes they were a self-contained unit of production, most usually in manufacturing cloth but also in shoemaking, capmaking, glove-making, and tailoring. In cloth-making, merchants' agents gave out raw wool on credit and collected and paid for the spun yarn. Similarly they distributed the yarn to weavers and collected cloth. It became the practice to hire out looms to weavers. Often a family did both spinning and weaving. Either way they became virtually employees of the merchants, or clothiers as they were called. At the same time, as well as a special low 'woman's wage', the tradition of a 'family wage' was established, a merchant or his agent paying the head of the household for the finished article, instead of each member of the family separately for their work in helping to produce it. In this way the law giving a husband a right to his wife's property, in this case her earnings, began to affect working people.

The subjection of women within the family and the lower cash value placed on their work, irrespective of the degree of skill or strength needed to perform it, was a boon to merchant and customer alike. The 'sweated' home-worker was already a feature of the late fourteenth century. Women's cheap labour enabled merchants to keep down prices for cloth especially in overseas markets, and so to undercut competitors.

A sort of running warfare went on. Spinners and weavers had many ways of trying to extract from their merchant customers more than their work was officially worth. The merchants on their side tried to pay less than the real value of the articles and so to cheat the working people of some of their earnings. Many efforts were made to regularize the trade. But the advantage was on the employers' side. For example, the burgesses who ran the City of London included many wealthy woollen-cloth merchants. In 1518, they enacted that a spinner who wilfully produced faulty yarn was to be brought before the alderman of her parish ward and sentenced to punishment.[25]

From the 1420s, two more forces were increasingly holding down earnings of both men and women. The population gradually grew as the incidence of plague abated. At the same time landowners deliberately destroyed villages and turned people out of their holdings in order to convert arable into sheep-grazing land. They wanted to profit from the great boom in wool and woollen cloth that developed.

The men, women, and children turned off the land were destitute. What began in the favourable conditions of labour shortage in the mid-fourteenth century as a voluntary flight of people of servile status from the land, turned into an involuntary abandonment of homes and countryside. People came to towns in search of work or to beg. Competition for available work increased and operated in favour of buyers instead of sellers of labour.

By the late fifteenth century the increasing number of women becoming prostitutes was worrying the City of London Council. At the same time, from the 1490s, the growing numbers of middle-class households were creating a growing demand for domestic servants. The Council tried to solve both problems by directing surplus women and girls to this work. An order of 1492 enacted

> that no single woman, being of good health and mighty in body [able] to labour from the age of 12 years, take nor keep from henceforth house or chambers by themselves ... but that they go to service till they be married ... [26]

The first conviction for non-compliance was to be punished with a fine, the second by prison. These girls and women would be kept in gaol until the City authorities had assurance that they would work as domestic servants. Anyone who tried to rescue them was also punished.

Town authorities were gradually forced to accept responsibility for the poor and destitute in their own parishes. We see from lists of cases that many of the poor and destitute were women and girls who worked in their own homes. For example, in a census of the Ward of St Stephen in Norwich in 1570 they included seamstresses like Agnes Nicholes, a forty-year-old widow, or An Bucke, in addition a teacher with two children of her own, aged nine and five years, 'that work lace'.[27] But above all these poor women, and often their children too, were spinners of white woollen warp thread. The prevalence of poverty among them was probably not altogether unconnected with the position of Norwich as the centre of the East Anglian textile trade. They provided a cheap product for the local weaving manufacturers.

Not all were local people. Many who had wandered from their home parishes were classed as vagrants, whipped, put in the stocks, and dispatched back to their places of origin.

In a 'Kalendar of all the Vagabonds Rogues and mighty valiant beggars' taken by the first watch on the night of 20 August 1571 in the Bassetlaw district of the town of Southcley in Nottinghamshire, for instance, women outnumbered men. There Johane Holmes, 'a valiant beggar', Isabel Cotton, Anne and John Draper, Agnes Gilbert, 'a mighty strong beggar', Millicent Walker, and Margaret Ridge with Reignold her eight-year-old son were examined, punished, and sent back to the places where they had been born. Some had come a fair distance, the Drapers from Bolton in Lancashire and Millicent Walker from Ilderne in Cumberland.[28]

Fortunes were being made in sheep-farming and the trade in wool and woollen cloth, but the economy was not healthy since, increasingly, it turned upon the export of one article, unfinished, white woollen cloth, to one major market, the Netherlands, Merchants grew rich, for until the 1540s cloth exports were booming. Some of the merchant employers went the length of setting up factories in which all the processes of cloth-making were carried out, by women and men, boys and girls. But because the foreign trade was unsteady, the livelihood of those women, men, and children who made the cloth, still mainly in their own homes, was insecure. When the Netherlands market was shut to English woollens in 1525 and again in 1528, there was unemployment followed by uprisings among the woollen-workers at home.

The capitalist clothiers, as they were called, combined together to pay one uniform rate to the manufacturing tradespeople who therefore could not take advantage of prosperity to raise their earnings. In their turn the workpeople combined together to present petitions to Parliament, asking for help against the clothiers. They asked in vain. The cloth manufacturing and exporting interests were well represented and increasingly powerful in the Commons. In this way, the country's economy was coming under the control of those who had capital, as well as those whose wealth was in land.

In the manufacturing trade in woollens, therefore, women as well as men were co-operating in protests and demonstrations aimed at maintaining themselves in work and protecting their standards of pay.

By the second half of the sixteenth century, the social and employment patterns were set for the next century and a half. The Weavers' Act of 1555 was intended to reserve the cloth-making trades for townsfolk and to reduce competition from the country districts where labour was cheaper. But it did not apply to large areas of the country, nor did it stop the operations of the big capitalist clothiers who lived in the towns, although the people who worked for them dwelt in the rural areas. The famous Statute of Artificers of 1563, four years after Queen Elizabeth I was crowned, and the Poor Laws were part of the series of edicts intended to compel men and women who were propertyless and who were not bred to a trade to undertake unpopular work like domestic service for which there was a big demand.

The tide of ideas set more strongly against women. The teachings of St Paul, which had justified the lower status of women in Roman Catholic feudal England, were similarly used by the Protestant ideologists among the rising capitalist class. The feudal view had been founded upon such Pauline pronouncements as: 'I suffer not a woman to teach, nor to usurp authority over the man, but to be in silence' or 'Wives submit yourselves unto your husbands, as it is fit in the Lord'.[29] John Knox the Calvinist argued in *The First Blast of the Trumpet against the Monstrous Regiment of Women* (1558) that God had made women inferior first because of Eve's rebellion in the Garden of Eden when she ate the apple of Knowledge and persuaded Adam to do the same; and secondly because she was created from Adam's rib, so that

> man was not created for the cause of woman, but woman for the cause of man, and therefore ought the woman to have a power upon her head.

Protestantism also emphasized individual effort and self-help as a means of improving one's personal fortunes and avoiding destitution. It strengthened the view that the propertyless were not merely unfortunate, but also wicked, and therefore sanctified the harsh treatment of paupers.

By the sixteenth century, all those features of the lives of working women condemned by nineteenth- and twentieth-century philanthropists, social workers, and supporters of women's emancipation, were established—the lesser value placed on 'woman's work', the 'woman's wage', the 'family wage', and 'sweating'. In the chief traditional women's occupations—farm work, domestic service, making textiles and clothes—they were now more and more employed as wage labourers. At the same time, some women were lucky enough to learn a trade and to gain membership of the organized craft gilds. In these they learned the need for self-discipline, co-operation, the joint financing of social security funds, and banding together to keep up the prices paid for their products.

Because of competition for work, and because increasing amounts of capital were needed to maintain independent businesses, they were driven into the ranks of employees. There they had to bargain with employers for their earnings. Craftswomen, like craftsmen, took with them into such negotiations the experience and traditions of their gilds. In these circumstances, in the second half of the seventeenth century, the British Trade Union movement began to evolve.

Notes

1 D. Stenton, *English Women in History,* 9: D. Whitelock, *Beginnings of English Society,* 150-2.
2 Stenton, op. cit., 11.
3 Whitelock, op. cit., 152.
4 Bland, Brown and Tawney, *English Economic History, Select Documents,* 7-8.
5 Bracton, *On the Laws and Customs of England,* vol. II, 31.
6 Bland, Brown and Tawney, op. cit., 28.
7 ibid., 60.
8 G. G. Coulton, *The Medieval Village,* 109, quoting Bartholomew Anglicus.
9 Bland, Brown and Tawney, op. cit., 71.
10 ibid., 73.
11 ibid., 164-5. Author's italics.
12 ibid., 172.
13 ibid., 177-8.
14 ibid., 169. Author's italics. Layer de la Hay is near Colchester, Essex.
15 M. Bateson, ed., *Records of the Borough of Leicester,* vol. I, 310-11.
16 F. Collins, ed., *Freemen of York,* Surtees Soc., vol. 96, 154-5.
17 Bland, Brown and Tawney, op. cit., 142.
18 M. Sellers, ed., *York Memorandum Book,* Surtees Soc., vol. 120, 201 (see also vol. 124).
19 *Tanners' Guild (4), Ordinances of the Guild,* 1541/2, Gloucester City Lib. Author's italics.
20 I. Pinchbeck, *Women Workers and the Industrial Revolution, 1750-1850,* 169, note 5.
21 *Stevenson's Gloucester Calendar,* 299/773.
22 M. Sellers, ed., *York Merchant Adventurers,* Surtees Soc., vol. 129, 64.
23 Southampton City Archives, *2nd Book of Remembrance,* SC/1/4,f. 26v-28r.
24 Tawney and Power, ed., *Tudor Economic Documents,* vol. I, 108.
25 A. H. Thomas, ed., *Calendar of Early Mayor's Court Rolls,* 658, para. 103.
26 ibid., 542, para. 77.
27 Tawney and Power, ed., *Tudor Economic Documents,* vol. II, 313-16.
28 ibid., 326-8.
29 St Paul, *Letter to the Ephesians,* ch. 4, v.21: *1st Letter to the Corinthians,* ch. 11, v.2: *1st Letter to Timothy,* ch. 2, v.8. St Paul, however, insisted that husbands should love their wives and treat them well. Women should not speak at meetings of Christian congregations, but they could be members.

2 Women in the Trade Union and Labour Movement before 1815

Women's part in the early history of trade union organization is shrouded in the same linguistic ambiguities as their part in craft gilds; masculine nouns and pronouns refer to women. In the case of seventeenth-century journey*men*'s combinations, it must be remembered that some of the journeymen were journey*women*. This became quite clear in connection with immigrant Huguenot silkworkers who settled in Spitalfields in London late in that century. The conditions of their employment were regulated by Act of Parliament in 1773 and again in 1792, reference only being made to 'journeymen'. But women weavers were paid the same rates as men and took on apprentices. Suddenly in 1811, 'a master refused to pay a journeywoman her price'. This caused a trial during which the question was raised of whether the term 'journeymen' included women.[1] It eventually led to the third Spitalfields Act in 1811 which definitely extended the earlier two Acts to women. Women were also taken on as apprentices and learners in the lace and woollen trades and in goldsmithying and gilding and so became journeywomen.

The evidence of women working in the skilled as well as the less skilled branches of textiles abounds along with evidence of industrial unrest and of workers' organization. The West of England weaving trade in the shires of Devon, Somerset, Gloucester, and Worcester was to a considerable extent in the hands of women in the seventeenth and eighteenth centuries. They were by no means confined to spinning. Women worked as handloom-weavers in the North and north-west of England and Scotland as well as in East Anglia in Norwich and Colchester. By the time the Civil War broke out, some London merchants and cloth-dealers operating in the West Country and East Anglia each employed on the 'putting-out system' up to a thousand spinners and weavers.[2]

With women forming so large a part of the labour force in woollen and worsted manufacture, inevitably some of them participated in industrial protests. Contemporary accounts seldom mention 'men', but speak instead of 'people', or of those working in particular trades, like 'spinners' or 'weavers'. Reports of processions and disorders must be considered with the presence of women in mind. Demonstrations of this sort became endemic from the early seventeenth century because of the expansion of overseas trade and the repercussions of its continuing uncertainties and fluctuations on the labour force. Interruptions in marketing, or overstocking and gluts, caused riots similar to those in the 1520s. There were violent protests, for instance, in Gloucestershire in 1615 because unemployment brought woollen-workers almost to starvation. In 1622 groups went to the houses of the better-off to demand money and seize provisions. There were minor uprisings in the south-west again between 1628 and 1631.[3]

When the country came to Civil War, Norwich, the East Anglian woollen centre, was a Parliamentary town. The maids of Norwich raised subscriptions sufficient to provide the eleventh troop of horse for Cromwell's Eastern Association which was accordingly named 'The Maiden Troop'. But the Norwich woollen-workers found their capitalist masters unchanged by the Commonwealth. In 1655 they put out a broadside accusing them of beating down their wages. Part of the heading ran:

> Combers, Weavers and Spinners for little gains,
> Doth Earn their Money by taking of hard pains.[4]

On the other hand, another broadside in 1666 depicting women spinners and throwsters among the working people, praised the woollen and worsted trades for providing work for everyone.[5]

During the seventeenth century, knowing that wages would be subsidized by the Poor Relief system, JPs in the clothing districts of Suffolk, for example, were in the habit of fixing rates of pay as low as possible. But realizing their importance to the economy, the workpeople became more demanding. In 1676 there were weavers' riots in Colchester and the following year in Trowbridge. A combination of London journeymen cloth-workers refused to work for less than 12s. a week.[6]

Nine years later there was trouble in the luxury trade of silk manufacture. London ribbon-loom weavers, women as well as men, burnt and destroyed new kinds of looms that were reducing the amount of work available for them.[7] In 1719, women and girls along with boys working in the silk trade demonstrated riotously against the menace of competition from 'Printed Callicoes and Linnens'. Men weavers petitioning Parliament against this threat, disassociated themselves from their violence.[8]

By the early eighteenth century in the West Country, many of those making woollen broadcloths, an occupation of nearly the whole population, had progressed from intermittent demonstrations, and were definitely organizing combinations. In 1700 one was functioning at Tiverton in Devon. By 1717 widespread combinations were reported to the House of Commons so that in February of the following year, an Act was passed to put them down.[9] But the very next year the Stroud weavers petitioned for the enforcement of the 1555 Weavers' Act against tyrannical capitalist clothiers. In 1728 Gloucester woollen-workers appealed successfully to JPs for higher wages. There was another serious uprising in Gloucestershire in 1756 because undercutting of established wage rates had become a problem. The House of Commons responded to operatives' appeals by passing a Woollen Cloth Weavers' Act to provide for the fixing of piece-work prices by JPs. The woollenworkers were still clinging to the tradition of Parliament as an arbiter in industrial disputes. But the master clothiers would no longer accept parliamentary interference. When the wage scales were duly laid down at the Quarter Sessions on 6 November 1756, they brought in troops to cow the operatives and successfully appealed for exemption from the Act.[10]

Working people were being put under great additional pressure because of the speed of technological change. This was particularly felt by women whose staple industrial occupation for centuries, the manufacture of textiles, was being disrupted. The development of new power sources caused the shift of industrial centres from one part of the country to another. Woollen and, later, worsted manufacture greatly diminished in East Anglia and Essex, and in the West Country. These trades moved to the North as coal was needed for the new steam-powered machines which replaced those powered by water.

Woollen and worsted manufactures were also under pressure from the competition of cotton. In cotton too, each new piece of machinery altered the existing allocation of work. Hand-operated machines were replaced by machines powered by water, first in Glasgow and the Clyde basin, the early centre of cotton manufacture. But employers there were slow to adopt steam-power so that Lancashire, quicker off the mark, surpassed the Clyde, and became the scene of many labour disturbances. The early spinning 'jennies' were worked in people's homes like the spinning-wheel; but gradually they were massed together on the premises of a single employer. 'Spinsters' of cotton yarn broke into the house of Hargreaves, inventor of the 'jenny', at Blackburn in Lancashire, destroyed his machines, and drove him south to Nottingham. In 1776 Arkwright's machines for facilitating cotton-spinning caused a riot and machine-wrecking at the first mill where they were introduced in Lancashire. In September and October 1779, there was further violence at Wigan, Bolton, Blackburn, Preston, Chorley, and Manchester. Labour-saving machines and all 'jennies' with more than twenty spindles, which were therefore too dear for cottagers to buy, were destroyed. Women and men were gaoled at Lancaster. A pamphlet, 'The Case of the Poor Spinners', published in 1780 explained that the new mass-production techniques forced them to work very long hours for very low pay, reducing them almost to starvation. The spinners enjoyed a good deal of public sympathy.[11]

Early spinning-engines were introduced somewhat later in the woollen and worsted trades than in cotton. But they had the same effect. In 1790, in Somersetshire, women, supported by their collier husbands, demonstrated against their introduction. However, the husbands were persuaded to return home and there was no violence.[12]

In 1601 a Poor Law had laid down that pauper children, girls and boys, should be taught a trade. From then on employers obtained servants and 'apprentices' from parish workhouses and the new factories hugely increased the demand for them. Yet there was no outcry about the conditions under which they worked until the second half of the eighteenth century when children of those adults who worked in the textile trades were also being dragooned into the new manufactories. Along with pauper children they were competing with adults, often members of their own families, for work. This development in 1780 provoked the Sisterhood of Leicester women wool-spinners to protest. They saw that once grown to an age when adult wages would have to be paid, their children would be discharged with no other means of earning a living. They also pointed out that as they themselves lost work to children, they would become destitute and would have to go into the workhouse. Like their children they had no other skills and would find it hard to learn a new trade. They argued:

> Were such changes gradual, the evil would be less; old persons would go off, and young ones be brought up to this new-fashioned employment.

They had heard that the markets were glutted with factory-made cottons, hence the sudden interest of manufacturers in 'turning their cotton mills into jersey mills'. Suspicious of masters' claims that machines did the work better than they did, the Sisterhood believed the real reason for massing machines in mills was to save labour costs. One of the masters threatened a member of the Sisterhood that he would in future send all his jersey to be spun at the mill and

insulted her with the pretended superiority of that work. She having more spirit than discretion, stirred up the *sisterhood,* and they stirred up all the men they could influence (not a few) to go and destroy the mills erected in and near Leicester and this is the origin of the late riots there.[13]

The new division of labour that emerged was that women and children were the main factory labour force in woollen- and eventually in worsted-spinning. Worsted, however, remained a cottage industry well into the nineteenth century. But on the new fabric, cotton, women lost spinning work to a considerable extent to men, who were helped by children. However, even on the later and more complex 'jennies', 'throstles', and 'mules', women were not completely ousted. Power-loom weavers of all fabrics were nearly all women and boys so that men and women handloom-weavers alike lost work, the women being forced into the factories where a few men worked as supervisors.

In a number of the clothing trades, just as in textiles, no sort of combined action would have been possible without the knowledge and, to some extent, the support and co-operation of women, girls, and boys who worked in them. In tailoring girls and women sewed; in felt-hat making they worked as wool-formers, hat-makers, and trimmers, and in shoemaking they stitched soles to uppers. In the small metal trades, pin-making, jewellery, bronze, and brass, in the building industry where girls and women toiled as clay-workers and brick-makers, in glassworks, in coalmining, and agriculture, the unit remained the family.[14] Everybody worked. If a strike or wage claim was to succeed, families had to co-operate and combine, even if the leadership and initiative came from the men. Unity was produced not by the proximity of individual workers one with another as in factories later on, but by the family and the community, for the early unions were small local associations.

Whether there was a continuous history of any formal organization involving women is unknown. But some sort of tradition of organization involving women persisted in Derby, Nottingham, and Leicester, in various London trades, and among northern and West Country woollen-workers. A formal union was certainly established at Manchester. The 'Articles' of the Worsted Small-ware Weavers of Manchester, a society set up in 1747, show women as equal members. These 'Articles', a set of rules for the conduct of the society gradually built up over the years, laid down that as from 6 April 1754

every Undertaker shall demand a Blank from his Journeyman, or *Journeywoman* when they come to work with them ...

(author's italics)

According to Article VI of 11 August 1755, every undertaker intending to bring up both sons and daughters to the trade, was bound to register them as potential members of the society. This would entitle them to a Blank at twenty years of age.

The 'Articles, Rules, Orders and Regulations' of the Friendly Associated Cotton-Spinners of Manchester and the surrounding area, printed in 1795, accepted women as equal members.

As well as joining societies along with men, women set up their own all-female Friendly or Benefit societies or Box Clubs. There were Box Clubs of women serge-weavers in the West Country by the 1790s as well as a Woollen-Weavers' Society in Gloucester by 1802 and a number in the main manufacturing towns and cities. That the members were working women is attested by rules dealing with sickness benefit. For instance, a Manchester Society dating from September 1795, meeting at the Blue Bell in the High Street, decided that any member who fell sick or was unable 'to work at her trade, calling or employ', should be paid benefit of 5 shillings a week for six months.[15] Another society set up in April 1799, meeting at William Barrow's house (i.e., pub) in Poole-Lane-End, in Failsworth near Manchester, similarly ruled that benefit be paid in case of sickness, old age, or infirmity to any member who was 'incapable of work seven days together'.[16] The Women's Benefit Society established in January 1795 at the White Lion, the House of Mary Adams, in Lichfield Street, Birmingham, required that a doctor's opinion be given before benefit was paid to a member unable to work because she was 'sick, lame, or blind'.[17]

Just like the men's craft societies, these organizations were the means by which the sober and industrious pulled themselves up and away from the Hogarthian squalor of working-class life, the quarrelling, drunkenness, illness, prostitution, and misery which drove some to suicide. Consequently only those below a certain age, in good health, and of respectable habits were eligible for membership and for benefits paid out of the common box. The Birmingham Society excluded from membership those over forty years old. No sickness benefit was paid to any member who became ill of 'the venereal disease or any other disorder contracted or occasioned by a loose and vicious life ...'.

The North Shields Society of 1825, meeting at Mrs Jane Swan's House in Wallsend, excluded the distempered or lame. Benefit was refused to any member

> lamed by quarrelling, ... or who bears a bastard ... And she who puts a period to her own days, shall forfeit both funeral charges and legacy to the box.

XVIII.

That if any member shall fall sick, blind, or lame, and thereby become incapable of working, he shall on making known his infirmities, provided the are not such as are brought upon him or her, by his, her, or their own intemperance, or debauchery, be paid the sum of five shillings and six-pence per week, during one whole year, in case his infirmities so long continues, or  more or less, at the discretion of the arbitrators for the time being, if the find his, her, or their situation may require, but if the member continue sick any longer he shall be paid the sum of three shillings and fix-pence, so long as he may continue sick, more or less, as the arbitrators for the time being may think proper; but no person shall be entitled to any relief till he shall have been a member of the society for one calendar month : and if any such member shall happen to be out of work (provided it be not through any default, or misconduct of himself), he shall receive such relief from the society, for the time he, she, or they shall be so out of employ, as in the direction of the arbitrators for the time being, shall be deemed sufficient ; and that in case any member being so relieved, shall be suspected of deceit in his infirmities, the arbitrators for the time being, shall be at liberty to call in some skilful physician to examine the member, who, if he shall refuse to be examined, or if upon such examination, on the report of such physician, it shall appear that such member shall have imposed upon the society, he shall be excluded any further benefit therefrom, nor shall he ever again be re-admitted.

XIX.

That in case of the death of any member or members of this society, his or their widow, or widows, or his, her, or their next of kin, shall receive from the fund of this society, the sum of five guineas for the funeral expences of

Page from 1795 Rule Book of Friendly Associated Cotton Spinners

The Blue Bell Society in Manchester was more lenient, laying down 'no unmarried to receive anything out of the box, for more than one lying-in'.[18] But it too banned from membership common prostitutes, women of 'vile character', thieves, felons, and so on.

Although the meeting-places were pubs and members were expected to spend a certain amount on drink, drunkenness and disorderly behaviour were prohibited. Any member who became 'disguised with liquor' was fined.

Some clubs only admitted men to meetings on payment of a fine. In general, strangers were not welcome, nor were children. The Wallsend Society would admit only babes being suckled at the breast.

The rules of these women's Friendly or Benefit societies were thoroughly businesslike, but, at the same time, democratic. The appointment of officials and admission to membership went by vote of the members, as in the Birmingham Society which ruled 'That a mother and treasurer to this society shall be appointed and elected for the time being by a majority of the members'. Whoever was elected had to give surety for all monies entrusted to her and keep accounts which she could be required to hand over to the Warwickshire clerk of the peace for vetting. A new member was admitted by a majority vote of two-thirds of those present at a meeting. She had to pay in for three months before she was entitled to benefit. No one who was already a member of another society could join. Any sick member 'on the box' at one of the annual divisions of the funds was continued 'as a sound member for the year ensuing'. But anyone who put added strain on the finances by leaving when the Society was having to pay out benefit to a sick member had to pay the very high fine of £1.12s. 0d.

Like the craft gilds, the women's Benefit societies had their convivial side. The Blue Bell Society held an annual feast on the First Tuesday in August, 'the landlord to provide the dinner, which is to be on the table exactly at one o'clock ...' The members of the Birmingham White Lion Society required

> That the mother ... shall keep a good fire during the winter season on the nights the society meet, and shall take care that all provisions, ale, etc. that may be wanted for the entertainment of the members at the feasts, etc. shall be of the best, or for every neglect shall forfeit One shilling to the fund ...'

These few examples, besides evoking the conditions of life of working women in the late eighteenth and early nineteenth centuries, prove their ability to organize themselves. They were therefore a refutation of the allegations being made by the early

1830s that women were incapable of organization. It was estimated that there were getting on for three-quarters of a million men and women in such societies in England at the turn of the century. Lancashire, with 820 of them, had the biggest single concentration. A few were supported and encouraged by employers, but the vast majority were the creations of working people.

Insofar as these clubs catered for people of any and every trade, they were not trade societies, although they had some affinities with the general unions of the late nineteenth century. They were not at first used for industrial action, so they were tolerated by the government. Some of the women's Friendly or Benefit societies sought official acceptance by protesting their loyalty to the monarch.

Throughout the eighteenth century, however, the government in its efforts to stop the setting-up of combinations of workpeople used both the Conspiracy Laws and Acts passed to regulate particular trades. There were said to be forty of these on the Statute Book by 1800.[19] At the beginning of April 1799, master millwrights, that is engineering employers, appealed to Parliament for an Act to prohibit a combination of journeymen in their trade in the London area. The occasion was seized to push the anti-trade union campaign to a new level. Nightmares were conjured up for property-owners by demands for 'liberty, fraternity, equality' from across the Channel. These were heightened by the writings of Thomas Paine and Mary Wollstonecraft on the rights of men and women respectively. The new manufacturing employers demanded more urgently absolute power over their workpeople and an absolute right to introduce new technical methods whatever the consequences to the currently employed workforce. The result was an Act forbidding unlawful combinations in all trades, rushed through Parliament in June-July 1799. Not content with this, Parliament passed a second Act in January 1800 making illegal 'conspiracies among journeymen', and therefore also among journeywomen, who aimed at raising wages. It further suppressed Friendly and Benefit societies. In practice employers winked at combinations and Benefit societies unless these seriously inconvenienced them. Even then the threat of prosecution under the Acts did not necessarily succeed.

Demonstrations continued, aimed both against industrial grievances and price rises which put food out of the reach of working people. Spontaneous protests and temporary local organizations bubbled up only to break under the attacks of government and employers. But the organizations continued a subterranean existence, sometimes merely in people's memories and

minds. Men, women, and children of Nottingham organized successful demonstrations against food shortages.[20] In Somerset in 1801
there were riots against a weaving innovation, the 'flying shuttle',
and then, all over the south-west, against the 'spring shuttle'.[21] Lancashire cotton-weavers began a campaign for a Minimum Wage
Bill and for the repeal of the 1804 Corn Law which virtually
prohibited corn imports until the price of English corn rose to 63s.
a quarter.[22] *The Times* of 25 June 1808 remarked that even after the
Lancashire weavers gained some concessions, there was still unrest:

> The women are, if possible, more turbulent and mischievous
> than the men. Their insolence to the soldiers and special con-
> stables is intolerable and they seem to be confident of deriving
> immunity from their sex.

The Friendly and Benefit societies' funds were lent to the strikers
on this occasion, as they had been in 1802 when the woollen-cloth
weavers of Bradford-on-Avon, Trowbridge, and places roundabout
threatened to prosecute anyone who tried to enter the trade
without having served a seven-year apprenticeship.[23]

In Manchester, under cover of the Friendly and Benefit societies,
a powerful union of all kinds of spinners existed secretly, probably
owing its ancestry partly to the 1794 Friendly Associated Cotton-
Spinners. It covered the area from Macclesfield and Stockport in
the south to Oldham, Bolton, and Preston in the north and to
Stalybridge, Ashton, and Hyde in the east.[24]

In 1812, because many employers refused to pay rates fixed as
fair by magistrates, all the weavers at an estimated 40,000 looms
between Aberdeen and Carlisle struck. The government stopped the
moves towards a settlement, arrested the leaders, and the combination disappeared.[25]

There was little sex distinction over prosecution of those involved in demonstrations. At Blackburn in September 1808 *The
Times* reported Elizabeth Walmsley as among those arrested, her
misdemeanour being the breaking of three shop windows with a
big stick.[26] In a further wave of disturbances five years later in April
1813, also in Lancashire, six women and girls were among those
sentenced to six months imprisonment. Most of those arrested at
Manchester during food riots were women and among eight
people condemned to hang was Hannah Smith, aged fifty-four,
who, like the men, died unrepentant. But Mary and Lydia
Molyneux, aged fifteen and nineteen years, arrested at West
Houghton because they were

engaged with Muck Hooks and Coal Picks in their Hands

breaking the windows of the Building and swearing and cursing the Souls of those that worked in the Factory were spared the death penalty because of their youth.[27]

Those who engaged in attacks on property, especially machines, came to be called 'Luddites' after a Ned Ludd, who was said to have been one of the leaders of such attacks in the Nottingham hosiery trade. These attacks were not only directed at securing higher pay. They were also protests at loss of work, mainly because of the diversion of the wide hosiery frames from fancy hose, no longer in fashion, to the making-up of small articles. As a result women and children gained work at the expense of men. Here the threat to employment was partly ameliorated by a growth in the lace trades. But lace-making was not free from combination. In 1811, women lace-runners in Loughborough showed

> A Spirit of combination to dictate to their Employers, and to raise the price of their wages ... Meetings have been called and emissaries sent into all the neighbouring Towns and Villages to unite, and to collect Money for their purpose

as the Rev. R. Hardy, JP, wrote. He described how the women were persuaded to desist by his warnings that their activities were illegal.[28]

The long hours and low pay established for home-workers and for the pauper children in factories, made nonsense of apprenticeship regulations. All through the eighteenth century these had been breaking down under the further pressures of technological changes and the employers' insistence. Although the Elizabethan Statute of Apprentices lingered until 1875, the government acknowledged the inefficacy of these old laws. In 1813 the regulation of wages by JPs was abolished. The next year most of the statutory apprenticeship regulations were repealed. Only where the workpeople were able to establish powerful trade societies as in the case of the men mule-spinners and the engineers, could a lengthy apprenticeship be enforced. Child helpers learned factory weaving 'on the job'.

New techniques and poor children, rather than, as has been suggested, the withdrawal of women from work to have children, kept these trades open to all comers. In a time of intense competition for jobs, women tended not to stay away from work during confinements for more than a few hours, or at most a few days, a practice that persisted into the 1930s Depression.

A new form of protection emerged, however, as a few middle-class professional men and manufacturers like Robert Owen and Sir Robert Peel, Senior, supported limitation of hours and control

of conditions of the pauper child 'apprentices' in the cotton industry. The first Act limiting their hours of work to twelve per day
was passed in 1802.

Coinciding with changes in technology, land- and property-
owners and new manufacturing interests stepped up the rate of enclosures of agricultural land. Those turned off their livings looked
for employment in industries old and new. They were said to have
flooded handloom-weaving just when it was meeting the
competition of the power-loom.

In addition, there was the relentless and speedy growth of the
population, which gathered momentum in the eighteenth century.
Not even the lack of sanitation in the new spreading industrial
towns, inadequate diets, gruelling hours, and conditions of labour
checked this rise, nor did wars diminish the numbers of women
seeking work as they did the numbers of men. The workers themselves deliberately contributed to this increase and so to competition for work, insecurity of employment, and low earnings.
They were slow to relinquish the notion that, since families depended for some of their income on children, the more they had of
them, the greater family earnings would be. Therefore they
married early and their children were earning by the time they
were five or six years old. The vicious circle created by large
families, acute competition for available work, and low earnings
was described in 1867, at the tail-end of the handloom era, by
William Felkin, a Midlands hosiery manufacturer. Referring to a
prematurely aged woman of fifty-three whom he found at work
between nine and ten at night, he remarked:

> She had been the mother of fifteen children, ten of whom, male
> and female, her husband and herself had bred up to be
> stockingers ...
>
> Here was the female frame-work-knitter; the mother of other
> female stocking-makers, and of sons too—ten in all—added to
> the numbers of a trade grievously overloaded with labourers ever
> since they had belonged to it...[29]

Because of all these pressures, the crises of unemployment that
had occurred intermittently when there were depressions of trade,
after 1815 lengthened into a common continual experience of job
insecurity, inimical to successful trade union organization.

There was inbuilt into British trade unionism from the start the
acceptance and practice of a graded organizational structure intended to protect those holding the best jobs within an occupational group at any given time. To this end the trade unions
took over the craft gilds' hierarchical structure and methods of

safeguarding work and prices paid for work. Restrictions on numbers coming into a trade and, to a lesser extent, restrictions on the
amount of goods produced, were both used by craft unions as a
means of keeping up employment.

These relationships at work and within the labour movement
were complicated by the fact that most occupations were still
family trades, so that hierarchical organization of work both
strengthened and reflected family relationships. Within a family,
men took precedence over women by law; at work, the male head
of a household claimed the best-paid work when there was any
question of specialization, as, for instance, in tailoring and
shoemaking, and it was still he who was paid, not the individual
working members of the family.

The tradition of subcontracting work also continued. If a member of the family did not perform ancillary work necessary to supply the most skilled worker with materials, some outside person
had to be paid to do it. This applied not merely in textiles and
clothing, but also in the small metal trades, in pottery, in
agriculture, and in mining. Although, for example, coal workings
grew deeper and the labour ever harder and more brutal, it was
still a family trade. The hewing miner, a man or occasionally a
woman, depended on others to get the coal to the surface. If members of the family did not do the work, the hewing miner had to
pay someone else, hence he himself was an employer. Rather than
pay away his earnings, a man in this situation married. As an old
miner bluntly told the 1842 Commission on Mines, he had been
'obliged to get a woman early' in order to avoid paying away his
profits. Or as a fifty-three-year-old Scottish woman coalbearer said:
'... it was the practice to marry early. When the coals were all
carried on women's backs, men needed us ...'[30]

So long as the traditional idea lasted that every member of a
family from the smallest toddler to the oldest worked to contribute
to the family income or to maintain herself or himself, all these
distinctions were blurred.

When too many people were chasing too few jobs in a particular
occupation, the hard decision then had to be taken on who was to
be kept out. In the craft gilds, the demarcation between those who
were allowed to exercise the mystery and those who were not, was
generally on family lines rather than on those of age or sex. In the
case of trade societies and unions, the first and obvious category to
be excluded was child labour, whether by raising the age at which
children should start work, or by shortening their hours of work;
policies based also on humanitarian motives. To begin with,
restrictions on numbers entering work were first directed at the

pauper apprentices. But it was also easy to exclude a physically distinct group such as women. Both hierarchical regulations and restrictions on employment also affected men and boys. But no male was excluded from work on the grounds of his sex, because some male apprentices and learners had to be taken on in order to replace men retiring from the top grades.

In the early stages of the development of trade unionism, there was no exclusion on grounds of sex. The highest-paid workers might as well be women as men. But during the eighteenth century this began to change. Evidence began to accumulate of men closing trades to women or restricting their employment. For example, from about 1725, a combination of men serge-weavers at Cullompton in Devon prevented women from learning the trade, although this low-paid branch of weaving was increasingly taken over by women.[31]

In 1769, an agreement written into a book of prices for Spitalfields silk-weavers shows that the men silk-weavers negotiated a price list which excluded women and girls from the better-paid kinds of work, unless and until there was another war, when it was anticipated trade would improve. The ribbon-weaving branch of the silk trade was almost wholly a woman's trade until 1770 when the Dutch engine-loom was introduced. Women were not allowed to work these looms and an attempt to set a journeywoman to work on one provoked a strike of men weavers. As a result, women were expressly forbidden to use any but the old handlooms. A great boom in ribbons together with the departure of many men weavers for the French Wars led to the breakdown of this embargo during 1812-15.[32]

In 1779-80 journeymen bookbinders founded a union, 'The Friends', from which women who worked in the trade as folders and sewers were excluded. The result was that in a strike in 1786, the women continued to work and did not support the men. But the women had established the right to an afternoon tea-break and secretly gave the men cups of tea. Encouraged by the women, in 1806, the men stood out successfully for a tea-break, but the women were still excluded from the union.[33]

In the agitation against the changes in the use of wide hosiery frames in 1811, which provided work for women and children and took it from men, Luddite frame-knitters were prepared to let the frames stand on condition that 'the owners discharged women employees and promised to prevent their working'.[34] In the same year, employers who were members of the Company of Tailors were complaining that journeymen tailors were prohibiting their wives and children from working in the trade. Thus women's economic inequality was more and more clearly defined.

The birth of trade unionism is sometimes equated with the appearance of factories. Yet combinations were rife where cottage handicrafts persisted because of the geographical closeness of the operatives, a characteristic also of small textile and mining towns. The growth of industrial cities, the movement of people to them, voluntarily or under compulsion, caused the breakdown of old community feeling and of organization. Taken together with men's restrictions on women entering some trades, this offset any encouragement given the nascent women's trade union organization through the concentration of people in factories.

On the other hand, the succession of wars during the eighteenth century and up to 1815, by absorbing men into the armed forces, increased overall the numbers of jobs available to women. Wars also tended to relieve unemployment by providing government contracts for equipment and clothing for troops and marine. Thus circumstances were not wholly unfavourable to the growth of trade union organization. Trade unionism among women continued to build in a modest way, hampered less at this stage by the attitude of their fellow men-workers, than by the opposition of employers and government.

Notes

1 S. Sholl, *A Short Historical Account of the Silk Manufacture in England*, 34.
2 C. Hill, *The Century of Revolution*, 21; I. Pinchbeck, *Women Workers and the Industrial Revolution. 1750-1850*, 157-8.
3 Hill, op.cit., 21, 27, 36. S. and B. Webb, *History of Trade Unionism*, 33n.
4 *The Clothier's Delight or The Rich Man's Joy, and the Poor Man's Sorrow*, Brit. Lib.
5 *England's Great Joy and Gratitude*, Brit. Lib.
6 Hill, op.cit., 208.
7 ibid.
8 *The Weavers' True Case*, Brit. Lib.
9 S. and B. Webb, op.cit., 34. Hill, op.cit., 269.
10 ibid., 50: J. L. and B. Hammond, *The Skilled Labourer*, 157-8. Pinchbeck, op.cit., 157. The evidence from *State of the Case and Narrative of the Facts relating to ... Risings of the Weavers in the County of Gloucestershire, 1727,* shows that women were widely employed in weaving, and contradicts the Webbs' claim that women took over only at the start of the nineteenth century (op. cit., 35). In general uprisings caused by distress due to stoppages of trade,

all workers including women took part. But men weavers used their combinations to try to stop the employment of women from 1725 onwards and women formed their own Friendly and Benefit Societies. A woman working within her own family was one thing; a woman employed under the putting-out system by some distant capitalist clothier and paid independently was another.

11 J.L. and B. Hammond, op.cit., 53-6, 149; *Annual Register*, 9 Oct. 1779: *Case of the Poor Cotton Spinners*, 1780, Brit. Lib.

12 J. L. and B. Hammond, op.cit., 149.

13 *Humble Petition of the Poor Spinners*, 2 May 1780, Brit. Lib. Author's italics.

14 Pinchbeck, op.cit., 1,2, 222, 271, 276, 291-3.

15 *Rules, Orders and Regulations to be observed by a Friendly Associated Female Society consisting of Women Only*, 8 Sept. 1795. A copy of the rules of a Women's Friendly Society in Didsbury in 1799 also exists. Note W. Marshall, *Rural Economy of the West of England*, 1806, 28-9, mentions Box Clubs among women serge-weavers.

16 *Rules and Orders to be Observed by the Sociable Friendly Society of Females*, 8 April 1799.

17 *Rules and Orders to be strictly observed and kept by the Members of a Woman's Benefit Society*, 12 Jan. 1795.

18 *The Articles Belonging to the Friendly Society of Women*, 1825.

19 S. and B. Webb, op.cit., 24n. J. L. and B. Hammond, *The Town Labourer*, vol. II, 78.

20 ibid., 112.

21 J. L. and B. Hammond, *Skilled Labourer*, 157.

22 ibid., 73.

23 Pinchbeck, op.cit., 165n 1.

24 J. L. and B. Hammond, *Town Labourer*, vol. II, 79.

25 S. and B. Webb, op.cit., 58-9, 82.

26 J. L. and B. Hammond, *Skilled Labourer*, 80-1.

27 ibid., 271; see also 309.

28 ibid., 262-3.

29 W. Felkin, *History of Machine-Wrought Hosiery and Lace Manufactures*, 459.

30 Report of the Commissioner ... to Inquire into ... Mining Districts, 1844, XVI, 452, 475. But there was great solidarity in coalmining families, see J. L. and B. Hammond, *Town Labourer*, vol I, 43-4 and *Skilled Labourer*, 43.

31 J. L. and B. Hammond, *Skilled Labourer*, 162. W. G. Hoskins, *Industry, Trade and People in Exeter, 1688-1800*, 35.

32 Pinchbeck, op.cit., 168-70; M. D. George, *London Life in the Eighteenth Century*, 182.

33 J. R. MacDonald, ed., *Women in the Printing Trades*, 30ff.

34 J. L. and B. Hammond, *Skilled Labourer*, 257.

3 General Union and Segregation

The ending of the Napoleonic Wars in 1815 brought the customary dislocation as war industries had to adjust to peacetime conditions and demobilized men from the armed forces flooded the labour market. The government met the ensuing protests over reductions in wages and rises in prices of food by further repressive legislation. The Habeas Corpus Act was suspended in 1816. The 'gagging' Acts of 1817 and the Six Acts of 1819 deprived people of most of their established rights of assembly and free speech. The quantity of such legislation was a proof of its ineffectiveness.

Women played a part in the accompanying wave of industrial unrest. In 1817, for example, a small group of Stockport power-loom weavers struck against being made to pay for the artificial light they used while they were working. These twelve women and eleven men chose to go to prison for a month rather than accept the deductions.[1] In 1818 Stockport power-loom weavers came 'out' again, but on a much bigger scale. Four men who were caught distributing strike pay were each sentenced to three months in Chester Castle gaol. But some young women who were merely receiving it, were, more leniently, only 'bound over'. The strikers, men and women, were not so lenient in their turn, however, with 'blacklegs', women and girls brought up from Burton-on-Trent. They held them under a pump and drenched them with water. Among spinners and other textile-workers, all over Lancashire; among woollen-workers in Leeds and the surrounding districts, and in the Rochdale flannel trade, occupations in which many women were employed, combination was rife. Agents provocateurs were engaged by government and local authorities to incite militants and force them into revealing themselves so that they might be arrested. Even those on the fringe of organized industrial protest were liable to be imprisoned.

But not all employers and authorities were opposed to combination. In the Coventry ribbon and Nottingham and Leicester hosiery trades, the employers saw unions as a means of reducing industrial strife and preferred to pay mutually agreed rates. William Felkin described how in 1819, because of four years of falling wages, and the resulting want and agitation, frame-work knitters of Nottingham 'In their extremity ... frequently paraded the town, women and children heading processions, one of which consisted of more than five thousand people'. It was with employers' help and approval that a union was set up in Leicester in order to avoid a strike, and in order to gather funds for those without work.[3] Ratepayers too, not all of whom were industrial employers, objected to subsidizing wages through the Poor Law, and were consequently intent that pay should be adequate.

This agitation immediately after the Napoleonic Wars elicited another Factory Act, both limiting the age at which *all* children, not just those from parish workhouses, were to start work in cotton factories, and restricting the hours during which they were to be employed.

As at the end of the eighteenth century and in the early years of the nineteenth, a mere list of occupations in which, between 1819 and 1834, there were strikes and protests against wage cuts and against the introduction of new machines, demonstrates that women must have participated. In terms of numbers, they dominated many of the trades concerned and were employed to some extent in nearly all of them. Among those who came 'out' were cotton-spinners of all kinds, and cotton power-loom and woollen-weavers in Glasgow and in Lancashire; Yorkshire woollen- and worsted-weavers; shoemakers in Manchester, Derby, and Northampton; pottery-workers in Worcester, Staffordshire, Derby, Bristol, Swindon, and Newcastle-upon-Tyne; hosiery-workers in Derby, Leicester, and Nottingham; Worcester, Nottingham, and Yeovil glove-makers; agricultural workers in the huge market gardens of Kensington, Walham Green, and Hammersmith; tailors in Birmingham and London; Kidderminster carpet-weavers, silkworkers in London, and women silkworkers on their own in the Liberties of Dublin.[4] In some areas, for example Banbury, Birmingham, Hull, Oldham, and in the whole of the West of Scotland, at times a whole range of trades—sometimes, it was said, every trade—was taking organized action and setting up combinations.[5]

The leaders of this activity were men in the building, plumbing, engineering, and agricultural trades, as well as in textile manufacture. They did the bulk of the work of organizing and they suffered most from the law. The assumption therefore has been that women had little share in this agitation. But the movement, in fact, was of the whole working class, women and children as well as men, since all were affected by high food prices and the impact of new machinery. As James Phillip Kay remarked in *Moral and Physical Conditions of the Operatives employed in the Cotton Manufacture in Manchester,* in 1832: 'Whilst the engine runs, the people must work—men, women and children are yoked together with iron and steam...' Bound together at work, they were bound together in their protests. If defeat, or victory, caused one group to retire temporarily from the fray, others were soon challenging the right of employers to dictate unilaterally the terms and conditions on which their employees worked.

Francis Place, an erstwhile breeches-maker and trade unionist, and Joseph Hume, a Radical MP, worked for legislation to restore the balance. The agitation, together with an improvement in trade, persuaded a majority of Members of Parliament in 1824 to force through Hume's Act to legalize all kinds of trade union activity and to repeal the anti-Combination Acts of 1799 and 1800. Released from fears of imprisonment or of transportation to penal colonies, workpeople, especially Lancashire and Yorkshire textile operatives, launched into a new wave of strikes to try to restore wage cuts. In Lancashire in 1825, hundreds of machines were wrecked and troops forced the people back to work. In a fright, employers and Parliament retorted in 1825 with a second Act in which the blanket right to organize was considerably watered down, and once more those who tried it were liable to prosecution for conspiracy.

It was at this moment that organization appeared in an occupation later regarded as totally unorganizable—domestic service. There had grown up two quite different categories of these workers. There were the pauper children, recruited mainly from parish workhouses, utterly at the mercy of their employers and maltreated for negligence or displeasing behaviour. For example, a century and a half previously, Samuel Pepys had recorded that on 30 November 1660, 'observing somethings to be laid up not as they should be', he took a broom and 'basted' his maid 'till she cried extremely'.[6] In January 1664 he directed his wife 'to beat at least the little girl' because the maids had been chattering to his servant, Will.[7] In February a year later 'the little girl' was again the scapegoat when his maids had let in 'a rogueing Scotchwoman' to help wash and scour the house. The child was beaten and locked in the cellar all night.[8] Small wonder that one little pauper girl he obtained from Bridewell workhouse ran away.

On the other hand, there were some domestic servants who retained their independence. With the expansion of overseas trade and progress towards Britain's first colonial empire, the class of people wealthy enough to afford domestic help increased. But the work was highly unpopular and those who had homes and were not consigned to the workhouse refused to do it, for example in 1655 during Cromwell's Protectorate: 'young people, both men and maids, fitting for service, will not go abroad to service without

they may have excessive wages, but will rather work at home ...'
Despite orders that 'the Justices shall proceed against them', the attitude persisted.[9] Daniel Defoe reported in 1725 that 'Women servants are now so scarce that from 30*s* and 40*s* their wages are of
late increased to six, seven, nay £8 per annum and upwards ...'
They left their employers without notice, but expected employers
who sacked them to give them 'a month's wages, or a month's warning'.[10]

David Loch, making a *Tour Through Most of the Trading Towns and
Villages of Scotland* some fifty years later, remarked on complaints in
Paisley that maidservants stipulated they should have the three
hours from 5 to 8 p.m. off every Thursday: 'The minute they were
free they hurried to a house where fiddlers and partners were
waiting for them and danced away merrily until eight; then with
cheerfulness and alacrity, they returned to work'. This practice, he
noted, promoted matrimony.[11]

How much more genteel an occupation it seemed to them than
coalbearing, for instance, or work in one of the new textile-mills,
or chain- or nail-making. A girl who found 'a good place' thought
well of herself. Work in affluent households was increasingly
sought after as the eighteenth century progressed, but the number
of 'good places' available was limited.

Although gentility was not usually accompanied by a commitment to trade union organization, nevertheless in 1825 some
Edinburgh maidservants organized the Maidservants' Union Society
and threatened to strike, putting out a broadside that was
published in the *Evening Post*. They demanded the restitution of
perquisites which they felt were being gradually withheld, including Sundays off 'no questions asked', and the mistress's old
clothes. A gown or any other item of dress had to be handed over
after it had been worn 'a sufficient time'. But in case of any difference of opinion between the mistress and the maid about the
condemnation of the dress, 'the servants of the house and those of
the two adjoining houses to be appointed judges'. The cook was to
have fat, dripping, hare and rabbit skins, so no skinned animals
were to come into the house. They also restricted entry into their
employment. No girl under sixteen years of age was to be taken
on, and beginners' wages were laid down. ' ... those taking less to
be considered KNOB STICKS, and treated accordingly'. Because a
recent strike among the Lyons silkworkers had driven up the price
of silk, and prices of furs and tooth powders were exorbitant, they
demanded higher wages, but accepted the current rate of 'tea
money' until the arrival of the free tea trade, 'when a change may
be deemed necessary'. They were prepared to enforce their

Ellen Richey's membership card, West of Scotland Power Loom Females' Society

demands by a strike, confident that 'Joseph Hume's Act will protect the maids should they be brought before the Justice of the Peace ... Court'. Each maidservant was to be supplied with a copy of the union rules 'to be hung up in the kitchen along with the Police Regulations ...'[12]

With some improvement in trade and jobs easier to come by, radical agitation kept up and produced some limited successes. In 1831 there was a third Factory Act limiting hours of juveniles as well as of children in cotton factories, followed by a fourth Act in 1833 which applied to all textile factories except silk. These did not give the operatives all they wanted, but the Factory Reform Movement and protective measures for workers were established. In 1832 the franchise was slightly widened and reformed.

The trade union activities of women and their militancy at times created alarm. The *Leeds Mercury* on 4 May 1833 reported a 'Turn-Out Extraordinary' of carders of wool for spinning:

the card-setters in the neighbourhood of Scholes and Hightown, chiefly women, held a meeting to the number of 1500, at Peep Green, at which it was determined not to set any more cards at less than a halfpenny a thousand. Alarmists may view these in-dications of feminine independence as more menacing to established institutions than the 'education of the lower orders'.

In 1833 in Glasgow, women spinners and power-loom weavers combined, part of their purpose being to claim the male 'rate for the job'. A cotton-manufacturer told the House of Commons Select

A VOICE FROM LEICESTER TO THE PIONEER.

Ah, Pioneer! I've often thought, and trembled
  At that same thought, that you were not sincere ;
I felt afraid, love, that your heart dissembled,
  When you wrote that address—it was the fear
That thou wert toying with our gentlest feeling,
And wounding our lone grief instead of healing.

You write as one who knew our degradation ;
  Who knew our helpless, hopeless, piteous, lot ;
Who, by the power of kindly, soft persuasion,
  Could wipe away our mind's deep cancer-spot ;
Give woman back what force has long wrench'd from her,
And placed on fickle chance, or man's false honour.

Art thou in thou in earnest, gallant Pioneer?
  Is all thou sayest the fruit of thy pure thought ?
Come tell me, bravest, art thou quite sincere,
  Or dost thou hold our intellect at nought ?
If false, you heartless rogue, we curse your knavery ;
If true, thy honied words relieve our slavery.

A thousand hearts will feel a pillow'd rest
  In your dear confidence, and hope will heal
The many sorrows which have long oppress'd
  And held imprison'd woman's weal ;
Long-buried hope will gladly re-appear,
And breathe its thanks to thee, good Pioneer.

One faithful token from your skilful pen
  That you are woman's friend ; and evermore
The galling yoke and harsh deceit of men
  Will lose the terror which it had before.
Till then we know not truly, loving scribe,
If 'tis thine aim to comfort or to gibe.

                      PIONEERA.

THE LABOURER'S PROPHECY.
(Continued from our last.)

How shall I curse the coward soul,
  Sunk down by thraldom's worst control,
Who yet admires his tyrant's fate
And calls the monster's vices great ?
Wisdom has lost her matchless prize,
And Virtue keeps her native skies ;
When foul approval soothes the fiend
Who plagues and derogates his kind.

Yet 'tis a loathsome dastard rage,
Wading through ev'ry worthless age
Since those abominable times
When Cæsar rose a king of crimes,
And pluck'd a mighty empire down
To glut his honour-fed renown ;
Then when the scythe of vengeance came,
And struck his crop of wrongs and fame,
War's lean-jaw'd hounds were all unyoked,
And Rome with desolation smoked.
The devilish priest bid Até blow
The whitest glare of honour's glow ;

THE PIONEER TO PIONEERA.

Ah, Pioneera! could the darksome dome,
  Which tops the region of my motley thought,
For once permit thy melting eye to roam
  Thro' every chequer'd trace which time has wrought ;
Could thy fair hand but lift it from its place,
Thou wouldst not, Pioneera, think me base !

The fiery spirit which resists all wrong ;
  The buoyant hope which flutters after right ;
The moist abode of Pity, and the throng
  Of deep imaginings engulph'd in night—
These, 'neath that cupola may find a seat,
But no dark spot to harbour bland deceit.

Thou askest, love, if I be woman's friend—
  And wishest, in thine innocence, to know :—
Ah, let thy sad misgivings have an end !
  I am no mocker of a woman's wo.
Thou wouldst not doubt the ardour of my love,
If thy impassion'd eye could see it move.

'Tis not for thee, my sweet, nor human breast,
  To know the mystic movements of the brain ;
The busy thought that despots cannot wrest,
  Nor gold, nor dread, nor penury enchain.
Good Pioneera, disabuse thy fear,
And doubt no more thy constant Pioneer.

TO THE PIONEER.

From your pretty epistle, address'd to the fair,
  The ladies of Leicester, I mean,
You're the king of good fellows, they boldly declare ,
  Your consort, of course, is a queen !
Of bliss the bright sunshine illumines her life,
  If we judge by the style of your letters ;
And the choice of your love 's the happiest wife
  That now wears of Hymen the fetters.
If fortune on me propitious would smile
  (I speak from a soul that's sincere),
I'd hope—fondly hope—from the youth of our isle,
  A spouse like the brave PIONEER !

                 A LEICESTER LADY.

The applications for information are showering upon
us from all quarters ; in faith, our jaw-bones are
threatening to strike against being over-worked. It
requires the lungs of an apostle to preach the doctrine
of unity. The hatters and wool-combers belong to
the Leicester division, which embraces all the miscel-
laneous trades. We refrain from mentioning the
embryo unions till time has made them invulnerable.

NOTICE.—*All communications must be addressed (if by letter,
post-paid,) to the Editor, at Mr. Morrison's, 170, Livery-street,
Birmingham. The* PIONEER *may be had at the office of the*
CRISIS, 18, *Duke-street, Lincoln's-inn-fields, and* 378, *Strand,
London, where communications may also be sent.*
    Cousins, Printer, Duke-street, Lincoln's-inn-fields.

Page of Poems from the *Pioneer*: two appearing in the 23 November 1833 issue, the
other in that of 30 November

Committee on Manufactures of that year: 'We had an intimation that they had meetings and I saw a letter signed by a woman, calling upon one house to raise wages to the same rates as paid to men'.[13]

The universal movement towards union had as its goal from 1819 the setting-up of one grand national union for all trades. The 1819 endeavour failed. From 1828, efforts of spinners to set up a national union covering their own occupation, culminated in the summer of 1830 in a National Association for the Protection of Labour for workers in general and not just spinners, under the leadership of John Doherty.

'Mixed' textile and clothing organizations of men and women and segregated societies for either sex subscribed to strike funds, for example for the Ashton spinners who were 'out' in January 1831. Such appeals for funds were carried in the newspapers and journals that sprouted as part of the trade union agitation, for instance the *Voice of the People,* the journal of the National Association for the Protection of Labour.

The movement for a national union for all trades rose to a climax with a third attempt inaugurated by a congress held between 7 and 14 August 1833 at the National Equitable Labour Exchange in London. At a further meeting in October, Robert Owen proposed the formation of a Grand National Moral Union of the Productive Classes of the United Kingdom. The *Pioneer,* edited by James Morrison, was particularly associated with this final phase of the movement for a great national union. From the first issue on 7 September, it displayed support for the 'women's interests':

> As women in great measure participate in the good or evil which accompanies any great movement of the community, he [i.e., the *Pioneer*] will not overlook their interests, nor fail to point out whatever may tend to promote their comfort and happiness ...

By the eighth issue of the journal, on 26 October 1833, Morrison had got wind of a women's trade union in Leicester, and his congratulatory editorial burgeoned in a correspondence of poetry.

From 1826 anti-union employers all over the country tried a new means of stemming the wave of trade union organization and activity. They required employees to sign a 'bond' or 'document' renouncing any part in such action and sacked or 'turned out' operatives who persisted in supporting trade unionism. One instance occurred at Derby where the employers in various occupations, acting together in a body, locked out or turned out all their employees at the end of November 1833. More women and children than men found themselves without work or wages. They received financial support from women's as from men's trade societies, as witness the lists of contributors published in the *Pioneer*. Not all the locked-out women supported the union. The *Poor Man's Guardian* reported on 12 December that some 'female hands' were complaining that although they had nothing whatever to do with the union, they were still deprived 'of the only means they possessed of providing for themselves'. But a great many did support it.

Early in 1834 five or six hundred women marched with thirteen hundred men round local villages to demonstrate the solidarity of their defiance to the employers. They received considerable public encouragement. A plane-driver described this procession which included '*Two hundred women*, four abreast, with crimson silk bands and knots over their shoulders'. and 'Women four abreast, with white silk bands etc ...' On the first day of the demonstration, after an open-air meeting at Duffield, they returned to Derby

> the females singing on the way, and through the streets of Derby, hymns and popular songs ... many remarks of good feeling was expressed by respectable people as the procession moved along, such as—'What sort of man can that be, who had the heart to starve such females as these?' And several others expressed their astonishment that, after ten weeks privation, the women could look so clean and respectable.[14]

Women had been charged at Wakefield in May 1833 with assaulting a woman 'black sheep'. The Derby women made another boisterous, impromptu protest against blackleg labour brought in by employers to break the trade unionists' resistance. With great speed and ingenuity they made an effigy of a black sheep and burnt it outside the door of the black sheeps' 'shepherd'. They made such a fearful row—'the baaing was deafening in the extreme'—that the shepherd invoked the authorities who ordered the arrest of three women deemed to be the ringleaders. But they were merely bound over for twelve months and fined 3s 6d each. While 'the whole of the black sheep absconded, with their shepherd, to the neighbourhood of Thorn Tree Lane accompanied by a band of music formed of various culinary utensils'.[15]

Of the 2,400 women, children and men originally locked out, by early May of 1834, a thousand were back at work without agreeing to give up the union; nor would they pay a £1 fine.[16]

The assumption that women had no feeling for trade unionism appears altogether extraordinary in face, not only of the Derby women's attitude to the lockout, but of contributions made by women to the Fund for them and their men colleagues. It ranged from the £3 from the Females of Earl Shilton to 6d from Margaret

Parrington of Barnsley, 'poor in pocket, but rich in principle!'[17]

Women trade unionists made their own protests in the other trade union *cause célèbre* of 1834. This was the case of the six Dorchester farmworkers sentenced to transportation to the Australian penal colony for trying to organize—the Tolpuddle martyrs.[18] Indeed it was a woman who gave the alarm when they were arrested.

Meanwhile, the *Pioneer* was being assailed with requests for help in forming a women's 'lodge' in London; the emphasis, with the *Pioneer*'s approval, being on the organization of non-working wives. A 'Mechanic's Wife' in London suggested 'Unions of females', more particularly married women. The *Pioneer* responded in gallant style:

> In the tough warfare of labour against the claims of capitalists, the mind is hardened into a forgetfulness of those finer sympathies which pervade the circles where women are the presiding influence ... Give us another week to build the fabric of a female lodge ...'[19]

A special meeting of Trade Union delegates was held in London from 13 to 19 February 1834, to try to establish unity of action particularly in face of the Derby lock-out. The delegates understood that 'a very large number of females among the industrious classes are exposed to great hardships and oppression in the disposal of their labour, by the competition for employment, which at present exists among them ...' It was this meeting that actually established the Grand National Consolidated Trades Union as a purely trade union body. But the delegates endorsed segregation within the trade unions. Their resolve to encourage women was limited to support for all-female lodges and duly incorporated in the third of the Grand National's 'Preliminary Articles':

> That lodges of Industrious Females be introduced in every District where it may be practicable; and that such lodges be considered, in every respect, as part of, and belonging to, the Grand National Consolidated Trades' Union.
>
> Announcing this on 8 March, the *Pioneer* also proclaimed
>
> A meeting of the members of the Grand Lodge of the Women of Great Britain and Ireland ... at No. 14, Charlotte Street, on Friday the 21st instant, at Seven o'clock in the evening for the purpose of initiating new members.
>
> All persons disposed to join this lodge may obtain information, and register their names, by application to Mrs. Brooks, at the Institution, 14 Charlotte Street, Fitzroy Square.

As a further earnest of its intentions, the *Pioneer* launched, also in this issue, what was probably the first 'Woman's Page' in any trade union journal.

Thus, in place of the old unity displayed in the 'mixed' unions of men and women Manchester smallware weavers and spinners in the eighteenth century and in the early nineteenth-century protests, more and more the idea of segregation of women into separate organizations was taking hold. Simultaneously with the drive towards a united national, general union of all trades, competition for work and friction were on the increase. The French Wars had created work for men, women, and children alike in addition to the absorption of men into the armed forces. But the situation had been suddenly reversed by the conclusion of hostilities. The effects of demobilization in 1815 had aggravated competition.

The sort of thing that happened was described by a woman straw-bonnet-maker, 'P.A.S.', in a letter to the *Pioneer* about her own trade:

> ... When the war ceased, in the year 1815, many useful men were thrown out of employment, their wives having to support them. The men, not wishing to be idle, were taught by the women to block; and in a very short time these men went round to all the principal houses in London, and offered to take home the work, and finish it for less money than the masters gave indoors, the latter finding everything for the girls' use. It was soon discovered by the women that these men were more tyrannical than their former masters; and, to get the business out of their hands, they offered to take it for less still. This mad competition has sunk the business from one of the best to one of the worst a woman can have ...'[20]

Journeymen handloom-weavers had been accused of excluding women from their organizations in 1825.[21] In the 1818 industrial unrest, some men mule-spinners went to the length of occupying a Scottish mill in which women were employed.[22] Eleven years later at a famous meeting on 5 December 1829 at Ramsey on the Isle of Man, the Grand General Union of Spinners, covering the United Kingdom, was formed. John Doherty had successfully moved a resolution to exclude almost all girls and women from coming into this occupation. The men agreed that the only women and girls to be allowed into the trade should be the poor relations, aged at least fifteen years, of the proprietors of mills. The hopelessness of entirely excluding women from work which they had once virtually monopolized was recognized, however, in a recommendation to them to form their own separate union.[23]

Men mule-spinners were able to keep down numbers of women in their trade. The Supplementary Report of the Factory Commissioners in 1834 stated that women mule-spinners were outnumbered by men.[24]

But four years later, they were already starting to fear the use of women as cheap labour, since the lower-paid women began to threaten their own standards of earnings. The 1833 stand of the Scottish women spinners and power-loom weavers for 'the rate for the job', was backed and inspired by the men spinners whose delegates were at the Isle of Man meeting. J. McNish, a member of the Glasgow Spinners' Association, explicitly told the Committee on Combinations in 1838 that it was the Spinners' aim to prevent the women being 'paid at an under rate of wages if possible'.[25]

Men's claims for 'equal pay' for women over the next hundred years were based less on notions of justice for women than on fears of losing work to women who undercut their wages; and even more on a determination to keep women out of their trades in order that they might have all the work available. Men supported the 'rate for the job', when they believed this would give them preference in employment.

Yet during the eighteenth and early nineteenth centuries, as Arthur Young, for example, had remarked in *A Six Months Tour Through the North of England* in 1771, the custom was to pay skilled women workers in woollen- and silk-weaving the agreed 'rate for the job'.[26] Wage levels in work done by both men and women fluctuated only in response to changes in the demand for goods. A tradition of 'the rate for the job' already existed in textiles and in other trades before the eighteenth-century industrial revolutions were in full swing. But the changes in the nature of jobs, their removal from homes to factories, and, above all, the growing competition for work led workpeople to undercut each other's prices in order, as P.A.S., the straw-bonnet-maker, explained, 'to get the business'.

Employers naturally took advantage of too many hands chasing too few jobs, and especially of girls and women who, because of their lower social status, were more vulnerable than men. They justified paying lower rates to women than men by arguing that women did less work and that of a poorer quality than men. Women workers were caught in a vicious circle for, on low wages and a lower standard of nourishment than men, their performance at work inevitably deteriorated. The claims of employers and certain male employees of women's inferiority as workers were thus often made good.

Attempts to exclude women from competing for work became

more direct. On 29 January 1832, Leigh Hunt's journal, the *Examiner,* went so far as to suggest that children under fourteen years and females of any age should be gradually excluded from manufactories. This provoked the Females of Todmorden in Yorkshire to ask why no suggestion was made for 'any more eligible and practical employment for surplus female labour ... for the thousands of females who are employed in manufactories who have no legitimate claim on any male relative for employment or support'. 'What', they asked, 'is to become of them?'[27]

In the two months between the *Pioneer's* announcement of the intention to build a Woman's Lodge on 11 January, and the Lodge's first meeting on 8 March, James Morrison and his readers were bombarded by letters from early supporters of women's emancipation. For example, the gentle 'Vesta' who believed that 'in proportion as woman is made a full sharer of the benefits of "Union", in such proportion will man discover his ultimate success will be hastened or retarded; for "Shall man be free, while woman is a slave?"'[28] The 'Initiated Weaver's Wife', however, more realistically pointed out 'that there is a great number of men that cannot bear the idea of a woman's union, and yet they are unionists themselves ...'[29]

There were two distinct forms of women's union being proposed. One was the trade union as we understand it today, of women in a particular occupation. The other, exemplified in the Grand Lodge of Women, was what today we would call a Women's Guild for housewives. It acknowledged their right to express their views and participate in the great trade union ferment, and provided them with a means of doing so. It was this trade union of wives that elicited a lone male protest from George Edmonds, a trade union tailor, in favour of occupational unions for women:

> I said that it was the duty of women in trade to form Unions, and thus protect their rights, and be paid for their labour; but to call wives and matrons away from domestic affairs is the idea I 'scout' ... the only way to make it [home] attractive is to have the wife's company in the evening, when man has done his day's labour; for if she goes out to spout, he will go to the public house...

Men's determination to assert a prior right to work over women created contradictory attitudes among them. On the one hand, it led them to connive with employers in depressing women's economic status. On the other, it trapped them both by creating the threat of cheap female labour and by adding to their own economic burdens. The idea of each member of a working-class family earning his or her own livelihood was being superseded by

that of the responsibility of some male relative for supporting
female relatives, children, and parents. The man's wage, therefore,
must be as great as that of an entire family. Henry Samuel Chapman, journalist, lawyer, and Assistant Commissioner for the West
Riding of Yorkshire in the 1840 Royal Commission on Handloom
Weavers, reported that it was universally found, where work was
such that it could not be done by women and children, that men's
wages were

> kept up to a point equal to the maintenance of a family. Tailors
> of London have not only *kept* up, but *forced* up their wages in this
> way, though theirs is an occupation better adapted to women
> than weaving.

He was using arguments and figures from a letter written by Francis Place to James Turner, a cotton-spinner. Place suggested men
working in mills and factories should follow those in other trades in
refusing to work with women and girls who would 'become all that
can be desired as companionable wives ...' The growing dependence of women on some male wage-earner posed a problem for
trade unionists which has still not been solved.[31]

It was at this moment that the 'marriage bar', the compulsory
withdrawal of women on marriage from some kinds of work, not
necessarily the heaviest, was explicitly proposed as a means of
work-sharing. The reasoning was that a woman with a husband
working already had a source of income. But men also aimed at the
kind of existence of the class above them in that they saw a non-
working wife as a symbol of their higher social and financial status.
They were contemptuous of those who could not 'keep their wives',
and wanted the exclusive concentration of wives on home and
husband to ensure them greater comfort, as described by George
Edmonds the tailor. At a time when there were no labour-saving
devices, and wives still shouldered an immense burden of domestic
work, most women were only too glad to be relieved of paid work
in addition to the multitudinous jobs they were expected to deal
with in their homes. They too wanted to live like 'ladies'.

Much more like unions than the married Women's Lodge were a
few lodges organized for women in different trades. The *Pioneer*'s
first Woman's Page of 8 March announced that a General Union of
Female Shoe-Binders and Closers would be meeting at 59 Poland
Street off Oxford Street in London. In May, 'thanks to some
spirited men', a Grand Lodge of Operative Straw-Bonnet Makers
was set up. This was a response to the appeals of 'P.A.S.', who must
have been one of the most advanced women trade unionists of her
day.

Her proposals have a very modern ring. She asked men trade unionists to enrol their women:

> ... I entreat fathers to teach their daughters the nature and value of union; brothers to lead their sisters into the midst of them; and you, husbands, who have seen your wives toiling early and late to get a bare subsistence for their children and you, rouse her from the lethargy her sorrows have sunk her into.[32]

The entreaty was being echoed more than a century later.

She criticized fellow-women workers for undercutting wage rates. She told them bluntly that the responsibility for improving their lot was their own and no one else's and she preached to them the importance of trade unions:

> Come to the Union, sisters, old and young, rich and poor, if you love liberty, study to deserve it. Let us set our wits to work, 'tis right against might. Children yet unborn must have to remember, there was woman as well as man in the Union.[33]

In May 1834, the Kensington washerwomen struck successfully for an advance of wages, followed by those working for big laundries in Horseferry Road, Westminster, who raised their wages from 2s. 6d. to 3s. 6d. per day, always, of course, with the customary allowance of beer for such hot and heavy work.[34] There were riots too in Oldham, in which people died and 12,000 textile-workers were put out of jobs. One woman was among those arrested.[35]

Yet, despite the continuing evidence of women's militancy, friction persisted. An editorial in the *Pioneer* mournfully predicted the evil effects of putting women out of work. If they were prevented 'from making clothes, binding shoes, spinning, weaving, etc., what shall they do? They must haunt the streets and prowl for prey, and then be reprobated by pious magistrates and other godly censurers of public morals ...'[36]

One of the main areas of battle was the tailoring trade. The hostility between men and women really came into the open in late March 1834. The men accused the women of undercutting, and fellow-workmen of what was later called 'sweating'. The women accused the men of taking work from them and of driving them out of the waistcoat-making trade.[37] To oust the women from the trade and protect their wage standards the London tailors struck work.

One unfortunate who had worked at the same West End house for eighteen years wrote in to say she had been told by her employer that the men 'intended to prevent the women from working in the trade'. They had held off doing so because some men opposed the measure since they were ailing and depended on their wives' earnings. Others were simply work-shy and preferred to leave paid work to their wives who got through so much they earned enough to keep the family, enabling them to 'loiter away half the week in a pot-house'.[38]

F. L. Lacon, a 'Unionist' tailor, countered this by saying they had given the women 'such satisfaction that they call loudly for a union of their own, and look to the journeymen tailors for protection, as they cannot rely on the masters'.[39]

The determination of many employers that those they employed should sign the document abjuring trade unionism, the huge number of strikes, and the consequent drain on the resources both of unions and of the Grand National Consolidated Trades Union, caused the collapse of the drive for a general national union. But unionism had been established in many trades, and it was not relinquished by women any more than by men, despite the extra obstacle they faced of men's hostility.

Notes

1 J. L. and B. Hammond, *Town Labourer,* vol. I, 133, quoting Report of the Select Committee on Artisans and Machinery, 418: vol. II, 87, quoting H.O. 42, 179.

2 J. L. and B. Hammond, *Skilled Labourer,* 94-6, 105, 115-16.

3 W. Felkin, *Hist of Machine-Wrought Hosiery and Lace Manufactures,* 441-3. S. and B. Webb, *Hist. of Trade Unionism,* 66; the Spitalfields Acts virtually sanctioned trade unionism among silk-weavers.

4 F. Devine, Sec., Irish Lab. Hist. Soc., Paper to the Irish Cong. of Trade Unions, Women's Advisory Committee, 10 May 1975, 'Women in Irish Trade Unions'. D.W. Bleakley, *Trade Union Beginnings in Belfast and District,* Thesis Queen's Univ. Belfast, 1955.

5 Webb. op.cit., 104-5: J. L. and B. Hammond, *Skilled Labourer,* 92. 109-19, 164-5.

6 H. B. Wheatley, ed., *The Diaries of Samuel Pepys,* 30 Nov. 1660.

7 ibid., 11 Jan. 1664.

8 ibid., 19 Feb. 1665.

9 Bland, Brown and Tawney, *Eng. Econ. Hist., Select Documents,* 360.

10 D. Defoe, *Everybody's Business, Nobody's Business,* 1725, *Coll. Works,* vol. II, 449-508.

11 D. Loch, *A Tour Through most of the Trading Towns and Villages of Scotland,* etc., Edinburgh, 1778, 35.

12 *Important Strike of Maid Servants of Edinburgh,* Broadside, Nat. Lib. of Scot. For hist. of Scottish maidservants see M. Plant, *Scot. Hist. Rev.,* vol. 29. 1950, 143 ff.

13 *Select Committee on Manufactures, Parliamentary Papers,* 1833, VI, 323, Evidence of a Cotton-Manufacturer.

14 The *Pioneer,* 22 Feb. 1834.

15 ibid., 15 March 1834.   16 ibid., 24 May 1834.

17 ibid., 15 March 1834. Lists not only include women specifically, but donations from trades like pin-making and wire-drawing in which women worked. For further proof of female devotion to the development of trade unionism, see also 24 May 1834 for Mrs Wastney, arrested with her husband for selling unstamped papers and imprisoned as he was. They were not permitted to communicate with one another. Also J. Ridgway, pamphlet, 'On Combinations of Trades', 1831, Account of money received by National Association for the Protection of Labour, including a number of donations from power-loom and small-ware weavers, and other trades in which women worked in large numbers.

18 ibid., 29 March 1834, Nottingham Women's memorial. See also 24 May 1834.

19 ibid., 11 Jan. 1834.

20 ibid., Letter from P.A.S., 24 May 1834.

21 J. L. and B. Hammond, *Skilled Labourer,* 257-8, 263, quoting H.O. 42, 118, 119.

22 W. F. Neff. *Victorian Working Women,* 30.

23 A Report of the Proceedings of a Delegate Meeting of the Operative Spinners of England, Ireland and Scotland, 50-1, Resolutions 18 and 24.

24 Pinchbeck, *Women Workers and the Industrial Revolution,* 186-7, 191-2.

25 *Parliamentary Papers,* 1834, VIII, qq.360, 1341-2.

26 A. Young, *A Six Months Tour Through the North of England,* 1771, vol. I, 137-8; vol. III, 187-8, 190: *Annals of Agriculture,* XXVIII, 620: XXX, 301: Rep. of the Select Committee on Manufacturers' Employment, 1830, *Parliamentary Papers,* X, 221, pp. 4-5. In cotton manufacture around Manchester equal pay in all classses of work in which men and women worked. Small-metal manufactures around Sheffield, scissors, open-knives, fenders, stove grates, etc., piece-rates in general use so that women's and children's earnings were considerable.
Thoughts on the Use of Machines in the Cotton Manufacture by a Friend of the Poor, Manchester, 1780, 14, for the increased wages of women spinners who could 'get as much or more than a weaver'.

27 The *Examiner,* 29 Jan. and 26 Feb. 1832.   28 The *Pioneer,* 8 March 1834.

29 ibid., 15 March 1834.   30 ibid., 29 March 1834.

31 Report of Commission on State of Handloom Weavers, *Parliamentary Papers,* 1840, XXIII, Pt III, 43-11, 583-4: J.A. Roebuck, *Pamphlets for the People,* 1835, Letter from Francis Place to James Turner, 5, 9.

32 The *Pioneer,* 12 April 1834.

33 ibid., 3 May 1834.   34 ibid., 14 June 1834.

35 *Leeds Mercury,* 19 and 26 April 1834. S. and B. Webb, op.cit., 152.

36 The *Pioneer,* 17 May 1834.

37 ibid., 29 March 1834: F. W. Galton, *The Tailoring Trade,* LXXXVII, 103, 191-2.

38 The *Pioneer,* 12 April 1834: see also 3 May 1834.   .

39 ibid., 31 May 1834.

4   Pegging away or 'Pay Up Lasses'

The middle of the nineteenth century from about 1835 until 1875 has been considered by some as a time generally barren of growth in women's trade unionism. There was indeed a decline in the pressure to set up trade unions. But this was general and not specific to women. It was a reaction to disappointments. In addition to the failure of the Grand National Consolidated Trades Union and the abatement of the ferment of organization that led to it, the 1832 Parliamentary Reform Act did not extend the franchise to the working class, so they still lacked a legitimate political voice. The 1834 Poor Law Act saved the ratepayers money, but at the expense of the poor. There was considerable economic distress among workpeople even in the new, mechanized manufacturing and engineering trades during trade recessions. These problems were not to be resolved merely by establishing trade unions. Working people sought to help themselves by setting up co-operatives, by agitating against the Corn Laws in order to bring down the price of bread, and by campaigning for political enfranchisement through the five demands of the Charter.

Chartist agitation was at its height precisely during the five years 1837-42 when privations were also greatest. The movement continued until 1848, ebbing and flowing in different localities at different times. But by and large, it was most strenuously advocated by workers from declining industries such as handloom weaving, framework knitting, or nail-making. The newer trades turned to it when they were depressed and the élite of the new working class let it be known through their trade societies that they preferred not to be implicated in it at all. Disraeli in *Sybil* described the support given by women in the Charter, in some cases stauncher than that of men.[1] In a Chartist petition of 1842, 8,200 out of every 100,000 signatures were those of women. A few Chartist leaders saw Universal Suffrage as including women.[2]

These activities diverted people from trade union struggles. But women's societies and unions continued to flicker into life and subside, suggesting an underlying continuity of thought and purpose, a cumulative folk experience.

Punch (1849, XV, 3) cartoon, 'The Way to Deal with Women Chartists'. 'A heroine who would never run from a man, would fly in dismay before an industrious flea or a burly black-beetle. We have only to collect together a good supply of cockroaches,

This continuity was conspicuously apparent in the flourishing, proliferating Friendly and Benefit societies, descendants of those of the late eighteenth century. In these years supposedly so arid of self-help among women, there were societies of Female Foresters, Female Druids, Female Gardeners, Female Rechabites, Odd Females, Odd Sisters, and Ancient Shepherdesses, while in the North of England female burial societies called 'life-boxes' were common.[3] Their stability improved with the publishing of yearly reports by the Registrar of Friendly Societies which began in 1857. Reforms that followed in 1865 helped them further.

Forceful and persistent efforts by women to establish conventional trade associations persisted in a range of trades in various parts of the country. Some turned to men's societies for assistance. For example, in 1836, in the West of Scotland, women winders of pirns, or spools for men weavers, showed some militancy. A correspondent calling herself 'Pirn Peggy' wrote to the *Weaver's Journal* in October 1836 saying that she suspected the men weavers and editorial staff had been too taken up with men's business to speak up on the pirn-winders' behalf. 'It was the least you could have done', she complained, 'when ye gained the least vantage ground, to have assisted your mothers and grandmothers and old aunts, who win' your pirns, in obtaining a share o' the benefit ...' For they were so wretchedly paid they hardly had enough to buy necessities. So on behalf of Bell Birr-the-Wheel, Katy Ca't-about, Sarah Speedy-head, Widow Win'-them-up, and many hundreds of others she asked the journal to take up their cause.[4]

with a fair sprinkling of rats, and a muster of mice, in order to disperse the largest and most ferocious crowd of females that ever was collected'.

David Brown, late of the 21st Scottish Fusiliers, who had turned carpet-weaver, described a pirn-winders' action at Kilmarnock which made clear that pressure was coming from the women. There the plain middle pirn-winders, following the success of another group of these workers, demanded a rise in piece-rates 'or they would know for what'. He was surprised by numbers of women congregating in his street. 'Our two Peninsular heroes, the town officer and drummer, in majestic array' proclaimed a meeting would take place to consider the matter. Brown, who was one of the deputation who negotiated an increase for these women, was a believer in the need for all to act in unison, men and women.[5]

Women pirn-winders in Hamilton and Airdrie in Lanarkshire, and Irvine in Ayrshire, set up unions undertaking for their part not to work for non-union weavers; while the weavers were to give them support.[6] The weavers' union, of course, did in fact include women as well as men workers.[7]

There was another instance in London among women bookbinders. The all-male London Consolidated Society of Bookbinders was praised for championing women in a series of disputes, first with the Society for the Promotion of Christian Knowledge in 1825, and then with the British and Foreign Bible Society which, in 1834, cut rates of pay for women book-folders and sewers to about half the men's rates. In 1844 the struggle recommenced and the following year over a hundred girls in one establishment were tricked into signing a statement that they were perfectly satisfied with the wages paid. Led by Mary E. Zugg, probably the first outstanding women workers' leader whose name we know, the women, when the trick was discovered 'against the advice of the committee of the men's Society, entered into a strike ...' The strike failed, although T.J. Dunning, the Secretary of the men's Society, claimed that 'it arrested a downward tendency in wages'. On 13 November 1861, Mary Zugg, aged thirty-three, died of consumption and was buried at Bow cemetery. T.J. Dunning in his obituary described her:

> Nothing could exceed the temper, moderation and firmness she displayed. Possessing great energy, strong sense and great acuteness of perception, detecting at a glance pretence from reality, she was not what was termed a strong-minded woman, commanding great respect and but little affection, for her goodness of heart and great regard for the feelings and welfare of others endeared her to all.[8]

The men's society was generous in that they subscribed to the women's strike fund and went the length of expelling 150 'finishers' from membership because they opposed this financial help. Yet, although the men's society had been interesting itself in women's pay for a number of years, at no time did they suggest changing their policy of the late eighteenth century to the extent of enrolling women.

It was in the early Victorian doldrums of trade unionism that one of the most heroic women's actions took place. This was the strike in 1840, of 440 home-workers, lace-runners or embroiderers, in Nottingham, organized and run without any help from men at all. It belonged to the tradition of community protest before the factory era and carried on the militancy displayed by the Loughborough lace-runners in 1811. Their 'turn-out' in November 1840, at the height of a recession, was not against capitalist entrepreneurs who ran the trade, but against the women who acted as their agents. For just as workpeople were of both sexes, so were employers and employers' agents. There was a chain of up to three of these women agents or mistresses between each lace-runner and the manufacturer. Each agent took a cut from the price so that little was left for the runners. The lace-runners considered that it would be reasonable to allow the mistresses a penny in the shilling from their earnings, 'for the trouble they take in going with our work to the warehouses'. They asked the manufacturers to price the lace-pieces and some began doing so.[9]

But the trade was depressed. The mistresses would not yield, 'no doubt under the hope that calls of hunger will eventually induce the turn-outs to succumb', as the *Nottingham Review* put it.[10] And the payments made to strikers were low. There was a bitter disappointment in December when it was found there was £2 less available in the strike fund than expected, so that each striker only received sevenpence for the week.

The *Nottingham Review* reporter was impressed with the lace-runners' determination:

> Notwithstanding this small pittance, they ... have with a tact and perseverance not expected from the female character, resolutely introduced various reforms and checks on the collection and distribution of their money, and persevere with a desperate devotion to carry their point against the mistresses ...
>
> As an instance of the general poverty of the female lower classes and the pertinacity with which they endeavour to appear clean and respectable, we know as a fact, that it is now the practice to let out gowns, shawls, bonnets, cloaks and shoes, at from halfpenny to a penny per day, ... such is their general honesty, that they are in almost every instance safely and carefully returned.[11]

The strike was called off on 18 December. But the women's spirit was not broken. They agreed to continue their association and intended to try the following spring 'for some regulation with the mistresses'.[12]

The first real and lasting success for women's trade unionism, however, came in cotton power-loom weaving.[13] Between 1830 and 1845 a big expansion took place in power-loom weaving with a concomitant decline in the numbers of handloom weavers. Not only did factory power-loom weaving come to predominate in woollen and worsted manufacture, but cottons superseded woollens as Britain's most important textile product. The number of handloom weavers put out of work by the power-loom, however, was nearly double the number of those absorbed into power-loom weaving at this time. In the resulting struggle for a livelihood, not only women but also men handloom weavers turned to power-loom weaving and by 1840 were quite commonly employed.[14]

The men in cotton power-loom weaving realized that organization would not succeed if, like the mule-spinners, they tried to exclude women, because in power-loom weaving, in contrast to mule-spinning, men were greatly outnumbered by women. On the contrary, some weaving associations, following the precepts of 'P.A.S.' in the *Pioneer*, made it a rule not to accept into membership any man unless all the female members of his family working in the trade were also union members.[15]

In the cotton-spinning and weaving unions there were a number of attempts in the late 1830s and 1840s to raise wages or to resist wage cuts. The aim of organizations of power-loom weavers was to bring their employers to accept negotiations on prices paid to workpeople for different types of work. That is, people thought as yet in terms of the method of payment in the old cottage industries in which they were paid a price for the cloth they wove. Or, to put it another way, their labour was worth a price. To stop employers arbitrarily and suddenly altering payments, they tried to establish lists of prices for the different kinds of cloth woven, so that when employers wanted to change them, they had to negotiate with the union concerned and they had to pay everyone making the same kind of material the same 'rate for the job'. It was a way of preserving unity since all were paid alike. It safeguarded rates of pay and it forced employers to recognize the right of unions to exist. Price lists were being established by the late 1830s, for instance at Oldham, but none of them lasted any length of time and women and men frequently struck work in protest at cuts in earnings. In spite of the 1825 Act recognizing the right of unions to exist, industrial stoppages were hazardous. At Stockport in a huge power-loom weavers' strike of 1840, 24 men and boys and 21 women and girls were arrested, while a further five women were not taken in charge, all of them accused of harassing 'knob-sticks'. They came out against cuts in earnings.[16]

The struggle for recognition and stable rates of pay was tough, and trade unionists were tough to those who refused to join and so weakened their bargaining power. They publicly named and so shamed non-members. For instance in 1859 in a strike of Padiham weavers, men were threatened with violence, but the women merely named in the strike committee's weekly balance sheet: 'Nan o'Sutting Nan's won't pay—shame! If Bill o'Pett's won't give over persuading weavers not to pay, Punch will deprive him of his top lip'.[17] Similarly in the Preston Spinners' strike of 1853, women defaulters on union dues were berated:

MILLS IN THE HYDES

Within these walls the lasses fair
Refuse to contribute their share;
Careless of duty, blind to fame,
For shame, ye lasses, O, for shame!

Come, pay up lasses, think what's right,
Defend your trade with all your might,
For if you don't the world will blame,
And cry, ye lasses, O, for shame!

Let's hope in future all will pay,
And Preston folks may heartily say,
That by your aid they have obtained,
The greatest victory. [18]

If women in the spinning trade were unenthusiastic about unions, the men trade unionists should hardly have been surprised after the way they had treated them.

Women themselves supported the withdrawal of married women from paid work in this dispute which culminated in a lock-out of 18,000 operatives. Female delegates travelled about and spoke at public meetings 'with all the energy, and perhaps more than the loquacity of their male coadjutors'. They preached the obligation of employers to pay men high enough wages 'to enable them to keep their wives in comfort at home, without the necessity of sending them to work in the mills'.[19]

In 1853 the Blackburn Association of Cotton-Weavers, Warpers, and Winders negotiated the first district price list for weaving that lasted.[20] Cotton was one of the new successful industries. Employers anxious to make the most of a profitable trade were more inclined to make concessions to their workpeople. Most of the earliest unions that endured were in expanding trades such as engineering, boiler-making, the iron and steel trades, coalmining, and building.

By contrast, the development of trade union organization in the woollen trades was arrested by their relative decline in importance. Many, including Sidney and Beatrice Webb, blamed women for the poor state of organization in this occupation. However, according to some statistics of the 1840s, while women outnumbered men in *worsted* factories, in the factory production of *woollens*, men outnumbered women.[21] The weakness of trade unionism was not attributable to the sex of the workers, but reflected the state of the trade and the tougher attitude of employers. Clearly a preponderance of female labour could not in itself inhibit trade union organization as successes in cotton-weaving showed.

In the same way the low wages of women have been continually ascribed to some innate peculiarity in the women themselves. It was true that it had become customary to pay women less when they were doing the same jobs as men, except in cotton-weaving with its price lists. They also suffered because, as the population rose, too many of them were chasing too few jobs. They were worse off than men in this respect, because all during the nineteenth century there was not merely an increasing total population, but a continuing small surplus of women over men. To this natural increase was added immigration into the factory areas of people from rural districts, and sometimes the forcible removal of country people to towns.

Often too, owing to pressure from fellow-men workers, women were employed on lower-graded, and therefore lower-paid, work. In Lancashire in 1834, the highest average wage for men was said to be 22s. 8½d. per week, but for women only 9s. 8¼d.[22] But if demand for items manufactured by women outstripped supply, their wages sometimes rose in response to market pressure. 'The demand for female handwork in Birmingham has so increased that women's wages have risen lately about twenty per cent. Here some are earning eleven shillings per week ...', as a writer remarked in Charles Dickens's weekly, *Household Words*.[23]

It has been contended that women were more likely to let themselves be used as strike-breakers than men. This was certainly not always the case. For instance, in the Northampton boot and shoe trades, women and men alike supported a Protection Society set up to try to arrest the introduction of the sewing-machine for 'closing' or fixing the 'uppers', or tops of shoes, to the soles. In 1858-59, the riotous behaviour of women and boys who were chiefly affected was too much for the men, an echo of the uproar in the silk trade a century and a half before. But women and men alike acted as 'blacklegs', taking work in new factories using the sewing-machine.[24]

The consequences of unregulated competition for work among a growing mass of workers were worst in those trades where trade unionism, or even a tradition of trade unionism, was most lacking, not in villages where there was at least an old tradition of communal action, but in cities. In the city clothing trades, far from the idyllically happy non-working wives prognosticated by Francis Place in his letter to James Turner, there was a mass of women as defenceless as they were desperate for work. And since such women would work for any wages, they forced down the wages of men. The London Tailors who had contrived to stop women working in their trade to a large extent by the early 1830s, were complaining fifteen years later:

> The masters have now learned that tailoring work, under the sweating system, can be done at almost any price; and hence those who are anxious to force their trade by under selling their more honourable neighbours ... give the articles out to sweaters to be made by women and girls. By such means the regular tailor is being destroyed ... Women and children who before were unemployed in the tailoring trade, now form a large proportion of the operative part of it.[25]

This particular conversation published in the *Morning Chronicle* on

6 November 1849 was only one of a number of conversations on the same theme, noted by Henry Mayhew. Needlewomen and seamstresses also suffered from the competition of inmates of parish workhouses who produced 'common' shirts at three for a penny.[26]

Yet men had not learnt from this experience. The solution still proposed to limit competition for work was to take jobs from women and give them to men. In 1845, the potters' unions were trying to prevent women being introduced to operate the new 'flat-press' machines.[27] Similarly in the Sheffield file trades, men tried and failed to exclude women in 1844 and were making a renewed effort against the two hundred women and girl workers three years later.[28] Women were forced out of the ribbon factories, not being allowed in dye-houses or to make pattern cards and books. And in the boot and shoe trade, the traditional female job of 'closing' was being taken over in the new factories by boys.[29] The day-to-day struggle for a livelihood hampered realization of the trade union ideal, 'Unity is strength'.

As an alternative to 'sweated' work, middle-class demand for domestic servants mopped up many of the workless women. But the number of 'good places' did not grow to the same extent. In many households only two servants were employed, or often only one girl. Such isolated workers were in the same situation as 'sweated' workers, except that, to an even greater extent, like the poor little girls from parish workhouses, they were open to intimidation and exploitation by employers. The element of personal servitude was emphasized.[30]

The growing scramble for employment led to a further deterioration in women's status. The growth of prostitution as a means of earning a livelihood among those who worked in the seasonal clothing trades[31] particularly, inspired Parliament to try to bring this under state control, as in France. It passed three Contagious Diseases Acts in 1864, 1867, and 1869. These Acts gravely infringed women's freedom, since any woman living in a naval or a garrison town could be denounced as a prostitute, and classification as such by the police was a lifelong sentence.[32]

The continuing pressure for shorter hours of work was one aspect of the policy of reducing competition from women for work. After the 1833 Factory Act was passed, considerably restricting the use of child labour in cotton factories, women replaced children.[33] So, similarly, it was hoped that a restriction on women's hours of work would cause employers to replace women with men. It was true that men trade unionists hoped in the long run to

reduce the length of the working-day for themselves, but the immediate battle was for work.

An agitation commenced for a 10-hour day for adult women,
known as the Short-Time Movement. In 1842 the Yorkshire Short-
Time Committee was demanding much more. The females of
Todmorden has been worried a decade earlier by proposals that
women should relinquish jobs to men. The Yorkshire Committee
asked for legislation to control the proportion of women to men
workers, including a ban on any married woman working while
her husband was alive.[34]

In its stated aim of merely limiting hours of work, the Short-
Time Movement had the support of women in textile areas. Female
Gardeners and Ancient Virgins rioted in support of an 8-hour day
in Oldham in 1840, for example. Shorter hours would spread work
among more women and women in cotton-weaving were too
essential a part of the labour force to fear that men would take over
their jobs. All warpers and winders were women, as well as large
numbers of weavers. This Oldham protest also proved, incidentally,
that the women's Friendly and Benefit societies still did not limit
themselves only to an interest in benefits, but were prepared to
take militant action in support of an industrial aim.

Women were, however, removed by Act of Parliament from one
traditional employment, coalbearing and ancillary work underground in mines, following the Report of the 1842 Commission
on Mines. The outcry about their conditions and complaints to the
Commission came less from miners than from scandalized coal-
owners and their stewards and from philanthropic Radicals. In
Lancashire and the West Riding, women and children had been
leaving the pits anyway as textile factories provided alternative
work. But in country districts men were still used to having them as
helpers, for the only other jobs available to them were in
agricultural work. Women continued to work above ground at the
pit-heads, cleaning and grading the coal.[35]

The very long hours worked by women and children were compared by contemporaries with the number of men unemployed, or
with time enough to hang about streets and pubs. But it was not
only unemployed men who enjoyed a pint of beer. A working wife
and mother also liked a drink and a chat, hence the popularity of
Friendly Clubs. Lord Ashley deplored the neglect of their families
which he felt sprang from this:

A man came into one of these club-rooms, with a child in his
arms. 'Come lass', said he, addressing one of the women, 'come
home, for I cannot keep this bairn quiet, and the other I have left

crying at home'. 'I won't go home, idle devil', she replied. 'I have thee to keep, and the bairns too, and if I can't have a pint of ale quietly it's too tiresome. This is only the second pint Bess and me have had between us; thou may sup if thou likes, and sit thee down, but I won't go home yet'.[36]

The report of this incident illuminated not only the current social disapproval of this reversal of roles, but also the confidence of the woman wage-earner, utterly at odds with the conventional, prototype, downtrodden, Victorian, housebound wife and mother completely dependent on her husband.

The 1844 Factory Act established a 12-hour day for women factory-workers. Trade union and radical pressure produced a whole series of such Acts. The 10-hour day for women factory-workers was established in 1847, but increased to $10\frac{1}{2}$ hours three years later. Limitations on hours of work were extended from cotton factories to textile print-works in 1845, and to bleach- and dye-works in 1860. In 1864 and again in 1867, the existing Factory Acts were applied to the manufacture of matches, munitions, iron, guttapercha, paper, glass, and tobacco products, and in engineering, printing, and bookbinding. The 1867 Act covered all industries in which more than fifty people were employed in one establishment. However, all those in 'sweatshops' and all home-workers were still without protection. But another Act in the same year regulated workshop conditions and so extended theoretical protection to 'sweatshops'. It also prohibited the employment of children under eight years old, restricted older children's hours of work and the hours women worked to 12 per day, if they were not covered by the earlier $10\frac{1}{2}$-hour limit. Enforcement of these Acts was another matter. The factory inspection system was not effective. Only in 1871 was a specialized Factory Inspectorate inaugurated. And home work was still excluded.

Middle-class and aristocratic support for trade unionism was growing. More of such persons came to understand that unions, and a trade well regulated by mutual agreements, reduced the amount of industrial strife. The philanthropically inclined were appalled at the results of free competition for jobs and the still almost absolute power wielded by employers over their workpeople. They saw that effective trade union power evened up the balance between capital and labour. So trade unionism was among the forms of self-help philanthropic, intellectual societies encouraged. The most noteworthy of these institutions was the National Association for the Promotion of Social Science whose president was Lord Brougham, and whose members included leading trade unionists.

The unions on their side, the better to co-ordinate their activities and support each other during strikes and lock-outs, set up in various towns and cities committees known as Trades Councils of delegates from local union branches. No one thought in terms of a single grand national union for all trades any more. But trade unionists began to consider setting up a national co-ordinating body. Encouraged in this idea by discussions of the National Association for the Promotion of Social Science, Sam Nicholson and William Wood, President and Secretary respectively of the Manchester and Salford Trades Council, called a congress to enable union members from different places to discuss trade union problems and publicize trade union work. The first meeting, at Whitsuntide in 1868, is regarded as the first Trades Union Congress.

Effective leadership of the trade union movement at this time was in the hands of five men, later nicknamed by Sidney and Beatrice Webb 'The Junta'. The use made of existing law to strengthen trade unions, and the help given them by radical politicians, gradually created an understanding between the leading trade union members and Liberal MPs who accepted responsibility for piloting through Parliament laws, like the Factory Acts, that unions wanted to see passed. The relationship came to be known as the Lib.-Lab. Alliance. Because of its partial alliance with Liberal statesmen and employers, British trade unionism was tacitly committed on its side to upholding the existing social system. The Labour movement had offered no serious challenge to the established order since the Grand National Consolidated Trades Union and Robert Owen had tried to substitute a co-operative system in the early 1830s. Thus the British unions held aloof to some extent from the revolutionary movements of western Europe. But they could not escape the impact of events there, culminating in the publication in 1869 of Karl Marx's *Das Kapital,* and the Paris Commune of 1870-71.[37]

The crowning achievement of the Junta and its supporters, following the Lib.-Lab. tradition, was in prevailing on the Royal Commission on Trade Unions of 1866-67 to recommend changes in the law so as to give trade unions greater legal rights. The resulting Trade Union Act of 1871 not only permitted strikes and afforded protection to union funds, but enabled unions that registered with the Registrar of Friendly Societies to hold property and bring and defend actions at law. A Criminal Law Amendment Act, also passed in 1871, permitted trade unionists on strike to mount pickets to try to persuade black-legs not to work. This legislation was the biggest step towards the complete social acceptance of trade unions since Joseph Hume's Act abolished the anti-Combination Laws in 1825. It went a long way towards repairing the limitations imposed on the unions by the amending legislation that followed (see page 31).

In 1871 the Trades Union Congress replaced the Junta's unofficial leadership with an elected Parliamentary Committee of ten members from among the officials of the strongest unions. The Committee adhered to the Lib.-Lab. Alliance. Its particular aim was to organize the trade union 'lobby' in Parliament.

Women were not without a voice in determining this conciliatory policy. A number of women were elected to the committees of the local cotton-weaving unions which pursued a curious course of, on the one hand, alliance with upper-class philanthropists like Lord Shaftesbury, people who did not want to be associated with the development of trade unionism, and on the other, opposition to the TUC Parliamentary Committee's moderate policy of emphasis on the Friendly and Benefit side of trade unionism. On the contrary, they shared with the mining unions the belief that wages should be the first charge on employers' profits. They went further, for they would not countenance, as the miners did, scales of wages that slid up and down automatically according to whether profits rose or fell. Their price lists, once agreed, should in their view only be altered by joint negotiations with employers.

There can be little doubt about the part of women in deciding the conservatism of the cotton-weaving unions. Nearly a generation later, women led a breakaway from the Blackburn Weavers', Warpers' and Winders' Association, to form a union nicknamed the 'Tory Club', in protest at the support given by the parent association to the nascent Independent Labour Party.[38] Women were on both sides in this dispute, living proof of female interest in trade unionism and the ability to lead unions. At one time the Wigan Weavers' Association was practically a women's union. Both there and at Oldham, women were elected union presidents.

Women therefore supported the cotton-weaving unions' alliance with the male cotton-spinners, formed on 1 January 1872, known as the Factory Reform Association, with the object of obtaining the 9-hour day. In order not to antagonize their anti-union supporters, they steered clear of the TUC Parliamentary Committee. The prime movers in the Association were the men cotton-spinners who were using the old tactic of asking for shorter hours for women and children first, in order to shorten their own working-day. The women approved because it was a genuine feint and not a

Blackburn Weavers' Banner. Since the price list negotiated with employers in 1854, this Association has been officially recognized — the first cotton-weaving union to have established continuous legal existence

disguised attempt to put them out of work. As Thomas Ashton, secretary of the Oldham Spinner's association, was fond of putting it, the battle was 'fought from behind the women's petticoats'.

The concern of the philanthropists and Radicals for women workers was expressed in a paper read at the National Association for the Promotion of Social Science's first Annual Conference in 1857.

> The absorption of the female sex into the industrial ranks has wrought itself out under every discouragement ... As a general rule, therefore, only women belonging to the lower orders have pressed into employment, and only the meanest occupations have been opened for these ...[39]

They reacknowledged that most women worked for their livelihood in the new factory-dominated economy as they had done earlier in their homes. It was true that in many cases philanthropy was not undiluted with an anxiety to make the best use of cheap female labour. But they believed in minimum standards of working conditions.

One old solution to competition for work which they actively encouraged was emigration to the colonies and the United States of America.[40] To working-class women they held out the hope of matrimony as an inducement to undertake domestic service in

Australia and New Zealand where there was a slight surplus of men. For daughters from lower middle-class families there were places as teacher-governesses. More and more of these girls from large families who could not provide for themselves and who could not find husbands faced the choice of 'sweated' work as seamstresses or prostitution.

There was an earlier instance of more direct help for working women in Britain. In the summer of 1846, Mr Samuel, and more particularly Mrs Courtauld, asked Miss Mary Merryweather to run classes for the 937 girls and women employed at their steam power-loom silk-mill in Halstead in Essex. The educational purpose of her appointment linked her to the radical middle class. But in addition, Mary Merryweather initiated welfare provisions, based on contemporary thinking. She was, in effect, an early welfare officer. The practices she introduced still formed part of the programme of aims of militant women trade unionists in the second half of the twentieth century.

Her charges were the womenfolk of agricultural labouring families. Although it involved them in long walks to and from their own work, the men came to the town in great numbers because of the work available there for the women and girls. These countrywomen, whose forebears had been hit by the transfer of the worsted industry to the North of England, lacking a skilled occupation, also lacked self-confidence. Like the men, they frequented pubs. They were thankful for small mercies:

> If we said to a poor woman who came for relief 'I hope your husband is kind to you', the answer often was 'Well, Ma'm he don't pay me' (beat me), implying that she was grateful for this amount of goodness. If we said, 'I hope your husband is good and sober', the answer most often was 'Oh, Ma'm, he can't get enough out of his wages to drink much!'[41]

The firm ran a doctor's club with a subscription of 1*d.* a week. But the girls complained that they were not given the necessary medicines because they were too dear and the doctor, being engaged with better-paying patients, left them to the care of his assistant.

The worst problem was the care of children while their mothers worked. All the customary difficulties encountered in the factory towns of the North appeared. Infants were left with slightly older children who had no idea how to care for them, or with old women who had not much more sense and tended to stuff them with suet puddings. Along with the common administration of 'sleeping doses' of laudanum, their ignorance contributed to a high infant mortality rate. Mary Merryweather's solution was to persuade the Courtaulds to run a crèche at the factory. It operated for nearly three years from December 1850 until September 1853. Crèches and day nurseries were advocated generally at this time, for instance in *Household Words*.[42] Mary Merryweather also opened a home for the unmarried girls, residence being voluntary.

Her main educational effort was an evening school. The girls started work at thirteen years of age and few had any schooling even at a local school largely supported by the Courtaulds, or at two church schools, although most began learning to read at the Sunday School. The wildest and roughest tried to obstruct the really interested by preventing their taking jobs as monitors. But they failed and Mary Merryweather, appealing to their emotions so near the surface with stories of well-known heroes and heroines, found the girls' interest in the domestic details of their lives gave chances for surreptitious instruction in domestic science.

Only in 1833 did schooling become compulsory for factory children and for a mere two hours a day. But employers often supported educational provisions, and not only for children. Once the 10-hour working-day for women was introduced in 1844 and they had more free time, evening schools were opened for them in London and in Birmingham, for example, where one was said to be flourishing in 1852. In 1845 the People's Instruction Society was established and provided evening classes for women as well as men. Women power-loom weavers were reported to be enrolling.[43] Like Friendly and Benefit Clubs and the trade unions, it was all part of the self-help movement.

Self-help was not a monopoly of the towns. A Mutual Instruction Movement began for farm servants at Rhyme in Aberdeenshire in 1846 and a class was formed for the women among them. They attended a conference at Rhyme three years later and the Movement went on for some years. But no new members came forward to replace the old ones as they left.[44]

In the northern textile towns, however, something more advanced could be attempted. In 1859, Miss Fanny Hertz of Bradford spoke to the National Association for the Promotion of Social Science on 'Mechanics' Institutes for Working Women'. Two on a very small scale, based on the principles of self-government, were then established, one in Bradford, and one in Huddersfield which had been steadily increasing 'in prosperity and usefulness' since it was opened in 1847.[45]

Because of its concern about the lack of work for women, the National Association for the Promotion of Social Science was connected in 1859 with the formation of a Society for Promoting the

Industrial Employment of Women, under the presidency of the Earl of Shaftesbury, formerly Lord Ashley. The secretary was Miss Jane Crowe and the offices were at 19 Langham Place in London. A periodical of the middle-class women's emancipation movement, the *English Woman's Journal,* edited by Miss Bessie Rayner Parkes, encouraged the Society. The women's emancipation movement itself was another middle-class movement which began to concern itself with working-class women in the late 1850s. The Society for Promoting the Employment of Women started an Employment Register to help educated women in search of work.[46] Bessie Parkes and Miss Emily Faithfull together succeeded in establishing a second Society for the Employment of Women in Edinburgh in 1865.[47] They also sought to increase employment for women in printing work which led to a clash with printing unions.

Women had worked as compositors from the time the printing press was introduced into Britain in the fifteenth century. It was a family trade carried on in villages as well as in towns.[48] The first attempt to introduce women into a big commercial printing house is though to have taken place at Messrs McCorquodale of Newton-le-Willows in 1848 when they were 'apprenticing and training female compositors and working them under the same rules as men'. Before the Children's Employment Commission of 1862-66, the firm had given this up.[49] But, meanwhile, in 1857 Emily Faithfull started a house in Edinburgh where the printing work was done by women and in which a kind of union, the Edinburgh Women's Typographical Society, functioned. This venture failed commercially and she came to London where she joined forces with W.H. Head who had set up the Victoria Press, employing women only. Named after the Queen, the work of the Victoria Press included printing the *English Woman's Journal* and the Reports of the National Association for the Promotion of Social Science.[50]

During the 1860s attempts to employ women in typographical firms increased. In 1860 the Typographical Association's executive was stopping its members from working in certain printing houses because they were employing women, but women were not driven out of the trade. A letter in the *Printers' Register,* the printing trades' journal, of 6 February 1869 attacked the Victoria Press for employing women at less than trade union rates. The writer feared that 'The mixture of sexes in a printing office would tend very much to injure the morals and minds of the innocent females, and aggravate all the baser passions of humanity ...' Men might be displaced by women workers and their wives and children become dependent on charity. 'Beware, then', he concluded, 'of Female Labour in the Printing Office'.

The same journal in April, however, in a series of articles on printing and publishing in Scotland, referred to women workers in bookbinding. They were accepted in the trade without any sign of a lowering of morals in their workplaces. They took charge of the printed sheets when they were brought from the drying-room and folded them with 'great expedition'. Then 'a staff of girls take the folded sheets and arrange them in order for binding ...'

It was in Scotland that women really established themselves in the printing trades. In Edinburgh in 1872 and in Aberdeen about the same time, women were brought in to break strikes of men compositors, thus giving the men a genuine grievance. In Edinburgh the issue was the men's determination to obtain a 51-hour working-week; in Aberdeen, apprentices. The result was that by 1899 there were about 540 women employed in 21 firms in Edinburgh alone, as compared with about 300 employed by 13 firms in the whole of England.[51]

As a result the hostility of men printers towards women working at their trade persists to the present day. In 1926 the Typographical Society was to block a move towards a merger with the Scottish Typographical Association and the National Society of Operative Printers and Assistants because those organizations had women members.[52]

The development of women's trade unionism in the printing and bookbinding trades respectively, disproves a long-held view, that craft workers were, and still are, automatically easier to organize than those in less skilled grades. For trade unionism did not flourish among skilled women printing-workers. All their efforts to organize at this time foundered on the rock of men's resistance. But trade unionism did take root among the less skilled bookbinders. The opposition of men trade unionists was strong enough to counteract any increase in self-confidence that training and exercise of skill engendered.[53]

The most obviously striking aspects of the development of women's trade union organization in the mid-nineteenth century were the triumphs of the cotton-weavers, warpers, and winders, the help from middle- and upper-class philanthropists, the extension of legal control of hours and conditions of work. But of equal and perhaps greater importance was the continuing grasp of sections and groups of women workers of what trade unionism could mean for them. Many came through these searing decades with their belief in trade union organization intact. The end of the period saw them struggling, as they had all the way through, to set up associations. In 1866, Sarah Gittens, Sarah Crawford, and Mrs Taylor succeeded in organizing tailoresses in Birmingham to the extent that they won a wage rise.[54] In 1872, the Edinburgh Upholsterers' Sewers' Society was established and continued in existence for many years.[55]

Notes

1 B. Disraeli, *Sybil*, Bk VI, ch. iii and ch. viii, See also the *Pioneer*, 14 June 1834, for universal suffrage advocated as a principle of union.
2 Hansard 1844, vol. 73, 1097; vol. 98. 290: P. W. Slosson, *Decline of the Chartist Movement*, New York, Columbia College, vol. 73, no. 2.
3 J. M. Baernreither, *English Associations of Working Men*, 225-7.
4 The *Weavers' Journal*, 1836. Note in 1837 women were admitted to the Bolton Assoc. of Cotton-Spinners' Piercers' Section, Neff, op.cit., 32.
5 The *Weavers' Journal*, 1836, 107: *Pioneer*, 31 May 1834, letter, all men and women should unite.
6 ibid., 104, 109.
7 ibid., 114. Letter about a Twisters' Meeting, one woman signatory. There were fewer women than men weavers.
8 J. R. MacDonald, *Women in the Printing Trades*, 32-6. Trades' Societies and Strikes, Report of the Committee on Trades' Societies of the Nat. Association for the Promotion of Social Science, 1859. T. J. Dunning, 101-2.
9 *Nottingham Review*, 4 Dec. 1840: also 18 Dec. 1840 for Employer's Letter in support of the strikers.
10 ibid., 11 Dec. 1840.   11 ibid.
12 ibid., 18 Dec. 1840.
13 H. A. Turner, *Trade Union Growth, Structure and Social Policy*, analyses the development of trade unionism in the cotton trades. See also S. J. Chapman, *The Lancashire Cotton Industry: E. Baines, History of the Cotton Manufactures in Great Britain* for a contemporary account.
14 Trades' Societies and Strikes, Report of the Committee on Trades' Societies. Committee of the NAPSS, 554, Frank H Hill.
15 B. Drake, ed., *Women in Trade Unions*, 119, the Blackburn Association.
16 *Northern Star*, 9 May 1840, 5; 16 May, 8; 23 May, 5, 8; 30 May, 2; 13 June, 2; 20 June, 1; 27 June, 5; 4 July, 3; 11 July, 3; 18 July, 8; 8 Aug., 6: H. A Turner, *Trade Union Growth, Structure and Policy*, 117. The strike caused the creation of the Power Loom Weavers' Association of Great Britain and Ireland. It began on 6 May, 4,000 coming out at once from 19 of the town's 25 mills. A further 3 mills were due to come out and the number on strike expected to rise to over 5,000: Hansard 1844, vol. 73, 1097, Sir Charles Shaw police commissioner, on women as leaders of riots, etc.
17 Trades' Societies and Strikes, Report of the Committee on Trades' Societies, NAPSS, 1859, 457. Another threat to a woman recalcitrant about paying her union dues ran: 'If Roger does not pay Punch will tell about her robbing the donkey of its breakfast to stuff her bustle with'. In other words, she was pinching coal intended for the fire for the donkey engine and hiding it in her bustle to convey it home. The

strike was partly aimed at raising weavers' rates to the prices
established for Blackburn; an East Lancs Amalgamated Power
Loom Weavers' Association covered the whole area and the
striking Padiham weavers joined it. Rule 32 of this union laid down
'That when any member of this association apply to the general
secretary *for the rate of wages per standard list,* he must communicate with
his or her employer on the subject'. Women were accepted into
full membership: 439. A deputation to the East Lancs Association
to dissuade them from ending the strike consisted of three women
and three men: 464.

18 ibid., 253-4. Women must have been among subscribers to the strike
fund, for they were certainly members of some of the contributing
unions such as the Manchester Finger Warpers; Manchester and
Glasgow Silk Small-ware Weavers; shoemakers from a variety of places;
the Ashton Industrious Sick and Burial Society. The list of unions
covered many trades in which women worked, e.g., tailoring, tin-plate
manufacture, glass-making, tobacco.

19 ibid., 219-20. In this dispute one employer broke ranks and secretly
agreed higher wages with a group of operatives represented by four
women and one man.

20 ibid., 433. Lists for separate trades were negotiated, starting with
spinners on 1 Oct. 1852, with 3 lists for the weaving trades in July and
August 1853.

21 Turner, op.cit., 199-200: 1833 Supp. Reports to the Factories
Commission as to the Employment of Children, *Parliamentary Papers*
1834, XIX, Pt 1, 37.

22 ibid., 29, 33-5 and 292.

23 Charles Dickens, ed., *Household Words,* vol. IV, 449: vol. V, 192-7.

24 Trades' Societies and Strikes, Report of Trades' Societies Committee of
the NAPSS, 3.

25 E. P. Thompson and E. Yeo, *The Unknown Mayhew,* 226, from the
Morning Post, Letter xvi, 11 Dec. 1849.

26 Neff, *Victorian Working Women,* 131, quoting *Punch,* vol. XV, 140.

27 W. H. Warburton, *Hist. of Trade Union Organisation in the North
Staffordshire Potteries,* 193-4. Drake, op.cit., 6.

28 Trades' Societies and Strikes, Report of Trades' Societies Committee of
the NAPSS, 554, Frank H. Hill.

29 ibid. 1, 3, John Ball. Everyone in the trade, i.e., women and boys as well
as men, was eligible for membership of the Northants Boot- and Shoe-
Makers' Mutual Protection Society, set up in April 1858. Voting in this
union was by districts and not by membership grades. The union ran
the strike the following Feb., 1859, p.6.

30 Pinchbeck, op.cit., 155.

31 Thompson and Yeo. op.cit., 176, 178, 201, 204, etc., Pinchbeck, op.cit.,
310, n 3; 311, n 3, from Select Committee on Factories Bill, 1831-32,
XV, 467: 1843 Report of Children's Employment Commission, XIV,
A10, A12, 172, 173, 225f.: *Pamphleteer,* vol. XXVI, 1827, 115-16.

32 R. Strachey, ed., *Our Freedom and its Results,* ch. 4 Alison Neilans, 173f.

33 Neff, op.cit., 26, quoting A. Ure, *Philosophy and Manufactures*, 466, 473:
    Peter Gaskell, *Artisans and Machinery*, 1836, 173. *PP.* 1842, XXII,
    365. Besides increasing numbers of townswomen going into factory
    work, there was immigration from the countryside. Poor Law
    Commissioners often arranged for Lancs manufacturers to
    take on surplus agricultural population. In addition to providing
    'hands', this brought down wages, since rural standards were lower
    than urban. See Pinchbeck, op.cit., 185: *Hansard* 1844, vol. 73, 1147-48:
    vol. 74, 970. J. Clapham, *Economic History of Great Britain*, vol. I, 582-3.
    Countrywomen, it was hoped, would reduce the incidence of
    'turn-outs'. The countrywomen sometimes preferred factories to rural
    workhouses: W. Cooke Taylor, *Notes of a Tour of Manufacturing Districts of
    Lancashire* and Letter to *Morning Chronicle*, 20 June 1842; C. Ryle Fay,
    Life and Labour in the Nineteenth Century, 174; F. W. Tickner, *Women in
    English Economic History*, 136-7.
34 Neff, op.cit., 31.   35 Pinchbeck, op.cit., 246.
36 *Hansard* 1844, vol. 73, 1096.
37 Louise Michel escaped to England. See M. Bondfield, *A Life's Work*, 47-8.
38 Information kindly supplied to the author by present officials of the
    Blackburn and District Weavers', Winders' and Warpers' Association.
39 Trans. of NAPSS. Paper read at 1857 annual meeting, 533.
40 ibid, 1861, 686n: 1862, 811-12, Miss Rye and Miss Hill: 1868, 342,
    Miss Lewin and Miss Layton.
41 M. Merryweather, *Experience of Factory Life*, E. Faithfull & Co., London,
    1862, 18-19.
42 ibid., 52f.; *Household Words*, vol. II, 110.
43 *Household Words*, vol. V, 78, 85-9: Ure, op. cit., 343-455: Neff,
    op. cit., 78: Pinchbeck, op. cit., 307n. 2.
44 *Scottish Farm Servant*, Jan. 1927, 171.
45 Trans. of NAPSS, 1859, Fanny Hertz, *Mechanics' Institutes for Working
    Women, with special reference to the Manufacturing Districts of
    Yorkshire*, 347f.
46 Trans. of NAPSS, 1861, 685. R. Strachey, *The Cause*, 93-9.
47 Trans. of NAPSS, 1868, 342.   48 Pinchbeck, op. cit., 284-5.
49 L. Barbara Bradley and Anne Black, *Women Compositors and the Factory
    Acts, Economic Journal*, 1899, 261ff.
50 Trans. of NAPSS, 1859, 819-22 and 1861, 685, E. Faithfull: H. Goldman,
    Emma Paterson, 78-9.
51 Bradley and Black, op.cit., 261-2: MacDonald, op.cit., 45.
52 J. Moran, *NATSOPA, 75 years*, 115.
53 A. Fox, H. A. Clegg, and A. F. Thompson, *History of the British Trade
    Union Movement since 1889*, vol. I, 149.
54 J. Corbett, *History of the Birmingham Trades Council, 1866-1966*, 172. For an
    account of a strike by women in 1861 who, besides letters, speeches and
    'wall placards', resorted to 'a liberal expenditure of forcible Saxon
    language', see 1861 Trans. of NAPSS, Bessie R. Parkes, 634.
    Unfortunately she did not state where it took place, nor the outcome.
55 S. and B. Webb, op.cit., 336n.

66

1 Emma Ann
  Paterson
2 Bessie Rayner
  Parkes
3 Emily Faithfull
4 Sir Charles Dilke
  and Lady Dilke

(Emilia Frances,
née Strong)
5 Gertrude Tuckwell
6 Margaret Hardinge
  Irwin
7 Margaret Bondfield

5   The Women's Trade Union League

For about half a century after the early 1870s, the history of women's trade unionism in Britain was dominated by a series of individual women of great strength of character. Most of them were middle class and because of their ability to speak in public and to obtain space in newspapers, they took the limelight from the ordinary women and men slogging away at trying to establish unions. They won publicity for working women, illuminating the conditions of the worst paid, those who were 'sweated' and worked in isolation in their own homes.

The first of them, Emma Ann Smith, was a direct successor of Bessie Parkes, Emily Faithfull, and the members of the National Association for the Promotion of Social Science.[1] She was born in 1848, the daughter of a headmaster of a Pimlico school attached to St George's Church, Hanover Square, in central London. Realizing her intellectual abilities, her father saw to it that she was well educated. Her training was also practical in that it included a spell as an apprentice bookbinder. But when she was sixteen years old, in 1864, her father died. She tried the usual recourse of the genteel girl who had to earn her own living, teaching in a school that her mother endeavoured to start, and working as a governess.

About 1866 she finally found work that suited her, as clerk to an elderly lady who was herself clerk to the secretary of the Working Men's Club and Institute Union. This was another of the middle- and upper-class creations intended to help and educate working people. Its first president was Lord Brougham, who also presided over the National Association for the Promotion of Social Science. The following year, Emma, aged nineteen, on her employer's recommendation was appointed assistant secretary of the Working Men's Club and Institute Union. She also met Emily Faithfull and worked with her trying to form societies of women printers. Thus before she was twenty she had close connections with the trade union movement.

But she gave up this work and in February 1872 was given the job of secretary to the Women's Suffrage Association. However, her new employers soon sacked her. In their opinion she lacked the personal magnetism, the emotional rhetoric, and polemical power to appeal to large Women's Suffrage meetings.[2]

Despite her genteel parentage, Emma Smith was a wage-earner. Her intellect and character were disciplined not only by her up-bringing and education, but also by the practical experience of the bookbinding trade. She understood working-class bread-and-butter issues, simple matters of life and death which were too mundane for the women's suffrage leaders. She had the virtues needed by working women: she was shrewd, commonsensical, level-headed. At the same time she had an excellent memory, and was indefatigable in the cause for which she chose to work. Like many other delicate and gentle souls, she had great determination. Although her matter-of-fact manner made it impossible for any man to make her a personal compliment, or to be rude, she inspired affection as well as respect. 'An aimiable lady', one of them called her.[3]

In July 1873 she married Thomas Paterson, a cabinet-maker and wood-carver of Scots origin. Paterson was one of the three honorary secretaries of the Working Men's Club and Institute Union. He became vice-chairman and helped to organize the Workers' International Exhibition at the Agricultural Hall in 1870.

Emma and Thomas Paterson went off for a prolonged honeymoon to the United States of America. It was there that she found the aim to which she wanted to devote herself, the encouragement of trade unionism among women. She returned inspired by successful women's benefit and trade union societies, particularly the Female Umbrella-Makers' Union of New York and the Women's Typographical Society. Along with her own experience in bookbinding in London and her realism, her observations there determined that she should follow the existing trend of separate all-female unions. She did not have first-hand knowledge as yet of the 'mixed' textile unions of the North. Nor, throughout her life, did she show awareness of the women's Friendly and Benefit societies, and other forms of self-help in Britain. For these were not the kind of organizations that could negotiate with employers. Neither she nor anyone else saw the first, faint signs that men's unions were being impelled to remove the barriers to women's membership. She knew that in her own trade, the London Consolidated Bookbinders' Society still refused to recruit women. She was not bitter towards the men. On the contrary, sensibly she sought help from all the men trade unionists she knew who had assisted women's organization. Through the Working Men's Club and Institute Union she had friends and contacts ready to support her efforts. She simply felt that if women could establish lasting societies in New York, they could succeed in Britain and so enable women to clamber out of their 'sweated' working conditions.

Emma Paterson did not make the mistake of appealing directly to working women. She first sought middle-class support, which she knew existed, for the setting-up of a National Union of Working Women. She used various means of publicizing the idea. Her arguments were nicely calculated to stir the sympathies of the manufacturers, property-owners, middle-class women philanthropists, and craft trades unionists to whom she looked for immediate help.

She opened her campaign with an article in *Labour Review* in April 1874, stating her belief that the solution both of women's problems of long hours and low pay, and of men's fears of competition for jobs from low-paid female labour, was the establishment of trade unions for women. She understood that it was this fear on the part of men that had led them 'to pass rules in many of their trade societies positively forbidding their members to work with women'. But if she understood men's fears of cheap female labour, she also mistrusted their intentions. Hence her opposition to a renewed attempt prompted by men's unions to limit hours of women's and children's work in factories and workshops. The classing of women with children perpetuated 'the idea that women are entirely unable to protect themselves' which was 'to a certain extent, degrading and injurious'. This legislation, which was then at the stage of a parliamentary Bill, was supported by well-meaning people intent on improving women's working conditions. But, she argued, 'if this is done by legislative enactments instead of by the combined action of the workers themselves, the result may merely be the reduction of wages, already often insufficient, and sometimes complete exclusion from work ...' Without trade organizations the women had no way of making known their views on such legislation. But recent combined action by men in the building and engineering trades to establish the 9-hour day had shown 'that no legislation was necessary'. Combination and trade unionism were the best means of improving wages and reducing hours of work.

The *Englishwoman's Review*, reprinting the article, added that she instanced a very successful New York women's union that had paid out in sick benefit alone 'during the three years of its existence, more than £200'. Whereas during a slack period in the bookbinding trade in London, in 1871, while two men's unions paid out £2,500 in unemployment relief to members, 'the women in the trade having no union to fall back upon, suffered the greatest distress'.[4]

The response to Emma Paterson's appeal was such as to justify the calling of a conference of sympathetic ladies and gentlemen on 8 July, under the chairmanship of Mr Hodgson Pratt, her own and her husband's friend, another of the honorary secretaries of the Working Men's Club and Institute Union. This meeting founded what came to be known as the Women's Protective and Provident League.[5] The first title chosen was the National Protective and Benefit Union of Working Women. A committee was set up which, as well as the Patersons, included Mr and Mrs Hodgson Pratt, the Rev. S. Hansard, and others. Later the League's committee came to include Mr Arnold Toynbee, Miss Harriet Martineau, and the Rev. Charles Kingsley. In 1875, Emilia Strong, or Mrs Pattison by her first marriage, who had begun to combine social reform with work as an art historian, joined the League. She was pretty, worldly wise, a devout churchwoman. Ten years later, after her husband died and freed her from an unhappy marriage, she married Sir Charles Dilke, a Liberal politician and old friend, just then ruined by accusations that he had entertained a young woman in his bedroom.[6] Dilke, a Radical, through association with his wife became one of the League's chief spokesmen in the House of Commons. Lady Dilke also brought her niece, Gertrude Tuckwell, into the League's work. Miss Tuckwell was a school-teacher, lacking her aunt's good looks but with all and more of her force of character, a sharper intelligence, and considerable business ability. She became editor of the League's journal.

The result of the first conference in July was the calling of a meeting of working women, chiefly bookbinders. As this was Emma Paterson's own craft, she knew and could contact them, and the London Consolidated Bookbinders' Trade Society gave help. Its secretary, Mr H.R. King, and two other members were among those who addressed the meeting. A further meeting of all the 5,000 women estimated to be then working in this trade in London was proposed.[7]

However, the first society sponsored by the League was set up not in London but in Bristol, following Emma Paterson's address to the National Association for the Promotion of Social Science's Congress there in September. It was called the National Union of Women Workers. But a national union was not then a possibility, because of the established segregation of women into local specialist all-female societies. Moreover, London alone was too big for a single general union like that in Bristol. There the trades had to be tackled separately.

From autumn 1874 to July 1875, 5 London societies were set up for bookbinders, upholstresses, shirt- and collar-makers, dressmakers, and hat-makers. Their secretaries became *ex officio* members of the Executive Committee of the League. Trade union support increased.[8] As well as the London Bookbinders, Edwin Coulson, General Secretary of the London Order of Bricklayers, and George Shipton, a member of the London Trades Council Committee and secretary of the Amalgamated Society of Housepainters and Decorators, lent help and encouragement. George Shipton's predecessor at the London Trades Council, George Odger, of the small Ladies Shoemakers' Society, the editor of a famous trade union paper, the *Beehive*, was to be of great help at the Trades Union Congress.[9]

The societies the League sponsored were open to all women over the age of sixteen provided two women of experience in the relevant trade vouched for their competence at work. The preponderance of middle-class philanthropists on the League's committee led to a very moderate policy. Since industrial disputes were to be avoided, there was no provision for strike or lock-out benefit. Between 1874 and Emma Paterson's death in 1886, the Women's Protective and Provident League claimed to have set up thirty or forty of these women's societies in England and Scotland. The upholstresses' organization, like the Bristol union, survived for twenty years. The bookbinders under the secretaryship of Miss Eleanor Whyte, a working bookbinder, for nearly forty.[10] Lady Dilke was largely responsible for establishing a general union in Oxford that included domestic servants and lived on until 1913. Miss Jessie Craigen, with the support of the Aberdeen Trades Council, set up a women's union there which gradually took in jute- and cotton-workers. It lapsed in 1891, but was soon revived.

But not many societies had more than a hundred members or lasted for more than a few years; about half disappeared within one year of their being set up. In 1886 the total membership of exclusively women's societies has been estimated as probably less than 2,500; at least half of them in the London area. The success of the League was not in these small women's unions.

Emma Paterson's first achievement in 1874-75 was simply the establishment of the League. Her second and greatest success was at the Trades Union Congress. The Bristol National Union of Women Workers applied for credentials for a male delegate, H. M. Hunt, at the Trades Union Congress held in January 1875. In spite of opposition from the Amalgamated Society of Engineers, the TUC Standing Orders Committee allowed Hunt as a delegate. The next Congress, held also in 1875, in October in Glasgow, saw Emma Paterson as a delegate herself, representing the Societies of Women Bookbinders and Upholstresses, and Miss Edith Simcox, representing the Society of Women Shirt- and Collar-Makers, as well as Mr Hunt, once again the delegate for the Bristol union. Once the entrée had been gained, the number of women delegates rose to reach ten in' 1881, the record until 1915. Except in 1882 when her husband was dying, Mrs Paterson continued to act as a delegate at each succeeding Congress until her own death.

The one issue on which Emma Paterson found little support at Congress was precisely the focal point of her original attack right from the time of her return from the United States. On special legislation to regulate hours and conditions of work for women, not only men opposed her at the 1875 Congress. Even Edith Simcox disagreed with her. The feminist lobby had managed to have the Bill killed in Parliament. But a Royal Commission was appointed and in 1875 inquired into the operation of the Factory and Workshops provisions. As a result a new Bill was proposed and approved by the TUC Parliamentary Committee. Their aim was to bring restrictions on the hours of work and kinds of work permitted for women and children, together with rights of inspection of factories and workshops, under one comprehensive Act. Emma Paterson stood by her views that women had a right to pronounce on legislation which affected them and that the way to improvement was not by paternalistic state action, but through the building-up of trade unions strong enough to negotiate agreements with employers. Moreover, she reiterated her suspicions that men trade unionists' support for the Bill was because they saw in it a means of curtailing further the occupations open to women.

Most of the League's delegates to the TUC, unlike Edith Simcox, supported Emma Paterson in her stand against the Bill. At her first Congress in 1875, in one of her few flamboyant outbursts, she interrupted one of the greatest trade union personages, Henry Broadhurst, secretary not only of the Operative Stonemasons' Society, but also of the TUC Parliamentary Committee. When he pronounced that 'To shorten the hours has ever been found the best way to improve the conditions of both men and women', she interjected a shout of 'By union!'

Broadhurst stated candidly that the improvement in the material circumstances of working men had effected a withdrawal of married women from the labour market. This had reduced competition for work and, he claimed, raised the wages of women who continued to work. He overlooked 'sweated' work, ever the recourse of married women who had to keep themselves and their families. In spite of the growth of 'sweating', Broadhurst like other TUC leaders thought in narrow terms of his own experience as a skilled craftsman.[11]

Removal of women from the heavy labour and grim conditions of underground work in the mines thirty years earlier was advanced as one of the beneficial effects of protective legislation for women. But public interest in relieving women of heavy work had stopped there. They still worked at chain-making and in the brickfields. The concern of most Congress delegates, was not purely for women's welfare, as Emma Paterson rightly surmised. Their interest in kinds of work done by women sprang also from a desire to keep them out of occupations wherever they thought they might take jobs from men.

The arguments about the Factories Bill continued at Congress for some years. In 1877, W.J. Davis remarked that in Birmingham women 'worked at the lathe and filed at the vice' and that this was harder work than chain-making and 'degrading'.[12] H.R. King of the London Bookbinders' Society, staunch to Emma Paterson and the League, replied very reasonably that the ladies had not the slightest objection to the Factories and Workshops Acts, nor to their consolidation into one Act, but 'what they wanted was that the men should not take it all to themselves to say what trades or portions of trades were or were not appropriate for women'. 'If', he said, 'the women were taken into consultation now and then by the Parliamentary Committee or by those who might be framing Parliamentary measures, matters might be very amicably arranged'. Emma Paterson and her colleagues by establishing women's presence at Congress and challenging the men's dictatorial views had moved women's trade union organization from the primary stage of simply establishing unions, to a claim for equality with men in union policy-making and leadership. It was the first such overt challenge since the agitation surrounding the Grand National Consolidated Trades Union in the early 1830s. Women's trade unionism in this respect fused with the Women's Emancipation movement.[13]

At the 1877 Congress, Emma Paterson was supported by one of the outstanding working women trade unionists of the day, Mrs Mason of the Leicestershire Seamers' and Stitchers' Society, which the League had helped into life. Mrs Mason illustrated both the hard necessities that set women to earning money and also, through her own success, the possibility of organizing home-workers within a limited geographical area. 'There were', Mrs Mason said, 'a great many villages connected with their Union, and the work they undertook was never done but in their own houses'. Some women did it 'merely for a pastime', but some widows or those like herself with sickly husbands depended on it for their own livelihood and that of their families. Increased wages would mean they need not work such long hours. She was not keen on inspectors popping into their homes since 'there were times when it was hardly desirable to have their houses inspected'. But she favoured a law enabling inspectors to see their husbands were out of bed before lunchtime. Her attack on lazy husbands brought the house down.

In villages with a stationary population home-workers not only *could* organize, they *had* organized all through the first century and a half of the development of trade unionism in Britain. Success was due to devoted men and women like Mrs Mason, prepared to trudge through wind and weather around the countryside to keep in contact with members and collect subscriptions. This required an immense physical effort, greater for women than for men in that it came not only on top of a day's work at earning, but was somehow squeezed in amongst all the work they had to do in their homes. Mrs Mason's organizational work was recognized by her election to her local Trades Council. She was the first woman known to have achieved this office. But she died young, three years after this Congress.[14] Organizing home-workers in city slums did not entail lengthy walks, but the population was more mobile, the workers more feckless and fickle. It was arduous and heartbreaking. Small wonder that trade union officials preferred the quicker returns from recruiting in factories and large works.

The resolution advocating the consolidation of the Factories and Workshops Acts and the extension of protection to women and children in new categories of work was, however, carried as usual. In 1878 the Bill became law. The League's fears appeared justified when, in 1882, in the case of the Black Country metal unions and then in 1885 through the Coal Mines Regulation Act in the case of the Miners' Federation of Great Britain, attempts were made to use legislation to exclude women from working. The miners wanted to stop them 'screening' the coal, that is, removing rock and other non-combustible impurities, a job they did at the pit-head.

The unions on their side considered that this middle-class opposition to a curtailment of women's working-hours and a more effective inspection of working premises, sprang from mixed motives. They saw that, for example, Mrs Millicent Fawcett, a member of the committee of the London National Society for Women's Suffrage, was also a shareholder in Bryant and May's match factory and that she was opposed to any restriction in the use of yellow phosphorus in the manufacture of matches, despite the fact that it caused necrosis, or rotting of the jaw-bones through phosphorus poisoning.[15]

Since opposition was useless once the Bill became law in 1878, the

League's committee shifted their line of attack, demanding women factory-inspectors to see the law was properly carried out. The bulk of TUC delegates were satisfied with only men inspectors. But in 1885, they bowed to the League's stubborn campaign and passed a resolution which included a demand for women as well as men sub-inspectors in factories. It was not until 1893 that the first woman factory-inspector was appointed. She was May Abraham, who married H. J. Tennant, Chairman of the Government Committee inquiring into Dangerous Trades. Both worked closely with the League.

Emma Paterson's own belief expressed at the end of her life was that the only real means of strengthening women's economic status, and that of men, was for both sexes to work together through trade union organization; to emphasize the unity and community of their interests as human beings instead of their physical differences. The League's committee therefore, notably Emilia Pattison, were determined to maintain good relations with men trade unionists. So during the 1877 Congress, Emma Paterson and her colleagues invited men delegates whose unions had an interest in the organization of women, to a social gathering to meet them and women trade unionists from the locality. This became an annual institution and survived the League; it continued until 1972.[16]

The League's standing at Congress was that of a Trades Council. When, therefore, in 1895 Congress took from Trades Councils the right of representation, the League also lost its right to send delegates. But its representatives came from the small societies it had fostered and not the League itself. These had the normal rights of bona fide unions to representation. Their delegates kept open the means for women to enter into Congress deliberations and maintained the League's presence there since their secretaries were League Committee members. By this time women also attended as members of 'mixed' unions.

In 1885, Emma Paterson proposed the formation of separate Women's Trades Councils, like those already established in the trade union movement, but linking together local organizations concerned with women workers. Besides promoting and encouraging existing unions among workers, she wanted them to collect and publish information on women's working conditions 'with a view to influencing public opinion, and promoting legislation' that would lead to improvements. She also suggested they should use all legitimate means to achieve 'fair and uniform wages, shorter hours, and sanitary workrooms'.

Several Women's Trades Councils were set up. The first was in

Glasgow in 1892. The one that lasted longest was the Manchester and Salford Women's Trades Council, established three years later.[17] It became a part of the main Trades Council in 1919 and was kept going as a sub-committee during the first half of the twentieth century to a large extent by the efforts of Miss Mary Quaile. In 1952 she was presented with the Trades Union Congress silver medal for the best contribution to Trades Council work.

The composition of these councils exactly mirrored the League committee. The members of the Manchester and Salford one were local worthies like the Rev. Dormer Pierce and Mr Campagnac, Warden of the University settlement, middle-class women who were local members of the Women's Trade Union League, and officials of the Trades Council. Mr F. Entwistle, President of the Manchester and Salford Trades Council, and Mr G.D. Kelley, the secretary, were also members, for example.

The Women's Councils promoted local women's unions. The 1897 Report for Manchester and Salford showed, for instance, that one had been set up for women in the printing trades and another for 'girls employed in machine works'. Efforts were being made to create unions for umbrella-coverers and laundresses. Once a women's union was established it was the policy of the League and of these offshoot councils to amalgamate it with a similar men's society in order to form a 'mixed' union. So Manchester and Salford had succeeded in the course of the year in bringing about a merger of the shirtmakers from the Federation of Women Workers and the Shirt- and Jacket-Workers' Society. By 1887 the League had become a federation of bona fide unions of women workers.

From 1882 when her husband died, Emma Paterson continued to work unceasingly in spite of growing ill-health for the single object of increasing trade union organization among women. On 1 December 1886, she died at her lodgings in Westminster; she was only thirty-eight years old. Among the trade unionists present at her funeral to show the great respect in which they held her, the TUC representative was her old adversary, Henry Broadhurst, by then an MP.

As relations improved with men trade unionists, to a large extent due to Emilia Pattison's efforts, the League became increasingly alienated from employers who were keener on the 'provident' than on the 'protective' side of its activities. In the year Emma Paterson died and in accordance with her wishes, the League officially decided to change its title. In 1889 it became merely the Women's Provident League and two years later, simply the Women's Trade Union League. Gradually it shed its 'provident' offshoots, a Halfpenny Savings Bank, the women's labour exchange, a workers' restaurant, a swimming club, and much more. Emilia Pattison, now Lady Dilke, and Edith Simcox ran it until, in 1887, Miss Clementina Black was appointed the new secretary and Lady Dilke became chairman.

Besides having prominent men trade unionists interested in women's organization on its committee, the League had all along accepted affiliations from unions. But it was no mere co-ordinating body of independent unions, 'mixed' or wholly female. It continued itself actively to encourage women's trade union organization, employing paid organizers of its own. Organizing for the Women's Trade Union League was just like any trade union organizing — a hard slog of much travelling, holding meetings, and distributing leaflets in bad weather and often only with poor attendance as a result.

For example, Miss Barry, one of the League's organizers, in the first week of February 1897 was organizing women workers in the Canada Docks area at Liverpool and in Birkenhead. While there she secured the support of Miss Julia Dawson, editor of the women's column in the *Clarion*, a socialist journal. Julia Dawson asked for a Women's Trade Union League organizer to open the Clarion Van campaign with a series of lectures.

At the start of the second week in February, Miss Barry was in Grimsby organizing the net-braiders who made fishing-nets for steam trawlers. Fishing was expanding and their work with it. In the third week she was tackling women boot and shoe-workers at Kettering, who 'like those in all the other trades where work is done in the home are very difficult to get at'. But again the boot and shoe industry was expanding, with more firms opening their own workshops. On 12 March she was at the Clarendon Press in Oxford inquiring into low rates of pay for women workers. The women were paid nothing for their first month's work when they were learning their jobs. Over the following six months their pay rose from 2s. 6d. a week to 12s., but 'at this sum they stop, even if they work for 20 years'. Three days later she was in Yorkshire where two meetings she arranged at Leeds were very poorly attended. And so on.[18]

But the League's organizers would not have had any success at all if there had not been all over the country a network of people, both middle class and trade unionists together with their wives, interested in building trade unionism among women. They helped arrange meetings, and followed them up. The League's committee kept in contact with these local sympathizers and the small women's societies by making a tour each autumn which took them all over the country and as far north as Aberdeen. Reports from different areas were published in the *Women's Trade Union Review*. It was indeed a national and not merely a London organization. But London was inevitably the centre of its activities because it was the seat of Parliament.

The League developed a parliamentary lobby aimed at improving working conditions. In this aspect of its work, the League did not limit its interest to women workers. Its concern was for all workers, irrespective of sex.

One of its longest campaigns, and ultimately to some degree a success, was that against lead poisoning in the pottery trades. The 1834 Children's Employment Commission noted that both men and women were engaged in the process of 'dipping' pottery and that arsenic was used in glazes. No protective legislation had been passed. During the 1891 Trades Union Congress held at Newcastle-upon-Tyne, the League's delegates and supporters followed their usual practice of taking the opportunity to find out about women's work in the city where Congress was held, with a view to encouraging organization. Their investigations on this occasion led them to the Newcastle and Tyneside lead-works, like Ismay's at Ouseburn, or Cookson's at Willington Quay, Gateshead, and Hayhold in East Howdon. The October 1891 *Women's Trade Union Review* carried a report on conditions there. The lead, after it had been baked in ovens for a week or more, was reduced to a fine white powder that worked its way into the pores of the skin and the lungs. In this way it caused 'a form of paralysis, eye disease and other maladies ...' to the workers. A woman when carrying the lead from the ovens wore a handkerchief over her hair and another over her mouth. Their employers had tried issuing them with respirators, but the women apparently found them too uncomfortable to use. Frequent baths would have helped them and all factories had bathing facilities. But the women were 'negligent' about using them, so that they seemed to make little effort to help themselves.[19]

In the Midlands potteries, however, the workpeople were trying to fight for themselves. In the summer of 1894, Mrs Goodwin, organizing secretary of the Potteries Union, along with thirteen men, represented the workers at a conference on the Special Pottery Rules. She wrote to the League:

Dear Miss G. Tuckwell,
... My chief desire was that the rules might be made more effective as regards *ground layers*, which might have been omitted, but are now inserted in the special rules; but a lot more wants doing; we *shall want more inspectors*, it is necessary to see that the

rules are carried out, the inspectors are scarce ever on the factories!

As a result of her stand, the workers were provided with overalls and head coverings to protect them from the dust. She was also trying to obtain more extractor fans.[20]

Mrs Goodwin explained why management welfare provisions were often not adopted, why the women were 'negligent': 'the prices are so exceedingly low for groundlaying that the workers have not time to look after themselves as they ought'.

Publicity brought supporters, notably the *Daily Chronicle* which published an article on conditions of work in November 1892. Five years later, the League, through its columns, appealed successfully for funds to help two girls and a boy blinded by their work. Some pottery firms offered help and a memorial asking for a woman inspector was organized, signed by hundreds of women workers and well-wishers, including the Duke and Duchess of Sutherland. A powerful deputation, headed by Sir Charles Dilke for the Liberals and Sir John Maxwell for the Conservatives, pressed the claim for a woman inspector in an interview with the Home Secretary. But they came away empty-handed. The League doggedly determined 'to see the whole question again raised and fought in the House of Commons'. But meantime news of two more deaths had come in.[21]

It was not until 1922 that the Women and Young Persons' Employment in Lead Processes Act was passed, a posthumous triumph for the Women's Trade Union League which had ceased to exist from May 1921.

By the mid-1880s, socialist parties were being established, the Socialist League, then the Social Democratic Federation with Marxist leanings. On Sunday 13 November 1887, this swerve to the left in the British Labour movement manifested itself in the form of a demonstration by radical clubs, trade unionists, socialists, even some Fabians, in defiance of a government ban. They marched on Trafalgar Square in protest against widespread unemployment. In the clash with police and troops detailed to prevent them reaching the square, one man was killed.

This episode, known as 'Bloody Sunday', had widespread repercussions. Among others it provoked the inauguration of a new left-wing publication, the *Link*. The editor of this journal, Mrs Annie Besant, visited Bryant and May's match factory in the East End of London and persuaded some of the girls to give her information about their pay and working conditions. As a result they were sacked, and their colleagues struck work to try to get them reinstated.[22] Not knowing what to do once they had left the factory, they went to Fleet Street in a body where Annie Besant saw them from her office window. She and Herbert Burrows, together with the Women's Trade Union League, formed the girls into the Match-Makers' Union, and started negotiations for improvements with their employers. They aroused public support to an extent then unknown and raised a large sum for distribution as strike pay. Consequently the employers had to make some concessions. This success in turn gave hope to other sections of low-paid workers. But it did not, as is sometimes assumed, result in reasonably healthy working conditions for workers in match factories. The Women's Trade Union League went on campaigning for those of both sexes as they did for the pottery-workers.

The dangers remained very grave. Parliamentary Reports of 1843 show that it was already known then that the workpeople in match factories were threatened with necrosis of the jaw. One of the first Lady Assistant Commissioners, appointed some fifty years later by the Board of Trade, Miss Clara Collet, compiled a report in 1894 based on visits to factories.[23]

But in 1898, ten years after the first matchgirls' strike, the *Women's Trade Union Journal* published a list of case histories of women and men suffering from this terrible industrial disease, in which the whole jaw was gradually eaten away by phosphorus.[24]

Real improvement only came in 1901 through provisions for dangerous trades in the Factory and Workshops Act of that year, and the 1908 Act forbidding the use of white phosphorus, which could then be enforced against the employers.

The 1888 union continued to function. At the end of 1893 there was a strike at Bell's match factory because the employers 'tried to get fifty per cent more work from the girls for the same wage!' One hundred and sixty of the girls were then locked out for no stated reason. After they were taken back, three members of the Trade Union Committee were sacked. 'The girls saw in the move an attempt to break up their Union', and came out on strike again. One girl, Ellen Conway, was sentenced to one month in gaol for breaking a window, although it was not certain that she was the culprit. The strike dragged on for months, with the League and well-wishers subscribing funds.[25]

The Women's Trade Union League was written off by many trade unionists during its existence as a collection of 'do-gooders', notwithstanding the members of unions affiliated to it and the presence of some eminent trade unionists on its council. It is still considered as such by some connected with the trade union movement today. But it was much more. It assured to women a place at the Trades Union Congress, in spite of the opposition of some trade union leaders. It pioneered the technique of long-term political lobbying on behalf of women workers, sustaining campaigns for many years. It claimed to have been instrumental in securing the 1895 Factory Act, the 1896 Truck Act, and the 1898 Workmen's Compensation Act. The 1898 Act enabled it to fight claims of injured work-women who did not know their legal rights, and made compensation compulsorily payable for industrial diseases such as anthrax. The League claimed credit for the 1904 Regulation of Conditions of Home Work Act and the Shop Hours Act of 1906. It certainly initiated the use of legislation to help workers who were unable to build unions; and it became a part of the great movement of working-class organization of the 1880s and 1890s. It was a great memorial to the tenacity of Emma Paterson.

Notes

1 H. Goldman, *Emma Paterson*, 20 ff.; B. Drake, *Women in Trade Unions*, 10 ff.; S. and B. Webb, *Hist. of Trade Unions*, 336-7n.; M. A. Hamilton, *Women at Work*, 51-2; J. R. MacDonald, *Women in the Printing Trades*, 36-7. Harold Goldman's detailed life of Emma Paterson, published 1974, must be considered the most authoritative account in so far as there are discrepancies, e.g. over her father's first name. His school was transferred from the authority of St George's Church, Hanover Sq., to St Peter's Church, Pimlico.
2 Goldman, op.cit., 28. She told Emilia Pattison that her employers had said: 'my bodily presence is weak and my speech contemptible'.
3 ibid., 27: Drake, op.cit., 25.
4 The *Englishwoman's Review*, New Series, Oct. 1874, 215-16: see also 1874 Trans. of NAPSS, 945-47, paper by E. Paterson.
5 *Englishwoman's Review*, Oct. 1874, 281-2.
6 Roy Jenkins, *Sir Charles Dilke*, 94, 197f., 296, 395. Hamilton, op.cit., 54, 56.
7 *Englishwoman's Review*, Oct. 1874, 282f.
8 List of unions affiliated to the WPPL, later the Women's Trade Union League, are at the back of each issue of the *Women's Trade Union Review*.
9 Goldman, op.cit., 45-6.
10 Drake, op.cit., 11-13.
11 1875 TUC Report: Goldman, op.cit., 70: H. Pelling, *A History of British Trade Unionism*, 86. In 1876 Emma Paterson started the *Women's Union Journal*, later called the *Women's Trade Union Review*.
12 See 1859 Trans. of NAPSS. *Household Words*, 152-3, 654: vol. IV, 141, 415; vol. V, 195-6; *Edinburgh Review*, vol. CX, 1859, 538-9.
13 1877 TUC Report 17-19, 42-3.
14 ibid., 19.
15 Strachey, *The Cause*, 234-40: TUC pamphlet, 'Women in the Trade Union Movement', 46; M. Ramelson, *The Petticoat Rebellion*, 102 ff.
16 Drake, op.cit., 16-18, 23-4.

17 *Women's Trade Union Review,* Jan. 1896., 13: April 1897, 12-13; K. G. Busbey, 'The Women's Trade Union Movement in Great Britain', *Bull. of U.S. Dept. of Labor Statistics,* No. 83, 1909, 15-16: Ramelson, op.cit., 130: A. Fox, H. A. Clegg and A. F. Thompson, *History of the British Trade Union Movement since 1889,* vol. I, 470, n1. C. P. Scott was among those who helped to start the Manchester and Salford Women's Trades Council. W. Diack, *Trade Unionism in Aberdeen,* 237-40. The two rival Manchester Women's Trades Councils merged with the Trades Council proper in 1919.

18 *WTU Review,* April 1897, 19-23.

19 ibid., Oct. 1891, 15; Jan. 1893, 12-14; Jan. 1894, 13. See W.H. Warburton, *History of Trade Union Organisation in the North Staffordshire Potteries,* 35-8, 43-4, 77-8 for potters' unions and women. The League was also campaigning against conditions in bronzing and the 'green sickness' in the rubber industry. There were also campaigns to help those working at fur-pulling, dressmaking, etc. See Annual Reports of Chief Inspector of Factories, particularly 1896 for Reports of Lady Inspectors. Also Hilda Martindale, *Servants of the State,* 51 ff. for work of early women factory inspectors.

20 *WTU Review,* July 1897, 7.

21 ibid., July 1898, 9.

22 There are many versions of this famous strike: A. Stafford, *A Match to Fire the Thames,* is the most complete account. See also R. and G. Frow and M. Katanka, *Strikes,* 101-4, quoting A. Besant's autobiography; B. L. Hutchins, *Women in Modern Industry,* 127-8; Drake, op.cit., 26; Hamilton, op.cit., 41f.; Pelling, op.cit.; etc.

23 Reports of Assistant Commissioners on the Employment of Women, 1893-94, *PP* c8694, XXIII, V. 37, Clara Collet.

24 *WTU Review,* May 1894, 7-9; Oct. 1898.

25 ibid., 1893, 14-15.

6 The Mass Organization of Women Begins

The activities of the Women's Trade Union League were the most publicized aspect of women's part in the general upsurge of trade unionism in the last thirty years of the nineteenth century. The success of craft and industrial workers in establishing organizations helped to revive among the vast unorganized mass of British working people the 'spirit of union' of fifty years earlier. Groups of them that had so far failed to set up lasting associations, gasworkers, builders, general labourers, railwaymen, and agricultural workers, were all making renewed efforts from the early 1870s. It was unorganized Sunderland shipbuilding workers, not the craft, élitist Amalgamated Society of Engineers, who, in 1871, forced employers to agree to a 9-hour day for their trade.

The Trade Union Act and Criminal Law Amendment Act of 1871, the crowning union achievements of the mid-nineteenth century, were the first spurs to renewed mass activity. But confidence in the protection of the Criminal Law Amendment Act was soon shaken by a famous case involving women. Among the new organizations was the National Agricultural Labourers' Union, founded in 1872. A few of its members worked on a 'Government Farm' occupied by Robert Hambidge, at Ascott-under-Wychwood in Oxfordshire. They asked for higher wages and when Farmer Hambidge refused to meet their demands in full, struck work. Employees of other local farmers followed suit. Hambidge then took on two non-union young men from a nearby village. On 12 May about thirty of the trade unionists' wives and women relatives, who themselves did seasonal farmwork, met these two as they were entering a field to start work. Although some of the women carried pitchforks and the lads were 'jostled' the women offered no very serious threat to them and are said to have invited them to go down to the 'pub' for a drink. The two youngsters apparently agreed to join the union, but inevitably informed Hambidge of these events. As a result sixteen of the women came up before the Rev. W.E.D. Carter and the Rev. Thomas Harris, magistrates at Chipping Norton, and were charged and sentenced under the 1871 Criminal Law Amendment Act for threatening behaviour. Seven were given 10 days and nine 7 days all with hard labour. Two of the women had babies who had to go to prison with them. During a meeting, reinforced, it was said, by Birmingham relatives of the women, who brought along friends, some of the demonstrators threw stones at Chipping Norton police station. There the women spent an uncomfortable night without lights and enough seats and, in the early hours, were removed to Oxford gaol to serve their sentences.

The weight of public opinion, however, favoured the women against the magistrates. *The Times* published a letter on the trial headed 'Impossible!'. In spite of the Liberal Home Secretary's refusal to intervene, the women were given a free pardon, along with 5*s*. and a flannel petticoat each, by Queen Victoria. £80 was collected for them and the union. They were taken home from gaol in grand style and, at a meeting outside Hambidge's farm, Joseph Arch, the secretary of the National Agricultural Labourers' Union, presented each of them with £5 and a silk dress in the union colour, royal blue.[1]

Like the small women's societies fostered by the Women's Trade Union League, the various unions of agricultural workers, of dockers, gasworkers, and others received middle-class help. Some have sneered at them for not being able to establish themselves unaided. No amount of middle-class encouragement, however, ever created a union. Only working people could do that and without their fixity of purpose no union could have come into existence. This inflexibility was shown by farm-workers, and by farm-workers' female relatives who formed the great reservoir of seasonal labour, but many of whom also worked full-time on farms. While the members of the agricultural workers' unions of the 1870s and late nineteenth century were mainly men, they were to a great extent family unions. Their womenfolk shared in large measure in union work as they still do today.[2]

Trade unions continued to secure legislative improvements. In 1875 a Conservative government headed by Disraeli came in, partly with trade union votes because many of its candidates appeared readier than Liberals to support further easing of conditions for organization. It honoured its pledges to the unions with the Conspiracy and Protection of Property Act which legalized peaceful picketing, and with further amendments to the law relating to registration of Friendly Societies.

A labyrinth of self-help clubs still existed, among them independent Friendly Societies. In addition, there were not only productive and retail co-operatives, but also Shop Clubs, Insurance Societies, Slate Clubs run in public houses, in workshops, in churches, and chapels, especially those of the Wesleyan persuasion.

Sometimes they were attached to an educational institute or polytechnic, and some were connected with Lending Clubs. Burial Clubs were particularly popular with women. People also united in calico and photo clubs, run by publicans or dealers in second-hand clothes.[3]

Trade union recruitment was facilitated by the conversion of many family firms into limited liability companies, and the breaking of the old, close, patriarchal ties of employers with employed so that neither a sense of loyalty nor employers' disapproval could inhibit union organization to the same extent as before.

At the same time the condition of working people became harder. By the mid-1870s, trade recession had set in. Economic growth became more unsteady as export industries felt the effects of growing overseas competition, particularly from the United States of America and Germany. Employees' prospects of continuous work were more uncertain. Many of the new small unions broke up under pressure from employers for reduced wages and longer hours to compensate for their business financial difficulties.

As population expanded, cities and towns spawned dormitory suburbs which in turn created public urban transport systems. The greater ease with which trade unionists from different districts could keep in touch with each other was balanced by the greater difficulty of getting members to meet after work. It was especially hard to persuade women to come out in the evenings in view of their domestic work.

In 1886, Charles Booth, a great merchant and shipowner, began a statistical inquiry into the social conditions of Londoners. He wanted to disprove allegations that thousands of men and women were not earning enough for subsistence. When the results of the huge survey were published in the early 1890s, they proved the contrary. Two-thirds of those living in the East End eked out an existence below the poverty line. Allied to a House of Lords Report on 'sweating', this forced the better-off to admit that poverty could not be ascribed to simple wickedness. On the one hand, legislation and upper-class interest in helping working women increased. On the other, there were instances in the last quarter of the nineteenth century of women's successes in establishing trade unions in spite of the uncertainties of trade and the ever-present fear of destitution.

In 1874 in Belfast, 40,000 textile-mill workers were out on strike from 6 July until 7 August against wage reductions. Their leaders were women like Miss Brown, who told them: 'I hope as I am informed that the gates are to be thrown open on Monday, that not one of us will be seen there, unless they put up a notice to give us

our old wages ...' A union developed from the strike, but within fifteen years had lost most of its members. In 1890 organizers from
the Women's Trade Union League visited Belfast and encouraged
the Trades Council to take an interest in organizing women. The
Trades Council was lucky in having a strong trade unionist in the
Belfast textile-mills, Mary Galway. Along with some men trade
unionists, she organized the Irish women textile-workers once
more. She became an active member of the Trades Council and of
the Irish Trades Union Congress.

Following the 1896 Truck Act, the mill employers put up lists of
rules, fines, and penalties to be enforced against their workpeople.
On 19 January 1897, Mary Galway, the union secretary, led a strike
of 8,000 operatives in protest against this definition of their
working conditions. She negotiated with the employers as a
representative of the Trades Council and obtained 'considerable
modifications of the rules originally posted'.[4]

Even more impressive than this example of successful leadership
by an ordinary working woman, there were at this time at least two
instances of women's action resulting in the setting-up, not of
segregated women's societies, but of 'mixed' unions.

The first occurred in the heavy woollen district around
Dewsbury, Batley, and the Spen Valley in Yorkshire. In the 1860s
mule-spinners in the area had struck twice to try to stop employers
from switching from piece-work to a time-rate system of payment.
They were locked out and failed. However, the Huddersfield
power-loom weavers were able to establish a union and were
followed in 1872 by the Holmfirth and New Mill power-loom
weavers. Thus there was a slow build-up of trade unionism. But
there was no union in the Dewsbury and Batley district until, in
February 1875, women weavers in the Dewsbury district struck
against a sudden and arbitrary decision of the employers to cut
rates of pay. They elected a wholly female strike committee with
Mrs Kate Conran as Secretary, Mrs Ann Ellis as Treasurer, Mrs
Hannah Wood as President, and Mrs Denman and Mrs Booth to
keep the accounts of strike funds received. But, as with the mule-
spinners, the employers quickly converted the strike into a lock-
out.

Over fifty manufacturers with two or three firms of finishers and
twelve of dyers were involved. The women were given financial
support by the Batley Carr Industrial Co-operative Society, some
middle-class sympathizers, including a niece of John Bright the
Radical, but most of all by working people from Lancashire to
Leeds and as far north as Hawick in Scotland. During attempts to
mediate by men 'tuners' of looms, it came out that some manufac-

Strike Committee of Dewsbury and Batley Heavy Woollen Weavers, 1875

turers had been giving out longer warps (vertical threads) than the
weavers knew. So they had been doing more work than they were
paid for. There were large protest meetings of 9,000 people on one
occasion and 7,000 on another.

On 3 April, two days before the strike ended successfully, a public
meeting agreed on the formation of the Dewsbury, Batley, and
Surrounding Districts' Heavy-Woollen Weavers' Association.[5]

A similar move by Dundee women jute- and flax-workers was
even more remarkable, given the terrible conditions under which
they had been working. The operatives had been virtually treated
as prisoners, tied to their jobs almost in the same way as Scottish
mining families were until the 1788 Act ended slavery in the Scottish pits. In evidence to the Factories Inquiries Commission, a witness stated that the operatives were crowded communally into
'bothies' without regard to age or sex. In order to keep the mill
going 17 or 19 hours a day, there were no meal-breaks. But
'women were employed to boil potatoes and carry them in baskets
to the different flats' (floors of the mill). The workpeople hastily
swallowed a potato while carrying on with their work. They had
brose, a thin porridge, at night, because it was quickly prepared.[6]

The workpeople were very frequently beaten, children who
made a slip through overtiredness, excessively, the House of Commons Committee witness said. Sometimes girls ran away. Two
escaped through the roof and left nearly all their clothes behind.
Another from Duntroon Mill was recaptured and kept seven months in Dundee jail for 'deserting'. She was then brought back to the
mill 'to make up her lost time and the expense incurred'. One day
the witness, alarmed by cries of 'Murder', discovered 'the master

had her by the hair of the head and was kicking her on the face, and the blood was running down'.[7] Conditions at Duntroon were particularly bad.

During the next forty or so years there was some improvement in hours and working conditions. In the summer of 1875, provoked by a threat of wage reductions, the workpeople were out on strike. Without any organization or strike funds, inevitably they had to return to work on their employers' conditions. In the 1885 depression in textiles, east of Scotland employers followed those of Lancashire in imposing a 5 per cent wage cut. There was at that time considerable unrest in the east Scottish textile towns. At the end of August, the Dundee jute-workers, the main body of them women, again came out.[8] The girls turned for help to some radical middle-class men and women who were speaking at strike meetings and trying to help these workers. A clergyman, the Rev. Henry Williamson, negotiated with the employers, without result. But he and one or two others, in late August 1885, helped the uneducated women to set up a Dundee and District Mill- and Textile-Workers' Union, with headquarters at the Rev. Williamson's mission rooms, and Williamson himself as Union Secretary.[9]

Williamson and the other radicals did not condemn all strikes as is sometimes said.[10] What they endeavoured to inculcate into the workpeople was that it was useless to strike against wage cuts during a recession. The best thing was to await an 'upturn in trade' and then put pressure on the employers to restore and possibly increase earnings. This precept he proved with the Dundee Mill- and Textile-Workers. The 1885 wage cut was duly restored at New Year 1889.[11]

More important, from this nucleus, union branches were formed in the surrounding textile towns, Arbroath, Montrose, Alyth, Brechin, Forfar, Dunfermline, and links maintained with an Aberdeen women's union (see page 71). By the late 1880s, these branches were breaking from the parent Dundee union and becoming independent.[12] From eight of these unions in 1892, the number rose to fourteen in 1900, many of them assisted by middle-class philanthropists. They were encouraged by committee members of the Women's Trade Union League on their annual tours through the East of Scotland. The women jute-workers' action resulted in another solid core of organized workers, like the Lancashire cotton-weavers, although the numbers were smaller.[13]

By the early 1880s various men's unions were being opened to women so that the trend was away from segregation and towards 'mixed' unions. As women were increasingly brought in to replace men in mass-production methods, unions were forced to rethink their exclusive policies. For instance in 1884, the National Union of Boot and Shoe Operatives, set up ten years before, resolved that:

> All women working at the shoe trade be admitted into the association upon the same terms and entitled to the same rights as men.[14]

In spite of the mule-spinners' restrictions on women's entry to the trade and union, there were nearly two thousand women in lower-grade 'piecers' sections of their unions, chiefly in the Bolton Provincial Association of Operative Cotton-Spinners. But by this time, ring-frame spinning was being introduced. About 1870, small card and blowing-room operatives' unions were being formed and finally amalgamated into one union, the Association of Card and Blowing-Room Operatives. Although at first they excluded women, or expelled them from the old local unions, women were employed in ever greater numbers. So the Amalgamation decided to enrol them and to acknowledge the interdependence of men's and women's work.[15]

Women were members of the Hosiery Unions then struggling to establish wage agreements in face of cheaper rural labour, both male and female. In 1892 women and men struck to establish their right to join the Leicester and Leicestershire Amalgamated Hosiery Union.[16]

Inspired by the success of Annie Besant and Herbert Burrows in gaining public support for the matchgirls in 1888, at the end of that year, Will Thorne and Eleanor Marx were organizing the gasworkers, along with John Burns, Thomas Mann, and Ben Tillett, a dock labourer. The following summer this same trio were organizing dockers in their famous strike for the 'tanner', that is, 6d. more a week on their pay. Both unions took an interest in women's organization, since they were not exclusive craft societies, but general unions.[17]

The increase in numbers of 'mixed' unions, however, was balanced by hostility to women in others. One aspect of their fear of cheap female competition was a reappearance of demands for 'the rate for the job' for women. In 1886 the Typographical Societies recommended the admission of women, but only on condition that they were paid the 'rate for the job'. The men were to some extent protected in the newspaper branches, since women were precluded from doing night-work. They still felt unshakeably confident that at the same rates of pay, employers would always prefer men to women workers. In 1892 the London Society of Compositors accepted its first woman member on these terms.[18]

But the alignment of those for and against 'equal pay' had

Emblem of Amalgamated Association of Card and Blowing Room Operatives, c.1890

become more complex since the 1830s. Not all men supported it because where competition for work was not keen, they could see no necessity for helping women to economic equality. Far more women did not support it, for they agreed with those men who saw it as a means of cutting down competition for work from women. For these women, the 'rate for the job' simply spelt 'unemployment'. But the middle-class women emancipators and educated women workers saw it as a mere matter of justice for women, since they had the confidence to assume that they stood an equal chance with men in any competition for jobs at equal rates. Finally a number of men trade union leaders believed, with the women leaders of the Women's Trade Union League, that the 'rate for the job' was a means of preserving existing wage standards for which they had had to fight so hard.

Some of these conflicting attitudes were apparent in the first Equal Pay resolution passed by the Trades Union Congress. It was moved by Miss Clementina Black, the secretary of the Women's Trade Union League, in 1888:

> That in the opinion of this Congress it is desirable, in the interests of both man and woman, that in trades where women do the same work as men, they shall receive the same payment.

She urged Congress to adopt the resolution, not only in the interests of men and women workers, but also of those employers 'who wished to do that which was right for their employés'.

She was seconded by Mr Juggins, a Darlaston delegate of the Chain-makers' and Strikers' Association, who spoke of a strike caused by women chain-makers in his district. The employer concerned had told him 'that when the time came that he had to pay women the same wages as men, he would refuse to employ them'. The resolution was carried unanimously.[19]

It was becoming clear that commitment to the political Left did not necessarily foster a belief in the equality of women as far as chances of jobs were concerned. Ben Tillett, who had become secretary of the Dock, Wharf, Riverside, and General Labourers' Union, and Alderman of the Borough of Poplar, was one of the more left-wing trade unionists. Yet in October 1896 he wrote in the *Women's Trade Union Journal* an article highly critical of married women working and fearful since unemployment coupled with 'the institution of machinery' was opening out to the employer greater possibilities 'to let the woman supplant the man as toiler ... The distinction between men and women's labour is becoming less with each piece of machinery introduced into industry ...' He saw the employment of married women as a threat to married life. For a woman life would be worse since 'domestic slavery — with some love at all events — is in the future to be exchanged for a worse taskmaster ...'[20]

In this he was supported by many women, including Lady Dilke, chairman of the Women's Trade Union League, who believed 'that our place, the place of women, is not here, but at the hearth'.[21]

Ben Tillett also warned 'the Trade Union of Women' of women's proclivity for hero-worship and their preference for men as union officials. And, forgetting the help given by the middle and upper class in the 1889 Dockers' Strike, and in 1888 by Eleanor Marx to Will Thorne over the gasworkers, he criticized women workers for looking for such help.

Implicit in the assertion of men's prior right to work was also sonetimes a positive dislike of women's economic independence. A jingle, probably by a carpet-weaver, summed this up. It formed part of the correspondence in a Kidderminster paper in 1891 about the right of men and youths who were unemployed to take over work being done by women:

Mary had a little loom, and unto it did go,
And every Sunday afternoon, you should have seen the show,
With veil, kid gloves and gaiters, too, she goes out on the mash,
She fairly knocks the men out now, because she gets the cash.

Men sometimes complained that once women were brought into their unions, they left all the work to men. Women's capacity for trade union work was, however, constantly demonstrated by the weaving and the newer clothing unions. Women members of the Dewsbury and District Woollen Weavers that eventuated from the 1875 strike, walked ten to twenty miles to collect contributions and interview employers, on top of long hours at paid work and a heavy load of housework. The month after the Dewsbury Woollen-Weavers' union was set up, the secretaryship passed to a man, Charley Grant. Then there were no further meetings of the union for over three years. Early in 1879 a woman was made treasurer for the following quarter. Mrs Ellis was the delegate to the 1882 Manchester Trades Union Congress and in 1883 it was two women who moved for amalgamation with the Huddersfield and District Power-Loom Weavers' Association which was officered by men. After the merger the women's activity lessened.

Aside from the call on women's energies of domestic burdens, the treatment accorded them in 'mixed' unions may have partly accounted for their inertia. For example, in 1885 the Leicester and Leicestershire Hosiery-Workers' Union was formed from various local unions including the previously successful women's Leicester Seamers' and Stitchers' Union. Yet the men in the new 'mixed' union then accused the women of apathy.[23] In the new union, however, as in the Amalgamated Society of Tailors and Tailoresses and many others, women were not equal members with men, but were given a lower membership grading.[24] This reflected women's lower earnings and their consequent inability to pay high membership dues, but at the same time it kept them out of union leaderships, and aggravated their sense of incapacity and inferiority.

In 1872 the National Union of Cigar-Makers tried to organize women in their trade, but found them unco-operative because they feared the men wanted to turn them out of work.[25] In 1884-86 the Journeymen Felt-Hatters, which claimed an ancestry going back to the seventeenth century, decided to organize women into a separate all-female union, the Association of Felt-Hat Trimmers and Wool-Formers, in order to prevent their performing the same work as men. In 1906, some women trimmers refused to join the women's Association. When the men threatened to strike to bring them in, the case went to arbitration and the women's representative, Miss Henshall, stated: 'We think we shall lose our individuality. We shall become part of an organization over which we shall have no control, and it will be of no benefit to us whatever...'[26]

They were quite right. The women were confined to trimming and wool-forming and prevented by the union from actual manufacture of hats. They were segregated into a special union of their own whose secretary, however, was the secretary of the men's union. But when mechanization eroded men's skills after the First World War, the differential rates of pay were maintained in the men's favour, although by the end of the Second World War the only skilled workers in the trade were women.[27]

Although men complained continually and often with reason that women let them down by undercutting their wages, there were instances of women being badly let down by men. For example, in February 1896, women and men workers in a vinegar and pickle factory in Gloucester came 'out' in protest at wage reductions. The men deserted the women and went back to work, while boys were brought in as 'blacklegs' to replace some of them. Incensed by the men's behaviour, the local officials of the Dockers' Union championed the women. Along with other members of the Trades Council, they managed to negotiate for the women smaller cuts in earnings than those originally proposed. All were given their jobs back and the women themselves were to control fines imposed for late arrival at work. Their right to join a union was established. The Dockers' Union branch, however, drew the line at enrolling them and called in the Women's Trade Union League to organize a separate women's union. But they did not relinquish interest in them. The employers agreed to discuss any future proposals for changes in earnings with the Dockers' local secretary as well as with the women's union committee.[28]

If women proved difficult to organize, or showed resentment at the kind of humiliating lower union grading that men often imposed on them, the men might have pondered the words of John

Burns, a member of the Amalgamated Society of Engineers, who became a socialist agitator. Speaking on the reactions of those men who were left out in the cold by élitist unions such as his own, he said: 'A spirit of revenge alone often prompts men to oppose or remain indifferent to Unionism, when if the Unions were wiser and more conciliatory, support would have been forthcoming where now jealousy and discontent prevails'.[29]

Elitism and snobbishness were not, however, a prerogative of men. The fastest-growing sectors of women's trade unionism in the late nineteenth and early twentieth centuries were the white-collar trades. Workers in these occupations were particularly prone to asserting their superiority over those in less well-paid, manual occupations.

The expansion of the Civil Service, especially the postal telegraph service, and of private insurance and other forms of office-work, widened the choice of work available to women since they were brought in to staff lower-paid, routine jobs. Universal primary education created for them a vast new field of employment as teachers, so that their situation became less desperate.

The white-collar unions of teachers, clerical workers, and civil servants were proving the immense importance of education and upbringing in establishing women trade unionists on an equal footing with men.[30] In white-collar work a 'marriage bar', that is retiral from work on marriage, was rigidly enforced by employers, supported by unions. Quite a number of unions, including the Shop Assistants and one or two general unions, operated 'marriage dowry' schemes. Through these, girl members, when they left work and the union in order to get married, were refunded part of the amount they had paid in union dues provided that they had not drawn out any benefits. These schemes were intended as incentives to encourage girls to join the unions. Women members of the National Union of Clerks, established in 1890, refused the 'marriage dowry'. They also insisted on paying union dues equal in amount to those paid by men.[31]

Their insistence on equality of treatment as union members and equality of pay as workers was an aspect of the commitment of many of them to the increasingly successful women's emancipation movement.

The major legislative breakthroughs that lifted women out of the legal, economic, and social inferiority that they had suffered since feudal times came in the last thirty years of the nineteenth century. New laws and court decisions particularly helped married women workers by giving them rights in their own property and earnings. The feudal supremacy of husbands, which was the basis of men's assumption of their prior right to work, or to the best-paid work, and to the receipt of earnings partly gained through their wives' work, was to a large extent destroyed. Legal steps to improve the status of married women had been taken in 1839 with the Infants' Custody Act, and the 1857 Marriage and Divorce Act. Neither had much effect, but as a result of agitation, a crucial amendment to the 1857 Act gave divorced women rights in their own property. It was not until 1870 that an Act gave married women ownership of the earnings. The independence of married women was asserted by an 1869 court ruling that restraint and confinement constituted cruelty and this was reinforced by the 1884 Matrimonial Causes Act and another 1891 court decision. In 1878 unhappily married women were given a limited legal right to obtain separation with custody of their children. From 1886 a married woman could proceed to law for maintenance from her husband without first having to go to the workhouse. And married women's property became their own without reservation in 1891 in England and Wales and the following year in Scotland.

Moreover, in 1870 the first Bill for women's franchise was given a first reading. Women were enabled to enter universities in 1875. Under Josephine Butler's leadership, and with the help of W.T. Stead, editor of the *Pall Mall Gazette*, the campaign for the repeal of the Contagious Diseases Acts that legalized prostitution succeeded in 1885.[32] Although it took some time to percolate into the minds of ordinary working people, all this legislation eventually transformed women's status.

Girls who came into commercial white-collar work were not by any means all middle-class. Country girls and manual workers sought to improve their status and earnings by coming to towns to the overcrowded professions of dressmaking and millinery and to shop-work. They were assisted in their aspirations by the advent in 1870 of universal primary education in England and Wales, and in 1872 in Scotland; in 1894 education was made free. But the more genteel occupations were by no means a sinecure.

Shop-work produced the first working girl to become a national official of a 'mixed' union started by men. Margaret Bondfield, born in the West Country, went to work in a local shop when she was fourteen. When she was eighteen years old, like thousands of others, she came to London to look for a job. She found one, working a 76-hour week for 10s., in a store which compelled its employees to 'live in', to stay at houses managed by women housekeepers who were also the firm's employees. Miss Bondfield, however, had unusual strength of character. Somehow in the rather squalid communal existence, she managed to educate herself and she joined the National Union of Shop Assistants, Warehousemen, and Clerks in 1894 as soon as she heard of it. It had been established five years earlier and was commonly known as the Shop Assistants' Union. It had 2,000 members and concentrated its efforts in the private trade. In 1898 she became its assistant secretary and waded straight into the struggle to end 'living in'.[33] In an article in the *Economic Journal* the following year, she attacked the system, disposing of any notion that it provided 'homes and guardians for the boys and girls who come up from the country'. She pointed out that employers operated a 'marriage bar' for men as well as women. They would not take on married men, or sacked those of their staff whom they found out had married, as married men required a higher family wage. Therefore men were chained to the system as well as women, since they could not set up homes of their own. That 'living in' was not essential to the welfare of the assistants was shown by Glasgow and other large Scottish commercial centres where it was practically unknown.

The houses where the assistants lived were governed by lengthy lists of House Rules. One contained 77 orders. In so far as they smacked of regulations enforced in cheap boarding houses, in obliging inmates not to stay out late, but to be up and out of their rooms early; not to break the furnishings or make a noise, they created conditions not much worse than those that shop assistants might have found anyway. But they were not allowed 'to sleep out' without permission. Worst of all, the housekeepers, who were the agents of the shops where the boarders worked, exercised a strict supervision over anyone claiming to be unwell. The house doctor's diagnosis alone was accepted.

Margaret Bondfield even went to the length of taking jobs in which 'living in' was compulsory, in order to produce a report that formed the basis of the 1906 Shops Act. As well as laying down for the first time a legal maximum number of hours to be worked, this Act also decreed the end of 'living in'. Gradually the practice diminished.[34] When she left the Shop Assistants' Union, it had 20,000 members.

From 1870 up until the outbreak of the First World War, the *rate of increase* of women's union organization was swifter than it has ever been before or since in general, as well as in some specific, occupational groups. In 1886, the number of women in trade unions was estimated, probably not very accurately, as 36,900, and this was said to be an increase of over 75 per cent during the ten years since 1876. The first official estimate of women's trade union membership in 1892 was much higher. It was put at 142,000, nearly four times the 1886 figure. But this was still only a tiny proportion of the

4½ million women workers in the 1891 census. By 1913, the number of women and girls in trade unions in the United Kingdom was over 433,000 and had risen more than another 300 per cent since 1892. The cotton unions accounted for nearly half of these with 214,109 women members. The second largest group was that of women teachers with 64,522 members, while commerce, distribution, and national and local government had another 45,016. The rate of growth between 1892 and 1913 was most rapid in the distributive unions, where women's membership rose 36 times, followed by the general unions in which it had gone up 33 times.[35]

Women became members of the Iron and Steel Trades Confederation, of the Amalgamated Association of Beamers, Twisters, and Drawers-In, and the National Society of Woolcombers which appointed two women to its executive in 1912. From 1900 they could join the Bolton Amalgamated Dyers' and Finishers' Association. In 1906 the National Society of Male and Female Pottery-Workers was formed from previous small 'mixed' associations.[36]

There was one further development in the latter part of the nineteenth century which was to help women workers. International links were created between the trade union movements of various countries. To a considerable extent this was connected with the establishment of an international code of standards for conditions of work for women and children.

In the early 1840s, Daniel Legrand, a Frenchman, was canvassing various European governments to persuade them to undertake special measures for the protection of workers who were children or girls, and, to a lesser extent, for women. The United Kingdom government had been among the first to introduce such measures, starting in 1802 with the limitation on hours of work of pauper apprentices. The British law first dealt particularly with women and girls in 1842 when legislation prohibited their employment underground in mines. The statutory 10-hour day for women in the textile industry followed in 1847. From then legislative restrictions piled up.

Women were taking an interest in the international working-class movement by the 1850s when Bessie Rayner Parkes studied Lyons silkworkers and read a paper to the 1859 Conference of the National Association for the Promotion of Social Science.[37] But it was not until a conference held in Berlin in 1890 that the protection of women workers was first properly discussed. The conference voted for five resolutions prohibiting the employment of women in underground work in mines, the employment of women and girls on industrial work at night, and the employment of women for four weeks after a confinement. It also adopted a maximum 11-hour day for women with a rest period of at least 1 ½ hours, and restrictions on their work in specially unhealthy or dangerous occupations. These resolutions were, however, merely pious expressions of hope. They had no force.[38]

In 1897, an International Labour Congress initiated by the Swiss Workers' League devoted much time to discussing conditions of work for women and young persons. The British delegation, mainly from London, included Miss Sullivan, representing the West End Tailoresses, and Herbert Burrows representing both the Match-Makers' Union and the Women's Trade Union League. A large number of men and women who had made a special study of labour legislation in their various countries attended. Miss Sullivan, for the British delegation, with the help of Frau Lily Braun of Berlin, nearly obtained support for the abolition of home-work. But the German Social Democrat Georg Heinrich von Vollmar narrowly managed to block this because on the continent large districts still depended on domestic industry.

However, the policies agreed went much further than in 1890. They included the 8-hour day and 44-hour week, legislative protection for women working in agriculture and domestic service equal to that for other workers, equal pay for equal work, and an extension of maternity leave for women from the original four weeks to a total of eight weeks before and after confinement. At least six weeks, the Congress felt, should elapse before a woman was re-employed in a factory, and pregnant women should be legally prohibited from working in some branches of industry. But this was not all. The 1897 International Labour Congress laid down as one of its aims public remuneration to a woman kept from work because of pregnancy and confinement:

> During this interruption of her labour a woman shall receive from the State or the Commune an indemnity at least equal to her wages.

Paid maternity leave from work in Britain was still merely a matter for discussion in the early 1970s.

The result of these international gatherings was the establishment in 1897 of the International Association for Labour Legislation, with its headquarters in Basle.[39]

Notes

1 E. Selley, *Village Trade Unions in Two Centuries*, 58-60; R. Groves, *Sharpen the Sickle*, 59-61; National Museum of Labour Hist., collection of cuttings.

2 Selley, op.cit., 82-3.

3 Edith M. Deverell, 'Slate Clubs', *Economic Journal*, 1899, 266ff. Some co-operatives excluded women. See G.D.H. Cole, *The British Co-operative Movement*, 87.

4 Devine, 'Women in the Irish Trade Unions': Bleakley, *Trade Union Beginnings in Belfast and District*.

5 Ben Turner, *A Short Account of the Rise and Progress of the Heavy Woollen District Branch of the General Union of Textile Workers*, 25ff. Hamilton, *Women at Work*, 53; Mrs Ann Ellis was sacked for her part in setting up the union. The WPPL believed she was the main force in the strike committee. See also Drake, *Women in Trade Unions*, 13-14. She was a delegate to the TUC.

6 James Myles, *Chapters in the Life of a Dundee Factory Boy*, 1951. Centenary ed., ch.6.

7 Rep. from the Committee of the Bill to regulate the Labour of Children in the Mills and Factories of the United Kingdom, *PP*1832, XV, 373-4: 1833 Factory Commissioners Report on the Employment of Children in Factories, *PP* 1833, XX, Section A, 22, 37-9.

8 *Dundee Courier and Argus*, 9 July 1885, 3: 16 July, 4; 4 Aug., 4; 13 August, 5. And see *Dundee Advertiser*, 29, 31 Aug.; 1, 4, 8, 9, 10 Sept.

9 Rule Book of the Dundee and District Mill- and Textile-Workers' Union, front cover and p.2. The Rev. Williamson would not at first accept men members, see *Mill and Factory Operatives' Herald*, May 1886, 2.

10 Rule Book, Dundee and District Mill- and Textile-Workers' Union, Rule, 'STRIKE OR LOCK-OUT'. *Mill and Factory Herald*, Sept. 1888, 3: Jan. 1889, 1-3, 4: Feb. 1889, 2, 4-6: March 1889, 4-5 for Kirkcaldy strike and appearance of new union for men. April 1889, 1-4: Oct. 1889.

11 ibid., 5 Sept., 2

12 ibid., Nov. 1888, 7; organization of rival Bleachfield Workers' Union, March 1889, 2. See also W.H. Marwick, *History of Labour in Scotland*, 55. In 1889 a Forfarshire Union of Textile-Workers was set up. A strike produced concessions, including a rise for lower-paid men. From this evolved the Scottish Mill and Factory Workers' Federal Union, a loose association of local unions based on the linen manufacturing towns of Forfarshire, Brechin, Forfar, Montrose. Two-thirds of this union's members were women. The Dundee and Aberdeen union later affiliated to it. *Mill and Factory Operatives' Herald*, Dec. 1888, 7, for unions at Arbroath, Brechin, Carnoustie, Montrose, also advert, p.8: ibid., Feb. 1889, 5; Mar. 1889, Kirkcaldy Union, 4-5: April 1889, 6.

13 Fox, Clegg and Thompson, *Hist. of the British Trade Union Movement since 1889*, vol. I, 188, for strong organization among Dundee jute employers and Rev. Williamson's shortcomings as a union secretary.

14 ibid., 25. Drake, *Women in Trade Unions*, 143. Unlike the Protection

Society of the 1850s (p. 52), this first factory union in the trade was set up by men for men only.

15 Fox, Clegg and Thompson, op. cit., vol. I, 120-1: Drake, op.cit., 29.

16 ibid., 29, 134. Fox, Clegg and Thompson, op.cit., 24, 191-2.

17 Fox, Clegg and Thompson, op.cit., vol. I, 65; T. Lane and K. Roberts, *Strike at Pilkington's,* 49.

18 Drake, op.cit., 32-3.   19 1888 TUC Report, 43.

20 *Women's Trade Union Review*, Oct. 1896, 7-9.

21 Lady (Emilia) Dilke, pamphlet, 'Trade Unions for Women', c. 1892, 12. Reprint of article from *North American Review.*

22 Arthur Smith, MS Hist. of the Powerloom Carpet and Textile Weavers' Assoc., Kidderminster Public Library, ch.1, 74b. See also Dilke, op.cit., 8; *Dundee Mill and Factory Workers' Herald.*

23 Drake, op.cit., 14-15: *Mill and Factory Workers' Herald,* Dec. 1889, 8: Rev. H. Williamson on breakaway unions: 'most of the trouble in some of the districts had apparently arisen from the fact that the men wished to take the whole control of the business, and leave the women simply as persons who supplied the funds (Laughter)'.

24 Drake, op.cit., 32. M. Stewart and L. Hunter, *The Needle is Threaded,* 149. Fox, Clegg and Thompson, op. cit., vol. I, 183.

25 Drake, op.cit., 18.   26 ibid., 39-41.

27 H. A. Silverman, ed., *Studies in Industrial Organization,* J. G. Dony, ch. IV, 166. Fred Worthington, Sec. of the men's and women's unions, told the author in 1966 that lock-outs in 1892 and 1907, when the union paid lock-out pay to women as well as men, helped to reconcile women to the union.

28 *WTU Review,* Apr. 1896, 13-15.

29 S. and B. Webb, op. cit., 388, 'John Burns's Address to Trade Unionists', 24 Jan. 1885. Dilke, op.cit., 8.

30 B. V. Humphreys, *Clerical Unions in the Civil Service,* 55, 135, chart opp. p. 135. Drake, op.cit., 175-9.

31 ibid., 171.

32 E. M. Turner, 'Josephine Butler', pamphlet for the Josephine Butler Centenary; R. Strachey ed., *Our Freedom and Its Results,* ch. 4, Alison Neilans, 194ff.

33 M. A. Bondfield, *A Life's Work,* 19ff.; M. A. Hamilton, *Margaret Bondfield.*

34 Bondfield, op.cit., 32, 62ff.: *Economic Journal,* 1899, 277ff., 'Conditions under which Shop Assistants Work': *WTU Rev.,* Oct. 1899, 9. Drake, op.cit., 58-9.

35 Abstract of Labour Statistics, 1911-12, 170: H. A. Turner, *Trade Union Growth, Structure and Society,* 25; S. and B. Webb, *Hist. of Trade Unionism,* 424; Drake, op.cit., 15 and Table 1.

36 Drake, op.cit., 29f. Fox, Clegg and Thompson, op.cit., 198. See also W. H. Warburton, *Hist. of Trade Union Organisation in the North Staffordshire Potteries.*

37 1861 Trans. of the NAPSS, 632ff.

38 International Labour Office, Studies and Report, Series 1, no. 1, 15 Oct. 1921, 1-2.

39 *WTU Review,* Oct. 1897, 10-15.

7 Margaret Irwin and the Scottish TUC

The second major female personality to emerge in British trade unionism was Margaret Hardinge Irwin, daughter of a Broughty Ferry sea captain. The Scottish TUC itself in large part owed its very existence to her.[1] Little is known of her early life, but Broughty Ferry is just a little north of Dundee and it is possible that the ferment among the East of Scotland textile-workers and the meetings held by Women's Trade Union League organizers first put into her head the idea of joining the Labour movement in order to help working women.

The assistance given by Emma Paterson to Emily Faithfull in the printing trades, and the contact she therefore had with Edinburgh, ensured the Women's Trade Union League's continuing interest in the organization of women in Scotland. The League always remained the Women's Protective and Provident League in this part of the country, and was supported by an array of intellectual, middle- and upper-class personages, including Professor George Adam Smith and the Countess of Aberdeen.

In 1887 Miss Clementina Black, secretary of the League, was in Glasgow. The Glasgow Trades Council had set up a committee:

> to try if something could be done to form a Trades Union for females, it having been felt that a great necessity existed for some organization to save them from the present fearful grinding down of the price paid for their labour, it being quite evident that no honest woman can live on the wages earned.

Miss Black was contacted and a meeting arranged. But only two people turned up. Mr Eddy of the Scottish Typographical Society, 'the energetic Convenor of the Committee', and those acting with him, 'resolved to persevere ...' A second meeting was held on 19 November and nearly a hundred people came. The result of the meeting was the formation of a Women's Trades Council, under the chairmanship of Mr Smart, a lecturer in political economy.[2]

From this joint Trades Council and middle-class effort two distinct organizations emerged: a branch of the Women's Protective and Provident League and a Glasgow Council for Women's Trades. From these in turn arose a National Federal Council of

Scotland for Women's Trades, whose aims like those of the League were to consolidate the interest then being shown in women's labour questions throughout Scotland and to promote legislative reforms to help women workers. This body confusingly came to be known as the Scottish Council for Women's Trades, sometimes abbreviated to the Scottish Women's Trades Council. All three bodies, the Glasgow Trades Council, the League, and the Council for Women's Trades, worked closely together. By 1895, the National Federal Council of Scotland for Women's Trades claimed to have in affiliation 16 Trades Councils and 25 trade unions representing a membership of 100,000.[3]

In 1891, the Scottish branch of the League appointed Margaret Irwin as its full-time organizer.[4] In the same year, she was appointed one of four women Assistant Commissioners responsible for gathering and supplying information on women's work to the 1891-94 Royal Commission on Labour. The *Women's Trade Union Journal,* reporting this, remarked on the unpopularity of Margaret Irwin's appointment which 'received unfavourable comment in the labour papers'. The League itself believed it had been due to wire-pulling, adding, 'she will doubtless justify the influence to which she had owed her appointment by a zealous discharge of her duties'.[5] It was not an encouraging beginning.

Her early critics had no conception of the strength of her personality. Along with immense energy and determination she had a powerful intellect and penetrating understanding which blazed out of her large, dark eyes. She was the last kind of creature in the world to submit tamely to accepting an inferior status. Her understanding and compassion impelled her to use her formidable qualities to help the poor and ignorant. There were others who felt the same but who lacked her ability and drive. Her report as Assistant Commissioner proved her interest in bettering working women's conditions. The Edinburgh Trades Council was the first to notice that it had been edited and altered. The Glasgow Trades Council protested:

> ... we express our indignation at the way in which the Scottish evidence collected by Miss Irwin, Sub-Commissioner, has been suppressed in the most important particulars by Miss Orme, Sub-Commissioner, acting with the authority of the Royal Commission on Labour; condemn the misleading footnotes of Miss Orme as tending to depreciate the evidence given by Scottish witnesses and declare the Report ... as published ... of little value ...

They intended to contact other Trades Councils to ask them to impress on the government the desirability of having the full, and accurate, version of her Report published.[6] No action seems to have resulted. The incident to this day causes astonishment and scepticism about a Royal Commission having done such a thing. But the evidence is incontrovertible.

In some ways this baptism of fire helped Margaret Irwin. Her relationship with the Scottish Trades Councils was strengthened. Her Report, along with those of subsequent investigations which she undertook, was published by the Scottish branch of the League and the Scottish Council for Women's Trades.

She carried out her surveys to a large extent alone, fumbling to strike matches to see her way up the dark stairways of the Glasgow tenements, past landings where communal sinks were frequently used as communal lavatories, along passages with numbers chalked on each door by the police specifying the maximum number of people allowed to sleep in each apartment. Perhaps the most astonishing thing she found was that here and there were 'sweated' home-workers managing to keep their single rooms sweet and clean.[7]

During the four years from 1891 when she was organizer for the League, the part played by ordinary working women at the annual conferences of the Glasgow United Trades Council increased. So did the numbers of small women's unions. Societies were set up of weavers at Napier's Mill in Bridgeton, pipe finishers at Alva, and handkerchief-hemmers and tailoresses in Glasgow. In February 1893 the Glasgow Trades Council unanimously resolved that additional factory inspectors be appointed, but they wanted 'women who have worked for a living in a workshop, factory, or warehouse, and that no other class of women be considered acceptable'. They put forward a candidate, Miss Isa Liddell, who had considerable experience in textile and laundry trades.[8]

At this time too the Trades Council backed the demand of the League and the Amalgamated Society of Tailors for a stronger Bill to protect home- and out-workers. They wrote off to the Secretary of State for Scotland to point out that the Public Health Act only required separate lavatory accommodation when more than ten women were employed, whereas it should apply if only one woman were involved; and they asked that the power of inspection be wholly in the hands of sanitary inspectors.[9]

When Emma Paterson launched her appeal for help in setting up all-female societies, she had little experience of organizing women. The League members soon found out how hard it was to establish unions of very low-paid workers. Margaret Irwin, as one of the second generation of the League, revealed the extent of the effort entailed when she told the first Scottish Trades Union Congress:

'She would rather organize ten men's unions than one woman's union', a sentiment endorsed by many men union officials. She did not blame the women for their unsteadiness of purpose, but their conditions. Her main criticism against them was 'their taking men's work at 50 per cent of men's wages', which undermined unity.[10]

Her aims then were to strengthen trade unionism in general both for the men's sake and also for the women's sake. But she followed the League's policy in simultaneously working for legislation to improve their pay and working conditions. Powerful unions would help to create a powerful lobby for legislative measures to improve women's conditions of work and so ultimately to bring about their organization.

She also believed that women like herself, if enfranchised, would have greater power to bring about the same object. Besides her trade union work, she was a pillar of Scottish women's suffrage societies.[11] Emma Paterson's devotion to women's trade union organization was equalled by her devotion to the cause of equality for women. But she confined her efforts solely to trade unionism once she set out to build the League. Margaret Irwin worked actively for both aims.

The 1895 British Trades Union Congress decided to exclude Trades Councils, and therefore the Women's Trade Union League, from affiliation (see page 75). The exclusion of Trades Council representatives disenfranchized the smaller trades who could not send delegates of their own. And there was resentment that a few of the large groups of unions, those for mining and textiles for instance, controlled Congress decisions with their votes. The Scots already felt that they had particular local problems and that the British TUC was handling too large a number of resolutions to allow time to raise these, so they decided to set up a Congress of their own.

In 1895 Margaret Irwin left her post as League organizer to take over the secretaryship of the Scottish Council for Women's Trades. The two bodies continued to work closely together. Through her work she had been in close touch with Trades Councils in a number of towns and cities. Naturally she bent her energies towards helping to create the new separate Scottish Congress. She was secretary of the Scottish Trades Union Congress Committee, and in order to give her more time to make the arrangements for the first Scottish Congress in 1897, John Brown of the Iron-Moulders' Society took over the secretaryship of the National Trades Federation Committee, apparently another of her appointments.[12]

The Scottish unions chose to strengthen the connection with the

Scottish Council for Women's Trades by specifically altering a Congress Standing Order so as to include 'Councils for Women's Trades', because societies like the Glasgow Council had done 'such yeoman service for the women's cause'.[13] Both the Scottish Council and the Women's Protective and Provident League were thus given the right to send delegates to the Congress.

On the proposal of the Govan and Falkirk Trades Councils Margaret Irwin was unanimously elected secretary for the Congress itself.[14] As one of the representatives of the National (Scottish) Council for Women's Trades, she was elected to the first Parliamentary Committee with the highest number of votes.[15] At the Committee's first meeting after the Congress on 27 May she was therefore offered its chairmanship. But there was another nomination, that of Robert Smillie, secretary of the Lanarkshire Miners' Association. There was thus the first faint clash. Margaret Irwin declined the chairmanship, but in words that showed she was conscious of her prior right: ' ... considering all the circumstances and that feeling was not quite ripe enough for a woman to occupy such a position, she thought it better to withdraw her name and allow Mr Smillie to be elected'.[16]

Less than two months later, it was Robert Smillie who proposed she become interim secretary of the Parliamentary Committee when the original secretary was forced to resign by his employers – H.M. Government. Other Committee members, however, asked her to take over as fully fledged secretary, but again she thanked them and turned the proposal down on grounds of existing 'heavy claims on her time and further that she feared that at this early stage of the Congress work it might be somewhat prejudicial to its interests were the position of Secretary to be filled by a woman'. She was, however, persuaded to act as interim secretary[17] and at the second Congress in 1898, held in Aberdeen, she was once more Congress secretary. She was nominated officially as secretary of the Parliamentary Committee by the Cabinet-Makers' Union and the National Operative Tailors of Scotland. There were no other nominations for either post. The Congress President, John Keir of the Basket-Makers' Union, a delegate from the Aberdeen Trades Council, presented her with a silver tea service and tray as a souvenir of the occasion and acknowledged her work:

It was not too much to say that to Miss Irwin, more than any man or woman in this country, was due the position of the Scottish Trades Unionists assembled there as a Congress ... He was satisfied that the work of Congress would continue to prosper in her hands ...[18]

The 1898 Congress also elected Isabella Blacklock, another member of the Council for Women's Trades, to membership of the Parliamentary Committee. As far as Congress was concerned, it was the height of the co-operation with middle-class radicals.

To begin with, the Parliamentary Committee rented a meeting-room at the Council for Women's Trades' offices at 58 Renfield Street, Glasgow.[19] Perhaps a feeling grew up that Congress was becoming too dependent on this middle-class organization. Possibly the presence of two of its lady members on the Committee was just too much for some of the other members. At all events, during 1898 the differences in priorities between the League and Scottish Council for Women's Trades on the one hand, and some of the men trade unionists on the other, began to come into the open and it became clear that they were fundamental.

For the Scottish Council for Women's Trades and the Women's Protective and Provident League one of the main concerns was to limit the 12- to 17-hour day worked by shop assistants, and the even longer hours, occasionally stretching to $37\frac{1}{2}$-hour non-stop shifts in laundries. But on the part of heavy industrial unions and their leaders, like Robert Smillie and George Carson of the Tinplate-Workers, there was a longstanding commitment to wresting an 8-hour day from the government.[20]

The main clash, however, was over parliamentary matters. From 1866 men trade unionists were chafing at their dependence on Liberal MPs The Lib.-Lab. Alliance had enabled a small but growing number of working men to contest general elections and some of them were successful in gaining parliamentary seats. But a movement built up outside the British TUC's Parliamentary Committee with James Keir Hardie at its head for an Independent Labour Party. Both the British and Scottish TUCs backed it. Margaret Bondfield, making her début at a British Congress, was one of the speakers who supported consideration of a Labour Representation Committee to promote the election to Parliament of independent Labour Members.[21] The Scots finally committed themselves to the idea in January 1900, when Margaret Irwin was still Parliamentary Committee Secretary. Their British counterparts followed suit in February.

There had already been criticism that Margaret Irwin was not sufficiently alert to the importance of the 8-hour Bill. And, at the 1899 Congress, the Parliamentary Committee Report was severely criticized for omitting reference to the Committee's efforts to promote Labour representation. In fact her name was not specifically mentioned and the whole of the Parliamentary Committee had approved the Report before it was published. The in-ference was, however, that because she had written it, she was responsible, and Robert Smillie, her colleague on the Committee, was one of the critics.[22] She defended herself obliquely while speaking to a resolution, insisting that 'it was against systems and not individuals that they should fight. To engage in personal warfare ... was ... demoralizing and had a deteriorating effect on oneself'.[23]

The Parliamentary Commitee and Congress on their side reversed an 1897 decision to support equal franchise for women, to which Margaret Irwin was so deeply committed. As Smillie pointed out at the 1898 Congress, the vote for women on the existing terms would enfranchise the middle class and aristocratic who had property, but leave voteless the mass of working women, since, unlike their menfolk, they were mainly propertyless. This strengthening of the upper-class vote might hinder efforts to establish a Labour Party in Parliament. In this the British Congress, where the matter received an airing later, was of the same opinion.[24] The Scots compromised by agreeing on universal adult suffrage, as extending to women as well as men; that is, on the demand of the 1848 Charter.

There was, however, an element of personal animosity to Margaret Irwin and to the idea of a woman as secretary of the Scottish TUC Parliamentary Committee. Emma Paterson had clashed with men union officials over the Factories Act and limitations on trades open to women, but she had not penetrated to the TUC leadership and her manner was placatory rather than bracing. No one ever described Margaret Irwin as 'aimiable'. In spite of her efforts to be self-effacing and helpful, her will and intellect and the facts and experience accumulated from her investigations made her authoritative, where ordinary, average women were submissive and pliable. Her commitment to the introduction of women's suffrage immediately enabled some of her male trade union colleagues to rationalize their resentment. The Scottish male character contained a strong patriarchal element. Furthermore, she strongly supported Conciliation Boards and condemned strikes as 'uncivilised' because of the suffering they entailed to the workpeople.[25]

An attempt was made to replace Margaret Irwin as Secretary of the Parliamentary Committee in 1899, with her support. But the Committee member offered the nomination refused it. So 'it was agreed that the present arrangement should be continued meantime', as she noted in the minutes. In 1900 she declined nomination because, she said, of the increasing claims of her other work and George Carson, secretary of the Tinplate-Workers, took over.[26]

Co-operation and mutual support, however, during her tenure of office had extended over a considerable range of issues. The whole Parliamentary Committee and Congress backed extensions of the Factory Acts to a greater number of trades. They voted for compulsory inspection of premises where outwork was done and for a wider application of the 'particulars clause' requiring employers to post up particulars of earnings for all those on piece-work systems, one of Margaret Irwin's pet campaigns.[27] Her expertise in drafting reports and memoranda was utilized on behalf of men working in railway marshalling yards.[28] Her determination helped to break down the persistent refusals of successive Home Secretaries of Lord Salisbury's Conservative administration[29] to meet Scottish TUC deputations, on the grounds that the British TUC covered the same subjects. To disprove this, she obtained, by some undisclosed means, the current British TUC memorandum to the Home Secretary, producing it triumphantly at the Parliamentary Committee meeting on 22 June 1898, partly as a gesture against her critics. As she pointed out, 'it demonstrated divergences of opinion'. She piloted her colleagues through deputations and built up the procedure of Committee meetings and Scottish TUC Reports.

Although no longer secretary, she was elected to the Parliamentary Committee in 1900 with the second highest number of votes, and was very active during the following year in campaigning for women home-workers and for improved working-class housing. The Scottish Council for Women's Trades had also taken up the case of seasonal workers.

But she only scraped on to the Parliamentary Commitee in 1901 and in 1902 did not stand for re-election.

The Scottish Council for Women's Trades still sent delegates to Congress and raised all the customary issues. Margaret Irwin was herself one of its representatives at the 1904, 1909, and 1910 Congresses. In 1910 her resolution condemning 'the scandalous conditions of housing which exist in some parts of Scotland amongst workers employed in potato gathering, fish curing, and fruit picking' was passed unanimously. She called for a government inquiry. She told Congress she had visited farms

> where from 25 to 30 men and women were lodged in some dilapidated, tumbledown barn, their only bedding some dirty heaps of straw on the floor, and the only window a hole in the wall over which sacks had to be hung to keep out the wind and the rain.

She also got in a dig about women's suffrage, explaining that appeals for an inquiry had failed 'because it was the case of voteless women who were of no value to a politician'.[30]

But deteriorating relations between some trade unions and the Scottish Council for Women's Trades were also evident. She moved for representation of Scottish labour or Scottish women on the numerous government committees of inquiry into industrial and social questions which had been recently set up. Congress, however, made it clear that its interest was not in Scottish women, but in Scottish women workers and trade unionists, before it unanimously passed the proposal.[31] For all her support for the Congress, Margaret Irwin was never a trade union member.

By this time a new organization to promote women's trade unionism had emerged, the National Federation of Women Workers. Like the Scottish Council for Women's Trades, it sprang from the Women's Trade Union League and it was created and led by the middle class (see chapter 8). But instead of seeing the Council as an ally, it became clear that the National Federation of Women Workers saw it as an obstacle. In 1906, the political Labour Party was established and to this the Federation was closely allied, while the Scottish Council for Women's Trades belonged to the era when the Labour presence in Parliament depended on the Liberal Party. Moreover, the Federation of Women Workers claimed to be a trade union. Its rights to affiliation to the British and Scottish Congress arose from this and not from any bending of the rules as in the case of the Scottish Council. The Scottish Council for Women's Trades, on the other hand, more nearly resembled the Women's Trade Union League, which had never used its right to send delegates to the British Congress. It was the small societies created by the League that affiliated.

In 1911, Kate McLean, one of the two Scottish organizers of the National Federation of Women Workers, became the third woman to be elected in straight competition with men to the Scottish TUC's Parliamentary Committee. By the summer of that year there were signs of coolness on the Parliamentary Committee's part towards the Scottish Council for Women's Trades.[32] Shortly before the 1912 Congress the National Federation of Women Workers challenged the right of the Scottish Council for Women's Trades to send delegates to Congress through the special arrangement made in the Standing Orders in 1897.[33] However, the Scottish Council's delegates duly came to the Congress. There, the young Emmanuel Shinwell, a representative of the Glasgow Trades Council, with the support of the Federation, moved that the right of the Scottish Council to affiliation to the Scottish TUC should cease. But the motion was defeated by 59 votes to 32, with the Scottish Miners' Federation as one of the Scottish Council's main supporters.[34] Robert Smillie, now one of the miner MPs, was also one of the trade union members on the Scottish Council, old differences having been forgotten.

However, Margaret Irwin and the Scottish Council for Women's Trades did not wait to be pushed. The Council ceased its affiliation to Congress. In a way the attack on its presence there was a token of success, a step towards ending the dependence on middle-class help. It was ironic that the Glasgow Trades Council, which had been one of the forces behind the setting-up of the Scottish Council for Women's Trades, and the National Federation of Women Workers, like the Council an offshoot of the Women's Trade Union League, should have been the organizations to press for the ending of this association of sixteen years' standing.

Kate McLean was re-elected to the Parliamentary Committee in 1912 and again in 1913. She persuaded her fellow-Committee members to relent in their opposition to women's suffrage so far as to let her represent the Committee at the Women's National Suffrage League. But she too ran into difficulties with the Committee members. In August 1913 the National Federation of Women Workers asked for their help in a prolonged strike of Kilbirnie net-weavers. Two Committee members negotiated a settlement which gave some of the women pay increases. But the Federation was censured for its handling of the strike[35] and Kate McLean failed to obtain re-election in 1914. The importance of pressure-groups and organizations devoted to helping women workers was then demonstrated. For women who struck at Kilsyth appealed directly to the Parliamentary Committee for help and received merely advice that they should return to work.[36]

Margaret Irwin went on working to help women earn a living in some degree of happiness. She became associated with their introduction into fruit farming, creating a model farm at Blairgowrie in Perthshire. In 1929 the Scottish Council for Women's Trades, of which she remained secretary, had turned its attention to finding work for unemployed women and was running a scheme to place girls as domestic workers in farmhouses. The wages were only £1 a month, plus board and lodging for beginners, but rose to £36 a year for girls who had gained some experience. Out of these, the girls gradually paid back money provided to them to buy suitable outfits. Despite some evidence of the scheme's success, the Scottish Farm Servants' Union was annoyed because Margaret Irwin had had a grant from the Board of Agriculture, through the Secretary of State for Scotland, for the scheme. It had therefore been put on the basis of charity. Employers, however, were gaining in having provided for them girls whose characters and qualifications were vetted by the Scottish Council for Women's Trades.[37]

Margaret Irwin never, therefore, threw off the middle-class philanthropic attitude of the Women's Protective and Provident League and the Scottish Council for Women's Trades. She was awarded the CBE in 1927, less usual then, just after the General Strike, than after 1939 among those connected with the Labour movement. The Council died with her. It was wound up in 1939 and she died on 21 January 1940, unnoticed by the Scottish TUC.

In addition to her role in helping to set up the Scottish TUC, she produced, often with very little help during investigations, a series of fine reports on work in laundries, tailoring and dressmaking, on shop-work, on printing and kindred trades, the operation of the Factories and Public Health Acts, children's employment, home-work in shirtmaking and finishing and in kindred trades, and also on minor trades such as 'charring' and seasonal work. Her inquiries on home-work extended to Ireland, on which she did a special report. The passage in 1899 of the Act making compulsory the provision of seats for shop assistants was, to some extent, due to her exposure of their conditions of work. Despite her early unpopularity, she became accepted as an authority on women's work, giving evidence to the Select Committee of the House of Lords on the Early Closing of Shops in 1901. She was a member of the Fabian Women's Council (see page 118).

She had a dry wit which flashed out, for example, when she demolished a main argument used by employers, and, it may be added, accepted by society at large and many employees, against paying women the 'rate for the job'. When she asked employers why they paid women less than men where both did the same work:

'the reply most frequently made ... was "Oh! well you know a woman's wage always *is* less than a man's". That may be so – I have heard it questioned', she went on, – 'but our industrial system is founded, theoretically at least on the principle of payment of the worker not according to his needs, but according to his production; and I fear many of these same employers would have felt both indignant and alarmed had they been told that ... they were advocating an extreme socialistic doctrine, and I do not think many of them would have cared to recommend its general application ...'[38]

The doctrine was, of course, that propounded as the ideal of work and payment in the *Communist Manifesto* by Karl Marx and Friedrich Engels:

from each according to his ability; to each according to his need.

Notes

1 *Glasgow Herald,* 22 Jan. 1940, Obituary: Scottish Dictionary of National Biography; Scot. Council for Women's Trades, 1904-05 Ann. Rep., 15-16.
2 Glasgow United Trades Council, 1887-88 Ann. Rep., 12.
3 ibid., 1889-90, 9: 1894-95, 13. Women's Protective and Provident League of Scotland, Rep. of Inquiry into Women's Work in Laundries, M. H. Irwin, 5: Scot. Council for Women's Trades, 1901-02 Ann. Rep., 5: Glasgow Herald Year Book, 1913, 222.
4 Glasgow Utd. Trades Council, 1889-90 Rep., 9: 1890-91, 7.
5 *WTU Rev.,* Apr. 1892, 2.
6 Glasgow United Trades Council Rep., 1893-94, 15.
7 Reps. of Inquiries for the Scot. Council for Women's Trades, see Council's Ann. Reps. for 1901-02, 6-7, 19: 1904-05, 5,9,12: 1905-06, 9-15. Inquiries on Women Employed at Home, 1900: Employment of Children, 1901: Women's Work in Laundries, 1907: Home Work in Ireland, 1909. Also pamphlet, M. H. Irwin's evidence to the Sel. Committee of the H. of Lords on Early Closing of Shops, 29 Apr. 1901.
8 Glasgow Trades Council 1893-94 Ann. Rep., 16.
9 ibid.
10 1897 Scot. TUC Rep., 35.
11 Letter Books and Minute Books and Ann. Reps. of the West of Scotland Women's Suffrage Soc.: Ann. Reps. of the Glasgow Soc. for Equal Citizenship.
12 Glasgow Trades Council Rep., 1895-96, 16.
13 1897 Scot. TUC Rep., 36, John Keir, Aberdeen Trades Council.
14 ibid., 11
15 ibid., 31.
16 Scot. TUC Mins. of Parliamentary Committee 27 Mar. 1897. 1897 Scot. TUC Rep., 11, 31.
17 Scot. TUC Mins. of Parliamentary Committee, 22 May: 10 July 1897. The first Sec. was Andrew Ballantyne representing the Nat. Federal Council of Scotland for Women's Trades, an employee of the Home Office. The government objected to his membership of the Scot. TUC Parliamentary Committee.
18 1898 Scot. TUC Rep., 63.
19 The Scot. TUC continued to meet at the Scot. Council for Women's Trades offices at 58 Renfield St, Glasgow until 1904. The WPPL also used the building.
20 1897 Scot. TUC Rep., 32-3, more seats for shop girls. In 1900 a Parliamentary Bill to make this obligatory became law. Also resolution against the intimidation of witnesses giving evidence to factory inspectors. 1898 Scot. TUC Rep., 53: resolution to bring laundries under the Factory Acts. A deputation consisting of M. H. Irwin and Robert Smillie saw the Home Sec. to press for action on these resolutions, 1899, Scot. TUC Rep., 9-12.
21 Scot. TUC Reps., 1898, 5-8: 1903, 40. 1899 TUC Rep., M. Bondfield, 64-6.

22 1899 Scot. TUC Rep., 23-5.
23 1899. TUC Rep., 56. George Carson of the Tinplate Workers, who took over the secretaryship of the Parliamentary Committee, made a much worse *faux pas* by sending out the Parliamentary Committee's Rep. before the Committee had approved it. However, he was forgiven, Scot. TUC Mins. of Parliamentary Committee, 20 Apr. 1901.
24 Scot. TUC Reps., 1897, 35: 58-60: 1903, 40, Mary Macarthur: 'As women would no doubt be loyal enough to contribute to the proposed Parliamentary fund (of the Labour Party) she thought they should ask for adult suffrage and not merely manhood suffrage'. TUC Reps., 1901, 80: 1902, 57, 75: 1903, 77: 1907, 165: 1912, 163.
25 1899 Scot. TUC Rep., 34-6.
26 Scot. TUC Mins. of Parliamentary Committee meeting, 18 Mar. 1899: 1899 Scot. TUC Rep., 56.
27 Scot. TUC Reps., 1897, 31-4: 1898, 49, 51, 56: 1899, 45-7, 50: 1900, 8-9, 39-40, 42-3: 1901, 49, 60, 65: 1902, 12, 35, etc.
28 1899 Scot. TUC Rep., 12-13.
29 The Home Secretaries during M. H. Irwin's term as Secretary of the Scottish TUC Parliamentary Committee were Sir M. W. Ridley, 1895 - Nov. 1900; then M. Ritchie until Aug. 1902, followed by A. Akers-Douglas.
30 1910 Scot. TUC Rep., 18-19. The Scot. TUC Parliamentary Committee took up the problems of seasonal workers on 20 Oct. 1910 Scot. TUC Rep., 63-4.
31 ibid., 69-70.
32 Scot. TUC Mins. of Parliamentary Committee meeting, 27 Mar. 1911.
33 ibid., 13 Apr. 1912.
34 1913 Scot. TUC Rep., 53. Shinwell moved that the Standing Order be amended by the deletion of the words 'Councils for Women's Trades'.
35 Scot. TUC Mins. of Parliamentary Committee, 28 June, 23 Aug., 13 Sept. 1913.
36 ibid., 22 Aug. 1914.
37 *Scot. Farm Servant*, Jan. 1929, 191, but see ch. 15, Bell Jobson of the Scot. TUC., Org. of Women Committee, p. 194.
38 M. H. Irwin, Paper for the Philosophical Society of Glasgow, 1907, 17.

8   'Our Mary' and 'Sweated Labour'

The third of the great personalities in the history of women's trade unionism, another Scot, Mary Reid Macarthur, was born in Glasgow on 13 August 1880. Her father took over a draper's shop in Ayr, where she eventually worked as a paid assistant.[1] John Turner, who became secretary of the Shop Assistants' Union, went to Ayr to start a new union branch in February 1901. At a meeting in the evening, he set himself to capture 'an animated group of young ladies, with a laughing vivacious, fair-haired girl in their midst'. He succeeded in recruiting the whole group from Mr Macarthur's shop, except the fair-haired Mary who hung back at first, feeling that as the employer's daughter she ought not to join. But Turner, and the fact that she was asked to be chairman of the new branch at Ayr, finally persuaded her to become a member.[2] In 1902, she was elected President of the Shop Assistants' Union's Scottish District Council and at that year's Annual Conference in Manchester she met Margaret Bondfield. The following year Mona Wilson resigned the secretaryship of the Women's Trade Union League. Margaret Bondfield suggested that Mary Macarthur would be the right person to replace her. Vetted by Gertrude Tuckwell, the League's honorary secretary, Lady Dilke, and Sir David Shackleton, she got the job.[3]

She was not gentle like Emma Paterson, nor did she have Margaret Irwin's cracking intelligence and persistence in piling up facts singlehandedly. But she had the determination and courage of both. She was emotional, highly strung, given to tantrums, exuberant, sweeping colleagues and workers along with her in her enthusiasm. She was also warmhearted and homely, qualities at which literary Fabians turned up their noses. But they help to explain why her supreme gift was organizing, and why she had so great a following among working women and men. They called her 'Our Mary'. And she never let them down. However bad the weather, if she had called a factory-gate meeting, she was there and she spoke, however few stopped to listen.[4] She also made the League's books balance for almost the first time. She had kept the accounts in her father's shop.[5]

She revived Emma Paterson's original idea of a national general union of working women. Lost sight of for a time in the work of establishing the League and in its multifarious campaigns and activities, the idea later developed as a federation of women's unions. Three years after she took over the secretaryship of the League, Mary Macarthur systematically amalgamated the small, often unstable societies it encouraged and created into the general, all-female union, the National Federation of Women Workers.

Announcing its establishment, she revealed the immediate cause as a strike by Edinburgh paper-bag makers against a wage cut. This was not, she thought, unfitting, in view of the long tradition of women's militancy in Scotland. It was, after all, her home territory. The girls were 'out' eight weeks, and they won. From the organization required for the strike, with the help of Edinburgh Trades Council, the first branch of the new union was formed, and in a few weeks had a membership of two hundred. Branches were then formed at London, Halstead, and Preston.

To try to stop agitation among their workpeople, the great Paisley thread combines announced they 'would transfer projected extensions in Paisley to foreign countries' to protect their shareholders. Undeterred by this threat to stop industrial expansion at Paisley, the mill-girls set up a branch of the National Federation. In her statement on the birth of the National Federation, Mary Macarthur was scathing about these firms: 'It would have been truly tragic if these poor shareholders, the victims of industrial agitation, had to be content with a dividend of less than 25 per cent. Be that as it may the Union has come to stay ...' Applications for help in organizing were coming in from all over the country. In typical style she concluded: 'The spirit that has been aroused will not die easily. The Woman Worker is awake in the land'.[6]

By 1908 the membership of the union had risen to 3,000, and by 1909 to 4,000. The report for that year states 'our organization has now £500 in hand, and is able calmly to face its increasing liabilities'.

The first President of this new union was Mary Macarthur herself, who retained the secretaryship of the Women's Trade Union League. Lady Dilke, the League's President, died in 1904 and was succeeded by her niece, Gertrude Tuckwell. In 1908 Gertrude Tuckwell also took over as President of the National Federation of Women Workers, Mary Macarthur becoming its secretary. So Gertrude Tuckwell was President of both organizations and Mary Macarthur secretary, a partnership that lasted until Mary Macarthur's death.

Some very able women joined the NFWW staff, like Dr Marion Phillips, Madeleine Symons, a young lawyer, and Susan Lawrence, a mathematician and educational enthusiast who in 1911 became the first woman member of the London County Council and organized its charwomen. The Federation had a dual membership policy. It accepted as members women who were already members of other unions, but who sympathized with the Federation's aims. Indeed, it would not accept as members anyone eligible for membership of a union affiliated to the TUC unless she joined that organization first.[7] They were not alone in this. Teachers might belong to a specialist union and to the National Union of Teachers. This policy increased membership for other unions.

But the Federation did carry on policies foreign to other unions, always with the aim of extending trade unionism among women. To this end it continued the League's method of bringing to an appropriate union branches of its members in specialized occupations. The Federation also, through a category of honorary members, who could not vote, provided a means whereby non-trade union sympathizers could help its work. All this was intended to promote friendly relations with as many unions as possible. But sometimes disparaging remarks were made about its middle-class leadership. Other general unions which were competing for members among the same poor, low-paid workers were particularly critical of the Federation.

The setting-up of the National Federation of Women Workers enabled the vocal, educated middle-class women who worked for it to be present at British Trades Union Congresses. Since their main goal in the first decade of the twentieth century was legislation to help sweated workers, it was very important to them to have this platform from which to try to win more trade union support.

The establishment of the National Federation of Women Workers reduced the number of all-female unions and societies. However, not all the League-inspired organizations were swept into it. The Manchester and Salford Society of Women in Bookbinding and Printing, for instance, founded in 1896, remained independent until 1942.[8]

Various women's societies were in any case unconnected with the League. These were mainly organizations of white-collar workers. Some women in the National Union of Clerks wanted special representation on its executive; when they failed to obtain it, they broke away to form the Association of Women Clerks and Secretaries in 1903. Women in a number of Civil Service departments formed their own associations. In 1901 the Association of Women Clerks in the Post Office was set up, followed by the Civil Service Typists' Association in 1903. Eight years later, women clerks in the Board of Trade felt the need to set up a separate organization. A fourth society, the Federation of Women Clerks, appeared in 1912.[9] In 1909 the National Union of Women Teachers was created as a breakaway from the National Union of Teachers because the parent union was not sufficiently energetic in supporting their claims for 'equal pay'.[10]

The most spectacular breakaway occurred for reasons quite unconnected with the leadership's indifference to feminine equality and emancipation. The Dundee Mill- and Textile-Workers' Union, initiated by women in 1885, almost fell victim to an unsuccessful strike in 1903. By this time a number of members were chafing because the Rev. Henry Williamson had turned to outspoken opposition to strikes as an ultimate means of altering employers' policies. He had gone to the length of accepting a 'no-strike' clause in union agreements. The employers did not soften their methods. Some women members, therefore, during a lock-out in 1906, applied to the Women's Trade Union League for help in forming a new union. The League obliged and the 'mixed' Union of Jute, Flax, and Kindred Textile Operatives emerged. Six years later it had 12,000 members, four-fifths of them women and girls. The original Mill- and Textile-Workers' Union dwindled away.[11]

There were signs, however, that the movement for women's equality had started to catch on among manual workers. In 1904 the newly formed Leicester women's branch of the National Union of Boot and Shoe Operatives felt the men members were giving them insufficient backing over a pay claim. The argument dragged on for five years until the employers introduced a new system of work which reduced women's earnings. This provoked them into breaking away and setting up the National Union of Women Shoe Operatives of Leicester under the leadership of Miss Lizzie Wilson. One member, Mary Bell, remained to the parent union, and eventually rebuilt the branch.[12]

The whole trade union movement was rocked in 1901 by the decision of the House of Lords over a strike that had taken place the previous summer on the Taff Vale railway in South Wales. Their ruling in favour of the railway company against some very effective picketing by the Amalgamated Society of Railway Servants, led to a huge fine on the Society totalling, together with legal costs, about £30,000. It made nonsense of the 1871 Trade Union Act and placed the funds of all unions at risk.

As a result of the case, an association of union officials was set up whose aim was to facilitate the exchange of information on the legal position of trade unions. Its Council of Management included Mona Wilson, at that time still secretary of the Women's Trade Union League, and Margaret Bondfield, assistant secretary of the

Shop Assistants' Union whose offices at 122 Gower Street, London, the association used. These were the only two women among all the seventy-four members, but the honorary members included Gertrude Tuckwell, also from the League, and Mrs Bridges-Adams of the London School Board. Although some of the most powerful unions supported the association, a great many trade union officials held aloof and it disappeared.[13]

The Taff Vale judgement finally pushed the unions into full support for a Labour presence in Parliament. Labour MPs were first elected at the general election of January 1906 when they helped the Liberals to a resounding victory over the Conservatives.

The main Labour aim was the reversal of the Taff Vale decision. It was achieved through the 1906 Trade Union Act, but only after some opposition from the Liberals. Trade union suspicions of the Liberals therefore increased.

This growing mistrust did not help relations between the unions and the middle-class people trying to improve working women's standard of living. The tensions and differences in priorities manifest in Scotland appeared nationally in the gathering campaign to end 'sweating'. From 1906 there were three major middle-class organizations concerned with women's conditions of work and their trade unionism as a means to improvement, the Women's Trade Union League, the Scottish Council for Women's Trades, and the new National Federation of Women Workers. In 1894, another body, the Women's Industrial Council, had been established, but instead of pressing for women's trade union organization like the other three, it worked for remedial legislation. It marked the concentration of the big guns of the radical, intellectual élite on a campaign to end 'sweating'. The campaign had been building up since 1864 through the amendment of existing laws and through the Factory Acts. But Charles Booth's survey together with the Report from a House of Lords committee and other independent reports made it impossible[14] to ignore conditions of home- and out-workers in London and other large cities and focussed attention on the poverty and cruel working conditions of a large mass of people, providing consumer goods for an increasingly affluent society. The leadership of the Women's Industrial Council included members from the other three bodies as well as eminent Fabians like the Webbs and Graham Wallas. It sponsored investigations into women's work by people of sufficient repute as to command some sort of official attention. On the bases of these it organized a powerful parliamentary lobby.

The immediate 'sweater' was not some wealthy capitalist, but a poor worker who had scraped together enough to set up as a sub-contractor of work for someone richer, or even for some West End store, as the London tailors had described in 1849. Some tried to blame the system on immigrants from the continent, refugees from oppression. But the system was far older. It was an extension and development of domestic, cottage industry as this became the sole means of livelihood of people who had no land from which to support themselves (see page 9). 'Sweating' existed in cities like Glasgow where there were hardly any continental émigrés.

Most trade unions were not really touched by 'sweating' in that they were created by craft and industrial workers and the employers were mostly middle or large-scale capitalists. Only a few men trade unionists trying to enrol members among the 'sweated' trades, like those from the Jewish Tailoresses' Union in the East End of London and in Leeds, the Society of Tailors and Tailoresses, or the Cigarette-Makers' Union, really understood the enormity of the problem, and worked with the Women's Trade Union League. They were resigned to the idea of legislation to fix minimum wages as the only means of lifting workers out of a hopeless, vicious circle. Whereas the trade union movement as a whole was beginning to dislike legislation. One of its most dearly held principles was that of voluntary wage negotiations and agreements with employers.

Four new Acts were passed between 1891 and 1901 to regulate hours and conditions of work. But control of small workshops remained ineffective, and the Acts did nothing to check the practice of 'giving out' work to the employees to take home to complete at night.

In Berlin in March 1904, an exhibition of 'sweated industries' was held with considerable effect, and the idea was taken up by supporters of legislation in Britain. Mary Macarthur played a leading part in bringing about the British Sweated Industries Exhibition. She spoke at fashionable West-End drawing-room meetings, and called on A. G. Gardiner, editor of the *Daily News*, a paper that had helped to publicize the plight of pottery-workers and could be relied on to support the cause of the poor. Soon afterwards Gardiner organized the *Daily News* Exhibition of Sweated Industries. It was opened in the Queen's Hall, in Langham Place in London, on 2 May 1906, by Princess Beatrice. Apart from George Lansbury and James Ramsay MacDonald, the list of speakers, and contributors to the illustrated handbook, were all middle-class. Besides Mary Macarthur, Margaret Irwin, and Clementina Black, they included reformers like George Bernard Shaw, H. M. Tennant, L. Chiozza Money, and Herbert Burrows.

The exhibition showed the range of 'sweated' trades. The *Women's Trade Union Review* reported that forty-five of them were represented at the Queen's Hall by at least one worker each. People knew vaguely about the low pay in clothing, box-making, sack-sewing, 'though a considerable proportion seemed much taken aback by the discovery that $2\frac{1}{4}d$. a gross and "find own paste" is the market rate of payment for matchbox-making, and that $5d$. is commonly paid for the entire making of a full-sized woman's skirt ...' What caused astonishment among visitors was that cigarette-making, the beading of ladies' shoes, the stitching of gloves, and the manufacture of hosiery, jewel-cases, tennis-balls, belts, ties, furniture, brushes, and saddlery were all homework trades, in which a 12- to 16-hour day brought in on average earnings of $5s$. to $7s$. a week.

The *Review*'s report also listed all the advantages of home-work to employers. They were saved rent of premises, other than a warehouse and office. They had no overheads, especially in the slack periods to which these seasonal trades were subject. The workers had to face these times of unemployment as best they might. Factory employers, on the other hand, not only faced all these expenses but had to observe laws and regulations about ages at which children might start work, and about hours of work for women and children. They also had to pay compensation for accidents. Competition from 'sweaters' forced them to cut the wages they paid 'to starvation point'.[15]

As a result of the exhibition, an Anti-Sweating League was formed with J. J. Mallon, now one of Mary Macarthur's friends, as its secretary, and Sidney Webb and other leading Fabians, and Mary Macarthur herself, on its committee. The Board of Trade commenced an inquiry into Earnings and Hours of Work. The House of Commons under pressure from Labour MPs set up a Select Committee to Inquire into Homework.

Mary Macarthur had been convinced by Sir Charles Dilke and Gertrude Tuckwell that the remedy for the low wages and long hours which were undermining trade union organization, especially of women, lay in boards with statutory powers to fix minimum wages and maximum hours.

The idea of wages boards had been introduced in Victoria, Australia, in 1896. The legislature there had been empowered to appoint special boards to fix wages or piece-work rates in certain trades. This power had been further extended in 1905 and by 1908 over forty such boards were in existence. They had also been introduced in New Zealand.

The Parliamentary Labour Party, created as a result of the successes of the 1906 election, had among its members Arthur Henderson, a member of the Friendly Society of Ironmongers, who now brought in a Wages Board Bill.

In addition to contributing to the pressure exercised through the Anti-Sweating League, Mary Macarthur personally assisted by saving from disruption a conference called in support of Wages Boards at the London Guildhall in October 1906. Many of the delegates, some of them members of the Social Democratic Federation, 'denounced Wages Boards as a middle-class dodge', a 'palliative' to postpone the day of revolutionary social change. A trade union speaker was shouted down. But Mary Macarthur, by drawing, in her emotional and graphic way, a picture of the miseries of women and children in the garret-industries of the London slums, brought the delegates to cheering acclamation and support of the statutory minimum wage. She also illustrated vividly the dangers to the better-off of 'sweating' by herself catching diphtheria from a visit to a girl making baby garments. The girl who had the disease possessed no bedclothes, and used the garments to cover herself at night.

The Trades Union Congress and Parliamentary Committee could not, however, be quite easy over a Bill which on its Second Reading on 21 February 1908 had the support of so powerful an employer as Alfred Mond, the armaments manufacturer and MP for Chester. He argued that all successful manufacturers 'had early grasped the fact that profits were not to be made out of low wages'. He told the House that England with an 8-hour day and higher wages had a lower labour cost per ton of product than any continental country and that 'Russia with the lowest wages and the longest hours had the highest ...' He thought the Bill if carried would only give 'the unorganized workers the same advantage as the organized' and that the penalty clauses for those employers who defaulted were not strong enough.[16]

By raising costs, Wages Boards which fixed minimum rates of pay and maximum hours of work would bear hardest on the smaller employers and so block this means of an employee raising himself or herself to the status of sub-contractor.

The Select Committee's Report, published a year later, came down in favour of statutory Wages Boards. In March 1909, the Liberal government brought in its own Bill, piloted through both houses by Winston Churchill, who then headed the Board of Trade. With many trade unionists and the TUC Parliamentary Committee still not very enthusiastic over it, the Act came into force on 1 January 1910. The Trade Boards, as they were to be called, were to be made up of employers' and employees' representatives. They were to settle rates of earnings and hours of work in four trades — chain-making, lace-making, paper-box making, and wholesale and bespoke tailoring in England and Wales.

The mere passage of the Act, however, did not mean that the boards would succeed or even function at all. Without wellwishers and unions to lead the negotiations on the workers' sides of the boards and to monitor the observance of prices paid to operatives for piece-work, or rates of earnings and hours of work, the boards might have been still-born. For many employers wanted to sabotage the Act and many employees were not well enough educated or strong-minded enough to argue successfully for themselves.

The test came in the chain and nail trades in the Birmingham area. Since the mid-nineteenth century there had been a big increase in the industrial employment of women in Birmingham itself and in the Black Country. They were brought in to manufacture chocolate and sugar confectionery. They were taken on in munitions works such as Kynock's, opened in 1862, with one man and twelve girls to make fog signals and cartridges. But their traditional work was in the small metal trades, in jewellery workshops in Birmingham, and in the chain and nail trades of the surrounding areas.[17]

In the 1850s there had been united action among chain-workers to raise rates of earnings uniformly to the highest level then paid, but this petered out because, with the end achieved, as in so many early labour struggles, no one could see any further reason for paying union dues.[18]

In 1886 an attempt had been made to organize the women separately in the chain and nail trades. About 200 out of the thousand estimated to be at work joined a union. But, as in the 1850s, this too failed, partly because of the indifference of men workers to the trade union organization of their wives and daughters. They were afraid, too, of their competition for work, as Mr Juggins of the male Chain-makers' and Strikers' Union indicated when seconding the TUC's first equal-pay resolution in 1888. The men preferred to enrol them in their own unions.

In the 1890s, Lady Dilke had reported that organization in the chain trade was fairly good, thanks to the efforts of Mr Juggins and Mr Smith. But women were very hard to organize in the spike-nail trade, although the union had obtained a 35 per cent rise in earnings for them. And in the nut and bolt trade they were not organized at all, although the Midland Counties Trade Federation had also tried very hard. In the late 1890s, there were four specialist 'mixed' unions for these trades listed by the Women's Trade Union

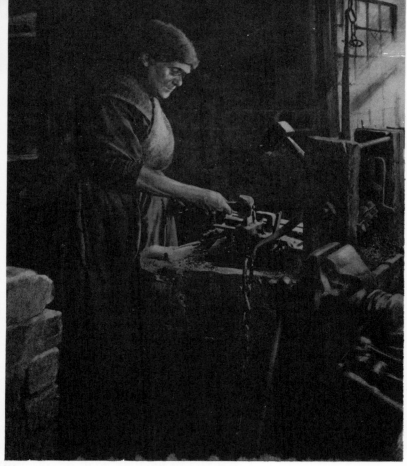

Woman Cradley Heath chain maker at work, 1910

League. They had not, however, succeeded in raising rates to a reasonable level when in 1910 the Trade Boards Act came into force. The men worked mainly for big employers, but the women worked mainly in their own homes for middlemen.

From February 1910 the Chain-making Trade Board set to work on the question of raising earnings for the thousand or so women in the Cradley Heath chain trade from their current level of from 4s. to 7s. a week. In August 1910 the board published new minimum rates which would bring weekly earnings to 11s. 3d. per week of 54 hours. However, these rates did not come into force automatically. For, in order to obtain the agreement of employers to the Act, it had been laid down that the rates should not come into force for six months. If any employer could induce work-people to agree to go on working at the old prices, the introduction of the Trade Board rates would be postponed for a further six months. Only then could those representing the workers again legitimately recall the board to have the agreed rates of earning republished. Thus the introduction of higher rates could by this process be indefinitely postponed.

About thirty firms and 150 middlemen were outside the chain trades Employers' Association. These now set about trying to force women home-workers, who could more easily be browbeaten than men, to sign a statement agreeing to work at existing rates. The Chain-makers' and Strikers' Union and National Federation of Women Workers believed that employers were trying to build up stocks of chain before the new higher Trade Board rates were enforced. Some workers, therefore, on instructions from the National Federation of Women Workers and the Birmingham Trades Council, refused to sign and were prevented from working. Effectively, therefore, though home-workers, they were 'locked out', from 17 August till early October.

Only around 500 women, about half those in the trade, were involved, but the unions felt that if this stand by the employers was not broken, the effect of the Trade Boards Act would be nullified. Union tactics were to split those employers ready to operate the Act from those who were not. The women were led by Mary Macarthur and organized by Helen Stocks, Charles H. Sitch, who had helped the men to organize and who became secretary of the National Federation of Women Workers' Chain-makers' and Strikers' branch, and Julia Varley.[19]

Julia Varley, a Bradford woollen-worker who became secretary of the Weavers' and Textile-Workers' Union there, was the first manual worker to rise to the ranks of the trade union leaders. In considering her early career, it must be remembered that in the woollen trades the 'half-time' system operated. That is, the employment of schoolchildren below the ordinary legal minimum age on a part-time or half-time basis was permitted. When a child so employed reached the statutory school-leaving age of twelve years, she or he was thoroughly acquainted with the working conditions of a full-time employee. All this would be pretty well known anyway in the close-knit textile communities. But actual, practical experience in the mills made it impossible for any twelve year-old half-timer to be ignorant of conditions or of union work. At twelve years of age, Julia Varley, tough and practical, was already committed to the idea of trade unionism. She not only joined the union, but by 1901, at the age of thirteen, she was on its executive and was elected to Bradford Trades Council when she was only fourteen. She remained a member for the next seven years. In 1908, after a meeting with Margaret Bondfield, she joined the staff of the National Federation of Women Workers as an organizer for the Birmingham area. Her first success in Birmingham was in establishing a branch at Cadbury's Bournville factory, Edward Cadbury having announced his support for women's trade union organization in 1908. This branch in 1909 elected her as its delegate to the Birmingham Trades Council. Within three months she had become the first woman member of its executive and remained a member, with a five-month break, for the next ten years, until the end of the First World War.[20]

In the Cradley Heath struggle there were the usual meetings and demonstrations to raise funds for those locked out and to encourage those still at work to strike for the Trade Board rate. For example on 3 September, with the Cradley Heath Town Band leading them, the demonstrators went to a section of workpeople, the coil chain-makers at Old Hill, and advised them to 'throw down their hammers'. This group had not realized the Trade Board Act applied to them.

The press supported the women strikers, some of whom appeared on the 1910 Trades Union Congress platform and held up the chains they made to immense cheers. The membership of the women's union rose to 1,700 and a durable organization was set up. After ten weeks of lock-out, the Trade Boards' rates were accepted. Thus the precedent was set that Trade Boards would not remain a dead fiction, but would become a reality.[21]

The immediate effect of the other Trade Boards was also beneficial to trade union membership. The membership of tailoring unions shot up; a Card- and Box-Makers' Union was formed. Campaigns to help other 'sweated' workers were organized. Charles Sitch found 'sweating' rife at Wolverhampton. A 9-month campaign, starting in March 1911, resulted in a National Federation of Women Workers' branch of 1,200 at the Lye hollow-ware centre.

Mary Macarthur also used the success of the initial Trade Boards in raising earnings to point out that they could be extended to more occupations, and the 'mixed' unions of tailoring and agricultural workers, along with the Shop Assistants, continued to campaign for them.

The Trade Boards had embodied official recognition of a principle. As A. Evans of the Printers' Warehousemen's Union pointed out in 1911 at Congress, it was 'practically the first time in our history that the Government has recognized that the workers are entitled to a living wage'.[22] So an agitation arose for a 'minimum wage' fixed directly by the government without the consultative machinery of Trade Boards.[23]

In 1913, another six trades were brought under statutory wage control, and many more in 1918. But, at the same time, the boards were not entirely popular with trade union officials. It was perfectly true that they 'put a bottom into wages': in that they were a definite success. But they did not stop home- and out-work. Nor did they necessarily bring in recruits; for the workers, particularly the women, believed their increased earnings were decreed by paternalistic governments. To the work of organizing, they added the preparation of the workers' case to be put at meetings of the Trade Board. For these reasons, non-trade union middle-class people continued to lead some of the workers' sides in negotiations until after the First World War.[24] These reservations were not shared by the middle-class leaders of the National Federation of Women Workers, committed to legislative intervention to raise women's earnings.

Home- and out-working, however, were not the only causes of 'sweated' working conditions and poverty. Mary Macarthur realized that, as she put it: 'Women are unorganised because they are badly paid and poorly paid because they are unorganised'. She told the House of Commons Select Committee on Home-Work in 1907:

> I wish to make it clear ... that the low rates of wages are not confined to Home Workers, and that the question of organisation is equally difficult with the similar class of labour in the factory — almost equally difficult when the wages are very low ...[25]

The early small local women's unions and societies, on the other hand, had proved that home-workers could organize, even without help. The years after the Second World War were to bear out the second part of her statement.

Notes

1 M.A. Hamilton, *Mary Macarthur;* and *Women at Work:* M. Bondfield, *A Life's Work,* 53-61: B. Drake, *Women in Trade Unions,* 44 ff.: *New Dawn,* Sept. 1965, 595-6.
2 *New Dawn,* Oct. 1965, 643: Hamilton, *Mary Macarthur,* 8-9.
3 ibid., 13-17, 27-8: *Women at Work,* 58-9.
4 Hamilton, *Mary Macarthur,* 33-8, 50-1.
5 ibid., 30-1, 47-8: *Women at Work,* 60.
6 *WTU Rev.,* July 1906, 10-13.
7 Drake, op. cit., 182.
8 C.J. Bundock, *The National Union of Printing, Bookbinding and Paper Workers,* 58.
9 B.V. Humphreys, *Clerical Unions in the Civil Service,* 55, 235, chart opp. p.135.
10 A.M. Pierotti, *The Story of the National Union of Women Teachers,* 1-4.

11 Information given the author by Mrs Margaret Fenwick, Asst. Sec. of the Union of Jute, Flax and Kindred Textile Operatives, 1967: Hamilton, *Mary Macarthur*, 52-4.

12 A. Fox, *Hist. of the National Union of Boot and Shoe Operatives, 1874-1957,* 309 ff.

13 Gertrude Tuckwell papers, 508 (TUC Library).

14 B. Seebohm Rowntree, *Poverty,* 1901: Mona Wilson, ed., *Rep. on Housing and Industrial Conditions,* 1905 (Dundee Social Union): Mona Wilson and E.G. Howarth, *West Ham, A Study in Social and Industrial Problems,* 1907: Members of St. Philip's Settlement, Sheffield, *The Equipment of Workers,* 1919.

15 The *Daily News,* May-June 1906. Reports on the Exhibition were given almost daily: Hamilton, *Mary Macarthur,* 65-7: Drake, op. cit., 56-7: *WTU Rev.,* July 1906.

16 *Hansard,* 21 Feb. 1908, 1216-19. Although politics was his first love, Mond went into the family chemical business of Brunner Mond in Lancashire. From it he created in 1926 the great Imperial Chemical Industries. He was very successful with labour relations.

17 *Household Words,* vol.IV, 141; 449: vol.V, 192 ff. 1859 Trans. of NAPSS, 654: *Edinburgh Rev.,* vol.CX, 1859, 538-9.

18 Trade Soc.'s Committee Rep., 1859, NAPSS, 152-3, Noah Forrest: *WTU Rev.,* Jan. 1895, 3-5, *Women in Cycle Manufacture in Coventry* for effects of intense competition for work.

19 R.H. Tawney, *The Establishment of Minimum Rates in the Chain-making Industry,* 37-8: Drake, op. cit., 47-9: Hamilton, *Mary Macarthur,* 80 ff.

20 The *Picture World,* 16 Dec. 1915: Bondfield, op. cit., 43-4: Corbett, *Birmingham Trades Council,* 91-2.

21 Mins. of the Birmingham Trades Council, 1910: 27 Aug., 3 Sept., 1 Oct. 1911: 20 Jan., 4 Feb.: 1910 Ann. Rep., 6: 1911 Annual Meeting of *Trades Council:* 1911 WTUL Rep.: Drake, op. cit., 58: J.H. Woolridge, *The Rise of the Black Country Chainmaking Industry,* History Special Study, Wolverhampton Teachers' Coll., 1965., Birmingham Loc. Hist. Library: *Express and Star,* 2 Aug. 1911.

22 1911 TUC Rep., 241-2.

23 TUC Reps.: 1911, 241: 1912, 64-5, 236-7: 1913, 267-310, 317-18: 1915, 298,314-16, 391. Scot. TUC Reps.: 1911, 54,59,62: 1912, 68-9,73,79: 1913, 55: 1914, 83: 1916, 66: 1917, 71: 1918, 24,72: 1920, 109. Most of the proposals and discussion were about a minimum living wage. The idea was not new, see Scot. TUC Rep., 1915, but the Trade Boards Act gave it a new lease of life and the impetus kept up all through the First World War. See also *Express & Star,* 9 Dec. 1911, Lye hollow-ware workers organized as a result.

24 J.J. Mallon, Sec. of the Anti-Sweating League, was also an Executive Committee member of the Nat. Fed. of Women Workers and shared with Susan Lawrence and Madeleine Symons from the Federation the work of acting as secretaries of the Boards.

25 Busbey, 'The Women's Trade Union Movement in Great Britain': Cd. 290, Rep. of Select Committee on Homework, Mins of Evidence, 134-44.

9   Unity is Strength!

Trade unionism from the turn of the twentieth century up to the outbreak of war in August 1914 was riven by two conflicting tendencies. On the one hand, unemployment was, as ever, creating tensions between workers. The ending of the Boer War in 1901 had the inevitable repercussions on employment, not only of men returning to look for work, but of the reduction of government contracts. Unemployment was also increased because of the introduction of premium bonus and speeded-up systems of work, pioneered in the United States of America. From 1904 onwards there were trade union protests about these, including a not very successful strike of women at the Leicester Gillette Safety Razor Works.[1] Unemployment had grown by 1905 to a point where Central and Local Distress Committees had been formed with the object of providing work for the unemployed.

A Women's Industrial Council memorandum of December 1905 revived the remedy of the City of London Council in the fifteenth and sixteenth centuries (see p. 9) by proposing domestic service as work for unemployed women and girls. No coercion was suggested. Necessity was driving women and girls to the work; the demand for their services in one-servant households continued to increase. The Women's Industrial Council emphasized training which would help to improve their status and earnings.[2]

Local authorities were urged wherever possible to undertake work which women could do, such as cleaning, upholstery, and needlework. Land colonies were being established to absorb men in need of work and the Women's Industrial Council urged that some of the work created, laundering, mending, making clothes, and cooking, along with lighter work on the land itself, should be given to women. It was this mounting unemployment that lowered wages, aggravated 'sweating', and spurred on the movement for Trade Boards.

On the other hand, the advent of representatives of organized labour, independent of either Liberal or Conservative parties, in Parliament marked a new era for trade unionism. With the great accession of women to unions, trade unionism at all levels was now a general movement among women as well as men. They were

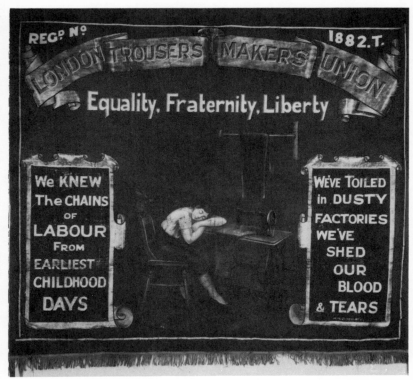

REG^D N^O

1882.T.

LONDON TROUSERS MAKERS UNION

Equality, Fraternity, Liberty

We KNEW
The CHAINS
OF
LABOUR
FROM
EARLIEST
CHILDHOOD
DAYS

WE'VE TOILED
in DUSTY
FACTORIES
WE'VE
SHED
OUR
BLOOD
& TEARS

Banner of the London Trousers-Makers Society, early twentieth century

part of the trade union world. They argued and fought resolutions through at Congresses on equal terms with men, just as, increasingly, ordinary women workers and rank-and-file trade unionists joined in the growing wave of trade union activity. Margaret Bondfield,[3] Mary Macarthur, Gertrude Tuckwell, Susan Lawrence, Julia Varley, and Dr Marion Phillips were all members of the Independent Labour Party exchanging ideas with leaders of the Parliamentary Labour Party like Ramsay MacDonald. Some of them were elected to the Labour Party's National Executive Committee. Margaret MacDonald, Ramsay MacDonald's wife, was secretary of the Women's Labour League which organized female support for the Labour Party. For it was by now accepted that women, though not enfranchised, could be of help in electioneering. On her death in 1911, the links between the Labour Party and these prominent women trade unionists became closer because Marion Phillips left the National Federation of Women Workers to take over Margaret MacDonald's political work.[4] In the same year, Mary Macarthur married Will Anderson, a member of the Independent Labour Party and the secretary of the Parliamentary Labour Party. They were close friends of the MacDonalds.

Since the 1871 Trade Union Act legalizing strikes and peaceful picketing, employers had been chipping away at the concessions gained by the unions. The reversal of the Taff Vale judgements in 1906, together with Factory Acts and Shop Acts, was a further victory for trade unionism and its radical supporters. Employers on their side were becoming increasingly uneasy at these union gains and at the spread of left-wing theories among working people.

On the Clyde, James Connolly, a disciple of the famous United States trade unionist Daniel de Leon, in 1905 started preaching workers' control of the establishments where they worked, a creed known in those days as syndicalism. A few years later Tom Mann was converted to it. Revolutionary Marxism was still advocated by the Social Democratic Federation, as well as anarchism. In spite of the insularity of British unions, the Russian uprising of 1905 did not pass unnoticed. There was a Marxist-led breakaway from Ruskin College for working men and women in Oxford. They founded the Labour College to preach the new faiths.

Trade union militants, encouraged by their successes, went on to new victories. The headlines in 1908 were about the miners who obtained the 8-hour day and a lengthy engineers' strike in northeast England. Much more humbly, in the East End of London, girls and women box-makers at the Corruganza factory struck in order to obtain the reinstatement of a forewoman. She had been sacked for protesting to the management on their behalf at swingeing cuts in pay that left them with earnings of only about 4s. a week. Mary Macarthur and the National Federation of Women Workers took over and ran the strike. They organized not only a strike fund, but a march to Trafalgar Square where a meeting was held, thought to have been the first such demonstration held by women on their own.[5]

At the British and Scottish Trades Union Congresses, delegates increasingly insisted on the 'Right to Work'. A 'Right to Work' Council was formed, with Mary Macarthur as one of the two women on its Executive Committee; the other was Anne Cobden Sanderson. At a 'Right to Work' Conference in the Guildhall on 4–5 December 1908, delegates from the Women's Trade Union League, the Women's Industrial Council, and the political Women's Labour League were present. The first of the three resolutions passed, underlined unity:

That legislation be immediately undertaken which shall establish the principle that every citizen *of either sex* is entitled to be provided with either useful remunerative employment or healthy maintenance.

There was talk of a Trade Union Charter. A second conference called by the Independent Labour Party on 27-28 October 1910 asserted the need for a 'Right to Work' Bill. By 1912 the Labour Party had sponsored just such a Bill.[6]

Inside and outside Parliament, organized Labour was sufficiently powerful to have much legislation altered to its advantage. A 1909 Bill proposing Labour Exchanges only gained Labour support when Winston Churchill, who was in charge of it, conceded that trade unionists should be among the supervisors in the exchanges.

Lloyd George's Unemployment and Health Insurance Bill, originally inspired by the Webbs, was accepted only when the government agreed that the benefit sections of unions should be converted into Approved Societies to adminster the Act. William H. Beveridge, drafter of the Unemployment clauses, saw state control of insurance as a means to greater state control of the workforce.[7] Trade unions feared this legislation less because it abrogated the long-established tradition of self-help than because there might be a wholesale exodus of members and a consequent drop in their funds if the state supplanted their own Friendly and Benefit activities. State provision against loss of work and ill-health, paid for partly by themselves and partly by employers, would provoke members to query why they should in addition pay dues to their unions for the same sort of insurance cover. But by insisting on acting as Approved Societies the unions gained a huge accession of members.

The National Insurance Act passed in 1911, however, did not have the approval of the Women's Trade Union League nor of the National Federation of Women Workers, although like other unions it converted its Friendly and Benefit side into an Approved Society.[8] The Act required insurance contributions of a percentage of wages. This bore hardest on low-paid workers, so much so, that after this deduction from earnings, Mary Macarthur claimed, some could not afford to pay union subscriptions. She and Gertrude Tuckwell through the Federation and the League campaigned for a non-contributory scheme for all earning less than 15*s.* a week, whether working full- or part-time. They suggested that employers and the state should pay the full amount. The resolution on these lines from the National Federation of Women Workers at the 1911 Trades Union Congress, was supported by the unions of agricultural workers and clothiers' operatives, and by Ben Tillett of the Dock-Workers, all of them concerned about the effects of the Act on their own low-paid members. But delegates representing the better-paid workers in the craft unions opposed it. W. F. Dawtry of the Steam-Engine Makers attacked

> ... the vicious principle underlying this proposal. It seeks to give nothing more than preferential treatment to the low-paid worker ... I believe it is better to help in the improvement of low-paid women by kicking rather than by the pampering process.

J. Cross of the Northern Counties Weavers' Amalgamation, who also opposed the Federation's plan, 'wanted the women to be discontented'. In a sense they were echoing Emma Paterson who wanted women to obtain improvements by standing on their own feet and organizing, not by their relying on legislative help from above.

Mary Macarthur, replying to these attacks, said the Bill already contained the principle of subsidizing low-paid workers and her resolution was passed, but only with a narrow majority. Through the campaign she and Gertrude Tuckwell led, the 1911 Insurance Act was altered to include special consideration for married women workers and exemption from insurance contributions for girls too poorly paid to be able to afford them.[9] They also pointed out women's need for old-age pensions. A destitute old age was one of the greatest nightmares, especially of unmarried, white-collar women workers.

Growing recognition of the power of the unions was shown by the setting-up of Conciliation Boards. They became all the rage as a way of working out settlements over pay, hours, and conditions, and of resolving grievances. The Board of Trade Labour Department staff frequently came to the rescue during negotiations. Since the rate of inflation, which had hitherto been moderate, suddenly doubled, pay claims (not only by the railway unions) became urgent and the boards offered a way of avoiding the miseries of strikes.

With such a high rate of inflation, however, unions were dissatisfied with the Conciliation Boards' pay awards. The possibility of a national stoppage by the railway unions became more imminent. There were threats of similar action by the Miners' Federation of Great Britain. A new trend, even more alarming to the authorities, manifested itself. The unions began increasingly to unite in federations. In 1910, a National Transport Workers' Federation was formed of seamen's and dockers' unions. Not only did both the Southampton seamen and London dockers strike in 1911, they were successful in raising their pay and the employers' Shipping Federation was obliged to recognize the dockers' union.

Influenced by the general militancy, and under pressure from in-flation, women took part in the outbreak of stoppages. In August 1910, twenty women struck against wage reductions at the English Sewing Company's Mills in Neilston, in Scotland. They were joined by nearly one thousand fellow-workers, all of whom were duly organized. Scottish trade unionists, particularly the Glasgow Trades Council, supported them. Under the auspices of the Board of Trade a satisfactory settlement was negotiated, while the National Federation of Women Workers gained a branch of twelve hun-dred.[10]

In the summer of 1911, 15,000 unorganized women working in Bermondsey firms 'came out' in protest at their very low rates of pay. Twenty-five or thirty firms were affected: glue- and size-makers, tin-box makers, box- and packing-case makers, metallic-capsule makers, bottle-washers, tea-packers, makers of pickles and canned food, perambulator makers, jam-makers from Pink's fac-tory, and biscuit-makers from Peek Frean's. Many of the employers were as little organized as the workers. The women belonged mainly to the families of dockers. Children and men were 'out' too. The Federation was among the general unions that went to organize them. Instead of simply asking for money contributions for the fund to compensate strikers for their lost pay, Mary Macar-thur asked the public for bread and milk. This ensured that the strikers were fed in a way that money might not have done. At the same time, it brought home to the public the basic needs of poorly paid workers who abruptly ceased to earn. The Bermondsey strikers with the help of the League and the Federation obtained wage increases amounting to £7,000 a year. J.O'Grady of the Fur-nishing Trades Union at the 1911 Congress moved a resolution congratulating the Bermondsey women along with the transport workers for their stand.[11]

The Women's Trade Union League reported altogether twenty-one strikes in 1911-12, in eighteen of which settlements satisfactory to the unions were obtained. In 1912-13 there were further strikes, but in many different places, in a shirt-and-collar factory in Taun-ton; a fishing-net factory in Bridport, as well as among the Kilbir-nie net-makers and in the London districts of Clerkenwell and Wandsworth. The men chain-makers brought the Cradley Heath workers out again. The total number of strikes of all workers in 1913 was nearly 1,500 and not far short of a thousand in the first half of 1914, most of them unofficial. At the same time, between 1910 and 1914, the total trade union membership rose by over 1½ million.

Demonstrations of trade union prowess caused an attempt to

stop unions using members' subscriptions to contribute to Labour Party funds. The House of Lords ruled that W. V. Osborne, a Liberal member of the Railway Servants' Union, could opt out of having his subscription used for this purpose. The precedent thus set threatened the source of Labour Party funds and so postulated a halt to all political activity by unions. The Liberal administration, however, was shaken, and thrown more than ever on Labour parliamentary support, by Conservative gains at the first general election of 1910.

With Labour more powerful in Parliament as a consequence, in 1913 an Act to some extent nullifying the Osborne judgement was passed. Unions might use their funds for political purposes on condition that each member was given the right of 'contracting out' or refusing to pay the political levy.

One of the few consolations of employers and governments at this time must have been that not many women trade unionists were involved in the more violent phase of the Women's Suffrage movement that developed from 1906 onwards. The main area of support for women's suffrage, other than the white-collar organizations of teachers, clerical and shop-workers, was the cotton-weaving unions and the preponderantly female spinners union of card and blowing-room operatives. In addition to the confidence of the women weavers, it must be remembered that the Women's Suffrage movement was functioning in Manchester by 1867 under Lydia Becker's leadership. The Pankhursts, who had by the early twentieth century assumed leadership of the movement, were a Lancashire family. They had stirred up interest in women's suffrage there in their early campaigning days.

In 1904 Christabel Pankhurst split the Manchester Women's Trades Union Council by insisting that women's franchise and political power, instead of trade union methods, were the way to improve women's status as workers. Six of the fourteen unions represented on the Council withdrew to form a Women's Trades and Labour Council committed to gaining political power for women. Within a year it had ten branches of 300 members each and one, the Weavers' Association of Beswick, with a thousand members. These working women, though not enfranchised, put pressure on their MPs and in 1901-02 presented to them a monster petition with nearly 70,000 signatures asking for the vote immediately.

They faced the same sort of hostility from union leaderships as Margaret Irwin did at the Scottish TUC. It became clear that the issue of women's enfranchisement went deeper than class differences. It was already cutting across political alignments. The

Wigan miners' union branch would not accept a candidate at the
1906 general election who represented not only Labour but also
women suffragists.[12]
   As far as individual women went, the most notable woman
suffragist was Annie Kenney, a Lancashire mill-girl. Her militant
suffrage activities led her into trade union activity. About 1905 she
'announced her intention of standing for the local committee of
the card and blowing-room operatives ... no woman had stood for
election in its (the branch's) memory'. Her fellow-workers tried to
dissuade her, but she stood and was elected. She later became the
chief lieutenant of Christabel Pankhurst and left off her union
work. Gladys Evans, a shop assistant, was another militant, and
Julia Varley was arrested for her suffrage activities.[13] Sylvia
Pankhurst organized a working-class women's suffrage movement
in the East End of London. But the Suffrage campaign, militant or
peaceable, had little real backing from the trade union movement.

   Labour unrest extended to Ireland, where there were major
developments in women's trade union organization. James Larkin
arrived in Dublin in 1908 to lead a transport strike. From this arose
the Irish Transport and General Workers' Union with himself as
General Secretary. James Connolly was secretary of its Belfast
branch. Delia Larkin, James's sister, followed him to Dublin, giving
up her own career to help her brother. After her arrival, Larkin excluded women from his union, although many men members
believed there was no necessity for sex segregation. Possibly Delia
wanted to emulate Mary Macarthur's success with the National
Federation of Women Workers. At all events, on 5 September 1911
another general union for women workers was set up, the Irish
Women Workers' Union, with James Larkin as President and Delia
as secretary.
   Light industries represented the major industrial growth area in
Ireland at this time, even more than in Great Britain. The majority
of their workforce were girls and women. There was a considerable
development of dressmaking and tailoring. Three-quarters of the
labour force in tobacco factories were women and girls and an
even higher proportion in sweet, chocolate, jam, and biscuit factories.
   In spite of the Larkins' ban on female membership, Connolly
himself was responsible for organizing women within the Irish
Transport Workers' Union. He assisted in the creation of an Irish
Textile-Workers' branch. In doing so he intruded on the Linen
Textile Operatives' Society, sponsored by the Belfast Trades Council and led by Mary Galway, who had built her union from the bet-

ter-paid Protestant workers in the 'making-up' section. Connolly claimed there were 18,000 women workers outside her organization.

On 4 October 1911, unorganized women struck at one factory against a speed-up. There were rules posted up in the 'shops' setting out a system of fines for singing, laughing, talking, even 'adjusting hair' during working-hours, while a girl who brought sweets to the mill was instantly sacked. Connolly insisted that these rules be abolished and made a wage claim. He organized the girls with support from some of Mary Galway's own members. He advised them:

> not to go back in ones and twos but to gather outside the mills and all go in as a body; to go in singing. If when at work one girl laughs and is reprimanded, they are all to begin laughing and if one girl sings and is checked, they are all to sing. And if a girl is dismissed for breaking the rules they are all to walk out with her.

The girls accepted the idea and went further than he intended, for they decided unanimously at a meeting to set up a branch of the Irish Transport Workers' Union.

They won their strike against the rules. But Mary Galway fought the new union through the Belfast Trades Council. She could not succeed against the much more powerful Irish Transport Workers' Union. She merely delayed the Trades Council's acceptance of Delia Larkin's Irish Women Workers' Union.

Connolly followed up his first success. On 23 November 1911, he issued a call to the workers in the Belfast linen-mills, castigating them for their 'slavish and servile nature' in submitting to very bad conditions, and comparing them unfavourably with 'their sisters on the farms of Ireland' who fought against Irish landlordism. There was an immediate success in obtaining improvements from the 'Linen Lords', but the girls were not wholeheartedly won to trade unionism. In 1913 the Flax-Roughers tried to break up meetings of the Irish Transport Workers' Union. Yet Connolly stood by the girls. He brought in outsiders as secretaries of the Textile-Workers' branch. First Marie Johnson from the Belfast Co-operative Society and Labour Party, then Winifred Carney from the Suffragette movement, one of his devoted supporters. The third secretary was to be a mill-worker and one of themselves, a 'doffing' mistress, Nelly Gordon.[14]

In 1913 the Irish Transport Workers' Union was fighting for recognition, for the right to exist. Connolly had joined Larkin in Dublin. The union employed the technique of the 'sympathetic' strike of trades unaffected in a dispute, coming 'out' in support of those who were on strike or 'locked out'. In the autumn of 1913 the transport workers were 'locked out' in order to break the union and James Larkin was imprisoned. Countess Markiewicz and a team of volunteers ran soup kitchens and the distribution of necessaries to strikers and their families from Liberty Hall, the Dublin headquarters of the Irish Transport Workers' and the Irish Women Workers' Unions.

Women and girls joined in the outbreak of industrial action in the summer and autumn of 1913.[5] Their strikes were encouraged by Delia Larkin's Irish Women Workers' Union. In July 1913, although unorganized, employees of the Savoy Confectionery Company in Dublin struck work against a 50 per cent wage cut. The management withdrew the threatened reduction, but the following week the strikers were locked out. Blackleg labour was imported and those locked out were accused of intimidation. Photographs of 'scabs', mostly girls, appeared in the Irish Transport and General Workers' Union weekly paper, the *Irish Worker*. The magistrate, however, refused to sentence the strikers and the paper continued to publish attacks on the company, including allegations of rats in the factory and in the pans of liquid chocolate, predicting a drop in sales due to the 'RATIFIED REPUTATION of the Savoy Confectionery Company'.

Women left off working in other 'sweated' trades. The movement culminated on 12 September in a lock-out over union recognition and victimization of union members at Jacob's Biscuit Factory. Here there were rules similar to those that provoked the Belfast textile-workers to strike. The Irish Transport and General Workers' Union backed up these members of the Irish Women Workers' Union by notifying all ports not only in Ireland but in Europe and the United States, of the lock-out so that Jacob's goods might be declared 'black' and not handled.

James Connolly, particularly, taught the Irish Transport and General Workers' Union to support women's efforts to obtain industrial and political rights and raise their economic status. For not all men backed the women strikers, as the Irish Worker explained:

> These heroic women of Dublin to-day are not alone and unaided by the men, but some male workers, members of trade societies, have actually assisted their enemies to defeat them. This state of things must cease ...
> We are all fighting, men and women, under one flag ...

In an attempt to break the union there were threats in Dublin of police violence against union members. The men thought it prudent to leave the city. The women, workers and non-workers alike, refused to leave their homes and stayed with the children and old folk. The threats were carried out against these three groups.

The Transport Workers were, however, forced back to work on the employers' terms, partly because of only lukewarm support from the British trade union movement. Delia Larkin toured Britain in 1913 with a company of singers and actors from Jacob's biscuit factory to raise support for those locked out, and for the campaign to secure her brother's release from prison. The TUC sent money and food supplies to Dublin, but 'sympathetic' strike action was discouraged.[16]

The Irish Transport Workers' Union, its textile branch, and the separate Irish Women Workers' Union all survived, however. In addition to the Irish Women Workers' Union, Delia Larkin founded the Irish Workers' Choir in 1912, ran dancing classes at Liberty Hall, and keenly encouraged the activities of her Irish Workers' Dramatic Company. She was a great organizer. But she resigned in protest at the growth of Republican socialism and its policy of breaking with Britain. She was succeeded in the secretaryship of the union by Helen Molony, who had been Countess Markiewicz's chief assistant in running soup kitchens and the distribution of stores from Liberty Hall.

Ireland had come to present the unconventional spectacle of a country in which Roman Catholicism was the dominant religion, yet in which a large section of people believed in radical socialism and trade unionism. Support for Catholicism was strong not only because of deeply felt religious beliefs, but because over most of the country it had become equated with opposition to Protestant Britain. A belief in Home Rule demanded loyalty to the country's original brand of Christianity. Irish workers easily reconciled patriotic devotion to the Catholic Church with devotion to James Connolly and trade unionism. The commitment to Connolly's revolutionary beliefs was, however, less widespread.

Meanwhile much time had been devoted at the 1912 and 1913 British Trades Union Congresses to demands for improvements in conditions of work which would primarily help women. There were protests that the Trade Board minima fixed for the tailoring trades were too low, especially for women. There were demands that dwelling-houses should no longer be licensed for tailoring; that 'shuttle-kissing' (threading shuttles by mouth) in the weaving trades should be stopped because of the risk of spreading tuberculosis; that conditions of work be vastly improved for girl telephone operators; that a minimum wage be fixed to stop the 'sweating' of theatrical choruses; and that deductions from women workers' earnings to pay for working materials, or fines for small and often unintentional mistakes, should cease.[17] Militancy and unity produced results. Four more Trade Boards were instituted and Old Age Pensions, school meals, and a school medical service as well as National Health Insurance were introduced.

But alongside this development of unity, the long standing causes of friction remained, causing not only disputes between unions enrolling the same kinds of workers, but also between men and women members and workers. All the established methods of reducing the labour force were proposed at the British and Scottish Trades Union Congresses. From 1904, the Scottish miners were again asking for an end to 'female labour' in surface work at mines. They wanted to substitute for women the growing number of men pitworkers disabled in accidents or through pneumoconiosis (dust turning their lungs to stone).[18] They could still do the lighter women's task of 'screening'.

The National Society of Amalgamated Brassworkers and Metal-Workers, after a silence of more than twenty years, suddenly, at the 1908 Trades Union Congress, proposed that women should not work at metal-polishing, screw-making, or turning. This led to a rumpus with Mary Macarthur and the National Federation of Women Workers. The Brass- and Metal-Workers were defeated, and voted down again in 1909, proof of the degree of acceptance of women since Emma Paterson and her colleagues fought the Factories Bill thirty years earlier.[19]

In 1911 the National Federal Union of Operative Bakers and the Dundee Calender-Workers were asking at the Scottish TUC for a reduction in hours of work for women and boys which would effectively take them out of their occupations.[20] The Paper-Mill workers and Woollen-Weavers in 1911, 1912, and 1913 at the British Congress were proposing various ways of cutting hours of work which, like the 8-hour day, might be used as a way of work-sharing.[21]

The women workers for their part were also pursuing this double policy of improvement in working conditions alongside reducing competition for available work. In 1910, the successful National Federation of Women Workers' amendment against the Brassworkers' resolution instructed the Parliamentary Committee to secure the prohibition of all young workers under the age of eighteen in trades scheduled as dangerous and unhealthy. There were resolutions asking for an extension of the length of time women should be excluded from work after childbirth, for keeping children out of jobs by extending the duration of schooling, for stopping the 'half-time' system of part-time child labour in the woollen trades. These were asked for on humanitarian grounds, but must also be seen as part of the now classic trade union reaction to growing unemployment and falling wages—the demand for raising the school-leaving age.[22]

Andrew Conley and W. E. Jancy of the Clothiers' Operatives' Union moved a resolution at the 1912 Congress opposing deductions from wages and fining. It asked the TUC Parliamentary Committee to seek the amendment of the 1896 Truck Act to make these illegal. Julia Varley, who supported them, told Congress of Midlands miners helping to break a strike of girl seamstresses at Hensford in the Cannock district during the previous four months. It was a strike against charges for articles necessary to their work – '3d. for the stools they sat upon, 1s. for cotton, and 1s. for the iron with which they pressed their goods'. She had appealed to the miners to stop their wives and daughters blacklegging. 'But', she told Congress, 'they excused themselves by saying they had no control over their daughters. Well, more shame to them...' The strike failed.

The miners' delegates at Congress hastily repudiated all knowledge of the incident and claimed it was an isolated case. But J. Cross of the Weavers' Amalgamation accused them of withholding help, in spite of repeated approaches from the Weavers, in organizing women in the Wigan district.[23]

Ben Turner of the Woollen-Weavers moved a resolution at the 1913 Congress for a minimum wage for all adult workers, calling on the government to stop giving contracts for textiles to firms paying women less than £1 a week, or to those which paid women less than men 'doing the same class of work'. He advocated a minimum wage for 'all adult workers, and especially women ... sufficient to provide the standard of life and comfort which they have a right to expect from their labour'. Congress cheered in response, and carried the resolution unanimously.[24]

The expressions of goodwill for women workers were weakened, however, when, a little later, a resolution for a minimum wage for adult *male* workers only, 50 per cent higher than that asked for *all* workers, also received the blessing of the 1913 Congress.[25]

The differences between men and women members were to some extent general problems. F. W. Lawson of the Gasworkers' Union, supporting Turner, pointed out that the issue of the 'rate for the job' applied also to youths who 'were competing with men in the same unfair way'. But women were bound to figure largely in issues that involved the less well paid and less well organized. Strong unions, however, would not necessarily support action to help them. For example, they were not keen on compulsory arbitration which would help the less well organized, but which might menace their own right to strike.

Men's determination to secure wage increases for themselves, even at the expense of women co-workers, caused an episode which seriously damaged the development of women's trade unionism and their relationships with men in the Midlands engineering trades. Julia Varley, in preference to the all-female National Federation of Women Workers, had joined the new 'mixed' general union, the Workers' Union, set up by Tom Mann in 1910. The Workers' Union, which recruited women in engineering, was involved in a settlement that was the outcome of a series of strikes. In 1911, there was a strike at the Birmingham BSA factory because women were being brought in at wages of 11s. to 15s. 3d. a week to replace men paid 28s. to 33s. The workers stood together, unskilled with skilled, women with men, and apparently the unions won this battle against cheap female labour.

The following year, unskilled workers working for the Birmingham Corporation and for Messrs Avery's gained wage increases. As a result, the Birmingham Trades Council called a conference of all branches of unions catering for unskilled men and women with a view to instituting minimum wages of 23s. for men and 15s. for women for a 48-hour week. The tactics of these unions, particularly the Workers' Union, were to carry out a great deal of propaganda for the men's 23s. minimum at a particular establishment, recruit as hard as they could, and, when they felt sufficiently strong, present demands to the management. They were successful at Messrs Tangye's, then in West Bromwich in the Spon Lane area, and above all at Smethwick, where the women began a movement which led to a huge strike. Starting at the Handsworth carriage-works, it spread through the Black Country to involve 30,000 workers. Ultimately in July 1912 the strike succeeded.

The following year, however, the Workers' Union and other organizations made an agreement with the Midlands Engineering Employers' Federation fixing the 23s. rate for men. But instead of the target 15s. for women, they settled for only 12s. a week, 6d. a week less than the current Trade Board minimum in the chain trade.[26] This was not only a sad recompense for the women's militancy. It set a precedent of very low wages for women engineering workers which dogged women workers and men trade unionists through war and peace for the next half-century.

Notes

1 1912 NFWW Ann. Rep., 10: 1907 TUC Rep., 194.
2 Women's Industrial Council Memorandum, addressed to the Central Committee and Local Distress Committee appointed to deal with unemployment in London, Dec. 1905.
3 Margaret Bondfield left the Shop Assistants' Union in 1906 to become a propagandist for the Independent Labour Party. But she continued to work with the Women's Industrial Council and to run campaigns to help working women.
4 Hamilton, *Mary Macurthur,* 114.
5 1908 NFWW Ann. Rep.
6 Scot. TUC Reps.: 1909, 20-6, Rep. of the Right to Work Conference at the Guildhall, on 4 May 1908 (author's italics): 1910, 60: 1911, 14-16, Rep. of the ILP Conference in London 27-28 Oct. 1910: 1912, 53, Lab. Party's Right to Work Bill: 1914, 63-4: See also 1909 TUC Rep., 192.
7 José Harris, *The Social Thought of William Beveridge,* Paper for the May 1975 meeting of the Soc. for the Study of Lab. Hist., see Soc.'s Bull., autumn 1975, 8-9. Beveridge himself supported saving and thrift but, for example, the Leicester miners abandoned their own voluntary superannuation scheme because it would disqualify them for the state scheme: Cd. 6179, Rep of Committee on Application of the National Insurance Act, 1912, Vol I, Mins. of Evidence, 73.
8 *WTU Rev.,* July 1911, 10-11. The WTUL and NFWW condemned the idea of basing Old Age Pensions on a test of thriftiness because so many women were paid starvation wages and were therefore unable to save. Nonetheless the Thrift Clubs and Co-operatives showed a great many women did save. Margaret Bondfield ran a parallel campaign which produced legislation in 1913 making Maternity Benefit the property of the mother.
9 *WTU Rev.,* July 1911, 7-13: 1912 and 1914 WTUL Reps.: Hamilton, *Mary Macarthur.,* 108-21: Drake, op.cit., 60: 1911 TUC Rep., 209-10.
10 1911 WTUL Ann. Rep.
11 1912 NFWW Ann. Rep., 5: Hamilton, op. cit., 101-6: Drake, op. cit., 46-7: TUC Reps.: 1910, 203: 1911, 227-8.
12 S. Pankhurst, *The Suffragette Movement,* 184 ff., 404 ff. R. Fulford, *Votes for Women,* 54-6, 61 ff., 109-12: R. Strachey, *The Cause,* 293-5, 297, 301. Drake, op. cit., 62 for assertion of women's equality in the Northern Counties Weaving Amalgamation. The two bodies, the Manchester and Salford Women's Trade Union Council and the Manchester and Salford Women's Trades Council, merged into the Trades Council proper in 1919.
13 Bondfield, *A Life's Work,* 143.
14 Devine, 'Women in Irish Trade Unions': Bleakley, *Trade Union Beginnings in Belfast and District:* S. Levenson, *James Connolly,* 203, 219, 222.
15 *Irish Worker,* July-Oct. 1913. The Women Workers' column continually gave news of women's strikes.
16 Corbett, *Birmingham Trades Council,* 99-100.
17 TUC Reps.: 1903, 89, 98-9: 1904, 118: 1905, 121, 152: 1906, 137: 1907,

177-8: 1911, 188: 1912, 235-6, 249-53: 1913, 205-6, 292-6, 312-14, 319.
Scot. TUC Reps.: 1903, 56: 1904, 61: 1906, 53, 69: 1907, 57-9, 64-5, 69-71:
1908, 52-3, 63, 79: 1909, 56-7: 1910, 12ff., 58, 63-5, 69-70: 1911, 30, 41, 56,
58, 61, 72, 83: 1913, 56: 1914, 79-80. The demands were on behalf of all
workers, men and women, boys and girls, but girls and women were
most affected by these abuses.

18 Scot. TUC Reps.: 1904, 49: 1905, 63: 1907, 62: *WTU Rev.*, Jan. 1912, 4.

19 TUC Reps.: 1908, 189-90: 1909, 167.

20 Scot. TUC Reps.: 1911, 46, 63: 1913, 56.

21 TUC Reps.: 1911, 186-8: 1912, 235, 236: 1913, 319, 401: 1911 Scot. TUC
Rep., 47.

22 1909 TUC Rep., 167. There was a general movement to raise the
school-leaving age and to improve education, see TUC Reps.: 1904, 120:
1912, 186, 258-9; Scot. TUC Reps.: 1910, 11: 1912, 61-2. For campaign
against 'half-timers', TUC Reps.: 1910, 165: 1911, 160-3: 1912, 326-7.

23 1912 TUC Rep., 249-50.

24 1913 TUC Rep., 244-5.

25 ibid., 267.

26 MSS of Corbett's *Birmingham Trades Council,* kindly lent to me. See pub.
book, 100-1: Drake, op. cit., 57, 186.

10   The First World War

The immediate economic effect of the outbreak of war on 4 August 1914 was to bring current trade and industrial production to a juddering halt so that people were thrown out of work. Local War Distress Committees were set up on which trade unions were represented and to whose maintenance they subscribed funds. But they sometimes complained that they did not have enough say on them.

The trade union and Labour movement therefore took measures of its own to deal with the disruptions of war. At a conference on 5 August, it set up the War Emergency Workers' National Committee. Mary Macarthur was the only woman member. Its purpose was to ensure that the emergency was not used to induce workers to accept any lowering of their established standards of living. To this end the Committee stood firmly for an equal rate of pay for equal work and for an adequate living wage for all women workers. It also insisted on adequate training for war work. The bulk of the trade union and Labour movement supported the war and, as a token of their support, agreed to terminate all strikes and lock-outs in progress when war broke out, and to avoid stoppages of work for the duration of hostilities.

Women were especially affected by unemployment at the outset of the war. The Lancashire cotton trade, dependent on imports of raw material and on export markets, along with the luxury and semi-luxury trades, and distribution, were the worst hit. The clothing-workers and home-workers were among the first to suffer as patriotic middle- and upper-class women set to work sewing and knitting comforts for the troops. Many women were dismissed from factories.

The agitation for help for the 'sweated' trades had increased the connections of the Women's Trade Union League and National Federation of Women Workers with influential people. The Princess of Wales, soon to be Queen, had toured the 1906 Sweated Trades Exhibition. She became Patroness of the Central Committee for Women's Training and Employment which before the war helped unemployed women through training schemes as well as by providing them with work, doing the same job as the Local Distress Committees, but more systematically and at a higher level.

Because of her continuing interest in working women, a strange alliance and friendship developed between the ultra-conservative Queen Mary and the radical Mary Macarthur, or, as Labour wags put it, between 'Mary M and Mary R'. Queen Mary by mid-August was holding consultations with people who had first-hand knowledge of the increase in women's unemployment, including representatives of working women. On 20 August, under the auspices of the Central Committee for Women's Training and Employment, the Queen's Work for Women Fund was launched to buy materials for unemployed women so that they could manufacture clothing for the troops.

By this time it was clear that women's work and pay were issues that cut across normal political alignments. The Central Committee for Women's Training and Employment was made up of people of very different political views. In order to save Queen Mary any embarrassment that might arise from attending meetings where political arguments were possible, the chairman, Lady Crewe, passed on to her information on the Committee's work. The Queen asked her to bring one other Committee member to see her, Mary Macarthur. At the first meeting she realized how much Mary Macarthur had to teach her, and Mary Macarthur appreciated the Queen's determination to help. She did not soften her gospel, but preached the trade union and Labour views of the War Emergency Workers' National Committee on the importance of work and standards of wages, hours, and conditions. 'I positively lectured the Queen on the inequality of the classes, the injustice of it. I fear I talked too much again', she remarked after a meeting. The Queen not only listened, she asked for books.[1] The lesson Mary Macarthur was expounding was the effect of well-meaning voluntary labour, not only on women workers, but on all those engaged in any kind of war work, heavy industry, munitions, textiles, as well as the manufacture of clothing for the troops.

Paradoxically, along with the mounting unemployment at the start of the war, there was also a growing labour shortage in war work. Unemployment soon eased. The needs of the armed forces for clothing, food, and leather goods created new jobs. By the end of 1914 women's unemployment was decreasing. Employers in war industries saw women as their main resource, not only for replacing men who joined the armed services, but also for an expansion of industry by means of increased mechanization and subdivision of processes. They hoped the war and appeals to patriotism might be used to force unions to abandon agreements on gradings and on earnings for skilled workers. Their first approach to the government was rebuffed. Then, in December 1914, they put proposals direct to the unions for the scrapping of all trade union regulations affecting demarcations between skilled and unskilled work. They also put forward suggestions for the ending of restrictions on the employment of non-union female labour and on overtime work. Not surprisingly the unions turned them down. The War Emergency Workers' National Committee in January 1915 countered with appeals to women coming into war work to join unions so that reasonable earnings could be negotiated for them and the threat of unorganized cheap female labour diminished.[2]

By February the undertaking given by trade union leaders not to call strikes during the war was being disregarded. In order to obtain a wage rise to compensate for a big increase in the cost of living caused by the war Clydeside workers struck. Their leaders were a new power on the trade union scene, shop stewards, elected directly by trade union members on the workshop floor. Trade union leaders' support for government policies made them remote from their members, whereas shop stewards reflected the true feelings of working people. The spread of the shop-steward movement demonstrated that union leaderships could no longer commit their rank-and-file members to policies they did not consider in their interests even during the emergency of the war. Four groups therefore were now involved in negotiations: government, employers, trade union leaderships, and rank-and-file representatives.

As a result of this Clydeside stoppage, Lloyd George, then Chancellor of the Exchequer, and Walter Runciman, in charge of the Board of Trade, called a meeting of trade union and TUC leaders. Neither the National Federation of Women Workers nor the Workers' Union, the organizations mainly concerned with recruiting women engineering and munitions workers, was represented at this conference. Delegates came from the craft unions, the National Union of Railwaymen, and the Gasworkers' and General Labourers' Union, an old supporter of the Women's Trade Union League. All, except the Miners' Federation, agreed to sign what became known as the Treasury Agreement, by which they accepted the 'relaxation of existing trade practices' for the duration of the war.[3]

Thus the government definitely aligned itself with the employers. At the same time the government set up a Committee on Production in Engineering and Shipbuilding Establishments, virtually intended to implement the employers' proposals. But before this inevitably fell apart because of union resistance, it produced four reports. One on *Shells and Fuses* recommended an extension of the use of women in this sort of munitions work. In March, the unions accepted this principle on condition that 'The relaxation of existing demarcation restrictions or admission of semi-skilled or female labour shall not adversely affect the rates customarily paid for the job'. Men whose earnings might be reduced as a result of the introduction of women workers were to have their rates maintained at the old level.[4]

The expansion in work was not sufficient to reabsorb all the unemployed. In February 1915, it was estimated that there were still 30,000 fewer women working in the staple industries than before the war. The Board of Trade, ignoring them, was now able to issue an invitation to *all* women, whether or not they were forced to earn a living, to volunteer for war work. Influenced by government propaganda, patriotic women who did not need to earn began rushing into war industries, ready to work at any jobs for any length of hours. Many others, although wage-earners present or past, lacked experience of trade unionism, for they were domestic servants, or working-class wives and mothers. If the unions permitted precedents to be set of 12-hour working-days, unlimited subdivision of jobs, and non-observance of apprenticeship agreements, all the work of the past century would crumble. As spring approached, they began to fear a complete breakdown of negotiated agreements. Women and men trade union leaders and active members were determined that these inexperienced women should not be permitted to undercut wages. The women trade unionists were also intent that they should not undermine the unity they were trying to build with men trade unionists. Flowery tributes to the endurance of women workers, real though their heroism often was, glossed over the dour reality of an intensified struggle between organized labour and employers supported by the government.

In April 1915, the War Emergency Workers' National Committee, reflecting alarm at the effects of the Treasury Agreement, called a conference of ninety-two unions, co-operatives, and other relevant organizations, including women's suffrage societies, which repeated demands for maintaining agreed levels of wages and working conditions 'in the interests of the highest patriotism'. They reiterated earlier demands that in order to achieve this 'adequate safeguards must be laid down for any necessary transference or substitution of labour', and once more advised women to join appropriate unions. In addition, the conference delegates also voted that women should be appointed to a newly set-up Labour Advisory Committee. Together with local Munitions Committees, it represented the government's latest move to assuage the unions' fears about dilution.[6]

In May, a Coalition Government replaced the Liberal administration. It made a new effort to secure union co-operation over alterations to agreements. Arthur Henderson, with the consent of his Labour and trade union colleagues, became President of the Board of Education. But his real job was to advise on Labour problems. Two other Labour MPs were given junior posts.

This new government, in which Labour was represented, quickly decided to drop persuasion and impose conditions on the unions. On 23 June 1915 a Munitions of War Bill was introduced into Parliament and was finally passed on 2 July. A Ministry of Munitions, headed by Lloyd George, was set up. The Advisory Committees on which the trade unions were represented were abolished. All real authority was transferred to three officials appointed by the new ministry. The Munitions of War Act made arbitration in disputes in trades concerned with war production compulsory, and thus strikes and lock-outs became illegal. It provided for the wholesale 'dilution' of labour, by the employment of untrained, non-union workers, and threw open to women trades, industries, and particular grades of jobs previously wholly staffed by men. The women, like low-paid men and boys, were virtually tied to their jobs.[7] To conciliate the unions, the Act limited war profits.

The government, however, discovered once again that, as in the decade before the war, the operation of legislation was limited by the power of the rank-and-file union members. Two hundred thousand South Wales miners struck work and since they could not all be gaoled, Lloyd George had to negotiate with them. There were further stoppages of work on the Clyde. The majority of women war workers, however, were still unorganized. For them there was nothing for it but meek acceptance of the Act.

The extreme uneasiness of men and women trade unionists, not least the leaders, over the Munitions of War Act and the Treasury Agreement was apparent at the 1915 Trades Union Congress in resolutions that dealt with the dilution of skilled male labour by women. Mary Macarthur, moving the most crucial, went to the root of union fears:

> ... When the Board of Trade asked for war service from the women of Great Britain a great number of women's societies rushed forward with unconditional offers of help. ... we ask you to say that it is very poor patriotism indeed which would allow the standard of life to be depressed in this way (Hear, hear) ... It is the profit-making people alone who would benefit, and they have already most shamefully exploited the interests and

necessities of the nation. We were told yesterday that, in the State-controlled shops at least, the profits were to be confiscated, but I do not think it was made quite clear that, under the Munitions Act, the profits are only touched when they are 20 per cent in excess of previous profits ... we are not satisfied that the Munitions Act has laid down adequate safeguards ...

She charged that where women replaced skilled men, employers were circumventing paying them the 'rate for the job' by sub-dividing jobs into many different small operations. Miss Isabel Sloan, assistant secretary of the National Federation of Women Workers, seconding, instanced a factory making lyddite, a high explosive for filling shells, where women were paid less than half the men's rates.

However, Isabel Sloan also showed Congress the means by which justice over pay could be done to both men and women. In Newcastle-upon-Tyne women were asked to volunteer for work on trams. They were offered a wage of 15s. a week. But the men refused to let them take the jobs unless they were paid their own full rate of 28s. Despite objections from the employers, the women were given the 'rate for the job' and all joined the union. This news of men's support for women was received with cheers.

The mood of Congress was by no means anti-feminist. J. T. Watkins of the National Gasworkers' Union had the resolution strengthened in women's favour. In place of yet another demand for an unspecified minimum wage for all women, he had Congress repeat their pre-war demand for the definite figure of £1 a week.

Nor was the resolution narrowly confined to women. The unions were suspicious of the Munitions of War Act's limitation on workers' freedom to move from one job to another. Therefore clauses were added asking Labour MPs to bring in a Bill 'to nullify all war-time emergency legislation that curtailed individual liberty', once the war was over.

The nervousness of trade unionists may be judged from the fact that this compendium resolution was followed by another from the Scientific Instrument-Makers and the Provincial Association of Operative Cotton-Spinners of Bolton asking for local committees of employers' and workers' representatives to be set up straightaway to ensure 'the replacement of women at the close of the war by more suitable male labour'. Mr Luckhurst of the Scientific Instrument-Makers thought 'it would be unfair to get rid of the women after they had served their country so well in time of national danger'. But they feared that before the war had ended, women would be established in every district.

Jim Battle of the Cotton-Spinners did not blame the women so

1 Staff of National Federation of
  Women Workers (*c* 1908):
  Mary Macarthur (seated);
  standing left, Marion Phillips;
  standing right, Julia Varley
2 Winifred Carney
3 Helen Molony
4 Louie Bennett
5 Mabel Talbot
6 Susan Lawrence
7 Dorothy Elliott
8 Alice Horan

much as the lack of support from men's unions for 'the rate for the
job'. He told the Congress the women had come to the Bolton
Trades Council to ask for information 'as to the proper wages for
their work'. The Trades Council referred them to the
Amalgamated Society of Engineers, which refused to recruit them
or help them. He said the same thing had happened in Birmingham, over work on hand grenades.

But he also made clear that 'the rate for the job' was not simply
an aspect of the sex war. For he instanced leather workshops in
Bolton working on government contracts where not a single man
was receiving the standard rate of wages. Congress supported this
proposal for stronger guarantees that demobilized men would get
back their peacetime jobs, by passing it with only 43 votes against.[8]

The war heightened tensions between various unions competing over the recruitment of women warworkers, so adding a new motive for inter-union disputes. Since the key union, the Amalgamated Society of Engineers, refused to accept women members, their enrolment was left to the general unions already organizing women in the engineering trades.

The problem was not simply women. It was a matter of work gradings. In 1886 the ASE had begun enrolling less skilled men. But in 1912 it had given this up because of the opposition of 'mixed' general unions which also recruited them. There was therefore a clear demarcation based on gradings at work: the ASE recruited skilled men, the general unions the rest. In the case of women war workers, however, the Amalgamated Society of Engineers ignored the unions with which it had made the 1912 demarcation agreement and made an alliance with only one general union, the all-female National Federation of Women Workers. The result was ill-feeling between the other general unions on the one hand, and the ASE and the National Federation of Women Workers on the other.[9]

In a symposium entitled *Women in the Labour Party,* edited by Dr Marion Phillips and published in 1918, Mary Macarthur expressed her views on the working arrangement with the ASE. Claiming that it was purely informal, in spite of a formal agreement signed by both unions in June 1915, she stated that the attitude of the Amalgamated Society of Engineers was preferable to:

> ... the attitude adopted by some other men Trade Unionists, who, while admitting women to membership of their Union and accepting contributions from them, have at the same time used the organization to which the women belonged — without consultation with the women who were members — to declare that under no circumstances whatever should women continue to be employed in their trade after the war.

The reaction of women to such an introduction to trade unionism, she said, was one of puzzlement and bewilderment.[10]

The National Federation of Women Workers, galvanized by Mary Macarthur's tremendous nervous energy, set the pace for all the other unions enrolling women, in pressurizing the government and in negotiations with employers. The Federation and the Amalgamated Society of Engineers sent a deputation to the Ministry of Munitions in the summer of 1915, before they had Congress support, to demand the £1-a-week minimum wage for all women who had been substituted for men in engineering and ship-building work.[11] The Ministry of Munitions refused at first to support this limited demand. It replied that it had no powers to enforce such a minimum other than in national, government-run establishments.

However, in September 1915, the ministry yielded to union pressure for restoration of joint consultation destroyed by the Munitions of War Act. It appointed a Labour Supply Committee — with Mary Macarthur on it. Through this Committee the £1-a-week minimum for women was partially achieved. To some extent also this Committee was able to control the operation of other parts of the Act. It drew up a scheme for dilution of skilled labour. It also produced a memorandum fixing women's rates in engineering and shipbuilding establishments on work not recognized as 'women's work' before the war. This was transformed into an agreement known as Circular L2. In addition L2 fixed the standard rate of £1 for a week of normal hours for all substituted women over eighteen years of age and also laid down men's overtime rates and Sunday, holiday, and night-work bonuses.

In November 1915 the government introduced a Bill to amend the Munitions of War Act so that the Minister of Munitions would have the power to fix rates of wages and other conditions for women war workers. But some of the proposals were opposed by the Amalgamated Society of Engineers backed by the trade union movement. Moreover, renewed rebellion was looming in the war industries of Clydeside and north-east England. In December Arthur Henderson and Lloyd George met with open hostility on a visit to Clydeside. The unrest spread to other war-production centres. There were strikes at Birmingham and Coventry, women coming 'out' with men. Sidney and Beatrice Webb accused the government of building up during the war 'a machinery of industrial espionage with agents provocateurs of workshop "sedition" ...' in order to remove militants. There were clashes with troops and a few of the leaders of the Clydeside revolt were not merely arrested, but deported.[12]

However, the government, concerned to stop such outbreaks, instituted a Commission of Inquiry which assigned various causes to the strikes, including the failure of wages to keep up with the rising cost of living and the unequal distribution of food supplies. Women's main grievances were poor wages, which were sometimes as low as 13s. a week, and the failure to implement Circular L2 properly. Among the men there was a complex of grievances concerning the women who had come into men's work.[13] Not only were there still fears that pre-war practices would not be restored when the war ended, and that women would lower piece-rates. There was also jealousy because women reached higher rates of earnings more quickly than male apprentices. Mary Macarthur explained that the men had some justification: 'The injury to his [i.e., a man's] self-respect is as great as that to his pocket ... often toolmakers and gauge-makers whose skill is the basis on which the machine operates ... were getting considerably less than the [women] pieceworkers ...' The Ministry of Munitions, and in particular Winston Churchill, were criticized for not calling a meeting of the National Labour Advisory Committee before all the trouble broke out. Joint Industrial Councils were advocated as a means of preventing it happening again.[14]

Because of the protests on the Clyde, the amendments to the Munitions of War Act were passed in January 1916 so as to give statutory force to the payment of the 'rate for the job' for those women who replaced skilled men. Women assessors were to sit on the ministry's tribunals to assess wages and consider working conditions. Regulations under which workers changed their jobs were also eased. The government set up a Clyde Dilution Committee which in turn decreed that £1 should be the starting-rate for all women 'put on any portion of a job customarily performed by a fully skilled tradesman'. It laid down that women only doing part of such a job should receive men's full rates after three months' probation. Thus the battle for the 'rate for the job' for substituted women in engineering, munitions, and other forms of war work was in effect won.

It was up to the unions to enforce L2 and these amendments. According to the Webbs the proliferation of committees and arbitration procedures was a government method of exhausting union officials and so of avoiding the full application of concessions the unions gained. The staff of the National Federation of Women Workers were energetic in exacting that the amended Act be applied. Something like a personal duel developed between Mary Macarthur and Lloyd George, who feared her adamantine determination which his Welsh persuasiveness could not corrode. They were two of a kind. Both used their charm to secure their political aims, both were wily. Mary Macarthur's main weapon was her tongue; when she wanted something done, she went to see someone about it, Lord Northcliffe, for example, to ensure that the Federation had adequate space and publicity in *The Times* for its activities. Lloyd George, too, relied on the spoken word. But none of his tricks could budge her from one simple demand, that if women were to be chained to their jobs by the Munitions of War Act, then they must have reasonable wages and decent working conditions. Mary Macarthur pointed out that while the minimum rates of earnings fixed by Trade Boards 'were hampered by consideration of what the sweated trades could bear', no such consideration limited earnings in the highly profitable war industries. There was no excuse in these for low earnings. The Factory Acts had been disregarded because of the emergency. A 14-hour day was usual and many worked a 70- or 80-hour week. The Home Office made no difficulties about applications from armaments firms for permits to employ women and even children on night-work. The persistence of the staff of the National Federation of Women Workers helped to produce a Committee of Inquiry which confirmed their accusations.[15]

It was not until July 1916 that the Ministry of Munitions began to fix 'fair conditions of employment', and even then paid no attention to payments for overtime, night-work, Sunday work, or for 'waiting-time', that is time spent in a factory waiting to be allocated work. Mary Macarthur attacked Lloyd George for smothering in 'radiant words' the fact that, far from operating a legal minimum wage, his ministry was enforcing a maximum rate above which a woman could not earn. Her husband, Will Anderson, renewed the campaign of pressure in the House of Commons for the enforcement of adequate standards of earnings.

By January 1917 it was apparent that even the low rates proposed by the ministry's Order of the previous July were not being enforced. Mary Macarthur thundered in *The Times* of 5 January 1917:

I unhesitatingly assert that there are thousands of women to whom no protection has as yet been accorded by statutory orders fixing wages ... The rates fixed for women on women's work, if valued according to the Board of Trade statistics of the rise in the cost of living, are worth less in real wages to-day than the rates fixed legally for some sweated trades under the Trade Board Acts before the War.

To strengthen the campaign for improved earnings for women, she took the initiative in June in forming, with other general unions, a Joint Committee on Women's Wages and Working Conditions. Margaret Bondfield joined the staff of the National Federation of Women Workers in 1915, and in 1916 became its organizing secretary. She now took a leading part on this Committee, of which Mary Macarthur was chairman [16]

However, the National Federation of Women Workers believed that the general unions contrived to stop any negotiations on working conditions. There is also some doubt as to how far the Workers' Union stood for the £1 minimum. Towards the end of February 1916, Julia Varley and R.E. Stokes, the union's Midlands District organizer, told a public meeting that the employers were consulting the union over women's employment. Almost certainly some of the women who were the subject of these negotiations were substituted war workers. Julia Varley and Mr Stokes said that while non-union women were only paid 8s.-9s. a week, the union members would now be receiving a 15s. minimum with 25 per cent extra on piece-work. Their total earnings were probably over £1 a week. But the minimum rate was less than the £1 stipulated in Circular L2.[17]

At the end of November, the *Daily Mail* reported another agreement between the Midland Engineering Employers' Federation and Workers' Union which raised the minimum to 16s. a week for women over twenty-one years, still below the L2 £1.[18] In addition there would be no restrictions on piece-work earnings, neither would output be restricted. Thus workers were left to set their own pace and hours of work. But this agreement was to remain in force until the end of the war, so any advance to the £1 minimum was ruled out. Julia Varley was conscious of the need to enforce the Circular. But there was opposition from men members, on which both she and the union's President, John Beard, remarked.[19]

At the same time as working for control of women dilutees, unions used their established policy of enrolling women in order the better to control them as competitors for work. A large number of unions decided to accept them into membership. In 1915 the National Silk-Workers' Association and other societies of silk-workers accepted women twisters and weavers, thus taking a step towards the restoration of the early nineteenth-century equality.[20] During a strike in 1913-14, the Bookbinders had followed their past policy of supporting the women strikers. But they left their organization to the National Union of Printing- and Paper-Workers. In 1915, however, the London branch of the National Union of Bookbinders and Machine-Rulers took them in.[21] At the end of the war, the Scottish Typographical Association decided to form a separate women's section.[22] In 1916 the Electrical Trades Union accepted them.[23] The National Union of Railwaymen, and two societies of vehicle workers, which merged into the United Vehicle Workers, began recruiting women in 1915.[24] The Amalgamated Union of Operative Bakers, which excluded women from making bread, enrolled them from 1915.[25] But in Dublin a separate Guild of Female Biscuit Operatives was set up. It was 1918 before the National Society of Brush-Makers admitted them.[26] And the Power-Loom Carpet-Weavers and Textile-Workers of Kidderminster, while screwing themselves up to enrolling women, laid down that it took the votes of twenty-five women members to

equal that of one man, so fearful were they of the effect of the
spendthrift propensities of women on union funds.[27]

In 1917 the government's Women's Employment Committee
reported that whereas in 1912, 204 unions admitted women members, by 1917 the number had risen to 310 unions. But in spite of
this expansion of women's trade unionism over a wide range of occupations, at the end of the war the cotton-weavers and spinners
still accounted for the largest single group of organized women.[28]

The government's agreement to the 'rate for the job' for substituted women in war work encouraged other unions to stand out
for the principle. It was not only an issue for munitions workers.
The tram, bus, and railway companies agreed to union requests
that women on men's work be paid at men's time-rates but refused
to pay women the same rate of war bonus as men. In 1918, rank-
and-file male members of the London and Provincial Licensed
Vehicle-Workers' Union struck along with women 'clippies'. With
Mary Macarthur and the League and Federation to help, they obtained an equal bonus.[29] The National Union of Journalists and the
Amalgamated Union of Co-operative Employees both established
the 'rate for the job', the Co-operative Employees going on strike
seventy times before they succeeded.[30] Three local authorities, at
East Ham and Tottenham in the London area and Mountain Ash
in Glamorganshire, conceded the 'rate for the job' for women
teaching staff.[31] The Shop Assistants' Union in private trade
agreements, and the wool- and worsted-workers, negotiated that
women should receive 80 per cent of the wages paid to men.[32]

But the 'rate for the job' was not obtained in the public services.
A Royal Commission on the Civil Service in 1914 under a Liberal
government had recommended the 'rate for the job' for a small
number of women in various Civil Service departments. Its Report
commented on the disparity in pay between women clerks and
'male clerks enjoying a much larger salary', and stated that 'ef-
ficiency in clerical, as in other forms of labour, depends in part
upon the food, housing, recreation etc. made possible by the salary
paid'. Gertrude Tuckwell, more detailed and practical, later
elaborated on this:

> Efficiency is impossible on a diet of tea and margarine ... it would
> be found that a considerable number of women clerks ... make
> their own clothes and perform many household duties in ad-
> dition to their office work ... to which many add — what is
> theoretically held to be the man's obligation — that of the sup-
> port of some other member of the family.[33]

She also pointed out that employers could not 'have it both ways —

a woman whose resourcefulness is dulled by excessive routine is not in the most favourable situation to respond to an emergency'.

During the war, the unions grouped in the Civil Service Alliance declared 'the rate for the job' for women was their aim.[34] However, like manual workers' unions their primary concern was to protect the jobs of men members from the threat of displacement by cheap female labour. And similarly they did not attach the same importance to women's fears of unemployment as they did to those of men.

The war created a demand for female labour in agriculture. In 1916 the authorities were being urged 'to consider the reasons why there has been a steady decrease in the number of women employed in agriculture in Scotland'. The women were taking the chances offered by the wartime demand for female labour to leave and the reasons were not far to seek. Not only were wages low and hours long, in the Lothians of Scotland and in north-east England, the conditions of work were still medieval.

In January 1916, the Scottish Farm Servants' Union organizer for the Lothians reported in the union journal that the bondaging system still operated in the Lothians. It was also prevalent in the area to the south over the Border. A man employed by a farmer was expected to provide women workers and to fix their wages with the farmers. 'A woman hired in this way is a bondager ... She cannot break her bargain owing to her father or brother contracting to provide an outworker at, say, 12s. a week without board'.

The system persisted because from the workpeople's point of view it kept families together and saved women and girls having to go to 'service'. Young men binding their sisters in this way got higher rates of pay since these were usually made up by the lower wages paid to the women. The farmers gained because it was said that women did the same amount of work as men. They were said to be much better workers than Irish labourers, and they cost only half as much in wages.

The people really harmed by the system were single women who had to live on their earnings. It led to the idea that there was something odd about a woman 'who had no men folks' to look after her. Consequently she was often imposed on because there was no man 'to speak for her'.[35]

There were, however, signs of a revolt by the women. The union was encouraging them to refuse to recognize any bargain made on their behalf by a third party. Wages of women in East Lothian, for example, rose from about 11s. a week in 1912 to 14s. a week by April 1916. A few women even obtained 15s.[36]

The National Federation of Women Workers extended its attempts to raise women's earnings to Ireland. Isabel Sloan, the assistant secretary, was there in May 1917, trying to bring Irish women munition workers' rates of pay into line with those in Britain. But she ran foul of the Irish Women Workers' Union, which was incensed at this encroachment, especially as anti-English feeling was running high. In the aftermath of the Easter Rising in Dublin in 1916, an abortive attempt to establish independence, the Irish Women Workers' Union and women's organization generally broke down. A Women Workers' Co-operative Society had been started to help unemployed women. Government troops looted stocks of materials from its workrooms at Liberty Hall when they attacked the building, leaving women without work. The Irish women trade union leaders were in the thick of the revolt. Winifred Carney, Secretary of the Irish Women Textile-Workers' branch of the Irish Transport Workers' Union, acted as James Connolly's secretary during the Rising and was the last woman to leave the besieged Dublin General Post Office.

In 1915, when Delia Larkin left for England, Helen Molony had been appointed secretary of the Irish Women Workers' Union by James Connolly. She was also a member of the Irish Citizen Army. She fought with them at Dublin Castle and at the City Hall and was imprisoned at Kilmainham and Holloway gaols. She became a member of the Sinn Fein executive after her release. While she was in gaol, someone had to be found to take over the secretaryship of the Irish Women Workers' Union.

One of the middle-class women who had come to dispense soup to women and children during the 1913 strikes and lock-outs was Miss Louie Bennett, a founder and joint honorary secretary of the Irishwomen's Suffrage Federation, established in August 1911. She was a pacifist and she disliked violence and class conflict. But James Connolly and Helen Molony had encouraged her interest in the organization of women in unions. The shooting of the leaders of the Easter Rising, including James Connolly, converted her to the cause of Irish nationalism. In 1917 she began organizing 'sweated' women workers. Helen Molony wrote to her from prison and asked her to take the lead in the trade union organization of women. Louie Bennett took over the secretaryship of the Irish Women Workers' Union and rebuilt it with the help of Helen Chenevix and in spite of opposition from trade unions, notably those in the printing trades.[37]

With the background of anti-English sentiment and with their own tradition of women's trade unionism stretching back at least thirty years, the Irish women did not welcome the intrusion of the

National Federation of Women Workers. The Irish Women Workers' Union joined the general unions in Britain in mounting an attack against the Federation and the Women's Trade Union League. [38] Given Mary Macarthur's outstanding leadership, this amounted to a personal attack on her. There was renewed criticism of the Federation's alliance with the Amalgamated Society of Engineers. The Federation was forced off the Joint Committee on Women's Wages and Working Conditions for the strange reason that it was an all-female union. So, of course, was the Irish Women Workers' Union. In effect, however, that organization was a women's branch of the Irish Transport and General Workers' Union, and so more acceptable, The function of this Committee was taken over by the National Federation of General Workers assisted by a women's advisory council, so that the women's presence in negotiations was diminished, presumably with the acquiescence of women officials and members of 'mixed' general unions. The men now ran the committee, the women merely advised. [39] Thus without Mary Macarthur's inexorable pressure on behalf of women's interests, the men' priorities inevitably prevailed in the male-dominated 'mixed' unions. All were agreed on the War Emergency Workers' National Committee's aim of protecting established standards of wages, hours, and working conditions and the jobs of men called up to the forces. But Mary Macarthur and the Federation also determinedly used the war and the increased demand for women workers to raise the levels of earnings of all women workers whether they were substituted or not. This was carrying the war into the enemy's camp. Like the employers they were trying to use the war to set precedents for peacetime conditions. It was also going further than many male-dominated unions wanted to go. [40]

Partly out of personal ambition and partly because she found direct contact with influential people the quickest way of achieving results, Mary Macarthur accepted appointments on a mind-boggling number of committees. As well as being the only woman on the War Emergency Workers' National Committee and a member of the Central Committee for Women's Training and Employment, she was the only woman on the Central Munitions Labour Supply Committee which tried to safeguard dilution schemes. She masterminded the Health of Munitions Workers' Committee. She became chairman of the Standing Joint Committee of Working Women's Organizations, established in 1916 to co-ordinate the work of various bodies concerned with improving conditions of life of working women and with gaining women's support for the political Labour Party. Along with Margaret Bondfield, she was on the panel of the Joint Industrial Courts. Her singleminded concentration on women's trade unionism was being dissipated. She was taken up by political hostesses. Her purpose of helping working women was unshaken. She was too practical and had too much commonsense to let lionizing go to her head. But she disregarded the government's known tactic of tiring and weakening its trade union opponents by involving them in large numbers of committees. Organization in the National Federation of Women Workers was increasingly left to Margaret Bondfield and the other members of the organizing staff.

The total number of women in unions in the United Kingdom trebled during the war, rising from 433,679 in 1914 to 1,209,278 in 1918. Women members who had risen to official posts in their 'mixed' unions therefore felt confident that they no longer required the help of middle-class women 'outsiders'. Those who had been able to show their abilities as organizers during the war felt that the Federation's policy of handing over to 'mixed' or all-male unions groups of women it had organized, impugned their capabilities of bringing in women members. Hence the Federation, from the summer of 1917, was experiencing the kind of hostility it had shown to the Scottish Council for Women's Trades before the war. Like Margaret Irwin, Mary Macarthur did not wait to be pushed. At the Federation's 1917 Annual Delegate Conference, in spite of violent opposition from some of the organizing staff, it was decided that the possibilities of amalgamation be investigated. As a general union, it could only sensibly be merged with another general union. Negotiations began with the National Union of General Workers because of Mary Macarthur's close personal friendship with its secretary, J. R. Clynes, but there was no immediate action.[41]

Margaret Bondfield now had an immense personal success. As a member of the National Federation of Women Workers she stood for election to the TUC Parliamentary Committee in October 1918. She headed the list of unsuccessful candidates. When Fred Bramley, one of those elected, moved up to the official post of TUC Assistant General Secretary, she automatically stepped into the place he left vacant. In this way she became the first woman member of the TUC leadership. The unions had not forgotten her presence at Congresses as assistant secretary of the Shop Assistants' Union, nor her part in ending the 'living-in' system. And she was one of them, an ordinary working girl. Thus Margaret Bondfield strengthened her contacts with unions when her middle-class colleagues were being cold-shouldered.[42]

As the war neared an end, the main fear of the Women's Trade

Union League and the National Federation of Women Workers, inevitably, was of the mass unemployment of women. At the 1918 Trades Union Congress, Mary Macarthur claimed from the men, for whose job security the Federation and League had fought, support for the women! 'If we stand by the men for complete restoration [of jobs], let them stand by us for guarantees and indemnities'. That is for guarantees of work and what is now called redundancy pay for women displaced by the men coming out of the forces.

But there was also official concern over the effects of the demobilization of women war workers manifested in the number of Reports that were issued at this time. There were the Report of the Gladstone Committee, the War Cabinet Committee's Report on Women in Industry, the Report of the Women's Employment Committee to the Ministry of Reconstruction, and the Ministry of Reconstruction's Report on Women in the Civil Service. In recognition of their war work, women at last got a limited right to the franchise. There was talk of increasing the number of Trade Boards and encouraging developments in joint consultation. The prospects of women workers in November 1918 were better than before the war and there were many reasons to hope that, in the normal conditions of peace, their improved status would be maintained.

Notes

1 James Pope-Hennessy, *Queen Mary*, 69, 491-3. See also *Burton Observer*, 1 Oct. 1914. Conference of local unions with Railway and Co-operative Women's Guilds to secure greater representation on local War Distress Relief Committee.

2 Drake, *Women in Trade Unions*, 69: *Cotton Factory Times*, 10 Jan. 1915: Hamilton, *Mary Macarthur*, 136-41. For withdrawal of women transport workers, see NUGMW *Journal*, July 1938, 84-5. Also Drake, op.cit., 106, for action of the London Tram United Vehicle Workers against summary dismissal of women.

3 Drake, op. cit., 71: S. and B. Webb, *History of Trade Unionism*, 638.

4 Drake, op. cit., 70-1.

5 ibid., 74: Hamilton, op. cit., 142.

6 ibid., 142: Drake, op. cit., 74.

7 ibid., 76.

8 1915 TUC Rep., 370-3. See also 301-3, 373-5, 398-9, 402, for union demands to keep women out of various trades. Drake, op. cit., 84-5, Mule-spinners advocated the employment of boys from Belgium, rather than women. 1916 Scot. TUC Rep., 6-7.

9 Drake, op. cit., 74-5: Hamilton, *Women at Work*, Mary Macarthur had notable support from G.D.H. Cole, then acting as adviser to the ASE.

10 Marion Phillips, ed., *Women in the Labour Party*, 23.
11 Drake, op. cit., 74 ff.: Hamilton, *Mary Macarthur*, 150-1.
12 S and B Webb, op. cit., 645.
13 Drake, op. cit., 80. There were 13,000 women employed in Clyde engineering firms in 1915.
14 ibid.: S. and B. Webb, op. cit., 641-2.
15 Hamilton, *Mary Macarthur*, 141, 149 ff. 155-6, 158. Drake, op. cit., 93.
16 Drake, op. cit., 104: Hamilton, *Mary Macarthur*, 159-60.
17 *Derby Express*, 29 Feb. 1916.
18 *Daily Mail*, 26 Nov. 1915: Drake, op. cit., 78.
19 *Derby Express*, 29 Feb. 1916: *Birmingham Gazette*, 12 June 1916.
20 Drake, op. cit., 135.
21 ibid., 151: Bundock, *Printing, Bookbinding and Paper Workers*, 104 ff.
22 Drake, op. cit., 154.
23 ibid., 115.
24 ibid., 147, 117.
25 ibid., 162.
26 ibid., 180.
27 ibid., 134.
28 Rep. of the Women's Employment Committee, 1917, Document 154, App. VII.
29 Drake, op. cit., 92, 106, 149. This dispute was one reason for the setting-up of the War Cabinet Committee on Women in Industry. B. Webb, Minority Rep., pub. as Fabian pamphlet, 1919, 'The Wages of Men and Women, Should They be Equal?', 3.
30 Drake, op. cit., 90, 169.
31 1944 Roy. Comm. on Equal Pay, sect. 1, Statement of the Nat. Union of Women Teachers, paras. 13-14, See also sect. 3, 68, para. 932: sect. 4, Statement 84, para. 2; p.88, para. 6.
32 Drake, op. cit., 89, 90, 95, 167. For great movement of organization among dressmakers, 96.
33 S. Webb, *Problems of Modern Industry*, 80 made the same point in 1888.
34 Drake, op. cit., 178.
35 *Scottish Farm Servant*, June 1913, 11: Jan. 1916, 13-14: Mar. 1916, 2: Nov. 1920, 157.
36 ibid., Sept. 1914, 5. A farmer who said he paid his women workers 2s. 6d. a day was answered by a woman who walked over to him and, with clenched fist to his nose, demanded an instance where he had paid over 2s. a day. See also Mar. 1916, 2.
37 F Devine, op. cit.
38 *Daily Express*, Dublin, 28 May 1917.
39 Drake, op. cit., 84-5, 94.
40 ibid., 99-100, 101-02.
41 Hamilton, *Margaret Bondfield*, 121 ff.: Bondfield was appointed Chairman of the Women's Council of Socialist and Labour Organizations, which seemed to duplicate the Standing Joint Committee of Working Women's Organizations.
42 Hamilton, *Mary Macarthur*, 197.

11   The End of the Women's Trade Union League and the National Federation of Women Workers

Women trade unionists shared the mood of unity and militancy during the two years that followed the end of the war. The balance of power within Congress had been altering, so that the textile unions, with their large female memberships, were overtaken in size by the mainly male mining, railway, and engineering unions. They now dominated Congress with their block votes and immediately the war was over forced the Parliamentary Labour Party out of the Coalition Government.

There had been a shift to the left in the Labour movement as a whole. The Russian Revolution of February 1917, finally persuaded the TUC Parliamentary Committee to take responsibility for international contacts. They participated in a meeting of the Labour leaders of the Allied Powers in February 1918. The left-wing Labour groups, the Independent Labour Party and the British Socialist Party, drew closer together. These moves helped to reconcile the union leaderships with the shop-stewards' movement, while co-operation with the government and employers diminished.

The Coalition Government hustled the country into an election called for 14 December 1918. Margaret Bondfield and Mary Macarthur joined Susan Lawrence on the National Executive Committee of the Labour Party, and along with other leading women party members became Labour Party candidates. The Conservatives and some Liberals, intent on preserving the Coalition, appealed to popular desire for revenge against the Germans. The preferred election slogan was 'Hang the Kaiser'. Any Labour candidate who could be described as remotely pacifist stood little chance. Many Labour Party leaders lost their seats, for example, Ramsay MacDonald, Philip Snowden, and Mary Macarthur's husband, Will Anderson, who had been chairman of the Parliamentary Labour Party. Mary Macarthur herself failed mainly for the same reason. The Coalition won handsomely. Nevertheless, the number of Labour Party members increased. With its mere 57 MPs, Labour was now the official opposition party.[1]

The expected steep rise in unemployment came. By November 1918 the contraction of war production and manufacture of clothing for troops had thrown large numbers of men as well as women out of work. On 19 November, two days before the Armistice, there was a big march from Woolwich and other London districts to the House of Commons to demand action to provide work or maintenance. The government promised that a new scheme to ease unemployment would be brought into operation in a year's time. Still dissatisfied and anxious about the fate of women dilutees who were being replaced in engineering, shipbuilding, and munitions, the National Federation of Women Workers, with the help of the *Daily Herald*, organized a meeting at the Albert Hall when it put forward its charter: 'The Right to Work: the Right to Life: the Right to Leisure' and followed this up with a deputation to Bonar Law who was acting for the Prime Minister, Lloyd George.[2] However, by March 1919 just over half a million women were officially admitted to be unemployed.[3] Labour exchanges were under orders to exercise 'extreme strictness' about accepting applicants for unemployment benefit and to weed out any woman whose right seemed doubtful. The true numbers of unemployed were thus higher than the acknowledged total. The new Coalition Government, forced to some sort of action, appointed a Select Committee

Mary Macarthur addressing crowd of unemployed, Trafalgar Square November 1918

of Inquiry into the extent of women's unemployment. But women representatives were excluded from it because, according to Sir Robert Horne, the new Minister of Labour, a Select Committee precluded the appointment of women.[4]

Yet in spite of the high unemployment, the numbers of women organized increased during the 1919-20 economic post-war boom, as women war workers transferred to peace time jobs. While the great munitions branches of the National Federation of Women Workers at Newcastle, Barrow, and Woolwich 'literally melted away', the demobilized women took their initiation into trade unionism with them into their new employments. So to compensate there was a great expansion of trade unionism among laundry-workers, for instance, which enabled the Federation in May 1919 to negotiate for those in London a minimum weekly wage of 28s. There were similar successes in the catering industry.

The General Union of Textile-Workers and the Amalgamated Tailors' and Garment-Workers' Union reported large increases in women's membership. There was a big rise in numbers of women in the Shop Assistants' Union, in which the women's strong support enabled officials to negotiate a 25 per cent pay increase with the Army and Navy Stores in London. In 1919 Miss Mabel Talbot, who worked in another of the big London stores, was elected President of the union, the first woman to hold this office in any 'mixed' organization. The Pottery-Workers' Union reported a total of 27,000 women members. The Boot and Shoe Operatives Leicester women's branch was now quite restored, thanks to Mary Bell. Rises in numbers of women members were reported by several other small clothing unions, by unions of clerks, agricultural workers, weavers, and other textile-workers.[5]

With these specific increases the relatively very high women's trade union membership in the two years after the war could not be ascribed merely to an unwillingness on the part of some unions to acknowledge that there had been a decline. There may have been some that kept lapsed members on their books to boost their female membership figures. But, by and large, although many women must have left male craft and industrial unions, like those of the railwaymen and the electricians, the women's membership still held. By 1920 the number of women in trade unions in the United Kingdom had risen to 1,342,000, an increase of over 140,000 since 1918. They represented 25 per cent of the total number of women then at work, as against 50 per cent of working men who were trade union members.

Many years later, Miss Annie Macdonald, a member of the Union of Shop, Distributive, and Allied Workers, gave a glimpse of this effervescence of organization working at grass-roots level. She described how the Glasgow District Council of the Shop Assistants' Union had set up a Women's Council, made up of women members from every branch. During 1919-20, the Council, with the help of organizers, mostly voluntary, held meetings at midnight because confectionery-workers were on a 72-hour week and did not finish work until 11 p.m. Annie Macdonald was proud to recall that they had cut this down to 48 hours:

> ... we had no funds, if the branches sent delegates to this Women's Council, they were allowed 2s. 6d. a year for the delegation fees. So you can understand we had to do a lot of dipping into our own pockets in those days ... which we did very gladly, because it meant we were raising our own status ...[6]

During these two crucial post-war years, the Coalition Government was endeavouring to weaken the trade unions by means of 'divide and rule' tactics. The wartime coalition had been very shaken not only by the socialist-led revolts on the Clyde and other industrial centres, but also by the support shown by British dockers and other workers for the Communist-led Russian Revolution of 1917. For the first time adherents of the new socialist creeds had overturned an established regime. The drawing-together of the left and right wings of the Labour movement at the close of the war seemed to them ominous in a much more profound sense than the accepted economic rough-and-tumble of capital versus labour. In December 1918, employers were instructed to try to control unemployment. The government's advice to them was that rather than suddenly and immediately discharging staff, production should be slowed down by the abolition of overtime, the suspension of payment-by-results systems, and by means of short-time working. To avoid labour trouble, and to get their old skilled craftsmen back, most engineering employers went back to pre-war methods of manufacture. Although some tried to cling to new mechanized methods using female labour introduced in the war, few if any cases were brought under the Restoration of Pre-War Practices Act. In addition, successive wage increases were granted to meet the rising cost of living. The government cushioned earnings that fell below fixed amounts. The Wages (Temporary Regulation) Act prevented employers from effecting cuts until May 1919. It was extended first until November and then until the end of September 1920. Industrial Courts, expressly freed from any hint of wartime controls, arbitrated in wage settlements. The right to strike was restored. In this way engineering workers were placated and industrial disputes in this key industry were discouraged.[7]

The government also wooed trade unions and their supporters. In the case of women, Gertrude Tuckwell was appointed one of the first women Justices of the Peace. Along with Mary Macarthur, Margaret Bondfield, and several other prominent women trade unionists and Labour Party members, she was also appointed to the Lord Chancellor's Women's Advisory Committee. Their inclusion was a gesture to make up for the exclusion of women from the Select Committee on Women's Employment.

The government's main concern at this time was with the transport, railway, and mineworkers' unions, which had come together in the Triple Alliance. The Alliance revived the awful pre-war spectre of strikes not just by one of these groups of unions, but by all three together.

But the Triple Alliance was never truly formidable. The new element in trade union-employer relations that arose from the war was not the political strike, but, on the contrary, joint consultation. In 1918, Ben Turner of the General Textile-Workers' Union and Alfred Mond were having unofficial discussions on this, a prelude to the conferences of 1928. In 1917, the Whitley Committee on the Relations of Employers and Employed, attempting to suggest means of avoiding the revolts in war industries, recommended joint consultation. As a result, voluntary employer-employee committees were set up for the naval dockyards and, most significantly for women, in the Civil Service and Post Office. In 1920, in private industry they were being established for a number of trades, those most important for women being the manufacture of matches, pottery, woollens, and hosiery.

As an aspect of joint consultation for the less well organized, the number of Trade Boards vastly increased. At a conference summoned in January 1919 by the Minister of Labour trade unions were promised that forty-eight new Trade Boards should be set up with the greatest possible speed, in addition to the nine that were already then in being. By the end of 1920, in fact about sixty boards had either been set up or had been proposed, covering an estimated 3 million workers of whom 70 per cent were women. The increased numbers of boards could not have operated if unions had not accepted most of the responsibility for the workers' sides in negotiations,[8] although a few non-trade unionists still led the workers' sides of boards covering small industries.

Queen Mary's Central Committee on Training and Employment was kept in being after the war ended, under Mary Macarthur's chairmanship. In the early months of 1920 she persuaded the Minister of Labour to recognize it as a body for supervising and devising training schemes for women whose earning capacities had been 'injuriously affected by the war' and for helping redundant women workers to find jobs.[9]

The war and its immediate aftermath brought increased concern for working women during and after confinement. Some women trade unionists, especially from white-collar unions, still viewed with deep suspicion suggestions for such special treatment. For white-collar women workers the 'marriage bar' largely obviated the predicament of pregnancies faced by many women manual workers. They did not want to raise additional obstacles to their employment, nor their claims for equal pay, when many women as well as men, including the intellectual Beatrice Webb, believed women generally were less inherently competent than men. They still saw in these proposals, although they were in accordance with the 1897 International Labour Congress programme, a threat by men trade unionists to put them out of jobs, by piling up extra complications and regulations for the employment of women, burdensome to employers. They felt that proof of equality as workers lay in emphasizing similarity in the performance of jobs and to do this, all biological differences had to be ignored. Few people then thought that equality lay partially in *not* penalizing working women for biological differences or for responsibilities thrust on them by society which might take them away from work.[10]

Voluntary health services for mothers and infants had grown up since the end of the nineteenth century. During the war, the Departmental Committee on Sickness Benefit claims under the 1911 National Insurance Act (popularly known as the Excessive Sickness Committee) published its Report. It gave proof of the poor state of health of a large number of working women and of risks to babies due to the absence of provision for rest before confinement. It recommended an allowance during the last four weeks of pregnancy. The law at this time prohibited employment of a mother for four weeks after childbirth. But no provision was made for her maintenance except 30s. insurance benefit. Norway, France, and some other countries were more generous. Mary Macarthur and Dr Frances Irens urged that this should be a charge borne by the Approved Societies, whose practices in respect of maternity allowances varied greatly. Trade union Approved Societies tended to limit maternity claims for fear of too great a run on their funds. Mary Macarthur and Dr Irens asked for a Royal Commission on ante- and post-natal care. In 1918 the Maternity and Child Welfare Act placed responsibility for maternal and infant welfare on the state.[11]

The Versailles Treaty established an International Labour Office under the auspices of the League of Nations, in which countries were represented by trade union, employers', and government delegates. The first ILO Conference was held in Washington at the end of 1919. Mary Macarthur and Margaret Bondfield were nominated as the two women members of the Labour delegation of four. Margaret Bondfield was on the Children's Employment Commission and Mary Macarthur on that for Childbirth and Maternity. The Conference considered a Convention extending the provisions advocated by the 1897 International Congress on women's work (see page 98). Mary Macarthur later explained these in a lecture at Bedford College. Women were not to be permitted to work for six weeks after a confinement. They would also have the right to leave work before a confinement provided that they produced a medical certificate stating the birth was expected within six weeks. All told, by the terms of the Convention they would be able to claim twelve weeks' leave as against the four then permitted in Britain. The Convention laid down that when off work, women should receive monetary benefit from public funds or insurance sufficient to maintain their own and their children's health. The mother was also to be entitled to free attendance by a doctor or a certified midwife.

The British government and employers' representatives at Washington, because of some minor point on the employment of nursing mothers, abstained from voting on these proposals. So Mary Macarthur, as the responsible trade union delegate, was the only member of the British delegation who voted for the Convention.[12]

A permanent International Working Women's Bureau was set up and Mary Macarthur was elected one of the five vice presidents. Mrs Raymond Robins of the American Women's Trade Union League became the first President.

The issue that aroused most interest among unmarried, white-collar women workers remained equal pay. The government made clear that it regarded the wartime concessions on the 'rate for the job' for women as merely temporary. The women, however, would not let the matter lapse. The Civil Service unions grouped in the Civil Service Alliance were said by the all-female Federation of Civil Servants not to be pursuing the principle vigorously, and the Federation left the Alliance in disgust.[13] But the number of other unions committed to the principle had risen, and now included the Boot and Shoe Operatives, the Clerks, the National Association of Local Government Officers, the London County Council Staff Association, and the National Union of Teachers, forced to it after a 1919 referendum of members.

In 1920, there was a majority vote in the House of Commons for 'equal pay' in all branches of civil and local government. The LCC granted it to their senior women staff. But the Tory-Liberal Coalition Government turned it down.[14] The Burnham Committee, set up to negotiate on pay for teachers, decided that women should have four-fifths of men's pay. So the three boroughs of Mountain Ash, Tottenham, and East Ham had to stop paying women teachers the full men's rate and conform to the national agreement.

The women's claims were strengthened when Article 427 of the Versailles Treaty dealing with conditions of working people enunciated a new proposal, far more radical than the 'rate for the job'. The seventh paragraph of this Article laid down:

> The principle that men and women should receive equal remuneration for work of *equal value*.[15]

This ran clean counter to the traditional practice of setting a lower value on work performed only, or almost entirely, by women, irrespective of the skill needed for its performance or of its economic importance. Militant women trade unionists had been discussing this principle for some years. But now for the first time it was given public, official sanction. It was a counterblast to all those, employers, men workers and trade unionists, and intellectuals like the Webbs who argued that women's capacities were inherently inferior to those of men. However, this wider meaning of 'equal pay' remained a pious aspiration rather than an aim capable of realization at the time.

By the summer of 1920, the situation looked more ominous than at the end of 1918. There was now no mistaking the fact of long-term unemployment, for which the unemployment benefit scheme had not been devised. The post-war boom began to die away and either workpeople found wages were being cut or unions found increases ever harder to negotiate. In the autumn of 1920, a deputation from the National Union of General Workers and the Amalgamated Engineering Union asked the Minister of Labour, T.J. Macnamara, for an extension of the Wages (Temporary Regulation) Act which prevented wholesale cuts. It also provided for an enforceable 'fair wages' clause for all kinds of work; that is, employers were bound to pay a 'fair wage'. But the Act expired on the last day of September.[16] Meanwhile there were large numbers of women still unemployed and employers were offering those in work the alternative of lower wages or dismissal. Women were also protected by the Industrial Courts Act until 11 November 1920 and the unions used part of this Act to prosecute employers who paid less than the agreed and guaranteed rates. But its expiry coincided with the collapse in wages.

In spite of the threatening economic storms, the merging of the National Federation of Women Workers with J.R. Clynes' National Union of General Workers, begun in 1917, was finally achieved![7] In 1918, Gertrude Tuckwell gave up the Presidency, believing that a President could by then be found from among the members. The merger was delayed by Mary Macarthur's manifold commitments, by the ending of the war, and then by a series of personal disasters which struck her. She had suffered cruelly from personal loss since 1913 when her first child, a son, was stillborn as a result of her hectic organizing work. Both her parents died during the war. Her failure in the 1918 General Election marked the beginning of real disaster. In February 1919, not long after he had lost his seat in Parliament, her husband, Will Anderson, died of Spanish 'flu. It was an enormous loss. Unmoved by her rages and tantrums, he had always supported her, believing she was the abler of the two. Mary had her daughter, Nancy, left, and her work which was her anodyne. She went to America in April where she spoke to vast meetings on the theme of peace. In October she went again with Stuart Bunning's delegation to the International Labour Organization Conference. She was back in January 1920, but she was extremely ill and in April underwent a serious operation. It was now that she applied herself to arranging the merger of the National Federation with the National Union of General Workers. It was an entirely personal matter between her and J.R. Clynes. The Federation became the Women's District of the NUGW as from January 1921 with Margaret Bondfield as its secretary and Madeleine Symons as assistant and negotiating secretary.[18]

The National Union of General Workers had, however, some women officials of its own, notably the beautiful Miss Leonora Cohen, who had been a militant suffragette and who joined the union's staff in 1919. She had much encouragement from Will Thorne and J.R. Clynes in her trade union work. But the National Federation staff, used to running things in their own way, did not really accept her. She was to leave the union in 1929. In June 1975 she celebrated her 102nd birthday at her home at Rhos on Sea, North Wales.[19]

Since 1918, the Trades Union Congress had been in process of transforming its Parliamentary Committee into a General Council to co-ordinate policies of affiliated unions and to help to resolve disputes between them. With the strong political Labour presence which the unions had created in Parliament, a committee to organize lobbies to press for union aims seemed less necessary. On 1 October 1918, just after Congress and Margaret Bondfield's success in reaching the Parliamentary Committee, the first meeting of an official TUC women's sub-committee was held. Besides Margaret Bondfield and Stuart Bunning, representing the Women's Trade Union League, C.W. Bowerman, MP, the TUC President for that year, Fred Bramley, the new assistant secretary, and E.L. Poulton, General Secretary of the National Boot and Shoe Operatives, were present. The business discussed was the merging of the Women's Trade Union League in some way with the TUC. There was some confusion on the TUC side because of a mistaken idea that the League was a trade union. Nothing was decided, but a week after this meeting, Mary Macarthur wrote to C.W. Bowerman about a closer working relationship between the League and the TUC Parliamentary Committee, and asked that discussions should continue. But, like the merger of the Federation with the National Union of General Workers, it was temporarily forgotten.[20]

However, a Women's Department was set up within the TUC, so that the need to pay special attention to women's membership was acknowledged. It was proposed that the new General Council should consist of representatives of seventeen industrial groups and an eighteenth Women's Group representing those unions that recruited women. The actual General Council representatives from this group were always to be women, so that two places were reserved for women. It was a safeguard against the exclusion of women from the leadership of the Trade Union movement through the indifference or hostility of men, once the two pressure-groups of the League and the Federation disappeared. These two women were not representatives of trade groups, however, like the other General Council members, but representatives of their sex. Their very presence was an admission that women had not won full equality in the Trade Union movement.

Similar segregation had already taken place within the Labour Party National Executive, on which four places were reserved for women. The Committees of the Women's Trade Union League and National Federation of Women Workers, however, looking at past experience, saw that without special help women's organization and special interests were given little attention in many occupations in which they worked with men. The constitution of the new General Council was agreed at the 1920 Congress before the Women's Trade Union League had definitely accepted the terms of a merger.[21]

Just after the Congress, Fred Bramley asked Margaret Bondfield for a statement. Mary Macarthur did not, however, accept Margaret Bondfield's offer to deal with this. She and Gertrude Tuckwell went out for a drive in a carriage and, secluded from the rest of the staff, finalized their views. On 22 October, at the last moment before decisive meetings of the Parliamentary Committee, Mary Macarthur wrote to Fred Bramley, telling him she was sure that the League would consider 'any suggestion that would bring it into closer relationship with the Trades Union Congress, even though it meant the complete absorption of the League itself'. She pointed out that the formation of the TUC Women's Group and Women's Department provided an opportunity for such a move.

In spite of the friendship between Mary Macarthur and Margaret Bondfield, two members of the National Federation of Women Workers who knew them both and who later themselves became illustrious women trade unionists, Dorothy Elliott and Alice Horan, both were convinced that Mary Macarthur mistrusted Margaret Bondfield's personal political ambitions as opposed to her commitment to helping working women and to trade unionism.

On 25 October, Mary Macarthur was in hospital for a second operation. She died on 1 January 1921 when she was only forty years old. She did not live to see the merger of either the National Federation of Women Workers with the National Union of General Workers, nor that of the League with the TUC General Council.

She was unquestionably the greatest woman in the history of women's trade unionism. Most of those who knew her loved her. Until the last few months of her life, she was still the same as when J.J. Mallon wrote of her in 1906:

> She has the habit of passing everything through heroic moulds. She shares in historic councils and earthshaking debates, and sees world movements come to birth. Breathlessness is her dominant characteristic. She is always at top speed. She whirls from meeting to meeting, strike to strike, congress to congress; the street shouting behind the dust and rattle of her car.

She loved movement and deeds for themselves, he said. She did not contemplate life, but lived it.[22]

The trust between the Women's Trade Union League officials and the TUC Parliamentary Committee was not absolute. On 20 May 1921, before the League Executive's final meeting, Susan Lawrence wrote to Gertrude Tuckwell that the League's Trustees 'did not desire that any part of the assets of the League should benefit the Parliamentary Committee of the TUC'. They wanted to transfer all the League's property to educational and other endowments. In conjunction with contributions from various unions, the League's financial assets were used to set up foundations in Mary Macarthur's memory, including a Mary Macarthur Convalescent Home for Working Women, of which Queen Mary was patroness.[23]

On 26 May, the League's Executive Committee agreed the details of the hand-over. They were to become the Committee of the new TUC General Council's Women's Group to carry on until the next Congress gave an opportunity for elections.

However, long before this, at the beginning of 1921, the TUC had excluded Gertrude Tuckwell, Violet Markham, and others from chances of election on the grounds that they were not trade unionists. The only ex-League Executive member to be elected to the first TUC General Council's Women's Group was Margaret Bondfield, now of the National Union of General Workers. Congress fulfilled its undertakings in making the second representative also a woman, Julia Varley of the Workers' Union. The other two members were men: E.L. Poulton of the 'mixed' National Union of Boot and Shoe Operatives, a valid enough choice, and, curiously, Harry Gosling of the Union of Watermen, which had no women members.[24] The composition of the Women's Group varied both in numbers and in personnel. By the following year, trade union secretaries more directly concerned in women's organization were voted on to it, Ben Turner of the Woollen-Workers' Union and Andrew Conley of the Tailors' and Garment-Workers' Union.

Announcing the absorption of the League at the 1921 Congress, the President, C.W. Bowerman, made a presentation to Gertrude Tuckwell of an illuminated address. She took the opportunity presented by her speech of thanks to tell Congress delegates: 'it will be long before you find anyone to do for you what our Mary did'.[25] But she also emphasized the special help that women workers needed for their own sakes and to maintain the living standards of the working class. She ended on a note of warning, heralding the battles to come, with the motto of the Women's Trade Union League: 'Look to it that ye lose not the things that they have wrought'.

The end of the National Federation of Women Workers and, more especially, of the Women's Trade Union League, which for almost half a century had helped and encouraged women's trade union organization, was the end of an era. There was to be no more help from outside the trade union movement. Women trade unionists faced the prospect of fighting on their own for attention to their interests in the world depression that loomed ahead.

Notes

1 Hamilton, *Mary Macarthur*, 179-80. See also Drake, *Women in Trade Unions*, 104-5 for growth of industrial women workers' support for equal franchise.

2 1918-19 NFWW Rep.: Drake, op.cit., 107-8 for sudden discharge of women war workers after the Russian collapse, 1917: see also 1918 Scot. TUC Rep., 50, Miss Adam: Hamilton, op. cit., march of unemployed munitions workers from Woolwich on Westminster, 170-2: Hamilton, *Women at Work*, 97. For women transport workers see NUGMW *Jour.*, July 1938, 84-5: also Drake, op. cit., 106 for London Tram United Vehicle Workers' action against summary dismissal of women.

3 *Hansard*, 1920, vol. 129, 1900-1.

4 *Hansard*, 1919, vol. 113, 2439; for whole debate on unemployment, 2403-2456.

5 WTUL Ann. Rep., 1919-20, 9-14: Hamilton, *Women at Work*, 99.

6 Rep. of the Proceedings of the 1953 Union of Shop, Distributive and Allied Workers' Annual Delegate Meeting, 10.

7 Drake, op. cit., 109.

8 Dorothy Sells, *The British Trade Boards System* and *British Wages Boards* and F.J. Bayliss, *British Wages Councils*, give detailed accounts of the expansion of Trade Boards.

9 Min. of Labour Gazette, 1923, 317-18. See Min of Lab. Ann. Reps. for reports on the Committee's work.

10 S. and B. Webb, *Industrial Democracy,* Pt 2, ch. X Sect. (d). See 1918 and 1919 Scot. TUC Reps., Textile-workers' proposals to extend maternity leave for working mothers. The 1919 resolution was passed with a majority of only 6. In 1920, however, there was a large majority, 113.

11 WTUL Ann. Reps. 1919-20, 6-7: 1920-21, 6-8.

12 ibid.: Hamilton, *Mary Macarthur*, 187-91.   13 Drake, op. cit., 178.

14 Rose Grant, unpub. Memorandum, *Story of the Equal Pay Campaign Committee*, for the Women's Service Library (Fawcett Soc.). A. Potter, *Political Studies*, vol.V, no.1, Feb. 1957. Equal Pay Campaign Committee pamphlet, *A Black Record*. Vera Douie, OBE, Librarian of the Fawcett Soc. (retired), Summaries. B. Webb, *The Wages of Men and Women: Should they be equal?*

15 Versailles Treaty, p.216, Seventh Principle listed. Author's italics.

16 1919 NFWW Rep., 13-14: 1919 WTUL Rep., 7-8.

17 1918-19 NFWW Rep.: G. Tuckwell Papers. See also Amal. Soc. of Gas, Municipal and General Workers *Jour.*, Feb. 1920, 6, for the merging of some NFWW members with this organization which also became part of the National Union of General Workers.

18 Hamilton, *Mary Macarthur*, 182 ff.

19 NUGMW *Jour.,* June 1973, 26: information from H. Goldman, NUGMW.

20 Correspondence and Papers relating to the merging of the WTUL in TUC's Women's Dept., TUC Lib.

21 G. Tuckwell Papers, *Memoirs* (unpub.), 282. TUC Rep.: 1920, 560-1: 1921, 290-4.: 1920-21 WTUL Rep., 9 ff.

22 The *Woman Worker*, 28 Aug. 1908: 1921 TUC Rep., 214-15 for obit.

23 Mins. of the WTUL Executive Committee Meetings, 20 May 1921: 26 May 1921. WTUL Rep., 1920-21, 19-20: 1921 TUC Rep., Appeal for funds.

24 1922 TUC Rep., 217.   25 1921 TUC Rep., 224-7.

12   The Fight to Hold Membership

In the two years 1920-22, the trade union membership of both men and women dropped enormously. From the peak of 1,340,941 in 1920, women's membership declined by about 470,000 and that of men by over 2¼ million. The two obvious causes of the drop were first a sharp fall in wages and secondly high unemployment. These huge problems dominated the minds of all union officials, male and female.

Hope of improving women's earnings were undermined when the number of new Trade Boards due to be set up was cut. A committee of all the unions concerned tried to ensure their continuance. But by March 1921, Macnamara was talking of only 36 new boards in place of 48. In the main the government's change of heart was due to an outcry from employers, chiefly those in the distributive trades. Mr Sidney Skinner of John Barker Ltd, the Kensington department store, remarked: 'even a large business like this cannot afford to pay the rates'. While the chairman of the Drapers' Chamber of Trade alleged that Trade Boards were the main cause of unemployment because employers could not afford to pay staff the proposed new minimum wages.[1]

The government investigated their complaints through the Cave Committee, which advocated that the boards should continue, but only for the lowest paid. Most of the unions involved were relieved that there was, at any rate, to be no wholesale annulment of boards, but were highly critical of the Report. At the 1922 Trades Union Congress Margaret Bondfield claimed that its effect had been not only to abolish some boards and to reduce minimum rates of earnings already fixed.[2] It had also made harder the negotiation of rates for special classes of workers and removed the power to improve industrial relations given to the boards under the Whitley Committee scheme for Joint Industrial Councils.

Some of the distributive employers were saved from the threatened extension of boards into their spheres, not by their own protests but by the National Union of Distributive Workers. It was against any statutory wage-fixing body in the grocery trade because its main membership was among men in the co-operatives who were well enough organized to negotiate voluntarily with employers. Statutory wage-fixing to help the lowest paid would, they thought, have infringed their freedom to raise their own rates. If employers could be persuaded to allocate funds for a wage increase, it was possible that more would have to go to the lower-paid to maintain Trade Board rates, and that they would gain less for themselves.[3] The National Union of Distributive Workers at this time was debarred from affiliation to the Trades Union Congress and so careless of pressure from other unions. But its opposition was unfortunate from the point of view of men because sometimes they were being replaced by lower-paid women and girls. Ex-servicemen claimed that they were not necessarily being reinstated in their old jobs.

The result of the reduction in the number of Trade Boards that had been promised was that by 1925 only 1½ million workers were covered, half the number proposed. But even of this reduced number, about three-quarters were women and girls, proof positive that they were the main labour force in the worst-paid kinds of work.

Mary Macarthur's dictum about the vicious circle of low pay and poor trade union organization was now amply illustrated. In Trade Board, as in non-Trade Board, occupations the factor governing the level of earnings was not the eloquence of leading trade unionists but the strength of union organization — both numerically and in the degree of determination to resist reductions and even to exact increases. Where organization and will were weak, the drop in earnings was dramatic. For example, Eldred Hallas, MP, reported in the *Monthly Journal* of the Amalgamated Society of Gas, Municipal and General Workers in the spring of 1922: the chosen battleground, he said, was the Midlands where women were the first to be 'attacked'. It was here that women engineering workers had felt sharply the men's tendency to sell them short in wage negotiations, as exemplified in the low wage settlements made by the Workers' Union before and during the war. In January 1921, Birmingham and Wolverhampton engineering employers cut the basic rates for adult women so that the total weekly wage, including cost-of-living bonus, dropped from 43s. 6d. to 35s. 9d. The Coventry engineering employers followed suit. What they were doing was trying to depress wages of women engineering workers to the same level as the minimum rates fixed by the Stamped and Pressed Metals and Hook and Eye Trade Boards. In April 1922, the National Engineering Employers' Federation cut rates for the whole country. The basic rate for girls of eighteen was to be 12s., rising to 16s. at twenty-one years, plus 20s. cost-of-living bonus, which was to fluctuate with the cost-of-living index.[4]

There was the same story in the clay industry and in a great variety of trades in Birmingham and the area to the west of it. The Trade Boards had minimized cuts in about sixty trades, but the rates they set for the least well organized were taken as the standard for non-Trade Board occupations. Thus the minimum of 24s. established for an adult woman of twenty-one years under the Pin, Hook, and Eye Trade Board, was applied in the cast-brass trade in which a Trade Board did not operate.[5]

By October 1922, at a conference with the unions held in York, the engineering employers also proposed a 24s. maximum for their women employees. The unions would not agree and the conference was adjourned until December. But the Engineering Employers' Federation instructed members to operate the new scale and the unions appointed a sub-committee to deal with the matter. They refused to accept any national agreement in order that they might keep open the possibility of improving rates by local negotiations.[6]

Eldred Hallas concluded that

... women were attacked first, and have been most severely dealt with, because from the point of view of organisation they are weakest, and it is equally important to note that women have fared best where their organisation has been most perfect ...

Even in engineering, if women were ready to go through the miseries of a strike, union negotiators could not only hold wages, but sometimes even increase them, for instance as a result of a 6-months' strike in 1922 when women supported men.

The Shop Assistants' Union gave further proof of just what a difference strong trade union organization made to women's earnings in some voluntarily negotiated agreements with employers where the union was especially strong. For instance, at Bourne and Hollingsworth, the Oxford Street drapers, women clerks and shop assistants obtained 63s. a week, or 81.8 per cent of men's rates: and at H.C. Stephen, the ink manufacturers, the union negotiated for women clerks 70s. a week or 82.3 per cent of the men's rates.[7]

Similarly the well-organized Leicester Women's District of the National Union of Boot and Shoe Operatives fared better than women generally in the footwear trade over wage cuts between March 1920 and June 1922.[8]

The second overwhelming reason for the sudden decline in trade unionism was unemployment. The post-war government had been successful in preventing sudden, drastic unemployment, but the numbers out of work were increasing. By 1920, ¾ million to a million people had been out of work for so long that they had nearly reached the end of benefits to which they were entitled under the unemployment insurance scheme. The numbers of jobless rose sharply in the first six months of 1921. By July over 2 million people were registered as workless and the unemployed were setting up a network of committees to press for their demands of work or maintenance.[9]

The government was still extremely nervous about the possibility of popular revolt, as they watched continental revolutionary movements, particularly the Spartacus uprising in Germany. To forestall massive working-class dissatisfaction, it introduced Uncovenanted Benefit, unemployment benefit beyond the amount covered by a person's insurance contributions, in other words the 'dole'. To obtain this, claimants, male and female, had to prove to a committee consisting of one employer, one employee nominated from names submitted by the unions, and a chairman likely to support the Establishment that they had previously been employed in insurable work. They were also obliged to evince readiness to accept any job offered to them although it might be in no way comparable with their previous work. They also had to show willing by trailing round to factories and other workplaces where there was patently no work available, simply to prove they were trying. They further had to submit to these committees their previous work record and details of the total incomes of their households. In short, the decision to allow uncovenanted benefit depended among other things on a test of their means of subsistence, or a 'means' test.

There were then no dependants' allowances, so that benefits did not always cover the needs of families. As a result, there were a great number of applications for outdoor parish relief to supplement insurance payments. Parish relief was administered not by the government but by local authorities, each of them allocating whatever amount they thought proper for this purpose. Some local councils for areas with high proportions of working-class residents were having to direct applicants for parish relief to workhouses because they could not meet their demands. The London County Council was supported partly by dues paid to them by London boroughs. The majority Labour group on the Poplar Borough Council, however, preferred to use money due to the LCC for local unemployment relief so that they ran up a large debt. Since the Council was unable to pay, the Labour councillors were gaoled. The five women among them, who included Susan Lawrence, were sent to Holloway. The London Unemployed Workers' Committee staged a demonstration to secure the Poplar councillors' release.

When they reached Whitehall, there was a battle with police. But the following week the councillors were freed.[10]

In November 1921, the local unemployed committees came together to form what was later known as the National Unemployed Workers' Movement. It included women, organized by Maud Brown. Its aims were adequate maintenance for those out of work, and measures to reduce unemployment. It pressed not only the government, but also the TUC General Council and Labour Party Executive. Its weapons were huge demonstrations, which often ran into trouble with the police. The year 1922 ended with a new form of activity, the first Hunger March.[11]

Women, however, were not suffering only from straightforward loss of jobs but from underemployment. In fact the amount of work available for them increased between the wars. But, chiefly because of the still rising population, the numbers of women coming on the labour market outpaced demand.[12] Women who had learnt skills were unwilling to take jobs which might damage their ability to work when the hoped-for improvement in trade came. Skilled weavers, whose jobs depended on their touch, for example, did not want to go charring or into domestic service because the work would coarsen their hands.

The greatest single women's employment until the mid-1930s was private domestic service. There was an insatiable demand for girls and women to do domestic work in private households, as there had been before the war. Yet this positively held back the development of women's trade unionism. It was the biggest stumbling-block at this time. The continuing decline of women's trade union organization coinciding with the large market for private domestic servants is a major proof that a high demand for workers does not of itself necessarily lead to greater trade union organization. The status and the conditions of work are more important.

No group of domestic servants had ever regained the pinnacle of confidence of the Edinburgh domestic servants' union in 1825. Even after the First World War they continued for the most part to be a most depressed section of working people because so many were isolated and closely supervised in households where only one or two of them were employed. In large wealthy establishments snobbishness and paternalistic employers with whose interests servants identified themselves were the impediments to trade unionism. From the late nineteenth century, various attempts were made to organize them. The strongest and most persistent society was the London Domestic Workers' Union. The *Woman Worker* reported in May 1910 the setting-up of another Domestic Workers' Union in London, the colours selected for its banner being 'Red for progress, Green for hope and Gold for dawn'. But these small unions failed.

The wartime impetus to organize affected these workers, however. In various cities individual women domestic servants tried to set up unions. For example, Miss Jessie Stephen started a small union in Scotland, going round to houses when she knew employers were likely to be out, to talk to staff.[13] Julia Varley, amongst her other professional organizing activities, set one up in Birmingham and claimed it was a great success. This union was able to obtain agreements from employers that minimum wages were to be reached at twenty-four years, that domestic staff were to receive paid holidays and have comfortable kitchens and bedrooms.[14]

Even before the outbreak of war, however, would-be employers complained of a shortage of female domestic servants. By the end of the war their concern was so great as to bring forth a government inquiry. In 1919, the Ministry of Reconstruction Committee on Domestic Service reported with marked sympathy for the workers. It recommended reasonable conditions of work, local joint committees of workers' and employers' representatives, and, eventually, Whitley Committees with an impartial elected chairman for any district where there were enough of each side to be found. It proposed training centres, and even the promotion of trade unionism. The Report suggested the local joint committees should negotiate to lay down working-hours, preferably no more than 48 per week, free time, and holidays, and opposed any payment in kind. But the Committee would not make any precise suggestions about rates of pay. For this reason Jessie Stephen and two other women domestic servants officially criticized the Report. And Dr Marion Phillips, who was a member of the Committee, refused to sign it.[15]

The Central Committee on Women's Employment between 1920 and 1922 trained a certain number of women in teaching, nursing and cookery, and in domestic subjects. But by far the largest number, 10,000 girls and women, were instructed in resident domestic service. In 1922 the Committee's own funds ran out so that it was entirely dependent on the Ministry of Labour. It had then to follow ministry policy in channelling even more girls and women to domestic service.[16]

With the growth in unemployment, inducements to women and girls to go into domestic service no longer appeared so essential to employers. Instead women were literally coerced into this work. The means used was the withholding of unemployment insurance benefits. The Coalition Government in 1920 had extended state unemployment insurance so that it covered 12 million of the 19 million or so people at work. Among the groups still excluded were home-workers, cleaners, and domestic servants. Anyone who went into service no longer had any insurance claim in virtue of previously insurable employment she might have held. Those in other kinds of work who could claim insurance benefit were offered domestic service. If they refused to take such work, they were classed as 'not genuinely seeking work' and so lost their claims to 'the dole'.

The level of women's unemployment was high enough in 1922 to prompt the TUC Women's Group to obtain General Council sanction for a conference of unemployed women. It was held on 6 March with Margaret Bondfield in the chair. A deputation, headed by Julia Varley and Madeleine Symons, was dispatched to Macnamara. They asked for provision for women of work or training and the inclusion of all workers under the Unemployment Insurance Act, since women figured so largely in the excluded groups. Delegates from the National Union of General Workers also protested against: 'the use of existing industrial depression to force women into domestic service without regard to their suitability or to the conditions of their work'. Some NUGW members working as cleaners in banks, offices, and schools discovered in January 1922, as a result of some High Court decisions, that they were classed as domestic workers and so were no longer insurable for unemployment, although most of them had been paying subscriptions since November 1920.[7] The Shop Assistants' and General Workers' Unions were dealing with legal cases of members directed to domestic service when they became unemployed, and who were refused unemployment insurance if they would not take such work. Now the government's policy was very similar to that of the City of London Council in the late fifteenth and sixteenth centuries when unemployed women were virtually being directed to domestic service (see page 9). Macnamara would give no assurance to the Conference deputation that its demands would be met.

A Ministry of Labour Report on the Supply of Female Domestic Servants in 1923 was consequently quite different in tone from the Ministry of Reconstruction Report of four years earlier, as indeed its title suggests. The committee recommended that all those employed in private domestic service should be brought under the unemployment insurance scheme. Long-term unemployment was, of course, less likely among these workers than in any other section. They also recommended, in view of the difficulty that even skilled domestic workers found in obtaining jobs after the age of fifty, that a pension fund should be set up to which employers should be required to contribute. Neither suggestion was implemented.

But their main concern was the reduction of unemployment benefit paid out to women as a whole. Through the restrictions on uncovenanted benefit, among others, all women whose first jobs had been making munitions during the war were excluded. Those refused benefit could appeal to Courts of Referees whose decisions were scrutinized by an umpire, who was a government officer, and therefore anxious to keep to a minimum the numbers whose claims succeeded.

The Report attempted to placate a section of the public who 'would appear to advocate that no woman should receive Unemployment Benefit at all, because they consider there are sufficient domestic vacancies to absorb all unemployed women'. Only 4 per cent of unemployed women as compared with 10 per cent of unemployed men received benefit, so the committee believed the machinery was working pretty well in keeping down numbers of claims. However, it felt that 'The public could do much to assist in preventing any leakage'. One lady informant stated that she had known of several girls who had been in service before the war and who were drawing benefit. She reported these cases to the employment exchanges, and 'in every case benefit was stopped immediately'. 'Such action', the committee lamented, 'is unfortunately rare'.

At the same time there was close co-operation between employment exchanges and Boards of Guardians or parish councils to prevent any woman who had failed to obtain extra unemployment insurance from being paid outdoor poor relief.[18]

All the old hindrances to the organization of domestic workers, their isolation, their openness to intimidation by employers or ties of personal loyalty, low pay, and low status still existed. They represented over a fifth of all employed women — more than 1¼ million of all those at work in the United Kingdom in 1921, according to the Census of Occupations.

There was, however, some trade union support for government direction of women to this occupation. Julia Varley, the TUC representative on the committee, signed the Ministry of Labour Report on the Supply of Female Domestic Servants. At the 1924 Congress when the first ever Labour government was in office, Ellen Wilkinson challenged the General Council. Julia Varley replied that women members of the Women's Group had been pressing the government to provide training for women other than in domestic service, but that as 'every trade had its quota of unemployment', they could not suggest what other training would be sensible in the circumstances. A TUC deputation had, in fact, been told that the government had no money to provide a wider range of training. The number of unemployed women in other occupations drawing benefit had also been pointed out to them. Ellen Wilkinson refused to accept the General Council's acquiesence. She persisted that the Labour government could have increased the amount of work available, for instance by creating more nursing jobs, and so have justified training for this profession.[19]

The previous Conservative government had excluded women from unemployment benefit more directly. In November 1921, following the release of the Poplar councillors, it bowed to the public outcry by instituting allowances for dependants of those unemployed. But by the following February, labour exchanges and committees adjudicating on claims for uncovenanted benefit were told to exclude aliens, married women workers, and others unless their incomes were 10s. a week or less when hardship was deemed to result. This instruction was confirmed in a circular in May, although the policy was officially denied for some years to come.[20] The 'means' test thus became more explicit for certain categories of people.

Just as the trade union and Labour movement accepted direction of women to domestic service, they also accepted this cutting-off of uncovenanted benefit to married women, although the best-organized sector of women's employment was the textile industry, in which the proportion of married women workers was always high. Trade unionists held to the traditional, rough and ready rule that one income going into a household had to suffice. It was said that most of the unmarried war workers for whom some responsibility had been accepted had married by this time and left work in any case to rear young families.

Similarly the majority of the Labour movement accepted the 'not genuinely seeking work' rule as a way of dealing with the work-shy. But the 1924 Labour government stopped the still unofficial 'means' test. It was, however, reintroduced in 1925 by the following Conservative administration, led by Stanley Baldwin.[21]

It has been estimated that in the early 1920s, 34 per cent of women's claims as compared with 15 per cent made by men for unemployment benefit were disallowed. On the other hand, fewer women were affected by unemployment than men.

This was because new employment opportunities were being created for women, partly by means of technological changes in working methods, partly through totally new kinds of work. Besides working in light engineering and electrical work, they were increasingly employed in grocery and provision shops where pre-packaging of goods had been introduced as an aid to women and boys in the First World War and in hairdressing and clerical work. Women were now manufacturing consumer goods such as electric-light bulbs, gramophone records, radios, and cheap, mass-produced clocks and watches. They provided the labour for the boom in cheap cigarettes, confectionery, and toilet preparations. A number of unions were slow to respond to these changes in women's occupations. Some still did not admit them to membership. The women did not impinge on the consciousness of men members employed in heavier work, or in jobs graded as having a higher skill, even when organizations like the Electrical Trades Union or Chemical Workers' Union enrolled them. Their growing presence was first acknowledged in offices and shops.

But in shop-work the preoccupation was with juvenile labour of both sexes and the reality of being 'too old at eighteen', or with the isolation of workers in small shops and offices where employers exercised a strong personal influence.[22] There was also the influence of supervisors, especially in large offices. A minority of these ladies might favour trade union organization, but most did not and positively tried to discourage it.[23]

At the same time, traditional occupations of women were declining because of the growing choice of work. Women were leaving one of the oldest of all, agriculture. Not even the Corn Production Act of 1917 setting up an Agricultural Wages Board to establish minimum rates of earning brought girls in in any great number. The demand for women workers in agriculture was diminishing too because dairy and field work was being mechanized and transferred to men, a reversal of the process in industry. Moreover, the working-day was very long — from 14 to 19 hours in some parts of the country. The girls' preference for work in towns and cities, even in jobs where hours were also long and pay was poor, indicated their feelings about working on isolated farms. So they continued to find work in shops, offices, or dressmaking, as they had done before the war, or went to the new light industries, or to domestic service.

The fall in women's trade union membership caused the TUC Women's Group to institute an inquiry in 1923 into how far women were active in unions and also into what was being attempted to encourage their interest. The findings bore out fears that not enough was being done.[24]

The experience of the National Federation of Women Workers' officials who now ran the Women's District of the National Union of General Workers was at this time anything but reassuring.

The other male district secretaries resented the way the Women's District cut across the geographical divisions of their own areas. They did not care for women organizers whom they did not directly control and who pushed the interests of women members instead of leaving it to them to determine priorities. The self-confidence and slightly aggressive feminism of Margaret Bondfield and some of the others, intent on proving their abilities were equal to those of their male counterparts, also grated on men used to running things all their own way. In spring 1923, the Women's District was reduced to a mere Women's Department. Margaret Bondfield, still Chief Woman Officer, was to attend General Council meetings to deal only with business affecting women. She now had to share control of the six women organizers who were kept on the staff with the district secretaries. A Women's National Committee was also set up to advise the Women's Department. Nominations for election to it were to come from branches in the proportion of one woman delegate to represent every 3,000 women members. The other large general union, the Transport and General Workers, had a similar Women's Advisory Committee.[25]

Margaret Bondfield, then the most illustrious of all women trade unionists, behaved in a way which did not help matters. In 1923 she was elected the first woman President of the Trades Union Congress. Later, in December of that year, she was elected to Parliament and asked to join the minority Labour government. Faced with this choice between trade unionism and politics, she chose politics. She left, under attack, the Women's Section of the Union of General Workers to function under the guidance of young Miss Dorothy Elliott, Madeleine Symons having fallen ill. In accepting government office she was behaving in no way differently from many men union officials, including her own union General Secretary, J.R. Clynes. What stuck in the throats of trade unionists was that she was prepared to give up the highest trade union honour of all, the Presidency of Congress, and that on the first occasion it had ever fallen to a woman.

During Margaret Bondfield's term in the government, in February 1924, the number of women organizers in the National Union of General Workers was still further reduced. When she returned to her job with the union after the Labour government fell, she threatened to resign, but was persuaded to stay on by the setting-up of a new committee to examine the boundaries within which women might still carry on independent organizing work.

The women's section, or more usually a special women's grade of union membership entailing lower subscriptions and benefits than those available to men, was still a feature of most 'mixed' unions. The chief exceptions were the National Union of Distributive and Allied Workers, the old Amalgamated Union of Co-operative Employees enlarged by mergers, the teaching and clerical unions, and Civil Service associations.

Occasionally, as with the mule-spinners, the distinction between higher and lower membership grades was that of particular kinds of work. In the Association of Engineering and Shipbuilding Draughtsmen, for example, the equivalent of the Mule-spinners' lower-graded piecers' section (see pp. 38, 89) was a tracers' section established in 1922. Since almost all the tracers were women, this was, in effect, a special women's section, although the union rules made no distinction between members on grounds of sex.[26]

Yet all over the country devoted women continued to act locally as union officials for many years, like the woman treasurer of the Aberdeen Branch of the National Union of Railwaymen. There were some who built up union branches from scratch, like Irene Pickup at the Rowntree sweet factory in York. Or those who encouraged women at shop-floor level like Mrs Platt of the National Union of General and Municipal Workers. She was secretary of the eighty strong Women Shop Stewards Group in the Northern District, which held its own annual meetings.[27]

Inequality rankled with women union officials and leaders throughout the Trade Union movement. It was proving much harder than they had expected to assert women's presence without the 'ginger' groups of the Women's Trade Union League and National Federation of Women Workers. The camaraderie built up with men in the war evaporated with the recession. They and some of their male counterparts felt not enough was being done to stem the drift of women from unions. At the 1923 Trades Union Congress, Miss Dorothy Evans of the Association of Women Clerks and Secretaries proposed that something like the special help given women by the Women's Trade Union League and National Federation of Women Workers should be revived. She asked for special consideration of ways and means of encouraging women's organization, in the form of a delegate conference of unions that enrolled them. Her suggestion caused impassioned debate.

The divisions that ensued were not simple male-versus-female ones. Mr A. Townsend of the Weavers' Amalgamation, with local instances of 90 per cent organization among women weavers in mind, supported the idea. But Ben Turner of the woollen-workers opposed it, blaming the men trade unionists for the low level of women's organization. The chief opponent of the special conference was a woman, Miss E.H. Howse of the Union of Post Office Workers. She pointed out that the setting-up of a special Labour

Party Women's Conference had simply meant that questions of importance to women were not discussed at the Labour Party Conference proper and prophesied the same would happen at the Trades Union Congress. She attacked the textile and other unions with high female memberships for not sending women delegates to Congress, for with more women there, more pressure could be brought to ensure attention to their interests. Most of all she feared worsening of relations between men and women. 'If you are going to separate women in organisations', she told Congress, 'you are going to pit them against the men'. In the long term she was quite right. Nonetheless, Ellen Wilkinson cajoled Congress into trying a conference as an experiment because women's general social inequality put them at a disadvantage in unions.[28] The need for pressure-groups had been proved again and again in the past. Male-dominated organizations left to deal with women's efforts to organize, or to secure attention to their concerns, too often showed, at best, only a perfunctory interest. It was this neglect that had kept the Women's Trade Union League and National Federation of Women Workers in being and provoked the all-female breakaway societies. These remained a living vindication of the belief that separate women's organizations were necessary.

With Congress agreement, on 25 March 1925 a conference of delegates from Unions Catering for Women Workers was held at Leicester. Fred Bramley, the TUC General Secretary, speaking on the first resolution calling on union executives and officials to make special efforts to organize women, remarked:

> The objection might be raised by the Executive Councils and officials that in requesting them to make special efforts there was the implication that they had not already done so. That was quite true, they had not made special efforts. The menace of cheap labour was not sufficiently recognised.

The angriest criticism of men's attitudes to women came from Miss Cooper of the National Union of Clerks, Miss Anne Loughlin of the Tailors' and Garment-Workers' Union, and Miss Mary Carlin, Transport and General Workers' Union, who found ' ... it very difficult to be an organiser in a mixed union' and thought 'that the men officials in the unions often regard the organisation of women as a side-line'.

The women were also annoyed because the Conference was not organized in the normal way, but was under the strict control of the General Council. This seemed to them to indicate that the General Council shared the view that women were inferior to men, although they and their like had proved their ability to further the cause not only of women's, but also of men's, organization. For, while the Workers' Union and National Union of General and Municipal Workers had women staff to deal specifically with women, most 'mixed' unions required their organizers, male or female, to deal with members of both sexes.

The women delegates' suggestions for redressing the decline in women's membership and activity harked back to the policies of the League and the Federation – to more special committees for women and increased segregation. They revived the League's recommendations to Trades Councils and to 'mixed' unions to set up women's sub-committees, like Annie Macdonald's in the Shop Assistants' Union. They asked for a National Women's Conference to be held annually during Congress week, a sort of resurrection of the League's annual conference. They showed implicitly that they considered the TUC Women's Group with its preponderance of male union secretaries was either ineffective or not very interested, by asking that four women be elected from the Conference as advisers and that a Chief Woman Officer be appointed to act as the group's secretary, with the special job of chivvying unions into increased consideration for women's organization. On a lighter note,

Women trade unionists' pressure-group, 1924. Front row from r.: E. Wilkinson, J. Varley, F. Bramley; 2nd row from l.: A. Loughlin, M. Quaile, M. Bell (4th l.); back row, 3rd r., D. Elliott

the Conference decided there should be educational and social activities for women on their own.[29]

There was a strong similarity between many of these proposals
and those made at the first conference of an International
Federation of Working Women set up after the First World War, to
which the TUC Women's Group affiliated. It is difficult to estimate
how far the British women representatives were influenced by the
International Federation's conference, and how far the conference
was influenced by them (see page 170).

As with the International Association for Labour Legislation of
the late nineteenth century, the welfare of women workers was one
of the International Federation of Working Women's primary concerns. But in addition it sought to promote the trade union
organization of women and encouraged education and recreation
for women workers. Marion Phillips was the first secretary of the
International Federation and Miss Edith Macdonald, of the Women
Clerks' and Secretaries' Association, the second, with Margaret
Bondfield as the vice president for England.[30]

But this International Conference showed that the segregation of
women from men trade unionists was an international feature
and not peculiar to the United Kingdom. At the same time it offered yet more proof of the ability of working-class women to
discuss and handle questions, to negotiate and produce agreed for-
mulae, just as well as the men. The inequalities that they continued
to suffer within the home trade union movement must therefore
have seemed all the more bitter.

The TUC General Council and the Women's Group did not
agree to the complete programme of action set out at the 1925
Conference of Unions Enrolling Women. The TUC Women's
Group was, after all, made up of union members. It was not an
outside pressure-group like the Women's Trade Union League.
However much Council officials like Fred Bramley wanted to back
the women militants, they could only go as far as the affiliated
unions would let them, through their spokesmen on the General
Council. The General Council felt they could not interfere in internal policies of unions so far as to ask them to set up women's
sub-committees. They deferred consideration of the appointment
of a woman secretary and they refused utterly to entertain the idea
of a national annual women's conference. Miss Varley defended
the decision at the 1926 Congress on the false premise that all the
unions represented at Congress had women members. She ignored
the fact that a number of unions still refused to enrol women and
that those that did, as Miss Howse pointed out, did not send them
to Congress as delegates, not even when, as in the textile unions,

the membership was predominantly female. Ellen Wilkinson, however, once more talked Congress round to agreeing to the annual conferences.[31]

The defeat of Labour in the election at the end of 1924 and the continuing decline of wages concurrently with rising unemployment, re-created something of the militancy that had been lost. To force the miners to agree to lower wages and longer working-hours, the employers staged a national 'lock-out' on 30 April 1926. On 1 May the TUC General Council honoured its pledge to the miners to meet this action with a 'sympathetic' general strike. It was never a complete shutdown, but a series of strikes in selected industries: transport, printing, building, iron and steel, heavy chemicals, and power industries stopped at once. By the seventh day of the strike, the engineering and shipbuilding workers were called out as well. Since textiles, the distributive and clothing trades, and post office workers were not called on to strike, fewer women were directly involved than men. The largest single group was the women's branch of the Paper-Workers' Union, then the largest union in the printing trade. The women made up half of its 70,000 members. Those of them on the staff of the Labour paper, the *Daily Herald*, worked like the men to put out the TUC's strike sheet, the *British Worker*, for only their strike pay. But as in many unions, with their lower rate of subscriptions, women received less when on strike than men, in this instance 5s. a week to the men's 10s.[32] This was accepted practice and in no way vitiated their support for the strike.

Contrary to some claims made at the time, the issues were purely industrial and not political, hence the tremendous support given to the mineworkers by those in other occupations. However, a TUC-Labour Party negotiating committee agreed to call the strike off unconditionally after nine days. The decision was an immense shock to the mass of strikers, many of whom were victimized. Worst of all, the mineworkers were left locked out.

In order to lessen the consequent suffering to miners' wives and families, a Women's Committee for the Relief of Miners' Wives and Children was set up by Labour, Trade Union, and Co-operative women. This developed from a League for Strikers' Children organized by Marion Phillips and Lady Slesser before the outbreak of war in 1914. As well as both these ladies, the Committee included Margaret Bondfield, Madeleine Symons, Susan Lawrence, and Ellen Wilkinson, both now MPs, with Ellen Wilkinson as chairman. They organized money-raising sub-committees, in whose work unemployed men and women played a big part. But they also employed Mary Macarthur's tactics in the 1911 Bermondsey strikes, of collecting food and clothing. The main work of distributing these items fell on women in the localities affected, many of whom wore their shoes out in the course of this work.

The principles operated to force women into domestic service were now applied with great severity to force the miners back to work. Dr Phillips described how frequently they were told of areas where grants received and distributed by the Miners' Federation were deducted 'from the Poor Law', that is from outdoor relief. In a few cases, mostly in Scotland, the grants of food and baby clothes made by this Women's Committee had the same harsh results of cutting off state aid. 'It was there', she wrote, 'that the Board of Health stopped Town and District Councils from giving milk to babies and children up to five years old'. The responsibility for these welfare items was placed entirely on parish councils, although some were already not paying anything to the miners' dependants. The hardships were increased in those places where education committees stopped feeding the children. One of the problems was the high birth-rate among the mining community. Dr Phillips estimated that between 15 May and 30 November 1926, when the miners capitulated, 40,000 new children were born among them.[33]

The unity of the Labour movement generally was further strengthened during the lock-out. One aspect of this was the increased support for measures to help women's organization. Margaret Bondfield declared at the 1926 Trades Union Congress: '... in all the years of the efforts to get women's questions dealt with effectively we have had more encouragement this year from the General Council than ever before'. She remarked on the great change in attitude. The lack of organization among women was no longer being regarded to the same extent as due to inborn feminine stupidity and weakness, but as a similar problem to that of other sections of working people where trade unionism was still not strong, for instance among the agricultural workers. Two of the 1925 suggestions were being implemented, a national organizing campaign for women and a joint committee with the Trades Councils Joint Consultative Committee to work out means of co-operating.

It was all the more shocking, therefore, when at the 1927 Conference of Unions Catering for Women Workers , Margaret Bondfield announced that the full-scale conferences would cease and would be replaced by the more modest social meetings traditionally held during Congress week by the old Women's Trade Union League, for secretaries of unions that enrolled women, and for women workers in the locality.[34]

There was no special women's group in the Scottish TUC's

General Council, thanks to the precedents set by Margaret Irwin and the Women's Trade Union League. Miss Grace Mewhort of the Edinburgh Trades Council, following the normal processes of candidacy, was elected for 1921-22. The Scots were a year behind the British Congress in expressing concern at the low level of women's organization. A number of delegates, like Anne Loughlin, attended both Congresses so that ideas flowed from one to the other. In 1925 the Scots agreed a resolution from the Glasgow Trades and Labour Council which not only laid down that all unions should admit women, but should accord them a status equal to that of men members in respect of both 'privileges and responsibilities'. It also stressed that the trade unions 'should support with their whole strength' the women's demand for 'equal pay for similar duties'. They proved that the proposals made at the 1925 British TUC Conference would work. They immediately set up the Committee and Annual Conference the delegates there had asked for. On 30 January 1926, some ten months after the first British TUC Conference at Leicester, they held their first meeting, at which the Scottish General Council itself proposed that an Organization of Women Committee be set up of five women elected at an annual conference. Its chairman was Joe F. Duncan, General Secretary of the Scottish Farm Servants' Union, and its secretary William Elger, the secretary of the General Council itself. Despite the General Strike and miners' lock-out, a second conference was held on 8 September of the same year. An Organization of Women Committee was duly elected. Miss Bell Jobson, assistant secretary of the Scottish Farm Servants' Union, topped the poll and so became the conference's first chairman.[35]

Whatever the attitudes of trade union leaders and active members, in Scotland as in the rest of Britain, opposition to women's organization was still rife among the rank and file. William Leonard of the Furniture Trades Association remarked at the 1928 Scottish TUC Conference of Unions Enrolling Women: 'In the workshops he did not find the help given that should be expected from men trade unionists'. On occasion he found that 'when men and women worked together, there seemed more antagonism to Trade Unionism among the women than when women worked alone...' The resentment against unions of the unorganized, lower-paid workers, in this case the women, of which John Burns warned, still persisted. Leonard stoutly stuck up for them. Their organization was not merely a means of protecting men's working conditions. 'The women themselves had the right to battle for improvements in their own conditions'.[36]

Notwithstanding hostility from some men, the Scottish TUC's

Organization of Women Committee and its annual conference were to enjoy an unbroken existence until the present day.

By 1927 the whole trade union movement was suffering reaction as a result of the General Strike and the economic depression. Because the high numbers of long-term unemployed were draining the Unemployment Insurance Fund, the government set up the Blanesburgh Committee to examine the operation of the unemployment insurance scheme. In the spring of 1927 it reported, and advocated cuts in the benefit rates. There were three trade unionists on this committee: Frank Hodges, ex-General Secretary of the Miners' Federation of Great Britain; Arthur Holmes, secretary of the Printing and Kindred Trades Federation; and Margaret Bondfield, Chief Woman Officer of the National Union of General and Municipal Workers. Her own union disowned her for being a party to the Blanesburgh Committee Report, and the Shop Assistants' Union, in which she had made her reputation, called through its Journal for trade union action against her, adding: 'early service does not justify anti-working class action'.[37] The cuts in unemployment benefit were made.

In May 1927 women trade unionists suffered the final blow within Margaret Bondfield's own National Union of General and Municipal Workers. The sub-committee considering the fate of the Women's Department now recommended that it should be abolished altogether. The union now had a love-hate relationship with Margaret Bondfield. They were proud of her status in the political world, but annoyed because she put her political career before interests of both union and working people. In 1928 she returned to politics and that year's Biennial Congress of her union carried a resolution giving effect to the abolition of the Women's Department. The rump of the National Federation of Women Workers disappeared. The remaining women organizers now worked wholly for the male district secretaries, dealing mainly with women, but also with men. Only the office of Chief Woman Officer remained as a reminder of the terms of the merger. It was disheartening not only for the women staff, but also for all active women trade unionists.

However, in 1927 much worse disaster overtook the trade union movement as a whole. Baldwin again had to bow to the diehards in his administration in permitting the passage of a Trades Disputes and Trade Union Act which prohibited sympathetic strikes and so any repetition of the General Strike. The Act also reduced the Labour Party's funds by laying down that those who wanted to contribute to the political levy made by unions must personally inform their unions: they must 'contract in'. The 1913 rule of 'contracting out' was thus reversed. The main effect it had on women's trade unionism arose from the prohibition on affiliation to the TUC for public service unions. These organizations were obliged to disaffiliate. Some of the most militant and fluent women trade unionists could now no longer take part in TUC debates, at a time when, with the general regression in trade unionism, women's trade unionism was under severe pressure.

Notes

1 P.C. Hoffman, *They Also Serve,* 206-7.
2 Rep. of an Inquiry into the Working and Effects of the Trade Boards Act of 1918, 1923: 1922 TUC Rep., 440-1.
3 Bayliss, *British Wages Councils*, 26ff.: 1950 Union of Shop, Distributive and Allied Workers, Annual Delegate Meeting Rep., 12-13, P C Hoffman.
4 Amal. Soc. of Gas, Municipal and General Workers' *Monthly Jour.,* Mar.-Apr. 1922, 11-12. See also ibid., Jan. 1920, 3: Sept. 1920, 4, Rep. of J.H. Davies: Oct. 1920, 5, Rep. of Exec. Council Meeting, 20 Sept.
5 ibid., Nov. 1920, 12-13: 1922 TUC Rep., 219-21.
6 NUGW *Jour.*, Jan.-Feb. 1923, 16. Information from Miss Alice Horan, OBE. The unions negotiating for women at this time were: NUGW; Nat. Amal. Union of Labour; Dock, Wharf, Riverside and General Workers' Union; Workers' Union.
7 Copies of actual agreements, by courtesy of Union of Shop, Distributive and Allied Workers.
8 A. Fox, *Hist. of the Nat. Union of Boot and Shoe Operatives, 1874-1957*, 309 ff., 410-16, 524-5. For others see, for example, NUGMW *Jour.*, Jan.-Feb. 1925, 16, Southampton aircraft industry, women's increase larger than that for male labourers. NUGW *Jour.* Mar.-Apr. 1924, 17, Tate of Liverpool, men and women given an equal wage increase. Sells, *British Trade Boards System,* 99, 171-2, women woollen-weavers voluntarily negotiated minimum higher than the Trade Board minimum for flax- and rope-, net- and twine-workers. But the Trade Board rate for women jute-workers was higher than the woollen-workers' rate.
9 W. Hannington, *Never on Our Knees*, 80ff., 103.
10 A. Deacon, 'Labour and the Unemployed: The Administration of Insurance in the Twenties. Paper for the May 1975 Meeting of the Soc. for the Study of Lab. Hist., and see Soc.'s Bull., no.31, 10-11: Hannington, op. cit., 110-13.
11 Hannington, op. cit., 121.
12 Abstracts of Lab. Statistics. There were about 5.4 million women employed in the U.K. in 1921, and 5.8 million in 1931.
13 *Woman Worker,* 11 May 1910, 965: Information supplied to the author by Miss Jessie Stephen: Drake, *Women in Trade Unions,* 22, 28, 180-1.
14 *Daily News*, 27 Jan. 1920: Drake, op. cit., 96,: during the war, domestic servants if they chose could dictate terms to employers.

15 1919 Rep. on Domestic Servants of the Women's Advisory Committee of the Ministry of Reconstruction, 6, 35-6.

16 Min. of Lab. Gaz., 1923, 317-18.

17 NUGW *Jour.*, Mar.-Apr. 1922, 14-15: See also Nov.-Dec. 1922, 15-16.

18 Min. of Lab. Report of Committee of Inquiry into the Supply of Female Domestic Servants, 1923, 27-8, para. 62: 29, paras. 65-6.

19 1924 TUC Rep., 209-310, 234, para. 203.   20 Deacon, op. cit.

21 *New Dawn*, May 1924, Mrs Bamber, National Organizer: the Labour government required no pledge from a woman before training was given in domestic service that she would accept this work afterwards. But a woman so trained and then unable to find work in her original occupation would be disqualified from unemployment benefit due to her because of her previous insured employment on the grounds that she was 'not genuinely seeking work'. The previous Conservative government exacted such a pledge, the penalty for breaking it being the forfeit of all claims to uncovenanted benefit.

22 T.W. Cynog Jones, 'The Regulation of Wages in the Retail Trade, 1937-57', 6-8.

23 Information from Miss Jessie Stephen, who later joined the Clerical and Administrative Workers' Union, and Miss Helen Walker of the same union. Both were office supervisors.

24 TUC Women's Group Pamphlet, 'Methods of Organising Women', 1923. Only 13 unions were mentioned: Nat. Union of Printing, Bookbinding, Machine Ruling and Paper Workers; Nat. Union of Distributive and Allied Workers; Tailors' and Garment Workers' Union; Union of Post Office Workers; Shop Assistants' Union; Assoc. of Women Clerks and Secretaries; Railway Clerks' Assoc.; Transport and General Workers' Union; Nat. Union of General Workers; Nat. Union of Furniture Trade Operatives; Iron and Steel Trades Confed.; Nat. Soc. of Pottery Workers; Workers' Union. The number of 'mixed' unions affiliated to the TUC that enrolled women was 87 out of a total of 209. Most were therefore unaffected by appeals for information from the Women's Group.

25 NUGW *Jour.*, Mar.-Apr. 1921, 25, Rep. of amalgamation arrangements with the Nat. Fed. of Women Workers: Mr Hugh Lynas, Sec. of the Northern District, complained that no member of the Women's District had been allocated to help organize Newcastle-upon-Tyne: ibid., Mar.-Apr. 1922, 5: H.A. Clegg, *General Union*, 83ff., 291. Information from Miss Dorothy Elliott and Miss Alice Horan.

26 J.E. Mortimer, *A History of the AESD*, 85, 90-1.

27 NUGMW *Jour.*, Aug. 1928, 116.

28 1923 TUC Rep., 315-19: 1924 TUC Rep., 232-3, 310-11, 379-81.

29 1925 TUC Rep., 222, para. 110, 421-2: Rep. of Proceedings of 1925 TUC Conference of Unions Enrolling Women.

30 1925 TUC Rep., 224, para.112.

31 1926 TUC Rep., 451-3: NUGMW *Jour.*, Sept.-Oct. 1926, 16: Rep. of Proceedings of 1926 TUC Conference of Unions Catering for Women Workers.

32 Bundock, *Printing, Bookbinding and Paper Workers*, 336. The union set up a special committee to deal with its part in the strike. It included three women: Mrs Taylor and Miss E. Kingsland, London, and Miss E.A. Hall, Lancs.

33 Marion Phillips, *The Story of the Women's Committee for the Relief of Miners and their Children*.

34 Rep. of 1927 TUC Conference of Unions Enrolling Women Workers, 3. There had been continuing conflicts between delegates and the TUC Women's Group representatives on the platform, see Conference Reps., 1925, 4, 8: 1926, 3, 7, 9. NUGMW *Jour.*, Sept.-Oct. 1926, 16, Rep. by M. Bondfield of the 1926 Conference. There was further trouble in 1927, see Conference Rep., 7, 8.

35 Mins. of Scot. TUC General Council Meetings 1925-26, 41, 13 July 1925: 1 Dec. 1925, 94: Scot. TUC Reps.: 1925, 170: 1926, 45, 105.

36 1928 Scot. TUC Rep., 45-6: also 75-80 for Organization of Women Committee's Rep., for the period 18 Sept. 1926-18 Feb. 1928.

37 1927 TUC Rep., 283-8: NUGMW *Jour.*, June 1927, 70. *Shop Assistant*. 23 Apr. 1927. For Margaret Bondfield's own interpretation see *A Life's Work*, 270-4.

13   The Depression, 1927-34

In the late 1920s there was a false dawn of improvement in the economy. By 1927 the numbers of people out of work had dropped to less than 1¼ million. Moves were made towards greater co-operation between organized labour and employers, because discerning employers felt reassured by the anxiety of a number of trade union leaders to end the General Strike. On the trade union side, Walter Citrine, General Secretary of the TUC, supported such collaboration. In 1928, Sir Alfred Mond, chairman of Imperial Chemical Industries, who had been the Minister of Health responsible for standardizing the rates of Poor Relief in 1921, and Ben Turner, secretary of the National Union of Textile-Workers, resumed their 1918 discussions. They brought together other employers and trade union leaders, most notably Ernest Bevin, by then secretary of the Transport and General Workers' Union. In 1928, the T&GWU had been strengthened by a merger with the Workers' Union, taking over its strong team of women organizers headed by Julia Varley. She and other leading women trade unionists supported the policy of discussions and co-operation, where possible, in place of confrontation.

In May 1929, a second minority Labour government was elected with Ramsay MacDonald as Prime Minister and Margaret Bond-field, still Chief Woman Officer of the National Union of General and Municipal Workers, as Minister of Labour.[1] The TUC General Council showed its intention of being a party to decisions on national economic policy which this government would be called on to make, by setting up its own Economic Committee.

But hopes that the Labour government would restore the cuts in unemployment benefit rates that followed the Blanesburgh Report of 1927 were soon dashed. The most the unions obtained was a Royal Commission on Unemployment Insurance. The Labour government's attitude on unemployment hardened. There was a polarization between Left and Right, not just in the country as a whole, but within the Labour movement, between those ready to collaborate with employers and governments whatever their politics, and those who felt that the only solution to their own and the country's problems lay in thorough-going social change. Not surprisingly, the Unemployed Workers' Movement and the Miners' Federation, both under Communist leaders, were in the van of the large minority who were against compromise.

The long standing system of collective bargaining even in the non-militant woollen and worsted trades broke down under the strain of deepening depression. There was a big strike in Yorkshire in 1930. Margaret Bondfield as Minister of Labour refused to intervene further than to bring the two sides together for discussions. In this dispute and in others in the early 1930s, the textile unions were utterly defeated. The appearance of a women's contingent from Yorkshire and Lancashire in a 1930 National Unemployed Workers' Movement Hunger March reflected the worsening conditions in the textile trades.[2]

In June 1931, Margaret Bondfield and the majority of the Labour Cabinet accepted the recommendations of the Royal Commission on Unemployment Insurance. Chief of these were the overt operation of the 'means' test in assessing claims for 'transitional benefit' (the old uncovenanted benefit) and cuts that particularly hit women, not only by reason of their married status, but also as seasonal and part-time workers. Trade union opposition to these measures and to the government's deflationary policy caused the downfall of the Labour administration in August, and the splitting-away of Prime Minister Ramsay MacDonald and his supporters from the Labour Party.

MacDonald led an all-party National Government brought in by an October election. Labour, with a mere 46 MPs, had to endure the operation of deflation, higher unemployment, the 'means' test, and the cuts in unemployment benefit. As a result, within two months. 78,000 women and nearly 200,000 men had their transitional benefit stopped. The following month the total affected had risen by nearly another 100,000. The women who bore the brunt of these policies were the textile-workers.

Because of a feeling that the majority of the TUC General Council did not appreciate their desperation and were not pressing for improvement in unemployment rates with any sense of urgency, the Unemployed Workers' Movement even organized a march to the 1931 Trades Union Congress. They demanded support in the form of industrial action by those still employed. But Congress was divided and they failed to gain any promise of such support. The bitterness of the unemployed increased when the following week there were attacks by police, reminiscent of the 1913 attack in Dublin, on working-class homes in Birkenhead and Belfast, both areas badly affected by unemployment. As a result of the Belfast attack, two men died.

Women's contingent of Hunger March, October 1932

By the beginning of 1932 the number of people registered as out of work had risen to 2,800,000. In the cotton and synthetic fabrics industry, unemployment was running at 30.4 per cent and in woollen and worsted manufacture at 26.4 per cent. In a march in October 1932, the women's contingent, led by Maud Brown and Lily Webb, coming south from Burnley in Lancashire, had a clash with the town council of Burton-on-Trent when they were offered accommodation in the common wards of the workhouse instead of the usual school hall.[3]

It was estimated that about a third of the total number of *insured* women workers were married and thus likely to be affected by the more stringent regulations on the granting of unemployment benefit. In 1933, Miss Bondfield reported that since the passage of the 1931 Act, over 250,000 married women had in fact applied for unemployment benefit, 29 per cent of them in the textile-producing, north-western division of the country. Only about a fifth of these applications were allowed, a third of them in the north-west. The area was affected by the first major cotton-weaving strike since the turn of the century, a protest at the employers' demand that each operative should work more looms. This meant not only a greater strain on those who had work, but also that more workpeople would lose their jobs. Like the miners in

1915-26, they stood out against such a policy.[4] Precluded by the 1927 Trade Disputes and Trade Unions Act from sympathetic industrial action, the TUC nevertheless ran Cotton Fund Committees, and, in self-defence against the success of the Unemployed Workers' Movement, itself organized nationwide unemployment marches, enlisting the local Trades Councils in both activities.

Women were now threatened less with being directed to domestic service than with destitution unless they could prove they might obtain insurable work. Mary Carlin, in an article in the *Shop Assistant* in February 1933, appealed to girls to take advantage of their right to have a union official with them at the Courts of Referees. She wrote:

> I have many times seen girls come before the Court and because of their ignorance of the Regulations they have been gently led by the Chairman to make an admission which has made it possible to turn them down... A woman who... eagerly proclaims her willingness 'to do anything, domestic service, anything', is immediately written down as 'not likely to be mainly employed in insurable work'.[5]

She would then have to apply for Poor Relief, or Public Assistance as it was now called, unless she could get a job in domestic service.

Cotton workers coming out on More Looms strike, 1932

Under pressure of economic exigencies, government offers of training even for domestic service were no longer necessarily made. Opposition to compulsory domestic service weakened. The hard fact was, as Bell Jobson pointed out at the 1931 Scottish TUC Conference of Unions Catering for Women, that unemployed men, too, were being forced to unpopular work such as labouring on roads.

By 1933, women's trade union membership for the whole United Kingdom had fallen to 728,388, and that of men to not much more than 3½ million, a decline of 46 per cent for women since the high point of 1920, and of 48 per cent for men.[6]

In Scotland over the same Depression years, the Organization of Women Committee went from strength to strength. Its greatest contribution was that from 1928 onwards, to encourage women to join unions and to be active in them, it succeeded in setting up local committees of women trade unionists. Its method of doing this was to hold a Day School for women members along with the Annual Conference of Unions Catering for Women. The Conference was held in a different town each year and the appearance of these local women's committees charted the circuit of conferences in Glasgow, Edinburgh, Aberdeen, Dundee, and Kilmarnock.[7]

The Scots were building in some instances on the existing base created by the Women's Trade Union League, in that one or two of the old Women's Trades Council Committees were still alive, like the one at Edinburgh, for example, though in a weak condition. What was new was the special educational provision for women members through day schools. The idea of the special Trade Union School for women only, as opposed to 'mixed' schools, for which women as well as men were theoretically eligible, was also taken up by individual unions and later the British TUC.

The Women's Trade Union League funds, which had not been handed over to the TUC General Council at the time of the merger with the Women's Group in 1921, were administered by a committee of trade unionists and Labour and Co-operative Party members. Some of the money was allocated to Mary Macarthur memorial scholarships in Britain for working women to obtain further education. In addition, places were available for women trade unionists to study the history and procedures of trade union and labour movements and economics at summer schools run by the International Labour Organization at Geneva, and at Bryn Mawr College in Pennsylvania.

These few special educational schemes for women were a gesture to make up for the smaller numbers of women nominated by their unions to attend 'mixed' schools. For, at Ruskin College, Oxford, through the Boards of Oxford and Cambridge Universities' Extramural Departments, the Workers' Educational Association, and the National Council of Labour Colleges, women had to compete with men members for places. Nominations even for scholarships for women only had to come from their unions. A chance of obtaining one depended on a union's willingness to show an interest in women members' education. A number of manual workers' unions with women members in lower membership grades did not bother about them, however. Even in the second half of the twentieth century, married women members were sometimes prevented from going to 'mixed' schools by their husbands, jealous of their meeting other men. If their unions nominated them for places, their own feeling of inferiority made them so shy that in the 1960s many union officials still said that they could never persuade a woman to go to a school on her own. She had to have a female companion with her. Women made much less use of schools and courses than men and this was to some extent due to their own lack of courage.

The Scots' answer to this was the short day school held locally, with advance publicity for the annual Conference of Unions Enrolling Women to arouse interest, and energetic follow-up. Even so the local committees sometimes foundered. By 1931, however, at the height of the Depression, the General Secretary of the Scottish TUC, William Elger, and Joe Duncan, Secretary of the Scottish Farm Servants' Union, felt confident enough of the Organization of Women Committee to leave it to function on its own. The General Council continued to keep a tight rein on its activities. The new secretary, a member of the office clerical staff, Miss Agnes Richmond, was to attend General Council meetings as liaison when Organization of Women Committee business was discussed.[8]

Inevitably there was friction between the Committee and some unions, which came to resent a group whose activities cut across their own. A Transport and General Workers' Union delegate, for example, informed the 1931 Conference of Unions Enrolling Women that his union 'was not disposed to spend money to create organisation for somebody else to come in and sweep the pool'. Unions also resisted the General Council's and the Committee's efforts to force them to support the new local Women's Committees and generally to take more account of women's problems.[9]

But the activities of the Committee, in no way curtailed by the withdrawal of William Elger and Joe Duncan, delighted the Scottish TUC General Council. Their Annual Reports of the mid-1930s drew the attention of Congress to the repeated success of the annual Conference of Unions Enrolling Women. They also pointed to increasing numbers of women trade union members who were taking an interest in union activities.[10]

As far as the British TUC was concerned, both Walter Citrine and Vincent Tewson, head of the TUC's Research Department, were sympathetic to measures for extending women's membership and trade union activity. The interest was the more understandable in Vincent Tewson's case, since he was married to an ex-member of the National Federation of Women Workers, and he acted as secretary to the Women's Group on the General Council. In response to Congress calls that something be done to stop the continuing decline in women's membership, a consultative meeting of organizers of Unions Concerned with Organizing Women was convened in May 1930.[11] It recommended the revival of the annual conferences and the 1930 Congress endorsed the recommendation.[12]

What is now regarded as the first TUC Conference of Unions Enrolling Women was held in January 1931. The women officials obtained all that they had asked for in 1925, including a National Women's Advisory Committee to operate along with the General Council Women's Group. The Committee's five members were to be elected annually at the Conferences on the basis of one vote per delegate and the Women's Group asked that they should all be women. The Advisory Committee members always have been, although in the early 1930s a large minority of the delegates at the Conferences electing them were men.

It was made quite clear, however, that these five representatives of women trade unionists were not the body ultimately responsible for women's organization within the ambit of the General Council. They were to be called in purely to give advice, on the basis of which recommendations might be made by the Women's Group, still made up of union representatives who were mainly male. The predominantly male General Council might or might not accept these recommendations. Similarly the Conference had no powers to direct that any course of action be taken. It too was purely advisory and came in time to be known as 'the Women's Advisory'. Like other General Council groups, however, the Women's Group diminished in importance and, like other TUC committees, the National Women's Advisory Committee, or NWAC, gained in influence, but it has remained an advisory body.

Differences in attitudes between the women delegates and the General Council were not ironed out. The General Council still wanted to involve women who were not trade unionists but who were supporters of the political Labour movement in the work of organizing women and bringing them into trade union activity. Home-bound working-class wives and mothers were still 'the weakest link in the chain of working class power'. The unity of the whole working class in the late eighteenth- and early nineteenth-century struggles for union recognition, which re-emerged in the first decade of this century, had not been carried over into the new growth industries of the 1920s and 1930s. Women who saw their homes threatened by deprivations caused by strikes did not always support the strikers. Their own experiences as workers before marriage too often convinced them of the hostility of unions to female interests. Worse, the unions were equated with the poorly paid dead-end jobs in which so many of them passed the years between leaving school and marriage, for did not the unions work with employers in eliminating a choice of occupation for girls and in keeping them in lower-graded jobs? Increasingly encouraged by the mass circulation press and the movies, in their own natural tendency to dream of a fairy-tale meeting with a Prince Charming and living happily ever after, girls saw marriage as an escape from work they disliked and from the union. Work and union were synonymous in their minds. Unions were now generally regarded as only 'a man's world'. But wives and mothers who maintained some sympathy with unions and the Labour movement were frequently members of Co-operative and Labour guilds. The National Union of Railwaymen and the Transport and General Workers' Union ran guilds to encourage interest on the part of members' wives. The General Council wanted to see the practice extended.

The women delegates, on the other hand, with the experience of the First World War in mind, correctly felt that the key to engaging women's sympathies lay in obtaining real backing from unions for recruiting women and for paying attention to their women members. They asked for more willingness to encourage women to take office and to do union work. Mary Bell, the highly successful secretary of the Leicester women's branch of the National Union of Boot and Shoe Operatives, suggested that the national executive committees of unions should be made responsible for their own non-members. She proposed that they call 'Trade Union Conferences of Women' from all their Districts because 'great work could be done in the light of the different experiences which could be exchanged'.

Discussion was not, however, limited to procedural matters. Delegates showed at this first conference that they were intent on practical steps to improve women's organization by pressing for measures to bring domestic servants into unions. The numbers of women in this occupation in Great Britain, including those out of work, had risen from approximately 1,270,000 in 1921 to 1,325,300 by 1931. They still accounted for about a fifth of the total female labour force.

In 1928, women were finally given the vote at twenty-one and so put on equal terms with men in the matter of the franchise. Because of this, the Labour Party, jogged by their Women's Section, showed a flurry of interest in the trade union organization of private, resident, domestic servants. In a pamphlet, the party pointed out that they accounted for a quarter of the female electorate aged twenty-one and over in Kensington and Hampstead, and for a third of all women voters in Westminster and Chelsea.[13] The 'daily helps' who did not 'live in' were only starting to replace resident servants in the early 1930s.[14] Hence the emphasis in the pamphlet on those who 'lived in':

> How can we combat the scattered nature of the trade?
> How reach the workers in one-servant houses?
> How reach those of the servants' hall?

In 1931, the Labour Party Women's Section and the Standing Joint Committee of Working Women's Organizations endorsed the proposal that 'living-in' should cease.

The TUC Conference of Unions Enrolling Women asked the TUC National Women's Advisory Committee 'to consider a campaign to ensure that domestic servants are brought within the Trade Union Movement'. The two main unions concerned, the Transport and General Workers and the National Union of General and Municipal Workers, however, refused their support. They considered, in the words of the T&GWU, 'the difficulties in the way of organising these workers too great'. They felt that they could not afford to divert either money or officials to make the effort to contact private domestic servants.[15] The NUGMW women officials privately wanted to help. Dorothy Elliott, with the assistance of Hampstead residents, the Trades Council, and even the TUC General Council, succeeded in the spring of 1932 in setting up a Domestic Workers' Guild for that borough. It had two hundred members, but it petered out.[16]

The General Council was prepared to push unions over women's organization to a much greater extent than in the mid-1920s. It accepted the National Women's Advisory Committee's commitment to encourage union branches and Trades Councils to set up their own women's committees on the lines developed in Scotland.[17] It also joined the chorus of appeals still being made, particularly by the distributive trades unions, to trade union parents to see that their daughters joined appropriate unions.[18]

During 1931-32, the General Council was finally persuaded into appointing a secretary for the Women's Group and National Women's Advisory Committee. Red-haired Ellen Wilkinson, affectionately regarded by trade unionists as a little firebrand, played an important part in obtaining this concession. She also had great charm. Alice Horan recalled how winningly she extracted General Council backing. At a social gathering to celebrate the instalment of Miss Mary Sutherland as secretary of the Labour Party Women's section, Ellen Wilkinson cornered Walter Citrine and gently but inexorably persuaded him to agree to the Women's Advisory Committee appointment. Even so, Citrine told the 1932 Conference that none of thirty-five applicants for the job was considered suitable. The delegates at once resolved again that a Woman Officer (i.e. secretary) should be appointed. Anne Loughlin expressed their determination 'to change the mentality of the men including those on the General Council from whom they got sympathy and sympathy only'. She made clear that they would not be fobbed off with a mere clerk, but wanted someone who would 'go out and support the Advisory Committee's work'. The choice finally fell on Miss Nancy Adam, a former organizer for the National Federation of Women Workers in Scotland, who took up this post in July 1932.[19]

The General Council had fewer reservations about publicity. Four leaflets were sent out, including one entitled 'Many a Miss Misses Marriage'. 'Commonsense Beauty Hints' sold 179,800 copies. In 1934, the London Trades Council Women's Advisory Committee joined in with a Pageant of Labour, involving about a thousand performers, which they ran for a week at the Crystal Palace. The publicity campaign culminated in 1936 with the issue of a million leaflets and 5,000 posters free to Trades Councils, along with a personal letter from Walter Citrine to Trades Council secretaries. A series of articles was featured in *Reynolds' News,* the Co-operative movement's national Sunday newspaper, urging girls and women to join. The General Council turned down requests for a film van, but agreed to three loudspeakers for the National Women's Advisory Committee to use at meetings. The crowning success in this publicity drive was a report of the 1936 TUC Women's Advisory Conference on the BBC.[20]

The General Council also agreed to a proposal from the 1934 Conference that Trades Councils be allowed representation, which they had not had at Congress itself since 1896. Many of the union leaderships were still worried by the Trades Councils' left-wing tendencies and Walter Citrine pointed out that the Conference already had a link with them since they had appointed Julia Varley to the Trades Council Joint Consultative Committee. She was a staunch supporter of union-employer co-operation and a member of the General Council Women's Group, so the General Council considered her reliable. It was a great concession, therefore, when the General Council agreed that Trades Councils could send a maximum of two delegates from their Women's Advisory Committees to the Conference. These Trades Council delegates were not, however, permitted to vote, nor could they send in resolutions. But the campaign to start up local Trades Council women's committees, now undertaken by the TUC National Women's Advisory Committee, would not have made much sense without this representation at the national Conferences. These local women's committees were a major success story in the early 1930s. Thirty-five were set up in 1931-32, in spite of the huge amount of work with which the Trades Councils were burdened at this time. But, as usual, persistent complaints came from them that the indifference of men trade unionists, and lack of support from union head offices, were hindering their efforts to establish women's committees. Union branches too often did not nominate women delegates to attend meetings, let alone encourage them to stand for election.

Women's participation in normal union activities therefore continued to present problems. Their attendance at branch meetings was generally low. Part of the trouble was that many such meetings were held in pubs and manners had changed since the mid-nineteenth century. The pub was no longer acceptable to many women as a meeting-place, as it had been to the Friendly and Benefit societies.

Alice Horan of the National Union of General and Municipal Workers pointed this out at the 1926 TUC Conference of Unions Enrolling Women: 'Women do not care to go to a meeting-room through the bar of a public-house, and I would suggest that unions make every possible effort to have their meetings in other rooms'. Miss Lil Grotier, London organizer of the Tobacco-Workers' Union, forty years later thought that women's antipathy to pubs might have been due to their husbands spending money on drinks when there was little in the way of family income. For the price of a pint in a pub, a man could escape for an hour or two from the nightmare of unemployment or poverty, and the squalor of a poor home. But a working woman had no such escape because every hard-won penny was earmarked for the family's needs. This was not universally true. A lot of women still enjoyed a visit to the pub. But there were places where pubs would not admit women at all.

Women were not allowed into some pubs in the Newcastle-upon-Tyne area, for instance, as recently as the 1960s.

Trade union women officials, on the other hand, sometimes did work which men officials in the mid-1960s considered quite beyond female capabilities. Mrs Martin of the Union of Distributive and Allied Workers foiled an attempt to get rid of her on account of her married status by sternly insisting on equal work. Miss Amy Wild, a Yorkshire organizer for the same union in the 1920s, was sent to contact men who worked in a slaughterhouse. The men flung offal at her and Miss Wild, looking at the resulting bloodstains on her legs, remarked: 'Gentlemen, if I go out into the street like this, people will think something has happened to me'. Immediately contrite, the men rushed with cloths and water to clean her up and offered to buy her a new pair of stockings. She had no further trouble after this initial horseplay.[21] Bell Jobson joined the Transport and General Workers' Union's Scottish staff when her own union, the Scottish Farm Servants, was merged with it at the end of 1932. She and Agnes Gilroy, a fellow-member of the Organization of Women Committee from the National Union of Distributive and Allied Workers, were elected to the Scottish TUC General Council in 1933. Bell Jobson was elected annually until her retirement in 1941. In 1936 she was chairman of the General Council and, in spite of her very quiet manner, an adroit President of a stormy Congress, riven by political squabbles between Left and Right. She herself, like Julia Varley, loyally supported the moderate policies of the Trade Union Establishment, as did the majority of Congress delegates.

The double-edged policy of unions towards women was now almost as institutionalized as the rest of their activities. The majority discriminated against them as workers and union members. But they disinterestedly pressed for legal and social changes to help women, provided these did not adversely affect men, or if they positively benefited men. Where there was any conflict, they gave priority to men's interests. This was comprehensible where the majority of members were men. But in quite a number of 'mixed' unions, the majority were women and girls - an apathetic, silent majority, acquiescing in the men's monopoly of policy-making.

The campaigns over hours and shift-working were a supreme example of this two-sided attitude to women members. Policies for shortening hours of work continued to be important not only as a means of work-sharing. The standard 47-48-hour week remained more or less unchanged between the wars. These were the hours applied by better employers and fixed through Trade Boards.

Women workers, whether union members or not, owed a good deal to trade unions in this respect. These standard hours were by no means universally observed, however, and unions were trying to establish them in trades which were badly organized and characterized by large numbers of women employees, such as domestic service, catering, and distribution.

Until the 1934 Shops Act, the only legal limitation on the hours of shop-workers was the 1912 Act laying down a maximum 74-hour week for those under fourteen, inclusive of meal-breaks, or a 65-hour week excluding these.[22] Even this limit was sometimes ignored. For example, nine years earlier in 1925, Messrs. Woolworths had been taken to court by the Shop Assistants' Union for sending girls under eighteen to work on Saturdays in the Woolworth factories from 7.45 a.m. until noon, and then to work a further 7 hours as assistants in the Woolworth shops.[23] The 48-hour week was only introduced as a legal measure in shops in 1938, although many employers, especially co-operatives, had been applying it for the previous 20 years. Sixty-five to 75 hours a week were said to be common in the hotel trade, and there were cases of 80 to a hundred hours a week being worked by domestic servants.[24] The Trade Board regulations left loopholes since they laid down hours per week, not per day. So in the mid-1930s, girl laundry-workers in the Midlands were working an 11-12-hour day.

The Washington Convention of 1918 had provided for the restriction of the amount of shift-work performed by women and young persons. The British government, instead of ratifying this proposal, persuaded Parliament to pass the 1920 Employment of Women, Young Persons, and Children Act allowing shift-work in 'essential trades'. This Act was kept in operation by the annual passing of the Expiring Laws Continuance Act.

A number of the trade unions fought it. An attempt had been made to introduce shift-work for girls working at Lever's Port Sunlight factory in 1922. It meant that those of them who lived in Birkenhead had to be up at 3.30 and 4 a.m. to catch the special train laid on to take them to work. The Distributive Workers' Union took the matter up with the Home Secretary and Lever Brothers dropped the idea, but other employers, for example in the Yorkshire textile industry, introduced shift systems. On 16 November 1928, when the government had to seek a vote in the House of Commons in order to keep the 1920 Act going, three Labour Members, Ellen Wilkinson, Rhys Davies, and William Mackinder, disputed it. Davies queried whether 'chocolate moulding, rivetting perambulator wheels, washing beer bottles, making pills and the manufacture of ice cream suckers, potato crisps, and fireworks' were 'essential trades'. There were just enough Conservatives left in the House to defeat the Labour attack.[25]

But the Labour government of 1929-31, intent on abolishing the Employment of Women, Young Persons, and Children Act, also ran into opposition from some of the unions, notably those in the printing trades. To this day, women members of printing unions are among the strongest supporters of shift- and night-work for women, against opposition from other unions.[26]

At the same time, international agreement on ending shift-work for women was being weakened. The 1933 Montevideo Convention of the International Labour Organization, signed by four governments, deprecated any restrictions on shift-work for women and removed distinctions for workers based on their sex. The 1919 Washington Hours Convention was revised so that it no longer applied to women holding responsible managerial posts, and who were not ordinarily engaged in manual work. But Julia Varley, who represented British workers on behalf of the TUC General Council, opposed the revision, partly on the grounds that it created a danger of 'opening the door to the employment of women at night'.[27]

One cause of unemployment and underemployment was the increasing pace of alterations in technology and methods of working. When unions were forced to accept such changes, there was a tendency to sacrifice women to preserve men's wage standards or jobs. The increasing introduction of time-and-motion study to speed up work, particularly the Bedaux system, produced several such instances. Most union leaderships accepted systems intended to save the operative fatigue, based on the observation of the amount of time and energy taken to perform a repetitive operation. But, since the development of these systems in the late nineteenth century, the unions had tempered their acceptance with a regard for the extent of unemployment (see page 128). They had also learnt that the workers' welfare was not the object of the Bedaux system. By this method, the time used by the fastest worker on, say, an assembly line, was set as the norm to which all must adhere, the object being to exact the highest possible amount of production per worker. No concessions were made to individual rates of working. The piece-rate method of payment left it to the workers to drive themselves and when the rates were very low, they overworked. The method was the same as that in the 'sweated' trades. But under the Bedaux system not even a notional choice was left to the individual worker. The amount and quality of work were closely checked and workers were supervised. If they could not keep up, they were sacked for, with the massive unemployment, there was no difficulty in finding replacements.

In the early 1930s both the British and Scottish Trades Union Congresses condemned the Bedaux system. Nevertheless, it was introduced in various occupations. In the hosiery trade at this time men were ousting women from the primary knitting process and leaving them the less well-paid work of making up garments. In the late 1920s, the hosiery firm of Wolsey in Leicester had already begun to introduce the Bedaux system. This was strongly opposed by the girls at the Abbey Park Works. They joined the Leicester and Leicestershire Hosiery Workers' Union and immediately struck work. Girls in other factories in the Wolsey group followed their example. In March 1931, a special meeting was held of all those working under the Bedaux system. By August an official strike against the system was in progress, and proving a strain on the union's funds. However, new time-and-motion study engineers were appointed, since the trouble was thought to be partly due to failure to explain terminology and there were some modifications made in the system as a concession to the union. The leader of the girls, Miss Moore, was trained in the system and became a link between the management and the girls.[28]

However, by January 1935, the lockstitch machinists were accusing the union of bad faith because the concessions were withdrawn. They were refusing to pay their union subscriptions. Two months later they were being offered a 15 per cent rise on piecerates as compensation for this. But the Bedaux system had taken hold and their attempts to avoid it failed because the union came to terms with the management. The late Miss Lily Kettell of the Hosiery Workers' Union remarked that in the mid-1960s some of the older women were 'very hard against the union' because they felt it had let them down in the late 1930s.

There was also a week-long strike in 1932 by girls at one of the Lucas engineering factories in Birmingham' in protest against an attempt to introduce the Bedaux system. The girl strikers sang 'Rule Britannia' with strong emphasis on the words: 'Britons never, never, never shall be slaves!' and threatened to throw the Bedaux rate-fixers out of the factory windows. But most of them were unorganized, there was no union to damp down their activities, and their protest was more like the rumbustious outbreaks of the nineteenth century than any other contemporary industrial action. It showed that, left to themselves, they had spirit enough. To persuade them to return to work, the management made some small concessions. But the following year the firm introduced 'speed-up' through a points system. When a whole group had accepted the system, wages were then reduced. And when sufficient stocks of goods had been piled up by the firm, a large number of women and girls were 'laid off' in 1935.[29] The local trade union protest was not strong enough to help the women. There were other examples in Birmingham, where the Trades Council opposed the introduction of the system and in 1933 supported a strike at Smethwick against it.[30]

The leadership of the Tailors' and Garment-Workers' Union sided with employers against their own women members in a strike in 1928. Rego, a clothing firm, moved from the East End of London to new premises in the northern suburb of Edmonton. There the girls and women were faced with new mass production methods which they said reduced their pay, as well as long journeys to and from work and the extra expense these entailed. They struck work chiefly to maintain their earnings. But the union was afraid this action would prejudice the success of national negotiations in which it was then engaged and would not back the strike, which failed. The National Executive Committee later disciplined the two strike-leaders.[31]

In the clothing trade the conveyor-belt, which was in use by 1918, had become widespread by 1930. In this trade a man acted as machiner and leader of the factory bench of women operatives. The union attitude to this new development was not that the conveyor belt should be abolished but that, since it was harmful to health and welfare, workers should be given compensation. The straight piecework method of payment was increasingly superseded in the 1930s by the production bonus system. In the cutting-room, where the men predominated however, payment was still on a time basis as a reward for skill. In 1934, the Tailors' and Garment-Workers' Union issued its Cutters' By-Laws, declaring piecework and the bonus system in the cutting-rooms to be 'pernicious'. In order to save the cutting-room from the system, the union apparently sacrificed the women, although in the end, after fierce resistance, incentive bonus schemes were introduced for men cutters too. In other trades the new commitment to rearmament helped to reduce opposition to speeded-up systems of production.

More clearly than in the campaigns to reduce hours and to establish the right to paid holidays, which equally benefited men, unions demonstrated their concern for women in their attitudes to their conditions of life and of work. Quite disinterestedly, since it had no effect in furthering memberships, they debated and pressed for increased pensions for widows and mothers in need of help.[32] They supported unequivocally a campaign against maternal mortality, the deaths of mothers in childbirth, in which Gertrude Tuckwell played a big part.[33] At this time there was a big rise in the numbers of deaths of both infants and mothers at birth in depressed areas, where it was sometimes double the national average. Women also feared to leave their jobs even for a day when births were imminent because high unemployment created strong competition for work and the chances of their getting their jobs back were sometimes nil. On the other hand, families might be absolutely dependent on their earnings because their husbands were out of work.

Mr R Doyle, General Secretary of the Union of Jute, Flax, and Kindred Textile-Workers, described conditions in his industry between the wars when 'women were to be seen at childbirth at their frames or were taken into lavatories to have their children'.[34] Mr Harry Kershaw, assistant General Secretary of the Amalgamated Weavers' Association, recalled cases of women leaving work at 3 p.m., being delivered of a child during the night, and being back at their looms again the following morning. The women weavers knew that if they stayed away from their work because of a confinement, their looms would be 'shopped' (allocated) to the woman next behind them in the queue, who was either unemployed, or waiting for more remunerative work. Sympathetic medical officers might give certificates to conceal pregnancy as, say, lumbago. If they could not get a certificate, women hid their condition and went on working. The threat of unemployment among Lancashire textile-workers between the wars led to the introduction of a 'marriage bar', so that women kept secret the fact that they were married: pregnancy might give them away.

Trade unionists campaigned for more nursery schools. The official TUC line from the mid-1930s was that more of these should be provided through local authorities since they were the province of the Ministry of Education, and part of general education. Day nurseries, available for children under two years old, and which came under the Ministry of Health, were less strongly advocated. They were not prepared to go to this length to help working mothers.

Local authorities' powers to provide welfare services at this time were merely permissive. In towns where 80 or 90 per cent of the population were out of work and on unemployment benefit or Poor Relief, they had little income from rates to spend on anything at all. The object of the campaign against maternal mortality was to force local authorities to use the powers they did have to provide medical care.

The public at large was ignorant of such conditions, or indifferent, because there were still 'two nations'. The monied class regarded the working class as a different race, capable of putting up with very rough conditions, in the same way as the British and other colonial nations saw the aboriginal inhabitants of the colonies. There was not the same concern with the miseries of working people as there had been before the First World War, although sweatshops and all the other abuses persisted. There were still too few white-collar women workers unaffected by snobbishness to bridge the gap between the leisured few and the mass of manual workers. The go-ahead, career women among them, who had paid the price of spinsterhood for their promotion, lacked sympathy with motherhood. The situation was exactly as it had been in 1919 when the British government and employers' representatives, on a technical point, failed to vote with Mary Macarthur for Britain's adoption of the International Labour Organization's Washington Convention on Motherhood (see page 170).

Unions independently of state or local authorities made some effort to help working women who fell ill. Some of the Women's Trade Union League funds were used to set up a rest and convalescent home for women, first at Ongar in Essex and in 1938, when that proved too small, at Stansted. Unions and other organizations endowed beds, although the TUC General Council took this step under pressure from the NWAC only in 1931. Some unions with large female memberships did not do so until twenty or more years later.[35]

In 1934, a women's wing was proposed at Manor House Orthopaedic Hospital. The hospital had been set up and was maintained by men trade unionists for themselves and their female relatives. The General Council appealed for funds, and, poetic touch, bought a house and grounds previously occupied by Pavlova, but were unable to go further with the idea at that time because of lack of finance.[36]

But unemployment, the fears it engendered, and the consequent acceptance of sometimes appalling conditions of living and working, which affected women and men alike, were only one side of the picture. Even at the 1933 low, women were in the trade union movement to an extent undreamt of before war broke out in 1914. Losses in their membership were at their greatest between 1921 and 1924. After that the rate of decline slowed down, so that there were only 150,000 fewer women members in the United Kingdom than nine years earlier. This was proof of the importance of unity – unity among unions in face of adversity, and unity and understanding between leading women trade unionists, active members, and the rank and file. These factors made certain the initial success of the Congress machinery set up to ensure attention to women. And they also helped to compensate for the tendency of men members to put their own interests first.

There were slight grounds for hope, too, about employment. Despite the drop in jobs in textiles and other work, the total number of women at work in the United Kingdom was up by about 400,000 in 1931 as compared with 1921. This contrasted with a decline of 300,000 in numbers of men workers, In paper and printing, woodwork and furniture, brick-making, pottery, and glass, in clerical and medical work, and to a small extent in clothing, the numbers of women employed had risen. In mining and the metal, engineering, and electrical trades, in food, drink, and tobacco, in chemicals, in banking, insurance, and finance, the female labour force had doubled or more than doubled. The numbers involved might be relatively small. What was significant was the rate of increase over the decade, particularly in light industries. The areas that prospered were primarily the West Midlands and the southeast of England.

Experience varied from town to town, district to district, depending on the kind of work carried on. In some places there was much more work for women than for men. The Dundee shipyards were badly hit by unemployment. But the women could still earn in the jute trade and Dundee men, left to mind their homes, were nicknamed 'kettle boilers'. In Londonderry there was work for women in textiles, and in making clothing and household linen, but little for men, so Londonderry was known as 'the petticoat city'.

Unemployment did not necessarily have a bad effect on women's trade union membership. In the small local unions based in Northern Ireland from 1921 until 1934 the numbers of women members were always in excess of those of men.

In the United Kingdom as a whole, in spite of the slump in employment in the cotton, silk, and synthetic fabric trades, the tradition of trade union organization held to a remarkable degree, both for men and women. Women's organization also remained strong in the boot and shoe trades. The community tradition still persisted in these occupations. In the other clothing trades, women were lapsing out of union membership to a much lesser extent than men.

It was in rapidly expanding trades that women's organization was poor, since the relevant unions still were careless of bringing them into membership. The only exceptions were the printing and paper trades, in which the unions had been forced to come to terms with women's employment half a century earlier.

Although 1933 was the worst year of the Depression as far as unemployment and trade union memberships were concerned, it also marked the start of the upturn. The rise of Nazism in Germany caused a crucial change in the British Labour movement. The TUC General Council, after discussions with the Labour Party National Executive, persuaded the 1934 Congress to give up its deep opposition to rearmament. The beneficial effects on industry were soon apparent. By 1935 gas-masks were already being manufactured in Lancashire and reducing unemployment among textile-workers.

Immediately in response to growing employment, the numbers of both men and women in unions began to rise steadily. Women imbued with the idea of union had not been brainwashed out of it by the Depression. Rather they had increased their power and effectiveness.

On the other hand, special efforts to organize women appeared less necessary to union leaders when from 1934 onwards trade union memberships began to increase. After 1935, Walter Citrine stopped his regular attendance at the British TUC's Women's Advisory Conferences. Like those of the Scots three years earlier, they were well enough established to function on their own. It was a tribute to the leading and active women trade unionists. Yet, despite the huge strides towards integration of women in the trade union movement, overall they were nowhere near being accepted as equals.

Notes

1 Bondfield, *A Life's Work*, 300,302 for Unemployment Insurance Fund.
2 Hannington, *Never on our Knees,* 227.
3 ibid., 259.
4 Min. of Lab. Rep. on the Operation of the Anomalies Regulations, 1933, 7-8, paras. 24-6: Min. of Lab. Gaz., 1931, 211, 296 and 1934, 234. Unpub. Proceedings of the 1932 TUC Women's Advisory Conference. 1933 TUC Rep., 351, Arthur Hayday, NUGMW and General Council. NUGMW *Jour*.: Jan-Feb, 1926 for examples of women losing unemployment benefit because they were married: Nov. 1933, 315, M. Bondfield, 'Women's Notes', the Anomalies Regulations of the Unemployment Insurance Act were amended to ease conditions for married women workers, but assessors of the Courts were not informed.
5 *Shop Assistant*, 11 Feb. 1933.
6 Min. of Lab. Gaz: author's Ph.D. Thesis, Univ. of London 1971, for employment and trade union statistics.
7 Scot. TUC Reps.: 1928, 75-6, 81-4, 45-6: 70 Scottish unions and divisions of national unions had affiliated to the OWC: 1929, 79-82: 1931, 61-2:

1932, 73-4: 1933, 39-40, 58-9, etc. The OWC Reps. were incorporated in the Scot. TUC Reps.: Mins. of Scot. TUC General Council, 21 Aug. 1934, 49: 19 Nov. 1934, 74: 17 Dec. 1934, 124.

8 1933 Scot. TUC Rep., 58-9: 1967 Scot. TUC Rep., 432-5.

9 Mins. of Scot. General Council Meeting, 29 Apr. 1932. 1932 Scot. TUC Rep., 61-2, 73-4.

10 1935 Scot. TUC Rep., 38-40: 1936 Scot. TUC Rep., 52.

11 TUC Reps.: 1927, 70, 198, para 130; 428-30: 1928, 361-3: 1929, 333-5.

12 There are no printed Reports of the May 1930 consultative meeting or any of the Conferences of 1931-35. The first printed Report is for 1936. See TUC Reps. for short summaries.

13 1930 Labour Party Rep., *First Steps Towards a Domestic Workers' Charter*, 19, presented by the Standing Joint Committee of Working Women's Organizations to the Nat. Conference of Labour Women, 3-5 June 1930.

14 Univ. of Liverpool, *Social Survey of Merseyside*, 1932, Booklet, no.4, 5-6, 20: *Survey of London Life and Labour*, vol. II, London Industries, notes on statistics, ch. viii, 428, 444-5, 452-5.

15 1932 TUC Rep., 106, para. 58.

16 Unpub. Reps. of Proceedings of TUC Conferences of Unions Enrolling Women and Women's Advisory Committee Reps., 1933, 1934.

17 1931 TUC Rep., Women's Group Rep., 121, para. 52 and Appendix for constitution of proposed Trades Council Committees: 1933 TUC Rep., 102, para. 48. In 1930-31, the NWAC and Women's Group arranged conferences in Newcastle, Bradford, Manchester, Birmingham, Bristol, Cardiff, Nottingham, and London on local organization to help the organization of women.

18 TUC Reps.: 1923, 315 ff.: 1924, 232-3 for text of circular sent by General Council to unions: 1925, 437: 1926, 224-5: 1940, 249-50. Scot. TUC Reps.: 1928, 190: 1936, OWC Rep.

19 1922 TUC Rep., 217, Miss I.M. Cowell, Corresponding Sec. of the WTUL, became sec. of the TUC Women's Group. She left in 1924 and was not replaced. *New Dawn*, 25 Oct. 1924, advt. of the post: 1925 Rep. of TUC Conference of Unions Enrolling Women: 1932 TUC Rep., NWAC Rep., 106, para. 59: *New Dawn*, 9 April 1932, 192, advt. Unpub. Reps. of TUC Women's Advisory Conferences.

20 TUC Reps.: 1932, 107, para. 64: 1933, 106, para. 59: 1934, 103, 44: 1935, 99, Resolution no. 7: 1936, 105, Resolution no. 15.

21 Information from Miss Amy Wild; survey, author's PhD thesis.

22 J. Hallsworth, *Protective Legislation for Shop and Office Employers*, 190-1: 1936 Rep. of Nat. Union of Distributive and Allied Workers, 6: NUGMW *Jour.*, Apr. 1935, 107: May 1936, 147.

23 *Shop Assistant*, 9 Jan. 1926, 34.

24 Min. of Lab. Rep., on the Result of an Investigation into the Rates of Wages, and Hours of Employment and the Degree of Industrial Organisation in the Light Refreshment and Dining Room (Non-licensed) Branch of the Catering Trade, 1926, 68, App. C, Table 44: 69, Table 46. Rep. of an Inquiry into Remuneration, Hours of

Employment, etc. in the Catering Trade, 1929. *Fact* pamphlet series, R. Postgate, ed., *Conditions in the Catering Trade by a Manager*, 1938, 7: 1939 Rep. of Ann. Conference of Trades Councils, 18.

25 1928 TUC Rep., 147-8: 1935 Scot. TUC Rep., OWC Rep., 71-3, para. 4. 1935 TUC Rep., 138-41.

26 1935 Scot. TUC Rep., 79-81: 1946 TUC Rep., NWAC Rep., 34.

27 1931 NUGMW *Jour.*, Aug. 1931; May 1933 Women's Dept. Notes. See also 1936 and 1937 NWAC Reps.

28 Leicester and Leicestershire Hosiery Workers' Union, Mins. of Exec. Committee meetings, 9 Jan. 1935: 18 Jan. 1935: 6 Feb. 1935: 7 Mar. 1935.

29 Joan Beauchamp, *Women at Work*, 24 ff. See also NUGMW *Jour.*, 1932, 143, Lucy Butcher, a London delegate to the union Biennial Conference on incidence of speed-up in rope, tin-box trades; in biscuit-making, and laundries.

30 Corbett, *Birmingham Trades Council*, 139-40.

31 Stewart and Hunter, *The Needle is Threaded*, 197-231: also information from Miss Sutton, National Officer, and Mr Mick Mindl, London Organizer of the Nat. Union of Tailors and Garment Workers.

32 TUC Rep.: 1919, 321: 1920, 78: 1922, 70-4: 1923, 74: 1924, 111, 113, 115, Rep. of a deputation to Prime Minister Ramsay MacDonald. Also 351, 360, 381-3, Point 7 of General Council's Industrial Charter. 1925, 202: 1927, 172, 406-8: 1929, 438: 1930, 330. 1930 Scot. TUC Rep., 42.

33 G. Tuckwell, art. in the *Copec News*, Jan. 1928. See also 1934 TUC Rep., Standing Advisory Committee on Soc. Ins. Rep., 117-18, para. 70: 1935, 119, and NWAC Rep., 99, Resolution no. 3.

34 1928 Scot. TUC Rep. 202-3, the Dundee and District Jute and Flax Workers' Union urged that a qualified woman should attend injured women at work. 1927 Rep. of TUC Conference of Unions Enrolling Women, 12-14: 1927 TUC Rep., Women's Group Rep., 147-8, paras. 1, 2.

35 1938 TUC NWAC Rep., 10-11, para. 9.

36 1934 TUC Rep., 345-6. NUGMW *Jour.*, 11 Feb. 1955, 41.

37 Abs. of Lab. Statistics and Min. of Lab. Gaz. for annual statistics.

14   The Mid-Thirties Turning-Point

In the mid-1930s the decision of the National Government to rearm, and the support of the Labour Party and the Trades Union Congress for that decision, created a watershed. Rearmament provided work and eased unemployment. It encouraged the *rapprochement* between union leaders and employers and led to the final institutionalization of the trade union movement. It was these five years, rather than, as is usually thought, the war itself which constituted a turning-point in much of British economic and social history.

By the late 1930s the TUC National Women's Advisory Committee had gradually become part of the trade union Establishment, loyally supporting its policies. Top-level acceptance of women was not only a sign of progress towards equality. It also meant that some of the ablest leaders, Anne Loughlin, Florence Hancock, Dorothy Elliott, Alice Horan, and Anne Godwin, followed many a male trade union official in exchanging militancy for respectability. Over the next twenty years and more, they were less and less assiduous in forcing men officials to try to understand the problems of ordinary working women. Like other members of the TUC General Council under the powerful influence of Bevin and Citrine, their commitment to the political side of the Labour movement increased.

The dominant trade unions were now the general workers' organizations, like the National Union of General and Municipal Workers, and above all the Transport and General Workers' Union, whose power was symbolized in the new Transport House in Smith Square, Westminster. Ernest Bevin had persuaded the Labour Party to share it with his union, a reflection of his own authority in the Labour movement. These general unions were based in London or the Home Counties. As far as women were concerned, the long experience and earthy good sense, stemming from close daily contact with the factory floor, of the northern English and Scottish textile unions went unused. Even women officials of the smaller white-collar London-based unions, such as the Guild of Insurance Officials and the National Union of Bank Employees, remained outside the trade union establishment. One of the few who did break into the inner circle was Miss Anne Godwin,

1 Florence Hancock and
   Anne Loughlin with
   Vincent Tewson
2 Nancy Adam
3 Ethel Chipchase
4 Anne Godwin
5 Margaret Mackay
6 Marie Patterson

who became one of the assistant secretaries of the Association of Women Clerks and Secretaries in 1931. While she and the university graduates Ellen Wilkinson and Dorothy Elliott possessed a trained intellectual toughness, most of the other women trade union leaders were womanly according to the convention of the time.

But intellectual or womanly, in the second half of the 1930s a gulf slowly began to grow between these leaders and the other women members, particularly those who were active and interested. It may have been widened by some men trade union leaders who saw these leading women as a race apart. Women like Ellen Wilkinson, Dorothy Elliott, Anne Loughlin, Florence Hancock were, in the phrase of both Tom Williamson, later General Secretary of the National Union of General and Municipal Workers, and Walter Citrine, 'goddesses'. The test of a union's attitude towards women as real or potential members, however, was its attitude to its rank and file. The very fact that women were mostly in lower grades of membership strengthened the opinion of many men members, and that of the women themselves, that they were inferior. The hardening of the divisions between women trade unionists, as part of the institutionalizing process, into the three tiers now traditional among men trade unionists, that is, top leadership involved with Labour Party politics, then militants, and finally the mass of the rank and file, just at this time was one facet of the fixing of the pattern in trade union development that continued for the next generation.

The start of the real battle on the key issue for women's equality — equal pay — was another aspect of this same setting of a course for many years to come. All the various groupings involved since the late nineteenth century crystallized their attitudes and adopted the positions that they were to hold for the next thirty and more years.

The small white-collar women's unions, the Association of Women Clerks and Secretaries whose members were drawn mainly from the lower grades of the Civil Service, the National Union of Women Teachers, and the Civil Service women's societies, had never let the demand slip, even during the vicissitudes of the 1920s and early 1930s. But it was in the middle of the decade that the 'mixed' unions began to campaign for the 'rate for the job' because of a marked increase in the number of lower-paid women brought in to do the same work as men, especially in the white-collar trades.

The divided views of men, and also of many working women, were illustrated by the attitudes of trade unions, the Labour Party, and the co-operatives in the role of employers. The policies of the co-operatives had been illustrated by the numerous strikes the Amalgamated Union of Co-operative Employees had to run during the First World War in order to establish equal pay for substituted women. By the end of the war, the Labour Party as well as the unions were well established as employers. None of them customarily paid women employees the same amounts as men. Wages of women staff were set by the standards of local practice in private firms, or the law of supply and demand, and rarely by the principle of the 'rate for the job'.

In the early 1920s, there were various indications of the lower value placed by the Labour movement on women workers, irrespective of skill or training. The National Union of General and Municipal Workers, for example, did not pay the women staff taken over from the National Federation of Women Workers to run its Women's District the same rates as the male staff of its other districts. In 1925, the Labour-controlled Rhondda Urban District Council went to the length of threatening members of the National Union of Women Teachers with dismissal for agitating for equal pay.[1]

The union custom was to make women staff members of the employing union rather than of an appropriate trade union, which rendered negotiations difficult. The Association of Women Clerks and Secretaries maintained a special branch for staff who worked in trade union offices. In 1921, the National Union of Clerks tried to obtain the agreement of Congress for setting up, for the purposes of negotiation, a Joint Board with trade unions as employers. They had had a serious dispute with the Association of Locomotive Engineers and Firemen, which was resolved in their favour. One result was that the Engineers and Firemen were one of the few all-male unions that paid women office staff the same as men. Another was their support for the Clerks on this resolution. But Jack Jones, MP, of the General Workers' Union opposed it and it came to nothing.[2]

The greatest impact unions had on women's pay was not through their policies as employers but in negotiations with the whole range of other employers, private and, at this time, more particularly public.

The only union in the public services which maintained an implacable opposition to equal pay for women was the National Union of Schoolmasters, whose strength lay in the secondary schools. They did so because they did not then feel threatened by the competition of the lower-paid women. Secondary schooling was not then compulsory and it was in the primary schools where attendance was compulsory that women teachers so heavily outnumbered men.

As the Civil Service expanded to staff the growing government departments and welfare services, the Treasury met the increasing wages bill by designating groups of workers as lower grades so that the number of grades proliferated. In the twentieth century these new lower grades were almost wholly staffed by girls and women, so that the unions, in agreeing to them, were in fact agreeing to their lower payment. It was a way of closing chances to women of competing with men for promotion to higher grades. In 1920 the Civil Service Clerical Association, for instance, accepted lower grading of work in which large numbers of girls and women were being employed, segregating them into a special shorthand typists' grade,[3] thus dodging the equal-pay issue.

The LCC Staff Association, more than any other organization in the public services, had made real efforts to obtain equal pay for women in the 'minor' establishment, i.e., lower-paid grades, first in 1920 and again a decade later. The Association established that they should be paid five-sixths of men's rates. Thus these women were within an ace of equality.[4]

The demands for 'the rate for the job' as a protection for men were being made in Britain by the second half of the 1930s not only by public service unions, but by various manual workers' organizations. The National Society of Pottery-Workers at its 1935 Annual Delegate Meeting considered a resolution from its Burslem branch that women should be paid the same piece-rates as men because, at lower rates, they had been undertaking the making of the larger sizes of plates since the First World War.[5] In the same year, the Amalgamated Engineering Union, although it was not contemplating the admission of women to membership, passed a resolution at its annual conference in favour of equal pay for women.[6] It could no longer pretend to be unaware of changing technology, which was bringing increasing numbers of less skilled workers into the engineering industry. The AEU were again recruiting unskilled male labourers and the semi-skilled men but not the mass of women who were graded as semi-skilled but whose earnings remained lower than those of the unskilled men labourers.

The interests of single and married women clashed over equal pay, just as they had done over maternity leave and state grants to help during confinements. Support among women for equal pay was strongest in clerical occupations, banking, and insurance where the 'marriage bar' operated most extensively. They did not look with favour on married women workers, because the large numbers of married women in the textile trades were said to depress men's rates of pay. One of the arguments in favour of equal pay all along had been the family responsibilities of single women. Married women workers living with their husbands were felt to weaken the case.

The proposition, especially in local government and Civil Service unions, was that the 'marriage dowry' paid by unions (see page 94) should be cancelled in return for an all-out campaign for the 'rate for the job'. But at the same time as they campaigned for equal pay, some women members demanded the ending of the 'marriage bar', thus challenging this aspect of the unions' policy of trying to reduce the number of women competing for work.

One instance of this occurred in a manual workers' union. In 1931 a group of women 'pickers' in the Power-Loom, Carpet-, and Textile-Weavers' Association accepted reductions in earnings for lower-quality work, partly to preserve higher rates for higher qualities, but also on condition that no more married women workers were made to leave work. They were clearly not overawed by their inferiority in voting strength (see pages 156-7).

The London County Council Staff Association in 1935-36 held a referendum of its members on the abolition of its own 'marriage bar'. Over two-thirds of the members voted in favour of continuing the 'bar'. But of the women members who voted, about three-fifths wanted the 'bar' lifted. In 1935 the LCC removed the 'bar' for women teachers and medical staff on the grounds that a lot of public money had been spent on their training and that marriage enhanced their professional qualifications. London, like the other conurbations, was growing at the expense of the countryside. More schools and medical services were required to meet the needs of the increasing numbers of residents. Therefore the employer, the LCC, had to waive the 'marriage bar' in order to obtain staff.[8]

In the early 1930s, the equal-pay issue was further complicated by attacks on the right to work of women and juveniles of both sexes, a facet of unemployment. The 1931 Census showed that the young were gaining work at the expense of adults. In distribution 40 to 50 per cent of labour in all branches was made up of boys and girls under the age of eighteen.[9] In 1933, the National Women's Advisory Committee remarked on 'the continuing displacement of men by women and girls'. At the following year's Advisory Conference Anne Godwin, moved a resolution for an intensive press campaign 'to safeguard the interests of women workers'.[10] Again, in 1935 at the Trades Union Congress, a composite resolution moved by the National Union of General and Municipal Workers and seconded by Anne Godwin's union, made clear the women's anxieties:

the problem of unemployment cannot be solved by transferring available work from one group of workers to another and [Congress] therefore opposes any suggestion that it can be solved by dismissing women from paid employment.

At the 1935 Scottish TUC Conference of Unions Enrolling Women, however, Miss Eleanor Stewart of the T&GWU, the chairman, voiced a new fear. She wondered if it was 'in the minds of some that we follow the example of Italy and Germany'. In Italy, she pointed out, recent agreements between the Federations of employers and employees specified 'the industries and types of occupations where women are to be displaced and their jobs taken by men'. This had occurred not only in agriculture and industry but also in office work, in insurance, and in banks. She quoted Nazi slogans: 'Motherhood is undeniably the aim of Feminine Education'; 'A woman's occupation is the recreation of the tired German warrior'; 'Kinder, Kirche, Küche'. Men who deplored the employment of women in heavy work, ought, she said, to go out 'charring'. She made clear that women were protecting their right to work precisely because at this time they felt more than ever threatened owing to the rise of fascist ideologies in countries also badly affected by unemployment, and their spread from the continent to Britain.[11]

At the 1935 Trades Union Congress Dorothy Elliott moved a resolution that unions should consider fixing 'a fair rate for the job', irrespective of the sex or age of a worker. Like other leading women trade unionists, she was playing on men's fears of cheap, female competition for jobs to advance the cause of equal pay. She put the male argument for the 'rate for the job' in conditions of growing unemployment, so successfully that the General Council subsequently circulated her speech as a memorandum to affiliated unions. But however much it was intended to promote women's economic equality, in fact it spelt out the threat of the 'rate for the job' to women's right to work.[12] The confident militants among women teachers and higher-graded civil servants might ask, in Emma Paterson's words, only 'a fair field and no favour' in competing for work with men. But nervousness that equal pay threatened their jobs was by this time affecting even some white-collar women workers. When equal-pay resolutions were debated at the 1932 and 1936 annual conferences of the National Association of Local Government Officers, women delegates spoke against them.

The clearest statements of all on equal pay as a protection for men's prior right to jobs came from the Irish Trade Union

movement, to which many British unions still adhered. The Irish
Free State was suffering from high unemployment. A Conditions of
Employment Bill was brought in the Dail to provide measures to
deal with this. It proposed among other things to give the Minister
of Industry and Commerce powers to prohibit women from employment in any kind of industry he thought fit, in order to provide
more work for men. Relegation to 'Kinder, Kirche, Küche' as in
Nazi Germany seemed a very real threat.

The Irish trade unions had developed strongly after independence was wrested from Britain in 1922, within the middle-
class nationalist Irish Free State, deeply influenced by the
powerful Roman Catholic Church. The Irish Trades Union
Congress General Council roundly condemned the Bill. It at-
tributed its conception to 'the advance of industrial systematisation
and mechanisation', and attacked it as condemning workless
women to a life of poverty and inaction. It claimed the proposed
Act would reduce them 'to industrial pariahs'. Working-class standards would worsen because daughters would have to be supported
by fathers or brothers. Low-paid workmen who took over jobs
from women would be as much a threat to the better-paid male
wage-earners as the women. The Irish TUC General Council
pledged that it would not 'leave its Trade Union sisters in the
lurch',[13] and Louie Bennett and her colleague Helen Chenevix led
the Irish Women Workers' Union in a campaign to secure the
reduction of the powers proposed for the Minister of Industry and
Commerce.[14]

But the Act was passed and men trade unionists supported it. As
the Irish fraternal delegate to the 1936 Scottish TUC told delegates,
in addition to reducing the working-week to 48 hours for adults
and 40 for juveniles, clauses had been put in 'to regulate the number of women and juveniles' who could be employed in new industries being established. 'There might be some difference of
opinion', he said, 'as to whether they should not have insisted instead of that on equal pay for equal work, but they had agreed to
try the experiment ...' It was a frank avowal that under pressure
British and Irish men trade unionists turned to the expedient of
sacrificing women workers to provide work for men, advocated
and practised a century earlier. They had not learnt from the
disastrous consequences to men of the ensuing growth of 'sweated
labour'. For the working class, being human and lacking the
security of inherited property, thought in the immediate short-
term. The destitution which would drive women to take any kind
of work at any rates of pay, the dead-weight of females on male
relatives, were regarded as lesser evils than an increase in men's

unemployment. The Act only applied to new industries, but the effect of increasing competition among women for jobs in old trades would be the lowering of wages and standards of conditions.

The British, with the economy improving, preferred to turn to equal pay. So what was to be the final lengthy campaign began where there was most anxiety about cheap female competition, in the civil and public services. Backed by women members in the 'common classes' intent on justice for themselves, as well as by worried men, the Civil Service clerical organizations raised the matter through their Whitley Council. But the Treasury in 1934 refused to deal with it through the normal Whitley negotiating machinery. So the only course seemed to be to try again to persuade Parliament to legislate. In 1936 there was a House of Commons vote in favour of equal pay in the 'common classes' of the Civil Service. But like the Liberal-Conservative coalition of 1920 (see pp. 170-1) the Conservative government refused to act further on this decision.[5] Therefore unions pinned their faith on the Labour Party which had always declared itself in favour of the principle.

Then simultaneously, in the same old way, while demanding the 'rate for the job' for the 'common classes', the Civil Service Clerical Association agreed in 1936, as it had in 1920, to the hiving-off of female staff into a separate, lower-paid, lower grade, instead of trying to maintain the notion of equality in existing lower grades as the LCC had done. Naturally this benefited the female minority in higher-graded work as well as men. It was just one more of the differences that arose among women over equal pay.

So the campaign started. The Civil Service Equal Pay Committee, which co-ordinated Civil Service union action, co-operated in this with the London County Council Staff Association and a non-union pressure-group, the Status of Women Committee, which was pressing for the full legal, economic, and political equality of women. But there was little progress at this time. The unions in the public services were still banned by the 1927 Trade Disputes and Trades Unions Act from affiliation to the TUC and the weight of the trade union movement was not behind the campaign. Too few unions were affected and the traditionally divided views of the late nineteenth century still prevailed.

But equally on this issue there was as yet no break in the traditional unity of most active women trade unionists at whatever level. If they were confident enough to take on union work, they were confident enough to uphold equal pay as they had done in the past.

Unity still obtained in other matters in spite of new methods of working in unions. Women had settled with the men of the trade union movement to working in committees after their initiation during the First World War. Gone were the heroic campaigns and dramatic gestures of the heyday of the Women's Trade Union League and the National Federation of Women Workers. Now with plodding, but nonetheless passionate, obstinacy, they argued for policies to help women. Still on the high wave of support from unions which had created the Women's Advisory Conferences and the National Women's Advisory Committee, they determinedly pursued the organization of domestic servants. They succeeded in persuading the TUC General Council to take a most extraordinary step. TUC policy was never to set up a trade union, but merely to accept into affiliation unions which the workers in an occupation themselves managed to establish. Under pressure from the National Women's Advisory Committee, however, they flouted this rule and in 1937, the TUC set up a National Domestic Workers' Union with a blare of publicity in the newspapers. It was formally launched in June 1938 with Mrs Beatrice Bezzant, who had been a domestic servant, as its national organizer. By July it was said to have 1,500 members. A Sunday Club was started in Shaftesbury Avenue for members and their friends and later moved to larger premises in Holland Park.

Simultaneously there were signs that a growing demand for women in other forms of work was lessening the supply of domestic workers. In London in January 1938, a Domestic Services Exhibition was held to try and persuade women to remain in this employment. Dorothy Elliott, speaking at the exhibition, showed that the old idea of joint consultative committees of mistresses and maids in areas like Hampstead, Kensington, and Chelsea was still in the minds of women trade unionists. More practically the TUC produced 'A Domestic Servants' Charter' proposing limited hours of work and conditions similar to those they aimed at for factory- and office-workers.[16]

Domestic service, however, was not the only occupation in which close supervision by employers impeded trade union organization of women. It was also characteristic of general nursing, a preponderantly female occupation. Supervision was exercised by senior nursing staff, especially matrons, opposed to any organization other than the professional Royal College of Nursing. In 1932 the reorganization of Poor Relief brought many hospitals under local authority control and raised union interest in recruiting nurses. But in 1937 the fear of intimidation was still so strong that on a sandwich-board march through the West End and City of London organized by the Guild of Nurses and the National Union of County Officers in protest at long working-hours, the marchers wore black masks to avoid identification. A TUC Nursing Profession Joint Advisory Council, set up in 1937-38, drew up a 'Nurses' Charter' demanding a 96-hour fortnight and other improvements. It was further evidence of the strong influence of women trade unionists in the General Council.[17]

Their influence was also apparent in union efforts to improve maternal and infant welfare. Maternity benefits were still nonexistent and the rate of maternal mortality higher than before the First World War. Accordingly the TUC General Council was prompted into setting up a joint committee with the British Medical Association. The Committee produced a plan to improve maternal welfare in 1938. But by this time local authorities had been made responsible for a midwifery service, and the plan was never implemented.

Further, the unions supported moves to increase women's unemployment benefits. By 1937 the national Unemployment Fund had a surplus and the TUC Social Insurance and National Women's Advisory Committees wanted the surplus used to equalize the contributions and benefits of men and women. They gave priority to ironing out anomalies in rates for married women and seasonal workers who had suffered most from the 1931 cuts. Although unemployment in 1938 was again over 2 million for the first time since 1933, the 1938 Congress agreed to this policy.[18]

The 'goddesses' were less successful over transferred workers, but the problem was not confined to women. It was another aspect of government efforts to deal with unemployment, like compulsory domestic service and compulsory labour on roads. The government set up a scheme to transfer people of both sexes compulsorily from depressed areas to places where there was work. The TUC General Council advised acceptance as 'a poor alternative' to providing work near their homes, but suggested unions should supervise transfers. Women officials of the Transport and General Workers' Union disapproved highly of the provisions for transferees. Mary Carlin, one of the critics of the scheme, remarked that it 'tended to place the transferee under an obligation to the employer with a consequent loss of freedom whilst the facilities offered by the Ministry [of Labour] tend to benefit employers in the manner of a subsidy'. Instead of living at home, girls had to pay for lodgings, often more than they could afford, a problem underlined by a strike at the Siemens factory in Greenwich when a number were left destitute. But transfers continued, although the numbers went down as the economy recovered.[19]

No amount of pressure from women trade union leaders and militants, however, would alone have persuaded unions to help women. The past had shown that a considerable willingness on the part of unions to be of help was also necessary. In the late 1930s the greatest advances that affected women workers were simply the result of long years of unyielding pressure by 'mixed' unions. The first of these was the national agreement concluded by the Shop Assistants' Union with the help of Sir Frederick Leggett, Chief Conciliation Officer at the Ministry of Labour, with the Multiple Shop Proprietors in the grocery and provisions trade in November 1937. Hitherto the only national agreements had been with the co-operatives. Otherwise agreements, some of them very good, had been merely with individual shops and enterprises. National agreements in retail footwear, tailoring, and outfitting followed this breakthrough. These were the basis of the retail trades Joint Industrial Councils set up during the 1939-45 war. Ultimately they led to a great extension of Wages Councils, that is, the old Trade Boards renamed and reconstituted. In this way the failure to set up boards for the distributive trades after the First World War was made good. The Shop Assistants' Union's national agreements therefore proved vital in improving wages for a rapidly increasing group of women workers.[20]

Similarly, without any spectacular industrial action, union pressure secured a huge extension of paid holidays. Bank and statutory holidays had been granted before the 1914-18 War. These were being pushed up to one week's and sometimes a fortnight's annual leave. By the 1930s, twenty-three unions had holidays-with-pay agreements. The three general unions, T&GWU, NUGMW, and the National Union of Distributive and Allied Workers, together with the Shop Assistants' Union and the National Society of Operative Printers and Assistants, were the main ones recruiting women. A government committee with strong trade union representation, including Ernest Bevin, was set up in 1936 to investigate legislation on enforcement and provision of paid holidays. It inspired the 1938 Holidays-with-Pay Act. This Act gave Road Haulage Boards, Agricultural Boards, and, most important of all as far as women were concerned, Trade Boards, the power to fix one week's paid holiday a year. Thirty-six Trade Boards had proposals ready by the summer of 1939. The war did not interrupt this development. The $7\frac{1}{2}$ million people who had holidays-with-pay in 1938 grew to 12 million by 1940.[21]

In 1938, the TUC General Council proposed to the Women's Advisory Conference that the numbers of delegates attending should be determined by numbers of women members in a union, and in 1939 this was accepted. The change would make the Conferences more like Congress, where the size of unions determined the size of the delegations and their voting strengths. The main bulk of women trade unionists were still in textiles with distribution some distance behind in second place. Of the individual unions, the National Union of Tailors and Garment-Workers was now running neck and neck with the Amalgamated Weavers' Association. The women's membership of the Tailors' and Garment-Workers' Union had dropped dramatically in the early 1920s, not only because of the recession, but also because of the hostility of men to women's presence, as Andrew Conley, the General Secretary, ever sympathetic to women's organization, frankly admitted. The strength of the union was still in heavy clothing, such as the manufacture of overcoats, and men's and women's suits. The light clothing trades, the main sphere of women, were not yet well organized and 'sweating' still went on. The restoration of women's membership within these limits was something of a personal triumph for the national organizer, Anne Loughlin, small, golden-haired, blue-eyed. She did it by carrying out union instructions to establish union rates and conditions, town by town. Her arrival in a clothing town in the late 1920s was said to bring employers to a hastily convened meeting in order that they might concert opposition to expected union demands, backed by threat of strike action. The confidence she inspired among operatives in union support for improved wages and conditions brought success and success brought them into membership.

The effect of the changes in the Women's Advisory Conference constitution, therefore, left untouched the influence of these traditional strongholds of women's organization. But they opened the way to the greater influence of the large general unions and left the small, militant unions of women clerks at a disadvantage.

By 1938 the numbers of women trade union members had been restored to almost a million and a good deal of the credit for this was due to the post-First World War generation of women trade union officials. But their very success had encouraged a new generation of active women members more numerous and more confident than ever before. A growing conflict was developing between the old generation and the new, who, in the normal way of youngsters, took for granted all the things for which the post-First World War women militants had had to strive so hard, and then went on to ask for more concessions.

Signs of restlessness appeared among delegates at the very tight control exercised over the Women's Advisory Conferences, echoes of complaints in 1925-27. Delegates from some unions revived the demand that the Conference agenda be circulated beforehand, in accordance with normal procedure, to allow of amendments to proposed resolutions. This request was ignored. Also at the 1939 Conference, when Charters were in the air, Mrs E. Edgar and Miss M. Crees of the National Union of Clerks first called for a general TUC Charter for all working women. They asked the National Women's Advisory Committee to prepare a report on 'wages, working conditions and the state of organisation among women in the main industries in Britain'. They wanted this circulated to the TUC General Council and to affiliated unions 'with a view to drafting an *Industrial Women's Charter*' (author's italics). They argued that 'it would be something for the women to work for' and that it would rouse public opinion against working women's conditions and help secure men's backing for 'equal pay for similar work'. Nothing was done about it.

At the same time there were signs that the TUC General Council and National Women's Advisory Committee were beginning to reverse earlier support for policies long held to be in women's interests. They were putting rearmament and support for the government, now Conservative, before the interests of women, and, in some cases, of men union members and workers. Thus, while attention was paid by the Women's Advisory Committee to resolutions on the key issues of welfare, hours, and wages at the 1936 Conference, similar resolutions in 1938, 1939, and 1940 did not have much support from the platform. Likewise proposals for equalizing women's insurance rates in 1938 came to nothing. Complaints over inequality in married women's insurance were still made in 1940.

Again, on the question of hours, in 1936 the Women's Advisory Committee stopped its opposition at the ILO to any relaxation of protective regulations already gained on hours of work and shift-working for women. Instead they accepted the argument that such restraints might be detrimental to women's right to work.[23] In 1937, a new Factory Act laid down a 48-hour week or 9-hour day for women and young persons over sixteen, and a 44-hour week for those under sixteen. Night-work was prohibited for women and girls and only allowed for youths over sixteen. It might have been claimed as an improvement, but 17 out of the 31 sections dealing with women and young persons were devoted to permissible exceptions. Some over-time allowances extended the working-week to 54 hours and the 44-hour restriction for under-sixteens only operated from 1 July 1939.

Many thinking women trade unionists were beginning to feel that their wishes and suggestions carried little weight with the TUC General Council. The National Women's Advisory Committee seemed no longer to have the power or the will to insist on attention being paid to them. Groups of men trade unionists without great influence were similarly disregarded. Women, however, rightly felt that lack of attention was due very often to ingrained prejudice about the inferiority of their sex. The new women's emancipation movement stirred into life in the late 1930s partly because active women trade unionists were finding their suggestions disregarded. It was the situation of the 1920s and early 1930s all over again, when Ellen Wilkinson, Anne Loughlin, Florence Hancock, and the rest thumped Congress into agreeing to the Women's Advisory Conferences. The same bitterness was welling up. but with a difference. This time it was directed not only at men, but also at these veteran women trade union leaders.

The outbreak of war in September 1939 accelerated the rate of change, but altered few fundamental policies. Women militants and unions abandoned opposition to various practices. For example, the transference of women workers was accepted as a necessity. The Midlands was the main area to which they were drafted. Already by 1939 nearly a quarter of engineering workers employed on munitions there were women. By 1942 the numbers of women had risen a further 150 per cent. From May 1940, when a Coalition Government with Ernest Bevin at the Ministry of Labour took over from the Conservatives, some attention was paid to raising their pay and allowances. A settling-in grant was arranged for transferees and industrial conscripts, and pay increased, although a Scottish Organization of Women Committee deputation in 1943 found girls under twenty-one still suffered financial hardship.[24]

All restrictions on hours of work and shift-working were waived. First the Home Secretary and then the Minister of Labour, who took over administration of the Factory Acts in 1940, issued orders under the government's war emergency powers, permitting longer hours than those laid down in the 1937 Factory Act for women and young persons. But also in 1940, the Chief Inspector of Factories reported a 24 per cent increase in fatal accidents over the 1939 figure, and a 20 per cent increase in non-fatal ones. He felt that the lessons of the 1914-18 War had been forgotten, 'particularly the lesson that excessive hours mean less production, and that proper breaks and rest-days are of great importance from the production standpoint ...' The control had to be reimposed and a maximum of 60 hours per week fixed.

Dorothy Elliott reminded the 1941 National Union of General and Municipal Workers' Congress of the weeks after Dunkirk when women worked 'twelve, fourteen, or, in some cases, eighteen hours, in order to make up the weapons that had been left in France and Belgium'. While this was going on in the winter of

1940-41 some women had to travel two or even three hours each way to work, sometimes through a blitz. She endorsed the Chief Inspector's opinion that what counted was not the number of hours worked, but the quality and quantity of goods produced. Neither quantity nor quality could be kept up on 12-hour shifts, or sometimes 11½-hour non-stop stints at work with no meal-breaks. Some factories were already shortening hours. But many, including those working for the Ministry of Aircraft Production, were not.[25]

In 1941, the TUC General Council agreed to relaxation of the restrictions in all factories, not merely those producing munitions, but only for extended day-work, not for shifts. However, the London Trades Council expressed alarm at the relaxation of the Factories Act in factories where there was no trade union organization, and called a conference. The outcome was an arrangement whereby, when a factory asked for permission to operate outside the limits of the Acts, the factory inspector had to notify the London Trades Council which directed him or her to the appropriate union, whether any union organization existed in the factory or not. In this way the unions could check that employers did not contravene the limits of the permitted relaxations.[26] A similar procedure was adopted on a national scale and continued after the war. The NWAC reported to the 1942 TUC Women's Advisory Conference its recommendation that the General Council suggest that employers be asked to consider a two-shift system; thus the labour force could be further augmented by including part-time women workers.

The First World War was scarcely a generation away. Men and women trade unionists, young then but now middle-aged, remembered the effect of the inundation of substituted, unorganized female labour on union agreements. They were determined to prevent the development of a similar threat, although men made huge concessions to secure victory, by waiving apprenticeship agreements in order to speed up training. As in 1914, they were early on considering the introduction of equal pay as a protection?[27] To a greater extent manual unions began to support the campaign which was still in progress in the public services. But their support was a response to the war. They did not join the Equal-Pay Campaign Committee that covered the public services. And ultimately a code regulating women's earnings in war industries was hammered out not by unions alone, but largely thanks to Ernest Bevin's granitic determination. This May 1940 Extended Employment of Women Agreement followed at once on the formation of the new coalition. Alice Horan, one of the union officials concerned, recalled that Bevin used a procedure, since become commonplace.

Each of the three parties: employers, the all-male Amalgamated Engineering Union whose agreements were to be affected, and the T&GWU and NUGMW, the two main unions recruiting women working on munitions and war equipment, was separately closeted at the ministry. Bevin simply kept them there with his officials running between each group until, out of exhaustion if nothing else, they reached agreement.[28]

All the old problems arose over the application of equal pay. The out-and-out opposition of men to any attempt to equalize women's pay was demonstrated in negotiations over an award in the co-operatives. In December 1942, the chairman of the National Conciliation Board, which helped in settling claims with co-operatives, gave more to women than to men. Mr A. Burrows of the National Union of Distributive Workers, spokesman for all the various unions involved, wrote ruefully in *New Dawn*, his union's journal, that the men had raised an outcry, 'and we know to allay this some societies gave so-called "merit increases" to the male staffs'. The responsible officials had to stand 'a barrage of criticism'.[29]

Amy Wild, Yorkshire organizer for the National Union of Distributive and Allied Workers, told a 1943 conference of women members that 'rationing and restricted supplies of materials had so altered work processes that it had become impossible to prove that women were doing exactly the same work as men did in peace time'.[30]

Florence Hancock, National Woman Officer of the Transport and General Workers' Union, explained to the 1944 Royal Commission on Equal Pay (see page 247) that she and Dorothy Elliott, her opposite number in the National Union of General and Municipal Workers, had come across 'cases where we have found a very slight degree of supervision provided for women and where the women themselves have said that they did not require it'. But it had been imposed on them 'to get over the necessity of paying them the full rate'.[31]

But neither of these unions was as assiduous in enforcing the 'rate for the job' as the all-male Amalgamated Engineering Union. As Sir Alexander Ramsay, Director of the Engineering and Allied Employers' National Federation, explained, also to the 1944 Royal Commission on Equal Pay, most of the cases brought against employers for defaulting on equal-pay agreements 'came from the AEU and not from the unions ... primarily concerned with the employment of women', that is, the Transport and General Workers' Union and General and Municipal Workers. He explained that they arose from the AEU's desire 'to protect the position of their male members after the war — and nobody blames them'.[32]

But equally the traditional advantages to employers of a mass of cheap female labour were made clear. Sir Eric Salmon, Clerk to the London County Council, explained that girls and women solved their need for a large number of employees to perform routine work, 'One cannot have an unlimited number of chief officers in order to provide outlets. They [the women] marry and they leave and you get fluidity'[33] Sir Alexander Ramsay was just as frank. He explained that if engineering employers were required to pay adult male rates to women on the same work, 'the price of the product would go up 50 per cent or more ...' This would seriously prejudice their 'export contribution to the national income'.[34]

The ambivalence of the bulk of the unions to equal pay was summed up by two agreements, one for and one against the principle. The General Council agreed that women civilians including, of course, working women, should share equally with men in fire-watching duties. But in return it exacted from the government a pledge that women civilians should have equal compensation with men for war injuries. The government was slow in implementing this promise and the General Council rounded on it, putting out its clearest statement on the equality of men and women:

> Woman's life is at least as valuable as a man's and her physical and mental well-being are just as important ... We feel that the life of a woman should be valued at not less than that of a man ... If disfigured or disabled, her chances of marriage have considerably lessened ...[35]

The claim succeeded. The heroic tone of this statement was, however, impaired when the General Council also agreed, apparently without demur, to lower rates of pay for injured women and girls than for men and boys during retraining. Adult women were to receive about three-quarters of men's pay. But the argument that males had always to keep themselves, while females were free of such responsibility, was undermined by a lower rate of pay for girls than for boys of an age when they were likely to be still living with their parents.[36]

On the other hand, in order to encourage women to join, unions were obliged to pay attention not only to those who could be proved to have taken over men's work, but also to all substituted women, and indeed all women workers. Even where women were not paid quite as much as men whom they replaced at work, unions negotiated for them a high proportion of the men's rate, 70 per cent being quite common as compared with levels around 50 per cent before the war. Where there was no question of substitution at all, unions negotiated higher wages for them to an extent they had never known before.[37]

But a rising cost of living diminished the value of wage increases. And, in fact, the greatest proof of union interest in women's organization during the war was not in the sphere of wages, but in welfare. Prodded by women officials, unions at last recognized the needs of married women workers and mounted a great drive both for nursery education and day nurseries. The Coalition Government allocated funds to local authorities to provide these facilities. By 1944, 1,550 nursery schools had been provided and there was a similar huge extension of day nurseries.[38]

The major departure from pre-war policies and women workers' chief gain was the massive provision of factory welfare. The 1937 Factory Act went some way towards providing medical attention for women workers and better toilet and welfare facilities. But real improvements only came after May 1940 once Ernest Bevin was Minister of Labour. Then the presence of women trade unionists in the Labour Establishment and on numerous government committees showed results. For Bevin was receptive to the information they passed on. So to compensate for speed-up and pressure of work, a Rest-Breaks Advisory Committee was set up, on which Dorothy Elliott represented the TUC General Council. Rest homes were made available, partly through contributions from the United States of America, for weary war workers. By 1943 Factory Welfare for women had gone the length of hot drinks after long, cold, and wet journeys, factory canteens, and treatment by factory doctors for colds which saved them having to visit their panel doctors in their spare time.[39] At last the modest plea of the woman jute-worker in May 1889 that 'we ought to have somewhere to hang up a shawl or a waterproof, which we are compelled to wear in wet weather' was backed officially and cloakroom facilities provided. The standards now set spread into private war factories. Factory welfare officers multiplied, many of them trade unionists, drawn to the work by idealism.

In women's trade union membership as in technology, the pattern was the same as in 1914-18. The war speeded up already existing trends. Indeed it was the changing technology as much as the need to replace men who went into the forces that accounted for a sharp increase in numbers employed and in unions, as it had done during 1914-18. The proportion of women workers who became trade unionists rose 7 per cent in the two years 1941-43. Women were encouraged by their unions to take a far greater hand in union management. As if to signalize the greater importance attached by unions to women members in the war, Anne Loughlin, as the longest serving General Council member, in 1942 became TUC General Council Chairman and so President of the 1943 Congress. She is held to be the first woman to attain these offices in view of Margaret Bondfield's preference for politics in 1923-24. In recognition of her wartime work, in 1943 she also became the first trade union Dame Commander of the Order of the British Empire.

Of similar significance, the post of Chief Woman Officer in the Transport and General Workers' Union, which had lapsed on Julia Varley's retirement, was revived under the title of National Woman Officer, the first appointment naturally falling to Florence Hancock.

An increasing number of unions took women into membership from the late 1930s onwards. The small craft National Union of Scale-Makers took them in in 1938. The Ironfounding Workers' Association recruited them during the war when the numbers of women working on light castings and core-making increased. The Association took its women members with it when it merged with the National Union of Foundry Workers and the United Metal Founders' Society in 1946 to form the Amalgamated Foundry Workers' Union. The Amalgamated Engineering Union decided to enrol women from January 1943. By the end of that year it had 132,010 women members. This was the reason for a spectacular leap in the proportion of women organized in the Ministry of Labour's estimates for the compendium category of metal, engineering, and electrical trades, of 2,120.8 per cent between 1939 and 1943. These new AEU members accounted for by far the largest part of the 171,000 women trade unionists in this group. The actual numbers of organized women engineering workers must have been considerably higher since the main unions which recruited them continued to be the Transport and General Workers and National Union of General and Municipal Workers in a different ministry category.[40]

But there was a difference in the women themselves. The patriotic acceptance of lengthy shifts, night-work, and fire-watching had veiled the spirit of independence already apparent by 1939. Now it increasingly appeared among rank-and-file women, not just among militants. For example, Bevin got the agreement of a meeting of trade union executives to a National Arbitration Tribunal which would settle disputes. In effect, it made strikes illegal and this was established through a government order, 1305. Nonetheless, women occasionally stopped work in defiance of men union officials. For instance, some hundreds of women at Player's cigarette factory in Nottingham in 1943 staged a sit-down strike against the introduction of a compulsory incentive bonus scheme. Even after their union agreed to the scheme, the women still refused to operate it.

Again at the 1942 TUC Women's Advisory Conference, the National Women's Advisory Committee produced its plan for post-war readjustment. It proposed that married women be encouraged to leave work by an offer of compensation, in the form of a return of national insurance contributions. It also suggested that women who were working before the war should have priority in jobs after it was over, and that efforts should be made to raise the status of domestic service. The delegates threw the plan back at them. They felt it was backward-looking, a repetition of policies pursued after the First World War. The NWAC was obliged to send a circular to local Women's Trade Union Organizing Committees emphasizing that there was no intention of restricting the right of any woman to work, and in 1943 they issued an amended version affirming that all 'women wage-earners who have contributed to the war effort either in industry or in the services', whether they had been trans-ferred, directed, or conscripted, or had volunteered, had an equal right to employment. They also declared that 'the sex of the workers should not be a factor determining payment'.[42]

When the war ended in 1945, the conflicts evident in 1939 were more sharply apparent. The crucial change in the six years was not that more women were in unions, but the growing number who un-derstood the help that trade union organization offered in im-proving wages and working conditions. There were far more of such women trade unionists than in 1939, committed to fighting not only employers, but also the trade union Establishment, male and female, for an equal place for women within the trade union movement. The situation was not at all the same as in 1918 when women, whatever their contribution to trade unionism, were unable to claim such an equality.

Notes

1 Clegg, *General Union*, 85: Pierrotti, *Story of the Nat. Union of Women Teachers*, 21.
2 1921 TUC Rep., 69 ff.: the *Clerk*, Jour. of the NUC, list of wage agreements, July 1920, 24: 1935 Exec. Committee Rep., Assoc. of Women Clerks and Secretaries.
3 B.V. Humphreys, *Clerical Unions in the Civil Service*, 153, 182-4. A. Spoor, *White Collar Union*, 466-8.
4 LCC Staff Assoc., *Progress Report, 1909-59*, 93.
5 1942 Ann. Rep., Nat. Soc. of Pottery Workers, 4-5: TUC General Council memorandum to the 1944 Roy. Comm. on Equal Pay, App.

VII, 67, 84, pottery-workers. See also Rules of Nat. Soc. of Potters, women only achieved status of half-members in 1947.

6   1944 Roy. Comm. on Equal Pay, AEU Mins. of Evidence, sect. 14, 235-6, para. 3365, Mr Jack Tanner.

7   A. Smith, *Carpet Weaving and Trade Union Activity,* unpub. MS, Hist. of the Power Loom, Carpet and Textile Weavers' Assoc., ch. Textile Sect., 21. This Assoc. dropped its 'marriage dowry' in 1931.

8   LCC Staff Assoc., op. cit., 93.

9   Cynog Jones, 'The Regulation of Wages in the Retail Trade, 1937-57', 6-8.

10 1934 TUC Rep., 105, Resolution no. 1.

11 1935 Scot. TUC Rep., 66-70.

12 1935 TUC Rep., 247-50.

13 1935-36 Irish Women Workers' Union 19th Ann. Rep., 14-18.

14 ibid., 12-14.

15 Equal Pay Campaign Committee, *A Black Record*: Rose Grant, *Story of the Equal Pay Campaigns since 1920*: V. Douie, Summaries: Potter, *Political Studies*, vol. V., no.1, Feb. 1957.

16 *Manchester Guardian* and *The Times*, 12 Jan. 1938: *Manchester Guardian*, 19 Jan. 1938, Letter: *Times,* 28 Apr. 1938: 30 May 1938. Letter: *Daily Herald,* 29 June 1938: *Manchester Guardian*, 15 June 1938: 30 June 1938: *Daily Telegraph*, 2 July 1938: *Daily Herald*, 21 Feb. 1939.

17 Spoor, op. cit., 478-9: unpub. Reps. of the TUC Women's Advisory Conferences, 1932-36: 1937 TUC Rep., 237: TUC *Industrial Newsletter for Women*, Apr. 1955, 6.

18 TUC Reps.: 1932, 114, para. 70: 1933, 119, para 69: 1934, 105-6, Resolution no. 5: 117-118, para. 70: 1935, 99, 119: 1936, 121: 1938, 127, para. 73: 1939, 149, para. 93. The General Council's proposals for the disposal of the surplus in the Unemployment Fund were: (i) abolition of the 3-days waiting period before a person could claim benefit. (ii) all round rise in benefit. (iii) reduction in men's contributions of 1d. and rise in women's benefits so as to establish equality between men and women. (iv) alteration of the anomalies rule so that married women with a good employment record qualified for insurance.

19 TUC General Council Document 1936: Ann. Reps. of Trades Councils Federation, 1937, 21-2: 1938, 25-6: 1939, 22-3: 1937 NWAC Rep., for T&GWU resolution against transfers.

20 Cynog Jones, op. cit., 10: *Shop Assistant*, 19 Sept. 1936, 766-7: Bayliss, *British Wages Councils*, 36 ff.

21 Min. of Lab. Gaz., Aug. 1920, 421, Summary of Extension of Holidays with Pay from the 1901 Factories and Workshops Act. 1937 TUC Rep., 200-1: Bayliss, op. cit., 41: *New Dawn*, 13 Apr. 1940, quoting *Hansard*, Mr F. Brown, Min. of Labour. The right was not universally recognized even after the Second World War, viz. 1947 Hosiery Workers' Union Ann. Rep.: NUGMW *Jour.*, Jan. 1965, 22, Irish notes.

22 Stewart and Hunter, *The Needle is Threaded.* 182.

23 NUGMW *Jour.*, Aug. 1931, May 1933, Women's Dept. Notes: 1936, 1937 NWAC Reps.

24 1942 NWAC Rep., 9: Scot. TUC Reps.: 1941, 52-3, 134-6: 1942, 61-2, 189-91.
25 1941 TUC Rep., 290-1: 1941 NWAC Rep., 45: NUGMW *Jour.*, July 1941, 309-10: 1943 NWAC Rep., 1-2, para. 9, 15-16, para. 5.
26 1941 TUC NWAC Rep., 45.
27 1940 Scot. TUC Rep, 67: 1942 Scot. TUC OWC Rep., 64: 1940 TUC Rep., 247-50.
28 1944 Roy. Comm. on Equal Pay, AEU Memorandum of Evidence, App. VIII, 79, paras. 26, 27: AEU Memorandum, App. V, 83, Text of the May 1940 Extended Employment of Women Agreement, Clauses 6, 7. Despite Alice Horan's evidence, the AEU claimed that they were not a party to the preliminary discussions. TUC Memorandum of Evidence, App. VII, paras. 56, 71, 95, 109, 119, 121. 1944 NWAC Rep., App. 19-22.
29 *New Dawn*, 3 July 1943, 210, 212.
30 ibid., 13 Sept. 1941, 300.
31 1944 Roy. Comm. on Equal Pay, TUC Evidence, sect. 13, para. 3161.
32 ibid., Mins. of Evidence of British Employers' Confederation, sect. 12, para. 2711.
33 ibid., LCC Mins. of Evidence, sect. 3, paras. 718-20. County Councils Assoc. Mins. of Evidence, sect. 3, para. 838.
34 ibid., Mins. of Evidence of British Employers' Confederation, sect. 12, paras. 2694-7.
35 1941 NWAC Rep., 20, 29: on 25 Nov. 1942, an amendment was moved on the Address to the King's Speech at the opening of Parliament, as it contained no reference to Equal Compensation for Women. This resulted in the setting-up of a Select Committee. 1943 NWAC Rep., 7-8, para. (f).
36 1942 TUC Rep., 43-4, para. 52.
37 NUGMW *Jour.*, Sept. 1940, 532: June 1941, 269, 271: Dec. 1941, 547-9. 1944 Roy. Comm. on Equal Pay, AEU Memorandum, App. VIII, 77, Table III: TUC Memorandum, App. VII, 66, paras. 75-6, 142: F. Hughes, *By Hand and By Brain*, 123-4, 126, 128: *New Dawn*, 20 Nov. 1943, 383.
38 TUC Reps. 1940, 354-5: 1942, 17, paras. 78-81: 1944 NWAC Rep., 6-8.
39 1943 NWAC Rep., 14: 1944 NWAC Rep., 15-16: 1945 Scot. TUC Rep., 55, para. 11. Finance for capital development of the scheme came from the United States-British War Relief Soc., and the two big American union organizations, the AFofL and the CIO.
40 Abs. of Lab. Statistics: Census of Occupations; Min. of Labour, including not only statistics published, but unpublished statistics for the war years kindly supplied to me.
41 *Tobacco Worker*, Nov.-Dec. 1962, 10.
42 1942, 1943 NWAC Reps.

15   Women Versus the Trade Union Establishment

In 1945 a Labour government came in, not just with a majority, but with a landslide victory. The Labour movement generally was hell-bent on avoiding the miseries of insecurity and deprivation of the inter-war years. The Labour government therefore had on the whole, the utmost loyalty from the trade unions. In the next six years it built the welfare state on the basis of proposals William Beveridge made to the wartime Coalition Government. As a result working people were better-off than ever before with a comprehensive National Insurance scheme covering most of them in respect of health, welfare, and unemployment. At the same time, under the Labour government the country entered into an epoch of material welfare such as had never been known before. The situation was totally different from that of the 1920s. The usual post-war boom in replenishing goods and materials run down in the war was merely the prelude to a continuing consumer boom. Working people were partly conditioned to it by the mass media, especially commercial television which began in 1956. The media were also used to develop the new mass market. The converse of the consumer boom was full employment.

In order to make good stocks depleted in the war, and to expand exports, the Labour government embarked on a 'productivity drive', probably planned by the Coalition before the end of hostilities. To provide labour, the government kept industrial conscription for women in being for some years after the war. A far more widely publicized decision, because men were primarily affected, was its perpetuation of Order 1305 prohibiting strikes. Women laundry-workers at Stoke, members of the Distributive and Allied Workers' Union, felt the weight of the Order when in 1945, troops were sent to break their unofficial strike.[1]

In March 1945, before the war ended, Ernest Bevin as Minister of Labour set up a Committee to inquire into 'the economic need for and social consequences of double-day shift working'. Two years later the Committee duly reported in favour of two shifts per day. The three union members dissented from its findings. The government, however, disregarded them and indeed the whole TUC when the General Council tried to limit shift-working. Under

1939 Defence Regulations, which were still in force, it authorized the system. Officially it claimed that it was to spread the load of electricity consumption after the calamitous cold weather of February 1947 and to circumvent a short-term fuel crisis as a result of depleted fuel stocks. But this new Factory Order not only enabled employers to introduce shifts. It also permitted very long shifts of 12 hours including meal-breaks, or 10½ without, where a 5-day week was worked. In factories on a 4-day week, women and young persons could be employed for 12½ hours to 11 hours at a stretch while spells of work could be as long as 6 hours with only one 15-minute break. It was putting the clock back to the conditions prevalent in some of the worst enterprises before the 1937 Act. The unions acquiesced without too much fuss purely out of loyalty to the government.[2]

But something of the unions' wartime concern for women remained. In 1945 the TUC General Council persuaded the government to revoke orders of the 1930s in recognition of the contribution made by married women workers during the war. As a result they no longer had to prove they were normally employed in insurable occupations as a condition of entitlement to unemployment benefit.

By May 1947 the government was making desperate appeals for 300,000 more women to work in hospital domestic service, transport, and various industries.[3] The TUC Industrial Newsletter backed the government's appeals with proffers of all the wartime inducements to women to work: factory welfare, more day nurseries, more part-time work at convenient hours.

From 1943 to 1946 as war industry was run down, there was a drop in the proportion of working women who joined unions. Women, wearied by their efforts in the war, were only too happy to relinquish one part of the burden they had carried. Nonetheless, the euphoria created by the Labour victory of 1945 and the support given women militants in the immediate post-war years by trade union leaderships, brought a further large accession of women to the unions. Between 1946 and 1947 the number of women members in the country as a whole rose by over 100,000. The proportion of working women who were union members also rose so that by 1948 it amounted to a quarter of the total female workforce, almost as high as in 1920. (Miscalculations in the numbers of women employed at the war's end prevent any exact estimate as to the extent of the rise in their trade union density.)

Because of the growing need for skilled staff, the Coalition Government in 1944 brought in a new Education Act making secondary schooling compulsory for all up to the age of fifteen. The impact on girls was greater than on boys, because in working-class families, if there was a chance of secondary schooling which inevitably entailed some sacrifices, it almost always went to a boy, not to a girl. The comparisons working-class families made on girls' training were not with the rushed, emergency training schemes of the war, but with the scarcity of training for girls in anything other than private domestic service before the war. Domestic subjects still figured largely in the new secondary schools, but now there was also mass education in secretarial work, and further reason for increased confidence.

Yet there remained a curious block in official thinking on women's employment. The high demand for women workers in spheres other than private domestic service and 'charring' was regarded as merely temporary. The Ministry of Labour estimated in May 1947 that over half a million women would have dropped out of industrial work by 1951. Backward-looking policies still prevailed even when in 1948 the new National Social Insurance legislation required the issuing of cards to all adult workers and the ministry found that its estimate of the numbers of women actually at work was 4 million short of the real total.

So certain were government and unions of a return to pre-war employment patterns that an Institute of Houseworkers was opened in April 1947. Ernest Bevin persuaded Dorothy Elliott to give up her job as Chief Woman Officer in the National Union of General and Municipal Workers in order to run it. The Institute embodied all the ideals of domestic service advocated since the first decade of the century.[4]

At the beginning of 1948, the Labour government introduced a policy of limited pay increases, or wage freeze. The unions affiliated to the TUC voted to accept it and the post-war party was over. As far as women workers were concerned, unions followed the government in rejecting a variety of steps to improve their conditions of employment. There were, however, two overlapping groups of women militants, the old one of the 1930s narrowly committed to achieving equal pay and drawn from many societies outside the unions affiliated to Congress, and the new one, emerging just before the war, comprising women trade unionists intent not only on equal pay but on maintaining the level of union interest in women's conditions reached during the war. They would not give up, despite the obstinate refusal of unions to support them against the Labour government.

The division in the history of women's trade unionism since the Second World War is between roughly the first fifteen years, 1945-60, when the militants made little impression on the traditional male domination of unions, except for one resounding victory, and the next fifteen years when a trickle of small concessions suddenly became a flood. It has been a characteristic of post-war Britain that concomitant with the big issues for the unions, the productivity drives and strikes for higher pay that caught the headlines, there went on almost separately the struggle of women for parity in unions and for economic equality. Active women members took sides in the debates on wider issues as they had done since Emma Paterson and Edith Simcox first appeared at Congress in 1875. But their differences over these were largely forgotten when fighting for women's equality. They maintained a common front against the trade union Establishment, male and female. Although this battle received little publicity, the reality was that the new women's emancipation movement rolled on, regardless of what the mass media considered newsworthy. The mass media both reflected and perpetuated the male domination of society, until the women's movement became so powerful in the late 1960s that it could not be ignored and they had to devote space to it.

In those first barren fifteen years, when on so many matters women were losing ground, women trade unionists benefited from one great success, the grant of equal pay in the public services. The 1944 Trades Union Congress voiced the wartime claims of its affiliated unions for the 'rate for the job' for women employed on men's work. But it was the debates on the 1944 Education Act that enabled teachers to have the issue of equal pay raised once more in the House of Commons. In March 1944, the House, by a majority of one, supported their demand for the 'rate for the job' as an amendment to the Act. True to past form, division of opinion cut across party political lines. Winston Churchill, head of the Conservative-Labour-Liberal Coalition Government, blocked any further action by making a decision for equal pay for teachers tantamount to a vote of no confidence in himself. Under union pressure, however, the government had to set up a Royal Commission on Equal Pay to investigate the claims of unions and women's organizations, not just for the public services but throughout the entire range of women's work. In 1945, the new Labour government's Chancellor of the Exchequer, Hugh Dalton, deferred any decision pending the results of this Commission's findings. When these were published in 1946, the Labour government refused to implement them on the plea of economic stringency.

The Labour government's view was that by increasing purchasing power, equal pay was itself inflationary. Moreover, they claimed it would lead to demands for increased family allowances from men, who, to a greater extent than women, had family

National Union of Women Teachers' Valentine

dependants. Their attitude deeply disappointed those trade unionists who had believed in Labour pledges of support.

The Royal Commission, in its Report in 1946, recommended only that women in the 'common classes' of the public services should be paid at the same rate as men for similar work. In other spheres the majority of the Commission shared the fears of the mass of ordinary women employees that many employers 'would take the first opportunity actually to replace female by male labour'.[5] They also feared that technical and other changes in the way work was organized, which had been helping women enter new areas of industry, 'would be inhibited and checked' if women became more expensive to employ.

The three women members of the Commission, however, Miss L. F. Nettlefold, Dr Janet Vaughan, and Anne Loughlin, by then General Secretary of the National Union of Tailors and Garment-

Workers, all disagreed. Faithful to the ideas of women who were better educated and professionally successful, they insisted that equal pay should be made mandatory for all kinds of work.[6]

However, the Commission had given the green light to the public service unions. In 1946, the 1927 Trades Disputes and Trade Unions Act was repealed and a number of these unions reaffiliated to the TUC, thus regaining the platform of Congress from which to pursue their campaign.

Meanwhile the application of equal pay was spreading in the public services. London and some other County Councils and the Civil Service were now paying men and women equally in certain grades. The tide was now running with the equal-pay campaigners. In April 1946, the National Association of Local Government Officers negotiated equal pay for all higher grades nationally through the Whitley Council.[7] Public services introduced it, starting with the Metropolitan Water Board in 1946, followed by the Fire Service.

The National Women's Advisory Committee in 1946 and again in 1947 declared itself absolutely in favour of a campaign to force the Labour government to implement the Royal Commission's Report. In 1946-47, together with the Standing Joint Committee of Working Women's Organizations, it ran regional conferences in support of the campaign. Florence Hancock at the 1947 Women's Advisory Conference stated that the 1944 Congress vote for 'the rate for the job' for women employed on men's work still represented TUC policy. The TUC General Council pressed the government to give the matter some priority because of 'strong feeling among the workpeople'. They were annoyed because the proposals of the Royal Commission omitted manual workers. Fears about women replacing men in engineering and related occupations were still prevalent. Unions like the National Union of Vehicle-Builders were among the strongest supporters of the 'rate for the job' at this time.

But in 1948 the General Council and its National Women's Advisory Committee endorsed the government's 'pay freeze', which ruled out pay increases of the size necessary to raise women's rates to those of men in the same work.[8] On this as on several other issues it had become clear that the unions were no longer leading the Parliamentary Labour Party as they had in the 1930s. Since their great electoral victory in 1945, Labour politicians, with Bevin the most forceful of all trade unionists now amongst them, had reasserted control over policies. The National Women's Advisory Committee executed a complete volte-face, in compliance with the General Council's support for government economic policy. Florence Hancock as chairman of the 1948 Women's Advisory Conference lectured the delegates on the need to put national economic policy before the demands for 'equal pay'. The equal-pay campaigners were the more annoyed because she was chairman of the General Council for 1947-48 and therefore the 1948 Congress President. And Ernest Bevin added insult to injury by coming and lecturing delegates on the need for increased productivity.[9]

There is no clearer illustration of the difficulties that beset the top women trade unionists than the dual role they played over the equal pay campaign at this time. Inside Britain, they loyally upheld the Labour Party and TUC leadership, opposing the insistent demands for immediate introduction of the 'rate for the job' in public services. But in 1949 Florence Hancock and Anne Godwin, as the two women members of the TUC Women's Group, represented the British Trade Union movement at the International Labour Organization Conference at Geneva and became members of the committee that drafted the first convention advocating 'equal pay', the famous ILO Convention 100 discussed below.

In Britain their opposition as TUC General Council representatives to practical steps towards 'equal pay' did not prevent further demands from the Women's Advisory Conference delegates. In 1948 a resolution from Miss Hancock's own union, the Transport and General Workers, on recruiting women to industry recommended 'equal pay' as an incentive and demanded equal training opportunities for women. Miss D. Steele of the Birmingham Trades Council's Women's Advisory Committee remarked: '... the operation of a full socialist programme included the emancipation of women, and that remained only a slogan till Equal Pay was achieved'.

For the next two years there was confusion. In 1949, for example, the Conference passed three resolutions demanding equal pay and a fourth accepting the TUC policy of wage restraint. The crux of the argument was timing: whether equal pay was to be brought in immediately, as the white-collar unions wanted, or relegated to some vague future.

At Congress itself, however, the issue remained clear-cut. Militant women delegates in 1948 were considerably irritated by the General Council's reaffirmation of 'unequivocal support' for the principle of equal pay and proposals that it be pursued through 'all normal channels of activity', i.e., wage negotiations, while on the other hand it not only adhered to the government's 'Statement on Personal Incomes, Costs and Prices', but positively refused to extend activities in support of the 'Equal-Pay Campaign'. The 1948 Congress supported the General Council's refusal to hold 'large public meetings', in other words the regional conferences proposed by the National Women's Advisory Committee.

Miss D. E. K. Jones of the Civil Service Clerical Association stressed that now they were asking only for the phased, in place of the immediate, introduction of the 'rate for the job' in the Civil Service. But not only had this been turned down, the Chancellor of the Exchequer, now Sir Stafford Cripps, had refused even to institute a government Court of Inquiry on the 'method of the eventual introduction of equal pay' which might have been accepted as an earnest of future intentions. In the view of the unions she represented, 'the treatment that we have had from Sir Stafford Cripps and from his predecessor in office [Hugh Dalton] has been quite indistinguishable from that of any Tory Chancellor for the last 25 years'. She concluded by parodying the poet Goldsmith:

> When lovely women stoop to folly
> And find too late that men betray,
> Ah, what can soothe their melancholy
> And boost production? — Equal Pay.

But at the 1949 Congress a card vote again produced a majority, this time of 2,070,000, in favour of the General Council's policies.

In 1950, Miss B. G. Jones of the Civil Service Clerical Association led the onslaught against official policy. Mr Lincoln Evans, replying on behalf of the General Council, revealed a new factor in the arguments. At the discussions taking place in 1950 at the International Labour Conference at Geneva, the United Kingdom government's stance was that 'equal pay' had to be included in a statement on:

> The structure and development of the social services .. in considering the obligations they were to assume under the proposed regulations [i.e., an International Convention] Governments could not avoid considering also the proportion of national income which they were in a position to devote to the social services generally.

The Labour government, in company with governments of other countries, was attempting no less than the linking of wage levels to the amounts spent on the social services. This fundamentally altered the attitude of the trade union leaderships who would not accept any such precedent. However, neither would the General Council support the composite resolution's demand for the immediate introduction of equal pay in all government work. Lincoln Evans asked Congress merely to refer the resolution to the General Council.

Another card vote was taken, and this time there was an overwhelming majority of 2,123,000 in favour of immediate introduction of equal pay in the public services.[10]

The vote did a great deal more than strike a blow for the recognition of women's role as workers. It also broke trade union support for the government's wage pause. This was quite incidental as far as the equal pay faction was concerned. But it was deliberate policy on the part of some unions who also forced votes of the Congress against the loyalist General Council on the wages issue. Even in terms of equal pay, the victory did not belong wholly to the public service unions affiliated to Congress. The somewhat bitter fact was that the unions opted for this limited grant not on the principle of justice for women, but out of pure self-interest, to prevent wage negotiations being tied to cash allocations for the social services. It was also true, however, that without the equal-pay campaign the matter would not have been raised so vigorously at Congress.

Again Congress support did not commit the government to any change of policy. Their chief representative at the 1950 International Labour Conference in Geneva, Sir Guildhaume Myrddin-Evans, with the help of Mr George Isaacs, had been endeavouring to defeat the adoption of the International Labour Organization's Convention 100. The convention, so crucial for working women, not only promulgated equal pay in the sense of the 'rate for the job', but also resurrected the principle of Clause 427 of the 1919 Versailles Treaty: 'Equal Pay for Work of Equal Value'.

The Labour Party lost the election of October 1951 without having taken any cognisance of the Congress vote. It carried its determination not to yield on the 'equal pay' issue into opposition. Its 1953 programme, *Challenge to Britain*, contained no reference to equal pay: it was said to have been omitted by 'inadvertence'.[11] The Women's Group on the Labour Party National Executive Committee saw that the omission was rectified. By then the party was lagging behind actual practice in the public services and its intransigence seemed all the stranger.

Ultimately the key factor in the introduction of equal pay in the public services was the state of the labour market, the huge increase in the demand for white-collar workers so that the public services were having to compete with private firms for adequately trained staff. Local authorities were the first to give further ground. It was on a Labour-controlled body that the great breakthrough came. In 1952 the London County Council introduced equal pay for all women in its 'common classes', including teachers, to operate immediately and completely. The other local authorities on the National Joint Industrial Council adopted this in principle in 1953.

The following year they gave equal increases to women and men staff and agreed to its phased introduction in 1955. The LCC had not, however, accorded equality in earnings with men to the ever increasing number of women manual staff. Typing and machine-operator personnel were ignored in spite of the LCC Staff Association's formidable President, the petite Miss Pat Knox, and her colleagues.

The Conservative government which took office in October 1951 was at first also deaf to pressure for the introduction of equal pay. But Charles Pannell, a Labour MP, introduced a motion into the House of Commons for equal pay in the public services to coincide with increased campaigning by the staff side of the National Whitley Council for the Civil Service. His motion was successful. The government agreed to introduce equal pay in the 'common classes' as soon as it could 'without serious prejudice to the national and economic recovery'. The reasons for this decision must remain speculative. But, as well as the desire to secure enough well-qualified women staff for the Civil Service, which had expanded enormously partly because of post-war social legislation, the Conservatives are said to have been concerned to secure the women's vote at the 1955 General Election.

Their intentions were shown to be serious when R. A. Butler became the first Chancellor of the Exchequer to receive a deputation from the Equal Pay Campaign Committee, exclusively made up of women trade unionists, one each from the National Union of Women Teachers, the National Association of Local Government Officers, and the National Association of Women Civil Servants, along with one representative of professional women. Hitherto women civil servants had only been able to discuss the matter with secretaries of the Treasury. When the grant was made in 1954, he also showed more generosity than the staff side of the National Whitley Council for the Civil Service expected. They had asked for phased introduction over 12 years in the Post Office and 18 years in the rest of the Civil Service. He phased it over six years so that equality was to be reached in 1961. Similar arrangements were made for teachers and the administrative departments of local authorities.[12]

The Civil Service Clerical Association succeeded where the LCC Staff Association failed. It established a 'notional' male rate for the all-female typing and machine-operator grades to raise their pay to what they argued men would have been earning had they been doing similar work.[13] Nurses were also included and in 1956 the arrangements were extended to women in government-controlled public enterprises of gas, electricity, and the Health Service.

Civil and Local Government Union members with banner, Millbank, 1954

The successful campaign for equal pay in the public services disposes of any notion that economic equality for women was a cause particularly espoused by left-wing unions or left-wing trade unionists. Just as in the late nineteenth century some of the most left-wing trade unionists would not accept women's right to work, so in the mid-twentieth century, unions with a tradition of militancy like the Electrical Trades Union, the Amalgamated Engineering Union, the National Union of Railwaymen, or the National Union of Mineworkers, were not among the protagonists of the 'rate for the job' once the war was over and their men members felt less threatened. At the Trades Union Congress in the late 1940s and early 'fifties, the battle was fought and won by sedate organizations like the National Association of Local Government Officers and the Civil Service Clerical Association. Outside Congress they were joined by the National Union of Teachers, still not affiliated to the TUC.

This signal victory did not alter the general hard line towards women in unions. In the executives of the National Association of Local Government Officers and Civil Service Clerical Association women remained a small minority. On the other hand, NALGO's campaign was not requited by a rise in the proportion of its members who were women, while in teaching the proportion of women who joined unions positively declined. What equal pay in the public services did establish was that in a solid block of white-collar work, women now had nominal parity with men.

But the wider group of women militants, enlarged by manual workers and encouraged to be active during the war, failed to move their own unions, Congress, or the government on any other issue, save one small one. Their irritation at being kept in leading strings at the Advisory Conferences erupted in a major row in 1947. The General Council made no mention of this episode in its 1947 Report. So Mr George Elvin, General Secretary of the Association of Cine-Technicians, challenged the Council on behalf of his union's delegates to the Conference at the 1947 Congress. Anne Loughlin replied astonishingly that there had been no time for the National Women's Advisory Committee to inform the General Council about it in the six months that intervened between the Women's Advisory Conference in April and the Congress in September.[14] But a General Secretary, albeit of a small, new union, had spoken for the rebels. The General Council would not democratize the arrangements over Standing Orders as they wanted, but did agree to have motions circulated in time to allow of amendments. An internal procedural matter like this could not adversely affect the Labour government. So it is difficult to understand the General Council's obstinacy other than as part of a general rigidity in face of all demands that were faintly progressive.

Once the unions had accepted the Labour government's pay freeze and austerity, the NWAC switched just as abruptly in deference to government policy, as it had over equal pay, from support to opposition over the provision of day nurseries, over married women's insurance, factory welfare, and hours of work and shift-work. Not only day nurseries but also nursery schools were closed wholesale after the war, in spite of protests from small unions like the Tobacco and Hosiery Workers. Even in face of the shortage of women workers there was little pressure on government from unions to keep them open. The 1944 Education Act did not make nursery education mandatory on local authorities.[15] The Labour government's policy was to keep day nurseries open only in areas where their 'productivity drive' required large numbers of married women to work. Anne Godwin at the 1953 Trades Union Congress summed up the prevailing trade union view: 'I do not think this Movement has ever accepted an obligation to maintain the children of those (mothers) who do go out to work'.[16]

Beneath trade union opposition to increased provision of day nurseries and nursery schools was the fact that many active trade unionists were also local councillors who did not want to arouse the hostility of ratepayers by increasing rates to provide funds for this purpose. As a male member of the Draughtsmen's and Allied Technicians' Association said: 'It is a very expensive way of providing labour'. Their view was that employers who wanted to employ married women should also provide facilities for the care of their children, but they applied little pressure for these.

The trade union Establishment, male and female, remained in- different on the important subject of married women's insurance. The National Women's Advisory Committee protested in 1946 that married women would be worse off under the new Beveridge proposals for national insurance than under the old regulations of the 1930s. A married woman opting to pay the full contribution would not get anything like the same amounts in benefits as single women or men.[17] But they soon came round to accepting that lower benefits for married women were justified because they did not normally have to pay rent, and because their incidence of sickness was higher than that of single women. Above all, they, like the Beveridge Committee, believed that lower unemployment benefits were balanced by an entitlement to maintenance grants during and after confinement. No account was taken of those women who had no children, nor of the numbers of years of paid employment of each individual. The National Women's Advisory Committee assumed, on no known evidence, that any increase in married women's contributions would have to be met by increased contributions from women alone, thereby raising the bogy of dissension between married and single women.[18] The change from Labour to Conservative government in 1951 brought no corresponding alteration in unions' outlook on married women's social insurance. In 1956 the matter was still being raised at the TUC Women's Advisory Conference. Meanwhile, most married women workers chose to be insured for industrial injuries only, relinquishing the chance of unemployment and sickness benefit. They virtually opted out of the scheme since the payment of full benefits was so disadvantageous to them. Possibly this was what the Labour government hoped they would do.

In the sphere of welfare the Rest-break Homes for women were allowed to close. It was said there was no demand for them.[20] Yet the demand for beds in the Mary Macarthur Home was so great that a second home was opened in March 1948 at Poulton-le-Fylde near Blackpool. The larger unions began to create their own rest- homes for women members and the demand for the women's wing at Manor House Hospital was revived.[21]

With a similar disregard for women's interests unions accepted 'speed-up' after the Second World War and 'speed-up' contributed to an increasing accident rate, which became a major pre-occupation of women trade unionists. Accidents were often the women's fault. For instance, they would not always wear caps provided for them in textile-mills, so that long hair was still caught in machines and they were scalped, a common injury before and during the Second World War. But the Reports of the Chief Inspector of Factories did not blame women's negligence. He placed the responsibility, as he had done in the war, squarely on the increasing speed of work expected from workers in mass production. In 1951 Women's Advisory Conference delegates were protesting because for the first time since 1893 there were no women factory inspectors.[22]

After the 1948 wage freeze, working people had more reason to accept shifts and overtime to make up for earnings which lagged behind a rising cost of living. Men eagerly sought overtime which prolonged existing shifts and for which they were paid at much higher rates than during normal working-hours. Their views on this were diametrically opposed to those of women. The average woman after her paid day's work had much work to do in her home, whereas the average man had little. Men trade unionists, however, expected their unions to arrange overtime agreements where possible to make up their wages. Where women carried on processes essential for their own work, the men compelled them to work overtime too by means of negotiated agreements. Their interests in this respect were much more nearly related to those of employers than to the requirements of women workers.[23]

After the Second World War, there was no fundamental change in union attitudes to women members as there had been in 1914-18. Then women had been brought into the TUC General Council, and into many unions for the first time, a very considerable advance. From 1945 the unions which still excluded women from membership, one by one accepted them. But ideas on how they were to be treated had not progressed.[24] In many unions they were still not accorded equality of membership. For example, the AEU and the Foundry-Workers set up special women's sections. A special AEU Women's Advisory Conference elected three women who attended the annual conference of their top policy-making body, the National Committee, but in an advisory capacity only. The Foundry-Workers did little to encourage them to do union work. In 1945 the Electrical Trades Union put the clock back by removing all women from its 'mixed' auxiliary section, where they had been since 1916, to a women's section set up during the war for 'dilutees'. In the Wood-Workers' Society, which admitted women in 1952, they did not qualify for union office.

Neither women nor men labourers could join the privileged Jacquard Section of the Power-Loom Carpet-Weavers' and Textile-Workers' Association. Women were restricted to working in the textile section of the trade in England, except during the Second World War, although in one Scottish factory they worked the broad Jacquard looms.

The Tobacco-Workers' Union, which terminated its special women's section in 1947, tried to keep them in repetitive processes. There was trouble in the Northern District of the National Union of General and Municipal Workers just after the war because work in light industry was being provided for women and the men wanted investment in heavier industry, which would provide them with jobs.[25] Men in Southampton solved a similar problem by simply taking over women's jobs. The textile unions of Overlookers and Tenters claimed women had not the strength to lift the heavy beams holding the warp threads on looms, although women did this work during the war. Nor were they allowed to attend to any faults on a loom. Miss Alice Foley of the Bolton and District Weavers' and Winders' Association observed that she had known cases of girls 'clouted for having spanners in their hands' with the intention of servicing their looms, and so in breach of union demarcation agreements.

The National Union of Mineworkers, as the old Federation was called after nationalization, persuaded the National Coal Board gradually in the 1950s to implement its longstanding policy of excluding women from 'screening' coal of impurities at the pithead, in order to provide work for disabled miners. It was claimed this was necessary when there was no redundancy provision. The women went reluctantly to work in the pit canteens or as cleaners, or were pensioned off on the same terms as men.

Along with some of the small-metal unions, the Mineworkers still retained the rule that benefits were available for the illegitimate children of full men members but not for half-members, that is, women and boys. Even unions like the Association of Cinematograph and Television Technicians, which considered it treated women equally, did not have a funeral benefit entitlement for the spouse of a woman member as it did in the case of a man.

Not all unions sent delegates to the Women's Advisory Conferences. The numbers of women in delegations to the Trades Union Congress and those reaching the executives of their unions continued to be disproportionately small when compared with their numbers in the total union memberships.

The difficulties in the way of women attending union branch meetings if anything multiplied. Unions timed meetings to suit men. They did not, for instance, when fixing meetings for Sunday mornings, take into account the fact that women generally cooked the main meal of the week, the ritual Sunday lunch. In the north-east of England, Saturday mornings were no use because traditionally women did their washing on Fridays and ironed on Saturdays. Evening meetings did not bring a good attendance from women since they carried the burden of domestic work. The best times seem to have been Saturday afternoons when men were at football matches or other sporting events, or straight after work or at lunchtimes. But segregated meetings were not conducive to extending men's appreciation of women members' point of view. And in any case there were difficulties about these times. Where women were on piece-work, especially if they worked part-time, for example in the clothing trades, they would not stop, or barely stopped, for lunch. Even when working full-time on a time basis, they traded their lunch-hours in exchange for a working-day that stopped earlier. Lunchbreaks might be cut to half an hour or less. Employers, who supplied special bus services to transport their workpeople to their homes, also put paid to factory-gate meetings.

Some trade unionists contended that shorter hours of work gave women more time to attend meetings. They found time and energy to go to entertainments, including the growing craze of Bingo, by the later 1950s. Not only women were affected, however. The family car and the spread of television also adversely affected men's attendance at union branch meetings.[26]

The effect of consumerism on working people was to make them more acquisitive, so that they progressed from buying real necessities and labour-saving devices for their homes to purchasing inessentials and to the middle-class fashion of 'keeping up with the Joneses'. The common pressures which had previously united them, more strongly than differences of politics or sex had divided them, were considerably reduced. As they became increasingly more comfortable individually, they also became more self-centred and society generally was more atomized.

At the same time, bigger unions were increasingly run as businesses with highly qualified staffs, less concerned with ideals than with a high membership. As a result, there had been a marked decline in numbers of women on the workers' sides of Wages Councils. The frustrations caused by exclusion from official union posts were more deeply felt because of the increased number of women in official positions in smaller unions, assistant secretaries

like Miss K. Edwards of the Civil Service Union, Alice Foley of the Bolton Weavers and Winders, and Mrs Joan Mineau of the National Union of Bank Employees.

In 1951, Mrs Margaret Mackay succeeded Nancy Adam as secretary of the National Women's Advisory Committee. There were many who thought the choice unfortunate. For where Nancy Adam was old-fashioned womanly, Margaret Mackay tended to an ostentatious femininity when what was needed was an unyielding intellectual capacity to argue for women's interests which would exact respect from male colleagues. The General Council control strengthened. More resolutions at the Women's Advisory Conferences were opposed by the platform or referred to the NWAC without an outright decision being taken, despite angry outbursts from delegates. The number of General Council members on the Conference platform rose from five in 1951 to nine in 1956, nearly twice as many as the five elected members of the National Women's Advisory Committee. In 1956, only five of the resolutions sent in by unions were adopted.[27]

The wartime gains had given conclusive proof of the decisiveness of union attitudes in determining the levels of both women's membership and their interest in their organizations. Yet in 1953-54 the National Women's Advisory Committee was moved to undertake

1 Joan Mineau
  addressing meeting
2 Alice Foley
3 Hilda Unsworth
4 Lil Grotier
5 Sister E. McKaig
6 Miss K.L. Edwards
7 Edith Sutton
8 Margaret Fenwick
9 Helen Liddell
10 Elizabeth McIntyre

yet another survey of unions to find out why women remained so indifferent to trade unionism. They duly reported the reasons, all the same as they had been in the other surveys since 1923, but gave little stress to the indifference of men members to women. Some of the delegates were indignant. Mrs L. Green of the Electrical Trades Union remarked in 1955: 'The men just turned aside any circular and said, "The women of our branch will not be interested in that" '.

There was current evidence that attention to women's likes and dislikes brought improved attendance at branch meetings. A pleasant hotel room where tea and biscuits were served produced better results than the pub or some Spartan public hall. A good attendance of women was commonest among white-collar workers, but such instances were still few.

In the mid-1950s the National Union of Bank Employees made a real drive to recruit women and girls and branched out in a major effort to win women's interest. In co-operation with the London Trades Council, it mounted a fashion show. Mrs Adams, chairman of the London Trades Council Women's Committee, explained to the 1955 Women's Advisory Conference that they

> had enlightened the men and told them they must organise in a different manner to what had been done in the past. If one went to a football match on Saturday afternoon in the winter time there were thousands of men, quite a number of whom were trade unionists and they were doing things men like to do and seeing things men like to see. No one suggested that they were any worse trade unionists because of that.

The female membership of the banking and insurance group of unions went up 114.7 per cent at this time. But when the same approach was used by Birmingham and Sheffield Trades Councils, it brought increased membership but not much growth in interest in unions. Anything that helped to increase the proportion of women coming into unions, however, should have been welcome because the new conditions of employment were certainly not making recruitment easier. It was not until after Labour lost the 1951 General Election that the real impact of the new consumer society was felt. In 1951 there were still well over 750,000 women in domestic service in Great Britain. During the following decade the number dwindled to less than 200,000. By 1955, as the shortage of hospital domestic workers became acute, a new source of cheap labour was brought in. In 1955, the first pilot party of girls arrived from Barbados to be trained in this work at the Institute of Domestic Workers.

With the decline in domestic service, conditions for recruiting women to unions should have eased.[28] The women moved mainly into distribution and clerical work, in which there was a vast increase. After 1948 the expansion of social services and the nationalization of coal, gas, and electricity entailed a huge growth in clerical employment in the public services. In the same way as after the First World War, men who had left shop-work tried to avoid going back. They were replaced by women. By 1951 in Britain about 14.54 per cent of all women workers were in distribution and 17.38 per cent in clerical work. In the next ten years, clerical work replaced domestic service as the largest single women's occupation, with distribution in second place. The expansion of these forms of work for women considerably blurred the rigid class hierarchy, the 'upstairs and downstairs' mentality of pre-war Britain. Women and girls enjoyed an independence quite impossible for a private indoor domestic servant and earned much better wages.

However, both the new major women's occupations, distribution and clerical work, were afflicted by the same problem as domestic service, though to a lesser degree. Workers were isolated in small shops and offices, often family enterprises, and they remained closely supervised.

There was also a vast growth of fee-paying employment agencies for nursing, clerical, and domestic staff especially. These agencies replaced unions in so far as they raised wages in order to increase their own commission fees and again made unions seem less necessary. The domestic service agencies preferred to employ men, a further reason for the decline of this old branch of 'women's work'. There were resolutions at union conferences and at Congresses asking for measures to check the growth of agencies. But nothing was done.[29]

The decline in numbers of men and women employed in the textile trades also continued, after a brief post-war recovery, because of increasing mechanization, 'speed-up', and mill closures. Protests, especially by the women, were in vain. The 'more looms' innovation of 1932 developed so that by the 1960s, on simple fabrics like bandages, women weavers in Burnley were 'minding' ninety-six looms each, or, on quality fabrics in Bolton, thirty looms. In spinning, much heavier loads were being lifted and fed into machines. The process was sometimes mechanized as in Stockport, but not in Rochdale, for example. Women spinners in any case described the pace of the work as 'killing'. In spinning these changes in methods followed on the Report of the Evershed Commission in 1945 which supported the prior right of men and boys to work. It stated that the employment of women had led to low wages and some confusion over skilled and unskilled functions. Incidentally, it revealed the same thinking as had incensed women when the threat of fascism loomed in the 1930s.[30]

Technical changes and shift-work had an adverse effect on women's trade union activity. Thus the composition of the Rossendale Weavers' Association Committee, for example, altered after the introduction of night-shifts from sixteen women and eight men to a majority of men. Similarly, women disappeared from the Accrington Weavers' Committee. Women spinners from the Card, Blowing-, and Ring-Room Operatives, said there were no women on branch committees in north-east Lancashire partly because of the increased capacity of machines and the greater weights operatives had to lift, and also because with shift-working, men were ousting women from the trade.

Much of the new work for women was low-paid and low-graded and presented unions and employers with the problem of labour turnover. Since more women than men were engaged in such work, they were the more affected. The unions' acceptance that women should largely staff these grades rebounded in the difficulties created over women's recruitment. But instead of equating these with the kind and conditions of the work itself, since men in these grades also displayed a low interest in unions, union officials tended to equate it with women. The high labour turnover of the post-war years bore out Mary Macarthur's dictum of the connection between low pay and a poor level of trade union organization. Low status in unions and low pay were also linked.

In addition, the high demand for women staff for dead-end repetitive jobs enabled the women to compensate for boredom at work by leaving for a job in a different sort of establishment. This was illustrated in the case of factory farming of poultry. At Perth in Scotland older married women pierced the throats of the birds to kill them as they came into the processing sheds hanging upside down on conveyor-belts. There was little choice of work for them and they stayed on in this unpleasant, repetitive job. In the East Midlands, however, the work was done by girls and there were plenty of alternative jobs. As a result, the Transport and General Workers' Union had to deal with high labour turnover.

For union organizers there was the constant, grinding effort to enrol, even in well-organized enterprises, because new staff were constantly coming in to replace those who left and lapsed out of membership. This in turn led unions wherever possible to arrange with employers that union dues be deducted from pay packets of employees who were members. But this rendered the union more remote, and linked it more closely with work and employers, so diminishing members' interest. Collecting had been a job very often undertaken by women because the small gratuities paid by unions for such work were a help for those with low wages.

Unions, by co-operating with employers in keeping girls in dead-end, low-paid jobs, by flying in the face of facts about married women workers, merely set up a treadmill for themselves. Girls still daydreamed through their routine days, seeing their work as no more than a hiatus between school and marriage, and the unions did not disabuse them because it was a time-honoured method of reserving promotion chances for men. But girls felt loyalty neither to employer nor to unions and slipped in and out of jobs, finding interest and variety that way instead of in the jobs themselves. It was increasingly easy for them to do this as the demand for workers of all kinds grew.

But perhaps too much was made of pay and grading as barriers to women's organization. During and just after the war, when the proportion of women in unions was rising, many had been employed on dead-end repetitive work. The women bookbinders had shown three-quarters of a century earlier that lower-graded workers could organize more strongly than the skilled. These were pointers to the crucial effect of the attitude of men trade unionists.

The effect of Labour's full-employment policy was to provide more work and high earnings for the young. Marriages consequently took place at an increasingly early age until they became common among couples in their late 'teens. Along with special hours to coax married women to work, over an ever greater part of the country where labour was in short supply, this younger marriage contributed to a growth in the numbers of married women in the workforce. How many women trade unionists were married at any given time is not known. But clearly, from the late 1940s in peacetime, as in the crisis of war, potential trade unionists included high numbers of married women.

Not only were their special problems, like day nurseries or insurance, given a low priority, some unions also agreed to the reimposition of the 'marriage bar' after the war. The Union of Post Office Workers continued to operate it among their own employees until 1963. In government and local government service, married women brought in during the war were retained in lower-graded clerical work with 'temporary' status.

At the same time, some unions still retained 'marriage dowries' in the expectation that women would retire from work on marriage. Trade unionists often expected that married women ought to be the first to leave their jobs when people were 'stood off' or sacked. For them the normal union rule — 'last in, first out' — did not apply. In 1966, Alice Foley, summing up union attitudes to married women workers, remarked: 'You would expect to have them on hooks to put them off and on as required'.[31]

The one concession made to married women was the 'twilight' or 'housewives' shift' inaugurated on 13 November 1950. Not greed, as trade union officials often asserted, but rather need brought them into part-time jobs. Before the war they had done 'charring', or become washerwomen or home-workers. Naturally now they took chances of better-paid or less arduous work. They slipped in and out of jobs if family illness required their temporary presence at home. They naturally wanted labour-saving devices flooding into the market which mechanized domestic work in their homes and made their lives easier. The working class wanted to take holidays abroad. Yet men union officials often wrote part-timers off as 'pin-money wives'. For most of them were married women and they vastly increased the problem of labour turnover. By 1958 the Ministry of Labour estimated that 11.8 per cent of the female labour force worked less than 30 hours a week. The England and Wales census for 1961 showed nearly 1¾ million part-time workers, about 20 per cent of them in government departments, where they made up the increased numbers of staff the new social legislation required. For example, the Treasury found it cheaper to employ them than to raise the pay and the numbers of full-time staff. Some Civil Service departments, for instance the Passport Office dealing with the greatly increased numbers of people holidaying abroad, became dependent on them.

Their attraction to employers was their cheapness. They were denied fringe benefits. Employers obviously preferred married women who opted to pay only Industrial Injuries insurance and saved them from paying the full contribution rate. There were also not uncommonly tacit compacts between employers and employees to conceal the fact of the women's work. The employer was absolved from paying social insurance and women gained not only a similar exemption, but also did not have to pay income tax. The demand for part-time work increased so that, by the 1960s, there was strong competition for such jobs, and various dodges to secure it. For instance women starting work mid-week would pretend they had worked elsewhere at the beginning of the week in order to ensure that employers did not feel burdened with paying their insurance contributions.

There were, however, other reasons besides those of convenience and a need for gainful employment that impelled married women to work. Few men, and indeed not all women trade unionists, appreciated their desire for economic independence, which prompted one married woman worker to explain to Eleanor Stewart in the 1930s that she wanted to work, 'because I have the turn of the money'. Or as a government office-cleaner said in the mid-1960s, 'I don't want to have to go to my husband every time I need a new pair of shoes'. Far less did they understand the joy that women, like men, found in using their skills at work, expressed by a 70-year-old woman weaver: 'I could fair eat my looms'.

Union attitudes towards part-timers remained dog-in-the-manger. The Civil Service Clerical Association resented the use of part-time labour to cut labour costs. Helene Walker of the Clerical and Administrative Workers' Union said she had a battle to persuade the men members that the union ought to negotiate a fortnight's paid holiday for them on a pro rata basis. The Union of Shop, Distributive, and Allied Workers excluded those members who worked part-time from all but industrial union benefits. Union officials complained of part-timers' indifference to organization. Yet Lily Kettell of the National Union of Hosiery Workers, a winner of the TUC gold medal for recruitment, and Miss E. McKaig of the AEU found no difficulty in recruiting them. As ever, the decisive factor was the attitude of the leading trade unionists. Alice Horan declared that if these women were 'treated like industrial auxiliaries or second-class citizens, they would continue to behave as such'.[32]

The women who fought their way through union elections at this time had a harder time even than their counterparts between the wars. There were no 'goddesses' now. They had to stand on their merits alongside men. The considerable gains for women in living standards and in a wider range of work were marred by unions' indifference or sometimes downright animosity. The consumerism and materialism that grew in the 1950s not only disintegrated what was left of the old unity, it encouraged the inexorable use by the stronger of their greater bargaining power at the expense of the weaker. Older men and women trade unionists, disturbed at the trend, felt that 'the Trade Union Movement was losing its soul'.

A determination to hang on to their new higher living standards brought the unions to co-operate with the Conservative government of this decade almost as much as they had with Labour between 1945 and 1951. This was the ultimate result of the decision to collaborate with employers made after the General Strike. Yet fundamentally the social, economic, and political system of Britain had not altered. Labour struggles never ceased; they merely diminished and any recession caused them to flare up. There was, however, one important exception to this general picture. The entry of women on a mass scale into new kinds of work and the change in their attitudes towards unions, which was maturing, in a few years time were radically to alter the Labour movement.

Notes

1 *New Dawn*, 27 Jan. 1945, 29 Feb., 15 June, 7 Sept., 21 Sept. 1946: 1945 Union of Shop. Distributive and Allied Workers Ann. Delegate Meeting, 17.
2 1948 Scot. TUC Rep., 77, para. 9. The majority Report expressed the view that machinery and plant were becoming more expensive and tended to become out-of-date more quickly. Extended hours would enable employers to get more back on their capital outlay. Min. of Lab. Gaz., Nov. 1947, 370-1: 1946 NWAC Rep., acceptance of the two-shift system other than for under-eighteens.
3 Min. of Lab. Gaz., June 1947, 183: Nov. 1947, 370-1.
4 NWAC Reps.; 1943, 19, App. I: 1945, 38-9: 1946, 21-2, 38-9: 1944 Scot. OWC Rep., 52-5, 63-4: TUC Memorandum to the Minister of Labour on the 'Post-war Position of the Domestic Worker'.
5 Rep. of the Roy. Comm. on Equal Pay, 1944-46, 157, para. 480: the TUC General Council upheld this view: Mins. of Evidence, sect. 13, 217, para. 3062, Mr George Woodcock, then Head of the TUC Research Dept., as did the employers, viz. Mins. of Evidence of the British Employers' Confederation, 204, para. 2858.
6 ibid., pp. 193-4 of the Rep.: also Dorothy Elliott, TUC Mins. of Evidence, sect. 13, 217-18, paras. 3066-9.
7 By this time in both the Civil Service and the London County Council, girl clerical workers, aged 16-21 years, had equal pay and the LCC and County Councils Assoc. paid equally at the top of their salary scales, while five provincial councils had introduced equality in some measure. See Rep. of Roy. Comm. on Equal Pay, sect. 3, paras. 682-5, and p. 51, Table B, Groups I and VII, evidence of LCC. It had raised the rates for all women on men's work from four-fifths to five-sixths of the men's earnings. County Councils' Assoc. statement, sect. 3, 59, para. (b): 62, para. 795. Hughes, *By Hand and By Brain*, 127, the Manchester City Council voted for equal pay for its employees in 1944. In April 1945, the Nat. Assoc. of Local Government Officers persuaded the new National Whitley Council to pay equally in the higher grades: Spoor, *White Collar Union*, 470: Roy. Comm. Rep., NALGO Mins. of Evidence, sect. 4, 69, paras. 9-10.
8 The TUC General Council recommended qualified approval of the Government White Paper, *Prices, Incomes and Economic Policy*, and this was endorsed at a Conference of Union Executives, in March 1948.
9 1947 NWAC Rep., 24-5, policy of support for equal pay: 1948 NWAC Rep., 1-4, F. Hancock and E. Bevin: but T&GWU Resolution in support of equal pay, 33-5: 1947 TUC Rep., 537-9: 1948 TUC Rep., 465-6: 1950 NWAC Rep. for Anne Godwin (General Council) on 'the duty of every woman trade unionist': *New Dawn*, 26 June 1948, 298 for suggestion of taking to suffragette methods.

10   1950 TUC Rep., 454-8.

11   Potter, *Political Studies*, vol. V, Feb. 1957.

12   The armed services and the police were excluded from the grant of equal pay on the grounds that women's work was lighter than that of men. Policewomen got 90 per cent of the men's rate.

13   E. Phelps Brown, *A Course in Applied Economics*, 155.

14   1946 NWAC Rep., 43-4: 1947 NWAC Rep., 7-8, 36-7: 1947 TUC Rep., 342-3.

15   Until the 1944 Education Act, local authorities were allowed to provide nursery education, but not compelled to do so. Clause 8 (a) of this Act made it obligatory for them to provide for pupils under 5 years of age. But this part of the Act has never been universally implemented. For the switch in TUC General Council policy see TUC Reps.: 1946, 168, para. 233: 1947, 343, 413-15. NWAC Rep.: 1947, 12-14.

16   1953 TUC Rep., 370-1.

17   TUC Reps.: 1941, 110, para. 47: 1942, 36, paras. 36, 48: 1945, 53, para. 61: 1946, 72, para. 92. 1946 NWAC Rep., 15-16, para. 6. Under NWAC pressure, the TUC General Council successfully persuaded the government to iron out one small anomaly.

18   1949 NWAC Rep., 41-2, Resolution no. 8: 1950 NWAC Rep., 3, sect. 5(a), 27 Resolution no. 1, which was an implicit criticism of the NWAC Rep. The majority of delegates to the 1949 Conference supported the NWAC and General Council. In 1951 the TUC Soc. Insurance and Industrial Welfare Committee refused support for a Women's Advisory Conference decision to equalize married women's benefits.

19   1956 NWAC Rep., 30, Resolution no. 11 and amendment: 1957 NWAC Rep., 2, sect. 7.

20   1943 NWAC Rep., 15, para. 14, the NWAC stated its dislike of special health measures for women. 1947 NWAC Rep., 17, para. (d): Scot. TUC Rep., 1948, 50: 1956 Scot TUC Women's Advisory Committee Rep. The Organization of Women Committee was renamed after the war.

21   1946 NWAC Rep., 21, para. 11.

22   Between 1952 and 1960-61 the incidence of accidents among women rose. Large numbers were unreported. Annual Reps. of the Chief Inspector of Factories: 1961, 14: 1964, 24-5. Miss Sutton, National Officer of the Nat. Union of Tailors and Garment Workers stated that women only reported to the union accidents which were serious and this accounted for the high amounts of compensation which the union obtained for them, in comparison with those for men. Details of compensation cases are given in the union's journal.

23   e.g., in 1961 'voluntary' overtime was made a condition of employment in a tobacco trade agreement.

24   In 1968 a study of the Rule Books of 97 unions revealed that in 33 women paid the same dues and received the same benefits as men. In USDAW, T&GWU, and the Soc. of Graphical and Allied Trades, which had amalgamated with other unions, dues and benefits were the same in some sections but not in others because the rules of the unions taken over were kept in being. In some the difference might be small, e.g., in

the Association of Cinematograph and Television Technicians.
In 25 unions women's benefits were roughly proportionate to their
lower dues. In 14, including some important organizations, women
received benefits proportionately lower than the dues they paid in.
But in 25 unions, again including some important organizations, they
received benefits higher than the dues they paid, i.e., for instance,
women's union subscriptions might be half those of men, but
strike and lock-out pay might be at three-quarters of the men's rate.
In 19 unions women had some choice as to scales of dues and
benefits. In 21 unions membership grades were determined by the
kind of work done; 9 unions made special provision to ensure
women's representation, rights to hold office and to vote. In 7
unions these rights were limited.

25 NUGMW *Jour.*, May 1944, 139: July 1946, 230.

26 These findings emerged from a survey of 46 of the most important
trade unions.

27 In 1947 the NWAC told the Women's Advisory Conference of efforts to
revive the Trades Council Women's Committees. By 1949, 48 out of a
possible 500 were functioning, see 1949 NWAC Rep., 6-7: by 1963 there
were only 6. NWAC Reps.: 1949, 44: 1954, 35, debate on Motion 7:
1955, 32-3, 39-40. Proposals for regional conferences on women's
recruitment such as were run pre-war, were turned down. The
roneoed Industrial Newsletter for Women which delegates continually
asked should be properly printed and circulated was discontinued, 1963
NWAC Rep., 52-3.

28 The close supervision by employers in domestic service was
diminishing. The new service flats concentrated workers. The local
authority Home Help service inaugurated by the 1918 Maternity and
Child Welfare Act and the 1946 Public Health Act expanded. They
were covered by the Local Authorities' Manual Joint Industrial Council
so that unions could negotiate for them.

29 Specialized employment exchanges were proposed to combat these,
Hotel Review, Nov. 1930. 1955 TUC Rep., 322-5, Helene Walker, CAWU.
1968 NWAC Rep., 10-11.

30 I am indebted for being permitted to see the MS *History of the
Amalgamated Weavers' Association* by Edwin Hopwood. Ch. IX, 147-52 gave
details of 'speed up'. Officials and members of local unions provided
much additional information. See Min. of Lab. Gaz., Dec. 1945, 220 for
summary of the Evershed Commission Rep.

31 The total number of married women workers was the same in 1951
and in 1945, but rose by 2 million between 1951 and 1966.

32 1959 NWAC Rep., 26-7: *Tobacco Worker*, Nov.-Dec., 1951, 15-16:
Mar.-Apr. 1952, 16: May-June 1952, 15-16 for cases of dismissal
of long-service part-timers.

The end of the 1950s and early 'sixties saw a shift in trade union leadership away from the Establishment that evolved in the 1930s, went through the war, and became the exponents of the Cold War and the consumer boom. Of the women, Anne Loughlin retired on grounds of ill-health in 1953 and Florence Hancock in 1957. The brightest star in the firmament of women's trade unionism, and the only one of the 'goddesses' left, was Anne Godwin. In 1941, her original union, the Women Assistant Clerks and Secretaries' Association, merged with the National Union of Clerks and she became assistant secretary of the 'mixed' union. In 1956, she took over as General Secretary. Majestic of manner, astute, experienced, she rather resembled a successful headmistress. She had none of the overwhelming characteristics of Mary Macarthur or Margaret Irwin. But, after years of attending international conferences, she was supremely confident, outwardly at least, and a good tactician in the humdrum committee world of the new, institutionalized trade unionism.

Margaret Mackay left the secretaryship of the National Women's Advisory Committee to become a Labour MP. Ellen McCullough from the Transport and General Workers replaced her, but only briefly. Her real interest was education and she left to run the TUC's new postal education scheme. Thus in 1962, Ethel Chipchase of the Transport Salaried Staffs' Association became secretary. She was a veteran delegate of Women's Advisory Conferences, with an attendance record stretching back to 1942, an abrasive manner, and, like Anne Godwin, an incisive mind.

These years were dominated by the Aldermaston Marches run by the Campaign for Nuclear Disarmament. The union rank and file largely remained aloof. A number of union leaders supported the campaign, however, and the bulk of the marchers were members of the Labour Party, but middle rather than working class.

At the same time, there were signs of the end of the honeymoon of comparative co-operation between government, employers, and unions so carefully nurtured by Ernest Bevin and Walter Citrine. As the union rank and file became accustomed to prosperity, they became confident enough to demand a bigger share of the profits in the new booming Britain. Strikes for higher earnings became more common. This Left-Right confrontation between employers and unions and within the union movement, along with the Aldermaston Marches, were the issues highlighted by the media. But in the background, the struggle for women's equality was brewing.

By the late 1950s militant women trade unionists were making headway with their demands both for union backing on welfare and for greater participation in union work. Ever since the war, very gradually more women had been winning elections to union offices, reaching not only branch committees but union executives. For instance, Irene Shears, diminutive, even mouse-like, who year after year went to the rostrum of the annual delegate meetings of her union, the Shop, Distributive, and Allied Workers, and, in most un-mouselike terms, crisply castigated her executive and fellow-members for not waging an all-out campaign for equal pay. As manageress of a shoe department in a London Co-operative Society store, she and her like felt the same sort of bitterness as the women in the 'common classes' of the public services. In this union and Anne Godwin's Clerical and Administrative Workers women were most adamant and most successful. In USDAW there were several very able men who backed them.[1]

More significantly, women manual workers were forcing their way through ordinary channels to union posts, so undermining Women's Sections. For instance, Miss E. McKaig in Dundee in 1951 and Miss Brigid Paton in Leicester in 1955 were elected shop stewards. Miss McKaig became factory convener in 1959.

Another small sign of changing times went almost unnoticed, although it would have been unthinkable between the wars. The National Society of Metal Mechanics, the stubborn opponent of the Women's Trade Union League from the 1870s, in 1959 decided to enrol women as half-members. It was a response to changing technology and the fact that women workers were now accepted as part of the labour force in the brass industry.

Conversely, the crucial decline in women's employment as private, indoor domestic servants, shown in the 1961 Census, was acknowledged by the winding-up of the TUC's National Union of Domestic Servants. The members were transferred to Dorothy Elliott's union, the General and Municipal Workers.

Margaret Mackay ended her tenure of the secretaryship of the National Women's Advisory Committee with an exhibition of women's work, 'With Women's Hands', in the summer of 1962, opened by Anne Godwin, that year's TUC chairman. By involving unions in the work of preparation, Margaret Mackay forced on their attention women's importance in the workforce and in union membership.

Union of Shop, Distributive and Allied Workers' Woolworths strike poster, 1961

By the late 1950s, the women's wing of the trade union Manor House Orthopaedic Hospital was open and proving very popular, especially with London Transport bus-workers.[2]

In 1958, the TUC General Council and National Women's Advisory Committee accepted a decision from the Women's Advisory

National Union of Agricultural Workers group, early 1960s

Conference for the revival of regional discussion conferences. The following year a significantly larger number of resolutions passed without opposition from the platform. In 1960, the Conference strayed well away from the confines of rigidly feminine topics by passing a resolution condemning the shooting of Black African civilians at Sharpeville while they were demonstrating peacefully against new South African government laws compelling them to carry passes.

The Union of Shop, Distributive and Allied Workers had some great triumphs. In 1961 it forced recognition from Messrs F.W. Woolworth, largely because of the loyalty of girls and women staff. The campaign, like many others, began in South Wales where the militancy of mineworkers spread to other kinds of work. A few years later, USDAW, through another strike, forced recognition from Messrs Foyles, the London booksellers. But the most remarkable gain for shop- and office-workers was the Offices, Shops and Railway Premises Act of 1963, the greatest step in welfare since the Second World War, and vital for masses of women workers. It embodied a great deal that the Women's Trade Union League and its multifarious offshoots had sought, and that the distributive, clerical, and railway unions had been pressing for since the end of the nineteenth century. It applied to offices and shops all the regulations enacted for factories on heating, space, lighting, and lavatory accommodation, so that there were now fixed, legal standards which unions could see enforced.[3]

This success helped to make up for the failure of the Agricultural Workers' Safety, Health, and Welfare Provisions Act of 1956. Ten years later the Agricultural Workers' Union, not least its women members, were still demanding that local authorities be statutorily compelled to provide portable lavatory accommodation for workers out in fields. They were also concerned about the growing risks of working with insecticides and pesticides.[4]

Perhaps more than factory- and office-workers, agricultural women workers compelled trade unionists to understand the necessity of care for children while their mothers were at work. In factory districts, if there were no elderly relative to help out, working mothers fell back on professional child-minders. There were not many of these in rural villages and laudanum had gone out of fashion as a sedative. Working mothers' problems were still those described by Mary Merryweather in the 1850s. Women members of the Agricultural Workers' Union were especially worried by accidents to their little children whom they had to bring to work. Deposited at the side of a large field, they had mishaps of which their mothers, working perhaps a quarter of a mile away, were unaware. In 1957, in response to oft-repeated resolutions and speeches at Women's Advisory Conferences, the National Women's Advisory Committee yielded in its opposition to day nurseries and to mothers of young children going to work so far as to publish a *Report on the Care of Children of Working Mothers*. Ethel Chipchase built on this precedent by producing a series of special reports on a wide range of topics, besides welfare. These were of considerable value not only to union members, but also to women generally.

It was disquieting, however, that in the mid-1960s conditions were still bad in trades in which the Factory Acts had operated for many years. Miss Sutton, who like Anne Loughlin had risen to be National Officer in the National Union of Tailors and Garment-Workers, stated that women were still ignorant of the Workmen's Compensation Acts and the help available to them through union legal departments. From about 1960 her own union was publishing information sheets on industrial safety and health. The first Women's Conference of the Amalgamated Union of Foundry Workers in May 1966 let loose a flood of complaints. Some delegates disclosed that they had taken to disappearing into the toilets when heating was inadequate. The cotton-weavers had long had a similar ruse. Mrs Margaret Abbot, secretary of the Rossendale Weavers' Union, remarked that when they found the weaving-sheds not heated to the statutory 60°F, they went off to the canteen and 'It's wonderful what half-an-hour's silence in the mills will do'.

In 1963 the battle for women's economic equality and for

equality in the unions reached a new stage. It came out into the open and for some years it revolved almost entirely around equal pay and job opportunities. While standards of welfare varied from one trade and one geographical area to another, problems over pay and job opportunities were commonly shared.

The opening of this new phase was signalled by the revival of the idea of a TUC Women's Charter, previously advanced in 1938-39. The National Union of Tailors and Garment-Workers raised it at the 1962 TUC Women's Advisory Conference in recognition of 'the importance of women's contribution to modern industry'. Mrs O. Smart, a delegate from this union, told the conference that the Tailors and Garment-Workers had already adopted an industrial charter of their own for women workers. The resolution asking for the charter called on the General Council to state 'clearly the policy and objectives of the trade union movement to raise the wages and conditions of women workers'. The Conference accepted the resolution and in 1963 the TUC Charter for Women was published:

> *Equal Pay* based on the value of the job and not on the sex of the worker.
> *Opportunities for Promotion* for women.
> *Apprenticeship Schemes* for girls in appropriate industries.
> *Improved Opportunities* for training young women for skilled work.
> *Retraining Facilities* for older women who return to industry.
> *Special Care for the Health and Welfare* of women workers.

Thus three of the charter's six points were for more and better education and training, and a fourth point, 'Opportunities for Promotion', arose directly from this.

Behind this claim lay years of patient insistence.[5] When war preparations and war production opened many kinds of technical education to women, women trade union leaders seized the chance to break down the severely circumscribed training opportunities that had characterized the Depression years. Even during the war, however, most private employers were reluctant to train girls for work recognized as skilled, and some unions, for example the Draughtsmen, would not countenance it. Women trade union leaders had pressed not merely for training for 'substituted' women, but for better training for 'women's work'.[6] After the war the Ministry of Labour provided a large number of courses for retraining and training women. But disappointingly few took advantage of them, perhaps because of war weariness.[7]

In 1944, the Women's Advisory Conference had made a more fundamental attack. They criticized the curricula in schools, especially the lack of science-teaching, as directing girl school-leavers into a narrow range of low-paid, low-grade ancillary work. Tackled by the TUC General Council over this, Ernest Bevin replied that state schools evolved their own individual curricula to meet the national need for various kinds of workers, so that enough girls were being trained to meet the number of jobs available for them and 'in this sense the teaching of science in girls' schools is already equivalent to that in boys' schools'. So he dodged the real issue of opportunity. But he was correct in that the obstacle to opportunities for girls was chiefly of the employers' making.[8]

However, during the post-war surge of respect for women, the unions did not let the matter rest. Three years after the 1944 Education Act provided secondary schooling for all, women trade union leaders and the TUC General Council attacked the use made of secondary schools to train girls for clerical work. In place of this narrow specialization, they asked for courses in a wider range of subjects.[9]

The Act had introduced a new inequality for girls through the 11-plus examination. This determined the numbers of boys and girls who went to the higher-grade grammar schools. In order to ensure that the numbers who passed the 11-plus examination each year miraculously matched the numbers of grammar-school places available for them, some local authorities 'weighted' the examination against girls. There were fewer of these openings for girls because there was less demand for educated female employees than for males.[10]

Once the reaction against women set in in 1948, women trade unionists made no headway on extending girls' training. However, united at least on this one issue, delegates and the National Women's Advisory Committee kept up the pressure. In 1954, they made the revolutionary suggestion of retraining and training for older married women, but without effect.[11]

With the growth of automation, electronics, and computer programming, and with increasing mechanization in old trades like tailoring, weaving, and spinning, employers' and trade unions' attitudes to excluding girls from jobs requiring higher skills began to change. The time-honoured assumption that women did not mind repetitive and monotonous work had been punctured in 1954 by an inquiry of the National Institute of Industrial Psychology. The Conservative government's Carr Report of 1957 suggested industry might make more apprenticeships available to girls as well as to boys. In January 1961, the Central Electricity Generating Authority awarded three out of twenty-four university scholarships to girls. That year a girl came out top in examinations in draughtsmanship at Sunderland Technical College.[12]

But the change was minimal. At the 1959 Women's Advisory Conference, Anne Godwin bluntly declared that the bulk of girls were only given technical training to enable them to become teachers, nurses, or shorthand typists and that industry wanted a pool of labour for repetitive, routine, and machine-minding jobs.

The following year the Crowther Report from the Central Advisory Council for Education in England and Wales confirmed both the inadequacy of science-teaching in girls' schools and the channelling of girls to work of a lower academic standard than boys. In 1962 the National Women's Advisory Committee estimated that employers were still giving four times as many apprenticeships and learnerships to boys as to girls.[13] In 1964 the Industrial Training Act theoretically provided as many training opportunities for girls as boys. But the inequalities continued. The only woman appointed to any of the Training Boards set up was Mrs Margaret Fenwick, Assistant Secretary of the Union of Jute, Flax, and Allied Workers.

Employers' arguments against giving equal training opportunities to girls were the same as those they advanced against paying the 'rate for the job'. They claimed that women were worth less because of the 'family break' and their higher sickness and absence ratio due to their responsibilities for sick members of the family. Giant trusts and combines like old family firms could still regard training as a long-term investment because choice of employers in their spheres was narrowing and employees were likely to stay within the company. Yet at the same time, industrialists were crying out for mobility of labour. So prospects of an employee's remaining with the firm that trained him or her were diminishing. Differences in the return on outlay on a woman's training in comparison with that of a man were lessening as men became more and more likely to change jobs.

However, it was not equal training and job opportunities but equal pay that became the focal point of the women's campaign. With men in the engineering and metal trades increasingly uneasy at the speed and impact of technological change, there was a revival of male demands for equal pay. By 1959 the Amalgamated Engineering Union, like the Metal Mechanics thoroughly alarmed, supported a resolution at Congress asking for the 'rate for the job for women'.[14] By 1960 the TUC General Council was backing this. The following year, they argued with the Conservative Minister of Labour, Iain Macleod, for its general introduction.

In addition to support from men trade unionists, the campaign for the extension of equal pay to all forms of work was helped by its final achievement in the public services in 1961. The National Women's Advisory Committee in 1962 revealed the results of an

inquiry among affiliated unions about the number of existing
equal-pay agreements. Like all such inquiries it was inconclusive
because not all affiliated unions replied. But it showed that even
with the achievement of equal pay in the common classes of the
public services, only a tiny fraction of the 7,980,000 women then at
work were being paid the 'rate for the job'.

In 1961, the Union of Shop, Distributive, and Allied Workers,
goaded by women militants, and a few men like Chris Norwood,
listed twenty-one trades, including six Wages Council occupations,
with which there were now agreements to pay the 'rate for the job'
to women. In a further ninety-one trades, women were being paid
70 per cent or more of men's rates. USDAW was a general union,
so that these agreements included women members from the other
two general unions and a variety of specialist unions. The equal-
pay faction was not assuaged. At the 1961 Annual Delegate
Meeting, Mrs Christine Page, a Norfolk grocery-store manageress,
demonstrated exasperation at the lack of a wholehearted campaign
by tearing up the Report as the finale to her speech at the
microphone.

Presaging the wrath to come, women telephonists in the Civil
Service, no left-wing hotheads and left out of the 1954 equal-
pay grant, worked to rule from September 1961 until June 1962.
Thus they forced the Treasury to reclassify them so that they won
both equal pay and the right to belong to the Civil Service Union,
instead of the Transport and General Workers which had no equal-
pay agreement with the Treasury.

There was now a new factor. On 25 March 1957, the Treaty of
Rome established the European Economic Community. Article 119
of the treaty laid down that 'men and women should receive equal
pay for equal work'. The application of this principle in the six
member countries seemed at first to some extent to justify
women's fears that for them equal pay meant unemployment. In
France, where a commitment to equal pay had been in operation
longest, women in some occupations were said not to have proper
legal protection in respect of pay. In Italy the number of jobs open
to women had been cut and there had been no collective
agreements incorporating equal pay. Equal pay had not been made
legally enforceable in Belgium or Holland.

The Council of Ministers, however, came to see that their interpretation of Article 119 was too narrow. They brought their
thinking and increasingly their practice more into line with ILO
Convention 100 and specifically condemned three practices as in-
compatible with this policy:

1. Systematic down-grading of women workers.
2. Adoption of different job-classification rules for men and women.
3. Use of job-evaluation criteria not related to real conditions of work.[15]

Even beyond the EEC, British women trade unionists could point to the fact that a small and relatively poor country, Israel, had adopted 'equal pay', while it was the policy of all the socialist states.

Britain had still not ratified ILO Convention 100. As Mrs Marie Patterson of the T&GWU and Miss Lil Grotier, London Organizer of the Tobacco-Workers' Union, pointed out, increasing mechanization was causing the re-evaluation of jobs in any case, so that the revaluation of women's work could be carried out at the same time.

Although the Labour Party when in power had done nothing towards equalizing women's and men's rates of pay, trade unionists who wanted to see equal pay extended to all forms of work persisted in believing that it was more susceptible to pressure than the Conservatives. But, just as after the war, when political power became a possibility, the equality of women's pay became less important. The Labour Party's election manifesto included a promise to implement 'equal pay for equal work', but not for work of 'equal value'. Even this more limited aim was shelved when Labour won the election of 1964. The Labour government embarked on a 'wage freeze' policy, a repetition of their own post-war policy, and that of the Conservative governments of the 1950s, aside from their one major concession to the women in the public services. In short, the Labour government continued to limit wage rises to a fixed percentage of anyone's existing wage, in this case to $3\frac{1}{2}$ per cent. Thus they not only prevented women obtaining wage rises high enough to close the gap between their own and men's pay, but also positively widened that gap in actual cash terms as successive governments had done since the end of the war, with union agreement. Women were aware that $3\frac{1}{2}$ per cent of a weekly wage of £8 was bound to be less than $3\frac{1}{2}$ per cent of a weekly wage of £15. And the Ministry of Labour's national averages of earnings of men and women showed that while in 1938 the differential between men's and women's pay was £1 16s. 6d., by April 1965 it was £7 19s. 4d. The gap had increased by over £5.

To some extent the national averages of wages within trade groups were depressed by the mass of women in lower-paid work. Employers argued that women earned less because they worked shorter hours than men. But in that case the percentage women earned of men's pay, and the percentage they worked of men's hours, should have roughly tallied. This was not the case. In 1965, for example, women nationally earned on average 60.2 per cent of men's rates, but they worked 84.2 per cent of men's hours.

The huge majority of women workers in the Wages Council trades, amounting in 1965 to about 3½ million, or 70 per cent of those covered, was further proof, if any were needed, that many women worked in low-paid jobs. Male negotiators and spokesmen now dominated the workers' sides of these bodies. They chafed at the endless round of finicky bargaining and privately endorsed the criticism made by Alfred Robens of Ernest Bevin's 1945 Wages Councils Act. Robens, an ex-member of the National Union of Distributive and Allied Workers, who had become a Labour MP, grumbled that 'the Trade Union Movement is spending its money and using its energies not only for its members, but also for millions of non-members ...' who still believed that ' "the Government fixes my wages" '. Union officials put up with the councils because they had become an integral part of wage-bargaining since, in the early 1920s, the unions in the tobacco trade began using statutorily agreed earnings as a platform from which to push up earnings in voluntary agreements. The technique brought results in big firms, chains, and multiples.[16]

Wage levels in the Wages Council trades reflected the amount of time and thought spent by union negotiators on each one. In spite of the fact that these statutory wage agreements were supposed to be tied to the cost-of-living index, there were wide differences in pay between the small trades and the large. Union negotiators would not give as much time to out-of-the-way trades like ostrich and fancy feather or fur as to larger occupations such as retail drapery and outfitting. This demonstrated the cardinal importance of unions to workers in raising earnings. But it also showed that the inequalities in pay were not just due to the sex of workers. They were also the products of economic and organizational weakness.[17]

Wages Council awards gave women a much more precise reason for resentment. They gave conclusive proof that they were not receiving the 'rate for job' when doing the same work as men in, for example, tailoring, flax- and hemp-weaving, hollow ware, laundries and food-retailing, and in cooking in industrial and staff canteens, because unions in Wages Council negotiations had agreed women should be paid less than men. Worse, the boast of union officials that women were getting a higher percentage of men's rates, thanks to their negotiating efforts, was utterly negated by the widening differential in cash terms. Ordinary working women and rank-and-file union members did not care about percentages, they cared about their take-home pay. In 1949, women serving in food shops, for instance, were paid 72.5 per cent of the men's basic rate and got 27s. less than men. By 1965 they were to get 74.1 per cent of men's basic rate, but the gap in cash earnings had widened to 49s. 6d.[18]

Joint Industrial Council settlements proved the same point, although the rise in the cash differential was often smaller. It was very small in engineering; yet the comparison was not made between semi-skilled women, still the bulk of the female engineering workforce, and equivalent semi-skilled men, but instead between semi-skilled women's rates and those of unskilled male labourers. A long term 'package' deal agreed on 22 December 1964 seemed to indicate a step towards bringing them to equality with this lowest men's grade. But four years later progress was reversed. The fears of the Engineering Workers' Union for the rates of pay of their male members were, as ever, to a large extent of their own making, since they continued to agree to a special low women's rate.

This growing cash inequality was also true of banking and insurance and other white-collar trades, including, strangely enough, the public services where the 'rate for the job' applied. For instance, the cash difference per week in National and Local Government, including teaching, and the National Health Service had risen by nearly £3 between 1955 and 1963. The application of equal pay in the public services was being eroded by the under-cover use of family allowances and other devices to maintain differentials in favour of men, as in the co-operatives during the war.[19]

In the continual revaluation of jobs taking place by the 1960s, women had the lower value of their work shoved right under their noses. Time and again, although the allocation of job points proved conclusively that to the employer a woman's work was as valuable as that of man, they were paid less. Hence their determination to stand out for 'equal pay for work of equal value' and not just the 'rate for the job'.

Mr Ray Gunter, the Minister of Labour, fulfilled the Labour Party's election pledge on the 'rate for the job' to the extent of appointing an interdepartmental committee to consider the effects of its wider application. Its findings were kept secret. However, he also set up a working party of representatives of the TUC, the Confederation of British Industries, and his own ministry. Although constantly pressed by Baroness Summerskill and Mrs Joyce Butler on the government side in the Lords and Commons, and Dame Irene Ward for the Opposition, he never divulged what progress it was making either in the 1964-66 Labour administration nor under that elected in 1966. However, on past performance there was some justification for Ray Gunter's reply to a Scottish TUC deputation, that the unions' attitude to equal pay in the past had been 'equivocal'.[20]

The TUC General Council returned to its policy of support for the Labour government over pay. In 1965, it stopped its commitment to ILO Convention 100 and 'equal pay for work of equal value', reverting to the 'rate for the job', as in the 1964 Labour Party election manifesto. But it wrote cautiously to affiliates, pointing out that if that minority of women who were on piece-work could achieve parity of pay with men through local negotiations, a considerable step would have been taken towards the 'rate for the job'.[21]

Women adherents of the Labour movement, while remaining loyal, struggled with increasing bitterness and intensity to remove their economic inequality, as they saw they were once more being pushed into the background. This relegation they absolutely would not accept. At the 1965 and 1966 Women's Advisory Conferences, there were landslides against the government's $3\frac{1}{2}$ per cent limit on wage rises in the form of numerous equal-pay resolutions. In most cases the effect on the pay-rise limit was not spelt out, but Mrs Monica Toye of the Association of Cinematograph and Allied Technicians questioned how precisely this was compatible with equal pay. In 1966, Mrs Christine Page of USDAW, forced through against the platform a resolution demanding that the TUC organize big demonstrations in Whitehall in support of 'equal pay'.

These militant women were encouraged by the growing extent of support within their unions. For example, the Association of Scientific Workers by 1965 was taking every university to arbitration in turn to establish the 'rate for the job'. The pressure was still nothing like strong enough to force any change in national policy. But it reflected not only union fears of women's cheap labour. There was also a fundamental change in the attitudes of ordinary women trade unionists summed up in a story told by a stocky, middle-aged North Country woman delegate from the National Union of Public Employees to the 1966 Women's Advisory Conference. She had been travelling home from work in a bus in which there was 'standing room only'. Alongside her stood a woman far advanced in pregnancy, while several healthy men occupied seats. The NUPE lady asked one of them: 'Why don't you get up and give her a seat?' The man retorted: 'You want equality, don't you? This is equality!' To which she answered: 'She's bearing a child. What are you bearing? Where's the equality in that?'[22]

The battleground was equal pay. But the battle was about a

Ford women machinists vote to strike, 1968

much more basic concept of equality. The rank and file had turned their backs on the old white-collar concept of equality with men, limited to similarity. They had advanced to the point of demanding consideration for physical differences, but without any vitiation of their assertion of women's equality as workers and therefore of their right to equal payment, equal opportunities to learn and exercise their skills, and equal status in their unions.

In April 1968, Mrs Barbara Castle replaced Ray Gunter and the Ministry of Labour became the Department of Employment and Productivity. She instituted a new working party, made up of CBI, TUC, and her department's representatives, to consider the introduction of equal pay.

Suddenly a lead for all women workers came in the form of a claim by some 187 women sewing machinists at Ford's Dagenham car factory.[23] As members of the National Union of Vehicle-Builders, they demanded upgrading of their work to take account of the skill involved. At the beginning of June they struck work: the first protest or industrial action ever undertaken about the *value* placed on 'women's work'. The Vehicle-Builders' Union had long supported the 'rate for the job' where women were on the same work as men, in order to protect men members' jobs. It had not succeeded in establishing even this policy.

The women's action coincided with the Vehicle-Builders' Annual Policy Meeting at Felixstowe. The Ford women machinists descended in coachloads, bearing banners, lobbying delegates, and invading the conference hall. They elicited impromptu and placatory speeches in support of equal pay. An emergency resolution supported their strike and deplored the absence of lady delegates at these annual meetings. The union had been arguing with Ford's for nearly a year about the whole pay structure and the women's demand was linked to this campaign for alterations. After the Vehicle-Builders made the women's strike official, they went on to press the Ford National Negotiating Committee union side into tabling a motion for equal pay for women.

The other unions on the Ford National Negotiating Committee, less immediately touched by the women machinists' wrath, did not support the Vehicle-Builders straight away. Barbara Castle invited the women to tea at her department, perhaps to dampen the urgency of their demand. This brought them more publicity for a strike already, for once, featured by the media. The public increasingly backed the women and so did MPs, swayed by the general mood. On 22 October at a meeting held at the House of Commons, union delegates pledged that they would 'strongly resist any attempt to sell down the river the women's claim to equal pay'. They insisted that whether or not the national wage claim then being negotiated succeeded, every District Committee covered by the Confederation of Shipbuilding and Engineering Unions should be told to 'apply to raise every woman's rate to that of an unskilled labourer in the next twelve months'. And they added the crucial rider on evaluation, that this application should 'be combined with skill classification'. The Coventry branch of the Vehicle-Builders' Union went so far as to claim that unless this condition was implemented, there should be a national strike in the engineering industry.

The negotiations on the restructuring of pay and gradings at Ford's were still going on in the mid-1970s. The effect of the women machinists' strike was less important there than on the trade union movement in general. At the 1968 Trades Union Congress a vague resolution for 'urgent progress towards equal pay' was amended, against General Council protests, to include a commitment to take industrial action to obtain it. The General Council was faithfully reflecting the opinion of union leaderships. Yet another of its equal-pay inquiries revealed that in 1968 nearly a third of the fifty-two unions who replied were against any form of equal pay. Even more could see no hope of progress. Yet over half of them said that 'they would not be satisfied until they had achieved equal pay for work of equal value'.

As in the 1930s and 'forties, pressure-groups developed outside the unions, supported by union militants. In 1968 four Labour MPs brought in a new Equal Pay Bill for all forms of work and Joyce Butler, with the support of MPs of all parties, launched an Anti-Discrimination Bill aimed at ending all forms of discrimination practised against women, not just in the matter of pay. She also sponsored a new Equal Pay Campaign Committee, replaced by the trade union and Labour National Joint Action Campaign Committee for Equal Women's Rights. This, a direct result of the Ford machinists' strike, was formed in response to demands from the National Union of Vehicle-Builders' London District Committee, the group that had called the equal-pay conference in the House of Commons. Mr Fred Blake, the East London Organizer of the Vehicle-Builders' Union, who had been the official chiefly concerned in the machinists' action, became secretary of this Equal Women's Rights Committee. Its co-chairmen were Mrs Audrey Hunt of the Association of Scientific, Technical, and Managerial Staffs and Chris Norwood MP, who had championed equal pay while a member of the Union of Shop, Distributive, and Allied Workers. At a meeting in Trafalgar Square, Edith Summerskill denounced the unions for their lack of support for equal pay. The Equal Rights Committee's Charter was much wider in scope than the TUC's 1963 Women's Charter. It demanded an end to sex discrimination and the inauguration of equal legal rights for women by 1969. It called on the TUC to lead and co-ordinate 'a national joint action campaign for equal pay and opportunities ...' in accordance with the 1968 Congress decision.

Men began to come out on strike with women, as in a 1968 stoppage of London lavatory-cleaners demanding the 'rate for the job' which the TUC General Council helped to squash. They were not forgiven.

The TUC General Council in its discussions with the government and Confederation of British Industries, would not press for adoption of ILO Convention 100 in order not to hinder investigations which the government was then carrying out with a view to the introduction of the 'rate for the job'.[24] But they sent a deputation to see Barbara Castle. They found that she was proposing to phase in equal pay over seven years, which they thought too long. Much worse, she informed them that it was not the British government's practice to ratify ILO Conventions until domestic law and practice already conformed to the ILO's standards. And, finally, she alarmed them by suggesting that equal pay could be obtained, but only at the expense of men's wage rises, and that labour disputes might hold back its introduction. Thus the government had no coherent policy, but tried both to frighten the Unions by threatening men's increases and to offer equal pay in return for fewer strikes.[25] Harold

Wilson, the Prime Minister, repeated the warning that it would mean less in pay settlements for men at the 1969 Trades Union Congress.[26]

Frank Cousins, General Secretary of the Transport and General Workers' Union, and the most powerful union leader, was stung into vigorous support for an equal-pay motion, in order to repudiate the government's policy. He had intended merely to move the resolution formally. But he took the chance to dipose of the argument that progress in raising wage standards of one sector of working people, women, could only be brought by restraint on the part of men. He asked if such a thing would be tolerated in the professions, among MPs, and government ministers. 'In a technological age', he went on, 'if ever there is an argument that ought to be thrown away by us, it is the one that there is such a thing as women's work'. He roundly condemned unions for still talking of women's wage-rates as a percentage of male rates, and ended by demanding not the 'rate for the job', but 'equal pay for work of equal value on behalf of all people employed'.

He was backed by other union leaders and what seemed a mass union revolt shook the government as the women and Joyce Butler's Committee had never done.[27]

Yet the unions were still not wholly committed to women's equality.[28] Along with the Labour government and employers, they were concerned in an attempt to frustrate the women's demands. This was over whether women should yield restrictions on their hours of work, particularly the ban on night-shifts, in return for equal pay. Trade union leaders, in supporting this bargain, were following the Union of Post Office Workers when they told the 1944 Equal Pay Commission that in return for equal pay newcomers to the service 'would be willing to perform night duty as they had during the war'.[29]

A lot of women manual workers, however, did not see why they should be paid less than men on day-shifts, just because they did not work at nights. In 1961, deep differences on this policy had already surfaced at the Women's Advisory Conferences. Mrs D. Jackson of the Inland Revenue Staffs' Association said her union felt that if women claimed special accommodation in the matter of hours and nursery provision for their children, they could not claim equal pay. There would, she said, 'be industrial chaos if hours were fitted round the home'. Yet the 'twilight' and 'housewives' shifts' were an instance of industrial employers making just such special accommodation.

The National Women's Advisory Committee view was still that of the late 1930s and of the Montevideo Convention that 'protective legislation should be kept to a minimum consistent with ... health and welfare. Over-concentration on protective measures could create and continue discrimination against women ...'

There was an alternative, but the only person who said anything about it was Ethel Chipchase. Querying the wisdom of night-working for women at the 1965 Women's Advisory Conference, she pointed to the example of Sweden. There, as part of the measures to implement equal pay, 'legislation against Night Work [for women] had been replaced by legislation against Night Work *for all*' (author's italics), except in work such as medical and transport services. This was the line taken by the cotton-weavers' unions, among the first to obtain legislation restricting women's working-hours.

The printing unions were still among the main opponents of restrictions on night-work for women. Miss M.A. Whewell of the Society of Graphical and Allied Trades, supported by Marie Patterson of the Transport and General Workers' Union, split the 1966 Conference by proposing the ending of all opposition to night-shifts provided these were agreed voluntarily and women's pay was no less favourable than that of men.[30]

On Barbara Castle's 1968 Equal Pay Working Party, the TUC representatives did not press for the ending of restrictions on night-shift work for women. They concentrated on improving conditions on these shifts for all workers, and on establishing for men the right to a break, after $4\frac{1}{2}$ hours of work, which women already had. They did support continued restrictions on night-shift working for women in exchange for equal pay, but not very assiduously.[31]

Negotiations at the beginning of 1969 gave a group of workers at the Ford plant at Dagenham the chance to comment on the proposals to cede equal pay in exchange for lifting restrictions on night-shift work for women. The firm offered this as part of a package deal. The fifteen union leaderships who carried on negotiations on 11 February accepted the offer and it was hailed as a victory for the women machinists. On the following day their members turned the deal down. Like the weavers, some women members could see no reason why they should lose concessions already won. It was the first of several similar disappointments for union negotiators.

A year later women clothing-workers in Leeds served notice that the new equal-pay campaign had lost nothing of its momentum. They struck work and men came out with them for a wage rise. But the women were intent that the rise should be the same for both sexes and their hostility to union negotiators who produced the usual unequal increase took officials and men by surprise. Starting

at John Collier's, the strike snowballed until 30,000 workpeople
were 'out'. Like the Ford women machinists, they thoroughly
shook up their union. The flat-rate increase was eventually gained
after they agreed to go back to work.

So the Labour government apparently gave in. On 29 May 1970,
Parliament passed 'an Act to prevent discrimination, as regards
terms and conditions of employment, between men and women'
for Great Britain and Northern Ireland. In fact, the concessions
amounted to the least that were acceptable and were riddled with
loopholes which would enable employers to avoid paying women
the same as men. The Act laid down that equal pay both in the
sense of the 'rate for the job' and of 'equal pay for work of equal
value' should be exchanged for women's acceptance of the lifting
of restrictions on their hours of work. Equal pay need not be paid
where 'any special treatment is accorded to women in connection
with birth or expected birth of a child'. It would not be required
where the law regulated 'women's terms and conditions of employment', nor would it be necessary on provisions affecting
retirement, marriage, or death.[32] In fact, it embodied the attitudes
of employers and unions shown in their evidence to the 1944 Royal
Commission on Equal Pay, a quarter of a century earlier. Ex-
pectations of marriage, the 'family break', earlier retirement age
imposed on women by National Insurance legislation, and many
other accepted practices would enable an employer to pay a
woman less than a man although she might spend the whole of her
working life of up to 35 years on similar work. She was still to be
penalized for her sex.

Equality had shown itself to be indivisible. The economic
equality of which equal pay was a part could not be realized
without social and economic equality before the law. The campaign of women trade unionists expanded. By 1968 they were
ceasing to talk about equal training and job opportunities and starting to take action to obtain them. For instance, when a number of
local councils began to lay off bus conductors and conductresses,
women demanded the retraining that they were giving men to
enable them to drive buses. The two unions mainly involved were
the National Union of General and Municipal Workers and the
Transport and General Workers' Union. The T&GWU in November 1968 decided positively to oppose the training of women as
drivers. In December twelve furious conductresses gatecrashed a
meeting on the subject, from which women had been excluded.
They demanded not only that this ruling be reversed, but also
equality with men members over pensions, sick benefit, and
promotion prospects. Seventy of the men delegates are said to have

walked out in a temper over the women's interruption. However, in 1970 men members of the General and Municipal Workers' Union in Huddersfield were persuaded to accept a woman driver and the ban was broken.

By this time the mass media and the general public were being forced to take notice of the most extreme wing of the new Women's Emancipation Movement, Women's Lib. While middle-class women were providing journalists with good copy about burning their bras, the working class, equally bitter, were preoccupied with lightening their load of domestic work. They joined in the demands for free abortions so that women should be able to decide whether they had children or not. They forced their unions to back demands for day nurseries.

The provision of day nurseries was going the way trade unionists wanted. By the 1960s, private firms, having to seek more of their employees among married women, were beginning to make up for the lack of public provision. Between 1960 and 1962 the number of local authority nurseries dropped from 462 to 447. But the number of registered child-minders rose from 1,351 to 2,208 and the number of private day nurseries from 601 to 932. A jute firm set up its own day nursery, reminiscent of Mary Merryweather's enterprise at Courtauld's Essex factory in the 1850s. By 1967 a Beckenham firm was offering to provide 'kindergartens for commerce', for firms accepting married women shop assistants and secretarial staff.[33]

But there was also a change in union attitudes. By the late 1960s they were discussing day nurseries as desirable not only for working mothers, but for all mothers. The National Women's Advisory Committee had come round to the idea that governments should not encourage married women to work on the one hand, and then deny responsibility for their children on the other. The International Labour Organization's Report *Women Workers in a Changing World* finally altered their views.

The new, much more basic, concept of equality, taking into account motherhood and women's work in the home, produced an Act of far greater significance than the Equal Pay Act: the Matrimonial Proceedings and Property Act, which followed almost immediately on the Equal Pay Act on 29 May 1970. It prescribed that in settling divorce and separation allowances which either party, man or wife, might have to pay the other, the courts should take into account 'the contributions made by each of the parties to the welfare of the family, *including any contribution made by looking after the home or caring for the family*. Settlements had to leave either party 'in the financial position in which they would have been if the marriage had not broken down'.[34]

The wheel had come almost full circle. In Britain, for the first time since the Anglo-Saxon laws, an economic value had been placed on women's work in the home. The 1970 Act was much vaguer than the old Anglo-Saxon laws. The amount a wife was to have in a settlement was left to the discretion of the courts and not fixed precisely at a half or one-third of the family property. But the whole basis of a woman's cheaper labour had been her unpaid labour in the home and in 'sweated' cottage industries. The anomaly that making clothes, mending, laundering, cleaning, and food preparation were valueless when done in the home by a member of the family, but had an economic value when some outsider was brought in to perform such jobs, was legally ended. Any pretence that despite the fact that men were engaged in all these occupations, they were 'women's work', was now finished.

1975 was designated International Woman's Year by the United Nations Organization. To mark the occasion, the TUC itself held a monster march and meeting in Trafalgar Square. Opinion had somersaulted since, nine years earlier, the General Council had recoiled in horror from Christine Page's call for a march and demonstration. The TUC also produced an updated Women's Charter embodying the whole of the programme of Joyce Butler's and Audrey Hunt's Women's Equal Rights Campaign Committee. For it now supported full equality in all spheres for women, including paid maternity leave, pensions, convenient working-hours, health and safety at work, facilities for women to return to their jobs after rearing children, and full citizen rights for women. In September 1974 the General Council proposed the abolition of the National Women's Advisory Committee. The Committee, however, insisted that it should be retained, but for a new reason. It was materially contributing to the new movement for women's economic equality by supplying women with detailed information to enable them to combat discrimination at their workplaces.

It was all too easy, however, to pillory unions for their slowness in reacting to changes in the kinds of work done by women and to their importance in the labour force. The fact was that their traditional attitudes were to a large extent justified, even in the mid-1970s. Most of the problems accumulated over the centuries had not changed. Employers had not completely accepted the responsibility of giving special protection to women workers. But industrial health was now seen as an aim for men and women alike. After considerable improvements during and just after the Second World War, standards in the later 1960s had seemed to deteriorate. By the mid-1970s the unions were campaigning for recognition of every worker's right to protection against health hazards at work.

Home- and out-work persisted in post-war Britain in spite of the establishment of minimum rates of earnings and working-hours. In the mid-1960s, H.A. Baker, Secretary of the Birmingham Trades Council, described the expansion of home-working in that city where it had hardly existed before the war, although the jewellery and small metal trades were home industries. The system in Birmingham largely resembled that described by the 'striking' Nottingham lace-runners in the 1840s. New and different forms of work were being undertaken at home, besides the traditional clothing trades. Occupations especially affected were clerical and typing work and draughting and tracing. Other home-work trades included the manufacture of electric switches, plastic handbags, and envelopes.[35]

Home- and out-work continued to exist because it was still the refuge of the married woman worker with small children, or of any woman with an invalid or elderly person in the family to look after and who could not easily go to work outside her home. In August 1975, the Low Pay Unit stated that it believed at least 750,000 women were engaged in out-working for manufacturing industries. Immigrants swelled the pool from which they could be recruited. Conditions of home-workers, the Unit claimed, were no better than those exposed by the Anti-Sweating League in the first decade of the twentieth century.

The numbers of local authority day nurseries were still low. In 1975 there were only 453. Only 7.7 per cent of British children aged three to four years had access to nursery schools, compared with 50 per cent in Britain's fellow-EEC countries, France, Belgium, and Italy.

The 'marriage bar' and union support for it still persisted in the late 1960s in areas like Northern Ireland and South Wales where work for women was scarce.

By the mid-1970s Britain's internal economic crisis had been overtaken and complicated by a world crisis. The progress of women towards equality had been made possible by the post-war boom. Workers were desperately needed, so concessions had to be made to them, and their domestic burdens eased to make it worth their while to accept jobs. They were still making advances in the aftermath of the boom. An Anti-Sex Discrimination Act of November 1975[36] was reinforced by a concomitant Employment Protection Act. Both of them asserted women's right to work, and the Anti-Sex Discrimination Act gave them equality in all spheres, including union membership presumably. Both seemed curiously at odds with the limitations of the Equal Pay Act.[37]

The question remains whether the new realization of both

unions and women workers of their interdependence will withstand the economic storms, or whether the disunity of the nineteenth century will reappear. As unions now understand how greatly they depend for growth on attracting women members, there is hope that support for women's equality will increase. Since women are so much more confident of their capacities as workers, there is more prospect of their not losing 'that which they have wrought'.

Notes

1 Rep. of USDAW Ann. Delegate Meeting 1955, 10, 60, Irene Shears. It became a continuing theme at the following ADMs.
2 *New Dawn*, 30 Aug. 1952, 554: 26 Feb. 1955, 140: TUC Industrial Newsletter for women, Feb. 1960, 5.
3 Rep. of Gowers Committee on Health, Welfare and Safety in Non-Industrial Employment and Hours of Juveniles, Mar. 1949.
   Scot. Home Dept. Committee Rep. on Closing Hours of Shops, Jan. 1947. Home Office Proposals, *Suggested Provisions for Amending Legislation*, HMSO 1953.
4 1966 NWAC Rep.: 1966 Biennial Conference of the Agricultural Workers' Union was considering measures to deal with insecticides. Chief Inspector of Factories Reps., *PP*. 1960-61, vol. XV, 260, 271-2, 389-91: *PP*. 1961-62, vol.XV, 302, 307-312, 375-6. Industrial Health Centres were set up in the 1950s partly on the employers' initiative, starting with Slough in 1951. By 1964 these were being closed. See also *New Dawn*, 14 April 1962, 234: 16 Mar. 1963, 174: 9 Nov. 1963, 712: 11 Apr. 1964, 250.
5 The Central Committee on Women's Training and Employment widened the range of courses it offered to include various kinds of office work and nursing, only for a brief period in 1929-31, NUGMW *Jour.*, Apr. 1930, 103. In 1939 the NWAC took up the question of training, 1939 TUC Rep., 126.
6 Janet M. Hooks, US Dept. of Labor Women's Bureau, Booklet no. 200, 'British Policies and Methods of Employing Women in War-time', 1944.
7 Min. of Lab. Gaz., Aug. 1950, 261-2, recruitment and training of young persons in industry gave opportunities for girls. But 1947 NWAC Rep., 7-9, para. 3 showed women still taking courses less than one-twelfth the number of men.
8 1945 NWAC Rep., 10.   9 1947 TUC Rep., 159.
10 Nat. Foundation for Educational Research Pamphlet, 'Trends in Allocation Procedures', 14: WHERE, no. S 16, Oct. 1968: Robbins Rep. on Higher Education, Cmnd. 2154 ch. VI, 50, Table 21, at all social levels the percentage of girls reaching higher education was lower than that of boys. But, 58, Table 26, the proportion was higher in Scotland.
11 NWAC Reps.: 1954, 27-8, 39-42: 1955, 15-16. The Nat. Un. of Boot and Shoe Operatives reported a recruitment and training scheme for both boys and girls at the 1954 Women's Advisory Conference.

12 TUC Industrial Newsletter for Women, Nov. 1960, 1: Jan. 1961, 2.

13 Rep. of the Central Advisory Council for Education (England), Cmnd. 7695, vol. I, 33, para. 49: 77, para. 116: 302-3, paras. 48-9. 1961 NWAC Special Rep. on Education and Training of Girls.

14 1959 TUC Rep., 440. Impatient delegates did not permit a seconder to speak for this Clerical and Administrative Workers' Resolution, but passed it unanimously.

15 1965 NWAC Rep., Rep. of Progress on the Implementation of Equal Pay in the Common Market countries.

16 *New Dawn*, 10 Mar. 1945, 70. Alfred Robens became a Labour MP in 1945. He was Minister of Labour and National Service in the short-lived second post-war Labour government. He later became Chairman of the Nat. Coal Board, 1961-71: Clegg, *General Union*, 241 and Bayliss, *British Wages Councils*, 146, give complaints of NUGMW and T&GWU officials against Wages Councils. See also Reports of USDAW Ann. Delegate Meetings, 1963 onwards. Total number of women on workers' sides of Trade Boards 1920-22 was 209, 134 single plus 75 married; the total number of men was 285. The total number of women on Wages Council workers' sides in 1962-65 was 111, 53 single plus 58 married; the total number of men was 439.

17 e.g., lowest rates on Retail Drapery, Outfitting and Footwear, and Retail Newsagency, Confectionery and Tobacco Councils in 1965 were £6 14s. 6d.: on the Linen and Cotton Handkerchief Council, mainly concerned with N. Ireland, the women's rate was £6 1s. 0d.: on the Ostrich and Fancy Feather Council, £5 19s. 0d., and for Fur-Workers, £4 17s. 0d. TUC Quarterly Summary of Minimum Time Remuneration fixed by Wages Councils for 1 Oct. 1965, General Minimum Time Rates for the lowest grade of adult worker.

18 Copies of Wages Council and Joint Industrial Council settlements, supplied by the Research Dept. of USDAW. USDAW was one of the three large general unions. The other two, NUGMW and T&GWU, along with various specialized unions, were parties to the Wages Council agreements, and to some of the JIC agreements. Engineering rates from the Jan. 1964 ed. of the Confederation of Engineering and Shipbuilding Unions' *Handbook of Nat. Agreements*, 121, 123, 173-4.

19 Min. of Lab. Gaz., Mar. 1967, 269, Table 125, Earnings of Monthly and Weekly Paid Salaried Employees: Mar. 1968, 204, Table 3, Average Earnings of Monthly and Weekly Paid Women and Men. See also Min. of Lab. Averages of Earnings and Working Hours of employees in Certain Industries and Services, pub. annually in the Gaz.

20 1967 Scot. TUC Rep., 66. The Scot. Women's Advisory Committee had so lost its influence that in 1965 delegates to its Women's Advisory Conference suggested special places should be reserved on the General Council to ensure women's representation. Experienced women trade unionists like Mrs Jean Glass of USDAW scotched the idea and the tradition of women standing in equal competition with men was preserved.

21 1965 TUC Rep., 408.

22 In 1967 the Abortion Act was passed.

23 The Nat. Union of Vehicle Builders merged subsequently with the T&GWU. The account of this strike was compiled from the Rep. of the 1968 Nat. Union of Vehicle Builders Conference, Mins. of Exec. Committee Meetings and other documents kindly made available to me.

24 1968 TUC Rep., 178-80. The government was carrying out studies on the 'cost implication' of equal pay.

25 1969 TUC Rep., 172-7.

26 ibid., 497.

27 ibid., 505-7.

28 J. Arnison, *The Million Pound Strike*, 18, an account of the 1966-67 strike at Robert Arundel, Preston, Lancs: Pauline Pinder, *Women at Work,* PEP vol. XXXV, Broadsheet 512, May 1969, 593-4, 598.

29 1944 Roy. Comm. on Equal Pay, Mins. of Evidence of the Union of Post Office Workers, sect. 15, paras. 3626-32.

30 1966 NWAC Rep., 49 ff.: 1968 Rep., 8-9, para. 11: T&GWU *Record*, Aug. 1965, 9-10, Marie Patterson on *Night-Work for women.*

31 1965 TUC Rep., 177. The government was proposing to weaken the Offices, Shops and Railway Premises Act of 1963.

32 Equal Pay Act, 1970, ch. 41, para. 1 (5).

33 V. Klein, *Britain's Married Women Workers,* 119 for a Scottish jute firm providing a day nursery: 1966 Scot. Women's Advisory Committee Rep., 16: *The Times Business Review,* 8 May 1967, 25, rep. of a Beckenham firm providing kindergartens for commerce.

34 Matrimonial Proceedings and Property Act, 1970, ch. 45, sect. 5 (1), sect. 37. Author's italics.

35 Nat. Union of Hosiery Workers 1949 Ann. Rep., Sect. G, out-workers in their trade alone numbered 12,790: 1956 NWAC Rep., 25-6: NUGMW *Jour.*, Mar. 1952, 66-7: Delegates to the 1966 Ann. Conference of the Draughtsmen's and Allied Technicians' Assoc.

36 This Act was inspired by ILO Convention 111 against Discrimination and supported by the TUC General Council from the late 1960s.

37 As usual the implementation of the legislation devolved on those who benefited from it. It was not automatically applied. The most important example of its enforcement was the strike at Trico-Folberth Ltd., of Brentford, Middlesex. The women were 'out' from 24 May until 15 Oct. 1976, almost 6 months. The case went to the Industrial Tribunal which ruled against the women's claim for the same rates as those paid to men, whether on day or night shift. The women would not accept the ruling and remained 'out' until the firm gave in. They had considerable support from the rest of the trade union movement.

Bibliography

Chapters 1-3

For the General Reader:

Alice Clark, *Working Life of Women in the Seventeenth Century*, F. Cass, London, 1968.

William Cobbett, *Rural Rides*, Penguin edition, London, 1967.

G. D. H. Cole, *A Study in British Trade Union History: Attempts at General Union, 1818-1834*, Macmillan & Co., London, 1953.

G. G. Coulton, *The Medieval Village*, Cambridge University Press, 1925.

Barbara Drake, *Women in Trade Unions*, Labour Research Dept., London, 1920.

J. L. and L. B. Hammond, *The Village Labourer* and *The Town Labourer*, 2 vols, Longmans, Green & Co., London, 1949, for the British Publishers Guild Ltd.

The Skilled Labourer, 1760-1832, Longmans Green & Co., London, 1920.

Christopher Hill, *The Century of Revolution,* Nelson, London, 1961.

E. H. Lipson, *Economic History of England*, A. & C. Black, London, 1947.

Ramsay MacDonald, ed., *Women in the Printing Trades*, P. S. King & Son, London, 1904.

Wanda F. Neff, *Victorian Working Women*, Allen & Unwin, London, 1927.

Marion Phillips and William S. Tomkinson, *English Women in Life and Letters*, Humphrey Milford, London, 1926.

I. Pinchbeck, *Women Workers and the Industrial Revolution, 1750-1850*, F. Cass., London, 1969.

Doris Stenton, *The English Woman in History*, Allen & Unwin, London, 1957.

Dorothy Whitelock, *Beginnings of English Society*, Penguin edition, London, 1952.

For Further Study:

Sir Edward Baines, *History of the Cotton Manufacture in Great Britain, etc.*, H. Fisher & Co., London, 1835.

Mary Bateson, ed., *Records of the Borough of Leicester*, Leicester U.P., 1927.

Bland, Brown, and Tawney, *English Economic Documents*, G. Bell & Sons, London, 1914.

Sir Sidney John Chapman, *The Cotton Industry and Trade*, Methuen & Co., London, 1905.

F. Collins, *Register of the Freemen of the City of York,* Surtees Soc., vol. 96, 1897.

Daniel Defoe, *Tour through the whole of Great Britain*, Peter Davies, London, 1927.

Everybody's Business is Nobody's Business, T. Warner, London, 1725.

Early English Text Society, *Roll of the Court of the City of London.*

Sir F. M. Eden, *State of the Poor*, F. Cass, London, 1966.

W. Felkin, *History of Machine-Wrought Hosiery and Lace Manufacturers*, London, 1867.

F. W. Galton, *The Tailoring Trade,* London School of Economics, 1896.

D. George, *London Life in the 18th Century*, G. Routledge & Son, London, 1931.

Mary D. Harris, *The Ancient Records of the City of Coventry*, Dugdale Society Occasional Papers 1, Stratford-upon-Avon, 1924.

   Company and Fellowship of the Cappers and Feltmakers of Coventry, Cornwall Press, London and Coventry, 1921.

   Coventry Leet Book and Mayors' Register, Early English Text Society, vols 134, 135, 138, 146.

Henry Hartopp, ed., *Register of the Freemen of Leicester 1196-1770*, Leicester U.P., 1927.

W. Marshall, *Rural Economy of the West of England*, E. Niev, ed., David & Charles, Newton Abbot, 1970.

James Myles, *Chapters in the Life of a Dundee Factory Boy,* John Scott, Dundee, 1951 ed.

Maud Sellers, ed., *York Memorandum Books*, Surtees Soc. vols 120 and 125, 1920.

   The York Mercers and Merchant Adventurers, 1356-1957, Surtees Soc., vol. 129, 1918.

Samuel Sholl, *A Short Historical Account of the Silk Manufacture in England,* 1811.

R. H. Tawney and E. Power, ed., *Tudor Economic Documents*, Longman & Co., London, 1951.

A. H. Thomas, ed., *Calendar of Early Mayors' Court Rolls*, by order of the Corporation of London, 1924.

F. Warburton, *History of Trade Union Organisation in the North Staffordshire Potteries*, Allen & Unwin, London, 1931.

Sir Frank Warner, *Silk Industry of the United Kingdom*, Drane, London, 1921.

S. and B. Webb, *History of Trade Unionism*, Longman & Co., London, 1920.

H. B. Wheatley, ed., *Diary of Samuel Pepys,* George Bell and Sons Ltd, London, 1906.

Arthur Young, *A Six Months' Tour through the North of England,* 2nd ed., 1771.

Pamphlets (The British Library):

'The Weavers' True Case 1719', W. Wilkins, London.

'Petition of the Leicester Worsted Spinners', 1788, British Museum Tracts, B.544 (10).

J. Ridgway, 'On Combinations of Trades', London, 1831.

E. Henry Tufnell, 'The Character, Objects and Effects of Trade Unions', 1834.

Newspapers:

The *Francis Place Papers*	The *Pioneer*
The *Leeds Mercury*	The *Poor Man's Guardian*
The *Leeds Patriot*	The *True Sun*
The *Manchester Mercury*	The *Voice of the People*

Government Publications:

1833 House of Commons Committee Report on Factories
1833 House of Commons Select Committee on Manufactures,
    Report and Evidence
1834 Supplementary Report of the Factory Commissioners.
1840 Report of the Commission on the State of the Handloom Weavers
1842 Report of the Royal Commission on Mines

Chapters 4-11
For the General Reader

Margaret Bondfield, *A Life's Work*, Hutchinson, London, 1951.
C. J. Bundock, *The National Union of Printing, Bookbinding and Paper Workers*, Oxford, 1959.
H. A. Clegg, *General Union*, Oxford, 1954.
John Corbett, *History of the Birmingham Trades Council, 1866-1966*, Lawrence and Wishart, London, 1966.
A. Fox, *History of the National Union of Boot and Shoe Operatives 1874-1957*, NUBSO/Blackwell, 1958.
R. M. Fox, *Louie Bennett: Her Life and Times*, Talbot Press, Dublin, 1958.
R. Fulford, *Votes for Women*, Faber, London, 1957.
M. A. Hamilton, *Mary Macarthur*, 1925; *Margaret Bondfield*, 1924.
H. Goldman, *Emma Paterson, Her Life and Times*, TUC, 1974.
R. Groves, *Sharpen the Sickle*, Porcupine Press, London, 1948.
P. C. Hoffman, *They also Serve*, USDAW, London, 1949.
Betty V. Humphreys, *Clerical Unions in the Civil Service*, Blackwell, Oxford, 1958.
B. L. Hutchins, *Women in Modern Industry*, Bell, London, 1915.
R. Jenkins, *Sir Charles Dilke,* Collins, London, 1965.
S. Levenson, *James Connolly,* Martin, Brian & O'Keeffe, London, 1973.
S. Pankhurst, *The Suffragette Movement*, Longman & Co., London, 1931.
Marion Phillips, ed., *Women in the Labour Party*, Labour Party, London, 1918
Ernest Selley, *Village Trade Unions in Two Centuries*, Allen & Unwin, London, 1919.
M. Stewart and L. Hunter, *The Needle is Threaded*, N.U. Tailors and Garment-Workers, 1964.
R. H. Tawney, *The Establishment of Minimum Rates in the Chain-making Industry*, London School of Economics and Political Science, Ratan Tata Foundation, 1914.
E. P. Thompson and E. Yeo, *The Unknown Mayhew*, Merlin Press, London, 1971.
S. and B. Webb, *Industrial Democracy*, Longman & Co., London, 1920.
Nora Vynne and Helen Blackburn, *Women Under the Factory Acts*, Williams and Norgate, London, 1903.

For Further Study

A. Fox, H. A. Clegg & A. F. Thompson, *History of British Trade Unionism since 1889,* Clarendon Press, Oxford, 1964.
M. A. Hamilton, *Women at Work,* Routledge, London, 1941.
M. Phillips, ed., *Women in The Labour Party,* Labour Party, 1918.

Dorothy Sells, *The British Trade Boards System*, London, 1923.
   British Wages Boards, Washington, D.C., 1939.
H. A. Silverman, ed., *Studies of Industrial Organisation*, Methuen & Co.,
   London, 1946.
Ben Turner, *A Short Account of the Rise and Progress of the Heavy Woollen District
   Branch of the General Union of Textile Workers*, National Union of Textile
   Workers, 1917.

Pamphlets

Mary Merryweather, 'Experience of Factory Life', 1862 (Brit. Lib.)
Lady (Emilia F.) Dilke, 'Trade Unions for Women', 1892, the *North American
   Review* (reprint of Article).
B. Webb, 'The Wages of Men and Women: Should they be
   Equal?', Fabian Tracts, 1919.
B. L. Hutchins, 'Home Work & Sweating: The Causes and the Remedies',
   Fabian Tracts, London, 1918.
Irish Transport and General Workers' Union, 'Fifty Years of Liberty Hall,
   Golden Jubilee, 1909-1959', Three Candles Press, Dublin, 1959.

Newspapers and Journals

The *Beehive*
Cotton Factory Times
Household Words, Charles Dickens, ed.
The *Printers' Register*
The *Weavers' Journal* (Glasgow)
The *English Woman's Review*
The *Women's Trade Union Review*
The *Shop Assistant*

The *Economic Journal*
The *Woman Worker*
The *Irish Worker*
The *Nottingham Review*
The *Dundee Argus*
The *Dundee Courier*
The *Daily News*

Transactions and Annual Reports of the National Association for the
   Promotion of Social Science

Articles

K. G. Busbey, 'The Women's Trade Union Movement in Great Britain',
   Bulletin of the U.S. Dept. of Labor Statistics, No. 83, July 1909.
Gladys Boone. 'The Women's Trade Union League in Great Britain', U.S.
   State Dept., N.Y., Columbia Press, 1942.
C. Saunders, 'The London Millinery Trade', 'Seasonal Trades', S. Webb,
   ed., 1912.

Trade Union Reports

TUC Annual Reports from 1868
Scottish TUC Annual Reports from 1897
Minutes of Scottish TUC Parliamentary Committee/General Council
Women's Trade Union League Reports
Women's Protective and Provident League/Scottish Council for Women's
   Trades Reports on Working Conditions in various Trades
Unpublished Correspondence between the TUC General Council and
   members of the Women's Trade Union League Executive
National Federation of Women Workers' Reports

The Gertrude Tuckwell Papers, TUC Library

Government Publications
Board of Trade Reports
Ministry of Labour Reports
1944 Royal Commission on Equal Pay, Minutes of Evidence and Report

Chapters 12-16
For the General Reader

F. J. Bayliss, *British Wages Councils*, Blackwell, Oxford, 1962.
Joan Beauchamp, *Women who Work*, Lawrence & Wishart, London, 1937.
J. B. Douglas, *The Home and the School*, MacGibbon & Kee, London, 1964.
V. Klein, *Britain's Married Women Workers*, London, 1964.
Margaret Morris, *The British General Strike*, Hist. Ass. Pamphlet G82, 1973.
Margery Spring Rice, *Working Class Wives*, Penguin, London, 1939.
F. Zweig, *A Woman's Life and Labour*, Pelican, London, 1952.

For Further Study

Story of the ETU, The Electrical Trades Union, Hayes, Kent, 1952.
H. J. Fyrth and H. Collins, *The Foundry Workers*, Manchester, 1959.
J. Hallsworth, *Protective Legislation for Shop and Office Employees*, London, 1939.
E. Howe & H.E. Waite, *The London Compositors,* London Soc. of Compositors, 1948.
F. Hughes, *By Hand and By Brain*, Clerical and Administrative Workers' Union, Lawrence & Wishart, London, 1953.
W. Hannington, *Never on our Knees*, Lawrence & Wishart, London, 1967.
J. Moran, *NATSOPA, Seventy-five years,* NATSOPA, Oxford, 1964.
New Survey of London Life and Labour, London School of Economics, 1930-32.
A. Spoor, *White Collar Union*, National Association of Local Government Officers, London, 1967.

Pamphlets
Central Office of Information, 'Women in Britain', No.R4498, 1960.
Equal Pay Campaign Committee, 'A Black Record'.
'Fact' Pamphlet Series, R Postgate ed., 'Conditions in the Catering Industry, 1938'.
C. W. Gibson, 'Sweating in the Catering Industry', Workers' Union, 1925.
T. W. Cynog Jones, 'The Regulation of Wages in the Retail Trade, 1937-57', USDAW, 1958.
M. Phillips, 'Story of the Women's Committee for the Relief of Miners and their Children', Labour Publishing Co., 1927.
Pauline Pinder, 'Women at Work', PEP, vol. XXXV, Broadsheet 512, May 1969, 593-4, 598.
Confederation of British Industry, 'Employing Women', 1967.

Newspapers and Journals
Labour Woman
Red Tape

The *Shop Assistant*
New Dawn
NUGMW *Journal*

The *Clerk*   *The Times*
The *Garment Worker*   The *Manchester Guardian/Guardian*

Trade Union Reports etc.

TUC Reports of the 1925, 1926, and 1927 Conference of Unions Enrolling
   Women
Unpublished Reports of the 1930-35 TUC Conference of Unions Enrolling
   Women
TUC National Women's Advisory Committee/Conference Reports 1936
TUC Industrial Newsletter for Women, 1930, 1939, 1940-62
Scottish TUC Organisation of Women Committee/National Women's
   Advisory Committee Reports, 1926
TUC Women's Group 'Methods of Organising Women', 1923
TUC Domestic Servants' Charter
TUC Nurses' Charter
Reports of the Annual Conference of the Federation of Trades Councils
Annual Reports of: National Union of Vehicle Builders, Pottery Workers,
   Union of Shop, Distributive and Allied Workers, Hosiery Workers'
   Union, etc.
Union Rule Books, Registry of Friendly Societies
Irish TUC: Reports of 1934 and 1935
Irish Women Workers' Union 19th Annual Report, 1935-36

Government Publications

Reports of the Chief Inspector of Factories
Report of the War Cabinet Committee on Women's Employment, 1919
Committee on Women in Agriculture Report, 1919
Ministry of Reconstruction Committee on Domestic Service Report, 1919
Cave Committee Report on Trade Boards, 1922
Ministry of Labour Report on the Supply of Female Domestic Servants, 1923
Ministry of Labour Report into Training and Apprenticeship, 1925-26 etc.
Ministry of Labour Gazette/Dept. of Employment and Productivity Gazette
K. S. Isles and N. Cuthbert, *An Economic Survey of Northern Ireland*, Belfast, 1957.
Report of the Royal Commission on Trade Unions and Employers'
   Associations, 1968, Cmnd. 3623.
Government Social Survey, 'A Survey of Women's Employment', Audrey
   Hunt, vol. 1, Report SS 379, 1968, etc.

Articles

Janet M. Hooks, U S Dept of Labor Women's Bureau, 'British Policies and
   Methods of Employing Women in War-time', 1944.
Hotel Review, 1930, 'The Catering Labour Exchange'.

Theses

L. Davidoff, *Employment of Married Women in England, 1850-1950,* University of
   London.
S. Lewenhak, *Trade Union Membership among Women and Girls in the United
   Kingdom, 1920-65,* University of London.

Index

Abbot, Mrs Margaret 275
Aberdeen 62, 71, 77, 88
Abraham, May (Mrs Tennant) 75
Adam, Nancy 208, 260
Aethelbert, 1
agencies (fee-paying) 263
agents provocateurs 29, 153
Agricultural Boards 232
Agricultural Labourers, Nat. Un. of 83-4
Agricultural Workers' Safety, Health and Welfare Provisions Act 275
Agricultural Workers' Un. 275
agricultural workers' unions 131, 166
agriculture, decline in women's work 186
Anderson, Will 130, 155, 164; 172
Anglo-Saxons 1, 2, 291
Anti-Combination Acts 21, 31
Anti-Sex Discrimination Act, 1976 292
Anti-Sweating League 120-1
apprenticeship 23, 147, 236, 277, 278
Approved Socs. of trade unions 131, 169
Ashley, Lord (Anthony Ashley Cooper, later 7th Earl of Shaftesbury) 54-5, 57, 61
Assistant Commissioners: Board of Trade 80; Royal Commission on Labour, 1891-94 102; see also Irwin
Assocn. of Card and Blowing Room Operatives 89, 135
Assocn. of Cine and Television Technicians 255, 258
attitudes to work 266

Baker, H.A. 292
Bakers: Nat. Federal Union of 139; Amalgamated Un. of Operative 156
Baldwin, Stanley 185, 195
Bank Employees, Nat. Un. of 221, 260, 262
banking, insurance, and finance 217, 282
Barker, John, Ltd 177
Bartholomew Anglicus 2-3
Battle, Jim 149-50
Beamers, Twisters and Drawers-in, Amal. Assocn. of 97
Beard, John 156
Beatrice, Princess 119
Becker, Lydia 134
Bedaux system, 212-14
Belfast 85-6, 200
Bell, Mary, see Richards
bell-founders 6
Bennett, Louie 159, 228
Berlin Sweated Industries Exhibition 119
Bermondsey strike wave, 1911 133, 192
Besant, Annie 79-80, 89
Beveridge, William 131, 244, 256
Bevin, Ernest 199, 221, 232, 236-7, 239, 240, 244, 246, 249, 250, 277
Bezzant, Beatrice 230
Birkenhead 77
Birmingham 52, 122, 124, 125, 140, 153, 178, 292; see also Friendly and Benefit Societies; strikes; Trade Boards; engineering; Varley, Julia; Workers' Un.
Biscuit Operatives (Dublin), Guild of Female 156
Black, Clementina 77, 91, 101, 119
Black Country, see Chain-makers

Black Death 3
Blackburn 51, 57
blacklegs 29, 35-6, 50
Blacklock, Isabella 106
Blake, Fred E. 286
Blanesburgh Committee Rep., 1927 195, 199
Bloody Sunday (13 Nov. 1887) 79
Board of Health and miners' lock-out, 1926 193
Board of Trade 120, 121, 132
Boards of Guardians 184
Bolton 89, 149, 151; see also strikes
bondaging 158
Bondfield, Margaret 95-6, 106, 117, 129, 155, 161, 164, 168, 170, 172, 174, 177, 187, 191, 192, 193, 199, 200, 201, 240
bondservants and unfree women 2, 3
bookbinders 26, 47-8, 70-1
Bookbinders and Machine Rulers, Nat. Un. of 156
Bookbinding and Printing, Manchester and Salford Soc. of 116
boot and shoe makers 30, 52, 53, 77, 217
Boot and Shoe Operatives, Nat. Un. of 89, 117, 170, 179
Booth, Charles 85, 118
Bowerman, C.W. 173, 175
Box Clubs, see Friendly and Benefit Societies
Bramley, Fred 161, 173, 174, 189, 191
brass (cast) trade 179, 272
Brass and Metal Workers, Nat. Un. of 132, 139
brick-making 217
Bridges-Adams, Mrs 118
Bristol 5, 70-1
British Medical Assocn. 231
British Specialist Party 164
Broadhurst, Henry 72, 76
Brown, John 104
Brown, Maud 181, 201
Brown, Miss 85-6
Brush-makers' Nat. Soc. of 156
Bunning, Stuart 172, 173
Burnham Committee (teaching) 171
Burns, John 89, 93-4
Burrows, A. 237
Burrows, Herbert 80, 89, 98, 119
Burton-on-Trent 201
bus conductresses 289-90
Butler, Josephine 95
Butler, Joyce 282, 286, 287, 291
Butler, R.A. 253

Calender Workers' Un., Dundee 139
Campaign for Nuclear Disarmament 271-2
cap-makers 5
Card and Box-makers' Un. 125
Card, Blowing and Ring-room Operatives, Assocn. of 89, 135
Care of Children of Working Mothers 275, 290
Carlin, Mary 189, 202, 231
Carney, Winifred 136, 159
carpet weavers 30, 92, 156-7, 258
Carson, George 106, 107
Castle, Barbara 284, 285, 286
Cave Committee Rep., 1922 177
Central Committee for Women's Training and Employment, 144-5, 160, 168-9, 182
Central Electricity Generating Authority, Girls' apprenticeships 277

Chain-makers' and Strikers' Un.
  122, 124
Chain-making Trade Board 123-5
Chartism 45
cheese-maker 2
Chemical Workers' Un. 186
chemicals 217
Children's Employment
  Commission, 1862-66 61
Chipchase, Ethel 271, 275, 288
Churchill, Winston 121, 131, 154,
  247
Cigar Makers, Nat. Un. of 93
Cigarette-Makers' Un. 119
Circular L2 153-4
Citrine, Walter 199, 205, 208, 218,
  221, 223
Civil Servants, Federation of
  (women) 170
Civil Servants, Nat. Assocn. of
  Women 253
Civil Service Alliance of Trade
  Unions 94, 116-17, 158, 162, 170,
  223, 225, 229, 253, 266, 279
Civil Service Clerical Assocn., 225,
  229, 253, 254, 267
Civil Service Typists' Assocn. 116
Civil Service Un. 279
Clarendon Press, Oxford 77
Clarion 77
clay industry 179
Clerical and Administrative
  Workers' Un. 267, 272
clerical work of women 217, 263
Clerical Workers, Nat. Un. of 116,
  166, 170, 224
clerical workers' uns. 94
Clerks, Board of Trade Women
  116-17
Clerks, Federation of Women 117
Clerks and Secretaries, Assocn. of
  Women 223, 224, 226
clothiers 10, 11
Clothiers' Operatives, Un. of 131
clothing trades 217; see also Tailors;
  Tailoresses; hosiery
Clydeside 146, 148, 153, 154, 167
Clynes, J.R. 161, 172, 187
Coal Mines Regulation Act, 1885
  74
coalmining 25, 54, 164
Cobden Sanderson, Anne 130
Cohen, Leonora 172
Combinations of Trades 23, 27,
  29-30; see also demonstrations;
  strikes
Communist Manifesto 111
competition for work 24, 25, 26,
  39, 40, 139, 258
Conciliation Boards 132
Conditions of Home Work Act 81
confectionery trade 122, 125, 186
Confederation of British
  Industries 282, 284
Conley, Andrew 140, 233
Connolly, James 130, 135-6, 138,
  159
Conspiracy and Protection of
  Property Act 84
Conspiracy Laws 21
Contagious Diseases Acts 53, 95
Cooper, Miss 189
Co-operative Employees, Amal.
  Un. of 157, 224
Co-operative employers 223-4, 237
Corn Production Act, 1917 186
Corruganza strike 130
cotton trades 54, 57-8, 144, 201-2,
  217, 263-4
Coulson, Edwin 71
County Councils and equal pay
  249
County Officers, Nat. Un. of 230-1
Courtaulds 59-60
Cousins, Frank 287
Coventry 153, 178
Cradley Heath 123-5

crèches 59, 60
Crees, Miss M. 234
Crewe, Lady 145
Criminal Law Amendment Act,
  1871 56, 83
Cripps, Sir Stafford 251
Cromwell, Oliver 14, 31
Cross, J. 132, 140
Crowe, Jane 61
Crowther Rep. 278

Daily Herald 165, 192
Daily News 79, 119
dairymaid 2
Dalton, Hugh 247, 251
Davies, Rhys 211-12
Davis, W.J. 73
Dawson, Julia 77
Dawtry, W.F. 132
day nurseries 59-60, 215, 255-6,
  265, 275, 290, 292
deductions and fines 139
Defoe, Daniel 32
demonstrations and protests 10,
  14, 15-16, 16-17, 21-2, 22-3, 29,
  30, 36, 50, 52; see also strikes
Derby 30, 35-6
Dickens, Charles 52, 60
Dilke, Sir Charles 70, 79, 120
Dilke, Emilia 70, 71, 75, 77, 91,
  115, 122
Disraeli, Benjamin 45, 84
distribution 186, 226, 232, 263
Distributive and Allied Workers,
  Nat. Un. of 177-8, 188, 237
Distributive and Allied Workers,
  Un. of Shop, 267, 272, 274, 279
Dock, Wharf, Riverside and
  General Labourers' Un. 91,
  93, 132, 167
dockers, organization of 89
Doherty, John 35, 38
Domestic Servants' Unions 181,
  182, 206-7, 230
domestic service 9, 31-2, 182-3,
  184-5, 203, 207, 230, 245, 246,
  262-3
Doyle, R. 215
Drapers' Chamber of Trade 177
Draughtsmen, Assocn. of
  Engineering and Shipbuilding
  188, 256
Dressmakers' London Soc. of 70-1
Dublin 30; see also Irish Transport
  and General Workers' Un.;
  Easter Rising
Duncan, Joe F. 194, 204
Dundee Jute and Flax Workers
  87-8, 117, 217
Dunning, T.J. 48
Dyers' and Finishers' Assocn.,
  Bolton Amal. 97

Easter Rising, Dublin 159
Edgar, Mrs E. 284
Edinburgh Maidservants' Un.
  Soc., 1825 32-3, 183
Edinburgh Upholsterers' Sewers'
  Soc., 1872 63
Edinburgh Women's
  Typographical Soc. 61
Education Acts 95, 245-6, 277
education of girls 246, 276-8
Edwards, Miss K. 260
eight-hour day 106, 139
Electrical Trades Un. 156, 186,
  254, 257, 262
electrical work for women 185-6,
  217
Elger, William 194, 204
Elliott, Dorothy 187, 207, 221, 223,
  227, 230, 235-6, 237, 239, 246
Ellis, Ann 86, 92
Elvin, George 255
Emancipation of women
  campaign 94-5
emigration 57-9

employers' support for trade
    unions 29; attitudes to Trade
    Boards 122-3; unions' co-
    operation with 267; breakdown
    of co-operation 271-2; dislike of
    equal pay 280; against
    protection for women
    workers 291
employment for women: growth
    of 185-6, 217; shortage of
    workers, post-1945 244-5; Min.
    of Labour miscalculations on
    246; reasons for growth of
    white-collar work 252;
    low-graded work and labour
    turnover 264
Employment of Women, Young
    Persons and Children Act 211,
    212
Employment Protection Act 292
enclosures 9
engineering, women's work in
    185, 217, 282, 284-6
engineering employers, 141, 156,
    178-79; see also Anti-
    Combination Acts; Ramsay
Engineering Un., Amal. 225, 237,
    240, 254, 257, 278, 282
Engineers, Amal. Soc. of 83, 151,
    152-3
English Woman's Journal 61
Englishwoman's Review 69
equal pay 26, 33, 35, 39, 89-90, 91,
    111, 144, 149, 151, 154, 157,
    170-1, 194, 223 ff, 227, 229, 234,
    236 f, 238, 246, 247, 248, 249,
    250-1, 287-8
Equal Pay Act 1970 289
Equal Pay Bill 285-6
Equal Pay Campaign Committees
    236, 253, 286
equality, struggle for 247
European Economic Community
    279-80
Evans 125
Evans, Dorothy 188
Evans, Lincoln 251
evening schools 60
Evershed Committee Rep. on
    spinning, 1945 263-4
exclusion of Women from work
    26-7, 38-9, 41, 42-3, 53

Fabians and 'swearing' 118
Factories, Reports of Chief
    Inspector of, 235, 256-7
Factory Acts, 73-4, 97, 155; 1st
    23-4; 2nd 30; 3rd and 4th 33;
    1844-67 Acts 55; 1895 Act 81;
    1937 234, 239, 245
Factory Inspectorate, 55, 75, 257
Factories and Workshops Bill 69,
    72-3
Faithfull, Emily 61, 67, 101
family as work unit 8, 24, 41
Fawcett, Millicent 74
federations of unions 132
Felkin, William 24, 29-30
Felt-hat Trimmers 93
Felt-hatters, Journeymen 93
Females of Todmorden 30-1, 40,
    54
Fenwick, Margaret 278
feudal tenures 2
fire service, 249
Foley, Alice, 258, 260, 266
Ford Women Machinists' 284-6
Foundry Workers, Amal. Un. of
    240, 257, 275
Foyles, 274
freewomen 5
Friendly and Benefit Socs. 18-20,
    21, 22, 46, 56, 84-5
furniture, women's work in 217

Galway, Mary 86, 135-6
Gardiner, A.G. 119

Gas, Municipal and General
    Workers, Amal. Soc. of 178
Gas Workers and General
    Labourers, Un. of 89, 146
General Strike, 1926 192, 195, 199
General and Municipal Workers,
    Nat. Un. of 195, 207, 221, 224,
    226, 237, 240, 289-90
General Workers, Nat. Un. of 161,
    171, 172, 186-7
gilds 5-6
Gilroy, Agnes 210
girls' dislike of trade unions 265
Gladstone Committee 162
Glasgow Council for Women's
    Trades 101
Glasgow United Trades Council
    101-3, 133, 194
glass, women's work in 217
Gloucester 6, 14, 15, 93
Godwin, Anne 221-2, 250, 255,
    271-2, 278
Gordon, Nelly 136
Gosling, Harry 175
grading at work 24-5
Grand National Consolidated
    Trades Union 37, 43, 45, 73
Green, Mrs L. 262
Grimsby 77
Grotier, Lil 209, 280
Gunter, Ray 282-4

Halstead 117
Hancock, Florence 221, 223, 235,
    237, 240, 249-50, 271
Handkerchief-hemmers, Un. of
    103
Handloom Weavers 13, 49
half-time system, textiles 139
Hallas, Eldred 178-9
Hat-makers, London Soc. of 71
Head, W.H. 61
Health of Munitions Workers
    Committee 160
Henderson, Arthur 121, 148, 153
Henshall, Miss 93
hiring fairs 4
Hodges, Frank 195
Hodgson Pratt, Mr and Mrs 70
Holidays with Pay, union pressure
    for and Act 232
Holmes, Arthur 195
Home Rule for Ireland 138
Home-work 8, 9, 292; see also
    sweating; Glasgow United
    Trades Council; Irwin;
    Macarthur
Horan, Alice 208-9, 221, 236-7,
    267
Horne, Sir Robert 166
hosiery 23, 24, 29-30, 89, 92, 213;
    see also Mason
hours of work 106, 210-11, 231,
    234, 235-6, 244-5; see also
    Factory Acts
House of Commons, Select
    Committee on Home Work
    120
House of Lords: Rep. on
    Sweating, 85; Osborne
    Judgement, 134; Select
    Committee on Early Closing of
    Shops, 1901 111
House Workers, Inst. of, 1947 246
Howse, Miss E.H. 188-9, 191
Hume, Joseph 31
Hunger Marches 181, 200
Hunt, Audrey 286, 291
Hunt, H.M. 71-2

immigration from rural to factory
    areas 51
Independent Labour Party 106,
    164
Industrial Courts 167, 171

Industrial Health, campaign for
    291
Industrial Training Act, 1964 278
Industrial Training Boards 278
Ine 1-2
Infants Custody Act 95
Insurance Officials, Guild of 221
International Assocn. for Labour
    Legislation 98, 191
International Conference on
    Protection for Women
    Workers, 1890 97
International Fed. of Working
    Women 191
International Labour Congress 98,
    169
International Labour Office 169;
    Convention on Maternity, 1919
    170, 216; Convention on
    restricted shiftwork 211;
    Montevideo Convention 1933
    212
International Labour
    Organization: Conference
    250-1; Convention 100 252,
    279-80; *Women Workers in a
    Changing World* 290
International Women's Year 291
International Working Women's
    Bureau 170
Ireland, Conditions of
    Employment Bill 228-9
Irens, Frances 169
Irish Transport and General
    Workers' Un. 135-8
Irish TUC opposition to
    Conditions of Employment
    Bill 227-8
Irish Women Workers'
    Co-operative Soc. 159
Irish Women Workers' Un. 135-8,
    159, 228
Irish Worker 137
Iron and Steel Trades Confed. 97
Ironfounding Workers' Assocn.240
ironmongers 5, 6
Irwin, Margaret H. 101, 102-8,
    110-11, 114, 119, 134, 161, 194
Isaacs, George 252

Jancy, W.E. 140
Jobson, Bell 194, 203, 210
Johnson, Marie 136
Joint Committee on Women's
    Wages and Working Conditions
    155, 160
Joint Industrial Councils 154, 232,
    282
Joint Industrial Courts 161, 168
Jones, Miss B.G. 251
Jones, Miss D.E.K. 251
Journalists, Nat. Un. of 157
journeywomen and men 13
Juggins, Mr 91, 122
Junta 56, 57
Jute, Flax and Kindred Textile
    Operatives, Un. of 117, 215, 278
juvenile labour 226

Kay, James Phillip 30-1
Keir, John 105
Keir Hardie, James 106
Kenney, Annie 135
Kershaw, Harry 215
Kettell, Lily 213, 267
Kilbirnie 110, 133
King, H.R. 70, 73
Kingsley, Charles 70
Knox, John 11
Knox, Pat 253

Labour Advisory Committee 147,
    148
Labour governments 185,
    199-200, 244, 246, 247-8, 251,
    280, 282, 284, 286-7

Labour Party 109, 118, 134, 164,
    195-6, 218, 221, 223-4, 229, 252,
    280
Labour Party Women's Group
    173, 188-9, 207, 252
Labour Representation
    Committee 106
Labour Review 69
Labour Supply Committee 153,
    160
lace-makers 23, 48-9, 122
Lansbury, George 119
Larkin, Delia 135-8, 159
Larkin, James 135-7
laundresses 76, 106, 166, 211
Lawrence, Susan 115-16, 129, 174,
    178, 192
Lawson, F.W. 140
Leeds 33
Leggett, Sir Frederick 232
Legrand, Daniel 97
Leicester 16-17, 128
Leonard, William 194
Lever Bros. 211
Lib.-Lab. Alliance 56, 106
Liberal Party 118, 134
Liddell, Isa 103
Liverpool 77
Lloyd George, David 131, 146,
    148, 153-5, 165
local authorities 215, 226, 230-1,
    252-3, 282
Local Government Officers, Nat.
    Assocn of 170, 227, 249, 253-5
Loco. Engineers and Firemen,
    Assocn. of 224
London Council, City of 8, 9, 31-2,
    128
London, strikes in 30, 133, 192
London County Council 226, 229,
    249, 252-3
London County Council Staff
    Assocn. 170, 225, 226, 229, 252
London Soc. of Compositors 89
London Trades Council 208, 236,
    262
Londonderry 217
Loughlin, Anne 189, 194, 208, 221,
    223, 233, 235, 240, 248-9, 255,
    271
Lucas Ltd 213-14
Luckhurst, Mr 149
Luddites 23, 26, 31

Macarthur, Mary 114, 115, 119,
    120-1, 124, 129, 131, 132, 144-5,
    148, 152-3, 154-5, 157, 160,
    164-5, 170, 172-4, 192, 203, 216,
    264; *see also* Nat. Fed. of
    Women Workers; Women's
    Trade Un. League
McCullough, Ellen 271
Macdonald, Annie 166-7, 190
Macdonald, Edith 191
MacDonald, James Ramsay
    119-20, 164, 199, 200
MacDonald, Margaret 129
McKaig, Miss E. 267, 272
Mackay, Margaret 260, 271, 272
Mackinder, William 211-12
McLean, Kate 109-10
Macleod, Iain 278
Macnamara, T.J. 171, 177
Mallon, J.J. 120, 174
Manchester and Salford Trades
    Council 56, 76, 134
Manchester Women's Trades and
    Labour Council 134
Mann, Thomas 89, 130
Manor House Hospital 216, 256,
    273
Markham, Violet 175
Markiewicz, Countess 137-8
Marriage and Divorce Act, 1857 95
marriage bar 41, 51, 94, 216, 225-6,
    265, 292
Marriage Dowry 94, 226, 265

married women workers 185, 201, 206, 225, 231, 245, 256, 265-6, 277
married women's property 1, 2, 95
Martin, Mrs 210
Martineau, Harriet 70
Marx, Eleanor 89, 92
Marx, Karl 56
Mary, Queen 144-5, 174
Mary Macarthur Convalescent Homes 174, 216, 256
Mason, Mrs 73-4
mass media 247, 272, 290
matchmakers 74, 79-80
maternal mortality, campaign against 214-15
Maternity and Child Welfare Act 169
maternity leave 98, 170, 216
Matrimonial Causes Act, 1884 95
Matrimonial Proceedings and Property Act, 1970 290-1
Maxwell, Sir John 79
Mayhew, Henry 53
medical services 217
Merryweather, Mary 59-60, 275
Metropolitan Water Board 249
Mewhort, Grace 194
Mineau, Joan 260
Miners, Nat. Un. of 254, 258
Miners' Fed. of Gt Britain 74, 132, 135, 139, 140, 148, 193, 200
minimum wage: for all 125, 140; for men only 140; for women only 149; see also Trade Boards
Ministry of Munitions 148, 154, 155
Molony, Helen 138, 159
Mond, Alfred 121, 168, 199
Money, L. Chiozza 119
More Looms strike, 1932 201
Morrison, James 35
Munitions Committees 147
Munitions of War Bill and Act 148, 153, 154
Myrddin-Evans, Sir Guildhaume 252

Nat. Arbitration Tribunal 240
Nat. Assocn. for the Promotion of Social Science 55, 56, 58, 60, 61, 67, 70, 97
Nat. Assocn. for the Protection of Labour 35
Nat. Conciliation Board 237
Nat. Council of Labour Colleges 130, 204
Nat. Federal Council of Scotland for Women's Trades, see Scottish Council for Women's Trades
Nat. Federation of General Workers 160
Nat. Federation of Women Workers 109, 115, 116, 117, 124, 125, 126, 129, 132, 139, 144, 146, 152, 155, 157, 159, 160, 161, 162, 166, 172-3, 186, 188, 189, 195, 230
National Health Insurance 139, 169
Nat. Inst. of Industrial Psychology Survey 277
Nat. Insurance Bill and Act 131
Nat. Insurance Scheme (Beveridge) 244
Nat. Joint Action Campaign Committee for Equal Women's Rights 286
Nat. Labour Advisory Committee 154
Nat. Soc. of Metal Mechanics 272
Nat. Unemployed Workers' Movement 181, 200
Nat. Un. of Women Workers, Bristol 70-1
net-braiders and makers 77
Nettlefold, Miss L. 248-9

New York, Female Umbrella Makers' Un. of 68
New York Women's Typographical Soc. 68, 69
nine-hour day 83
Northcliffe, Lord 154
Northern Ireland uns. 217
Norwich poor 9, 14
Norwood, Chris 279, 286
Nottingham 23, 48-9
nursery schools 215, 255
nurses 230-1, 253
Nurses, Guild of 230-1

Odger, George 71
O'Grady, J. 133
Offices, Shops and Railway Premises Act, 1963 274
Old Age Pensions 139
Oldham 30, 57; see also strikes
Ordinance of Labourers 3
Organization of Women Committee 194-5, 203-5
Osborne Judgement 134
outwork 108, 292
overseas competition 85
Owen, Robert 23, 35

Page, Christine 279, 283, 291
Pankhurst, Sylvia 134, 135
Pannell, Charles 253
paper-boxmaking 122
paper-making 217
Paper Mill Workers' Un. 139
Paris Commune, 1870-71 56
Parkes, Bessie Rayner 61-7, 97
Parliamentary Reform Act, 1832 45
Particulars Clause 108
part-time workers 266-7
Paterson, Emma 67, 68, 69-70, 71, 72, 75, 101, 104, 107, 114, 139, 247
Paterson, Thomas 68
Paton, Brigid 272
Patterson, Marie 280, 288
pauper apprentices 16, 26
Peasants' Revolt 3-4
Pepys, Samuel 31
Phillips, Marion 115, 129, 182, 189, 192-3
Pickup, Irene 188
Pioneer 35, 37, 40, 41
Pipe-Finishers, Un. of Alva 103
Pirn-winders' Uns. 46-7
Place, Francis 31, 41, 52
Platt, Mrs 188
Poor Law, 1834 45
Poor Relief (Public Assistance) 202, 215, 230
Poplar councillors 180
population increase 51
Post Office 116
Potteries 78-9, 217
Potters' Uns. 53
Pottery Workers, Nat. Soc. of Male and Female 97
Pottery Workers, Nat. Un. of 166, 225
Poulton, E.L. 173, 175
Power Loom 17, 49; see also demonstrations; strikes
Power Loom Carpet Weavers and Textile Workers, Assocn. of 156-7, 258
Printers and Assistants, Nat. Soc. of Operative 62
Printers' Register 61
Printing, Bookbinding and Paper Workers, Nat. Un. of 182
printing work 61-2, 159, 212, 217, 288
production bonus 128, 214, 258
prostitution 53
Public Employees, Nat. Un. of 283
pubs 54-5, 209-10

Quaile, Mary 76
Queen's Work for Women Fund 145

Railway Servants, Amal. Soc. of 117, 132
Railwaymen, National Un. of 146, 156, 164, 168, 188, 206, 254
Ramsay, Sir Alexander 237, 238
rearmament and industrial growth 218, 221
Rest-Breaks Advisory Committee 239, 256
Restoration of Pre-War Practices Act 167
revaluation agreements 282
Reynolds News 208
Richards, Mary Bell 117, 166, 206
Richmond, Agnes 204
Right to Work Conference 130-1, 226-8
Robens, Alfred 281
Robins, Mrs Raymond 170
Roman Catholic Church 138
Rowntree of York 188
Royal College of Nursing 230
Royal Commission on Equal Pay 237, 247, 248, 289
Royal Commission on Labour, 1891-94 102-3
Royal Commission on Mines 25, 54
Royal Commission on Trade Uns, 1866-67 56
Royal Commission on Unemployment Insurance 199, 200
Runciman, Walter 146
Ruskin College 130, 204

St Paul 11
Salmon, Sir Eric 238
Scale-Makers, Nat. Un. of 240
Schoolmasters, Nat. Un. of 224
Scientific Instrument Makers 149
Scientific Workers, Assocn. of 283
Scottish Council for Women's Trades (Scottish Women's Trades Council) 105, 106, 108, 109, 110, 111
Scottish Farm Servants' Un. 158
Scottish TUC 104, 108, 193-4, 204-5, 283
Scottish TUC Conference of Uns Enrolling Women 194, 203
Scottish TUC Women's Trade Union Committees 204
Scottish Typographical Assocn. 62, 101, 156
Shaw, George Bernard 119
Shears, Irene 272
sheepfarming 9, 10
Sheffield File Trades 53
shiftwork 234, 235-6, 244-5, 257, 287-8
Shinwell, Emanuel 109
Shipton, George 71
Shirt and Collar Makers 70
Shirtmakers, Manchester 76
Shoe-binders and Closers, General Un. of 41
Shop Assistant 202
Shop Assistants' Un. 211, 232
Shop Hours Act, 1906 81, 96
shop stewards 146, 188
Shops Act, 1934 211
Short-Time movement 53-5
Sickness Benefit, Departmental Committee on 169
silk (ribbon-loom weavers) 13, 14, 26, 30, 53
Silk Workers' Nat. Assocn. 156
Simcox, Edith 70-1, 72, 77, 247
Sitch, Charles H. 124-5
Slesser, Lady 192
Sloan, Isabel 149, 159
Smillie, Robert 105, 107, 109-10

Snowden, Philip 164
Social Democratic Federation 130
Socs. for Promoting Industrial Employment of Women 60-1
Southampton 6, 132, 258
Speed-up 212-14, 256-7, 263-4
Spinners, Grand General Un. of 38-9
spinners, mule 38-9, 188
spinning 8, 9, 10, 17
Spitalfields Acts 13
Standing Joint Committee of Working Women's Organizations 160, 249
Statute of Artificers 11
Statute of Labourers 4
Stead, W.T. 95
Steele, Miss D. 250
Stephen, Jessie 182
Stewart, Eleanor 227
Stockport 29, 50
Stocks, Helen 124
Stokes, R.E. 155-6
Straw-bonnet Makers, Grand Lodge of 41
strikes 29, 30, 42, 47-51, 110, 128, 130, 133-4, 136-7, 146, 148, 153-4, 167, 200-1, 231, 240-1, 244, 274, 284-5, 286
sub-contracting 6, 8, 25
substitution of women 145-7
suburbs 85
Sullivan, Miss 98
Summerskill, Edith 282
Sunderland Technical College 277
Sutton, Edith 275
Sweated Industries Exhibition 119-20
sweating 55, 118-19, 138
Symons, Madeleine 115, 172, 187, 192

Taff Vale dispute 117-18
Tailoresses, uns. of 62-3, 103, 119
Tailoring, Wholesale and Bespoke Trade Board 122
Tailors and Tailoresses, Amal. Soc. of 92, 103
Tailors, Company of 26-7, 38, 41-3, 52
Tailors and Garment Workers' Un., Amal. 166, 214; *see also* Loughlin
Tailors and Garment Workers, Nat. Un. of 233, 288-9
Talbot, Mabel 166
Tanners' gild 6
teachers 59, 94, 157, 247
Teachers, Nat. Un. of 116-17, 170
Teachers, Nat. Un. of Women 117, 223-4, 253
telephone operators 138
Tennant, H.J. 75, 119
Tewson, Vincent 205
textile unions 200, 221
Textile Workers, General Un. of 166
Thorne, Will 89, 172
Tillett, Ben 91, 131-2
Times 22, 84, 154-5
Tobacco Workers' Un. 258
Tolpuddle 37
Townsend, A. 188
Toye, Monica 283
Toynbee, Arnold 70
Trade Boards 126, 139, 154, 162, 168, 177-9, 210-11, 232
Trade Boards Act 121-2
Trade Union Acts: 1871 56, 83, 130; 1906 118
Trade Union Charter 131
Trade Union dues 264-5
trade union education for women 191, 203-4
trade union membership (women) 96-7, 133, 157, 161, 166, 177-9, 186, 191, 203, 216-17, 218, 233, 239-40, 245

Trade Union Officials, Assocn. of 117
Trade Union women's committee 207
Trade Union Women's Sections 156, 187-8, 190, 223, 257, 262, 272
trade union women's welfare 216, 272-3
trade unions as employers 223-4
trades, medieval 5-6
Trades Councils 56, 104, 141, 190, 193, 202, 208-9, 262, 291
Trades Disputes and Trade Unions Act, 1927 195, 196, 202, 229, 249
Trades Union Congress 56, 57, 73, 125, 138, 164, 172-4, 190, 200, 202, 218, 221, 231, 234, 236, 238, 246, 250-1, 282, 284, 285, 288, 291
Trades Union Congress, Conferences of Unions Enrolling Women 188-90, 193, 194, 205, 206-7
Trades Union Congress General Council 172-5, 191, 193, 199, 205-6, 207-8, 212, 216, 230, 234, 249, 252, 260, 273-4, 277, 278, 283, 285, 286
Trades Union Congress Nat. Women's Advisory Committee 205, 208, 221, 226, 230, 231, 234-5, 241, 255-6, 260, 262, 273-5, 278-9, 280, 290, 291
Trades Union Congress Women's Advisory Conference 218, 232-3, 234-5, 241, 250, 255, 258, 260, 273-4, 275, 276-8, 283, 288
Trades Union Congress Women's Charter: 1963 276, 286; 1975 291
Trades Union Congress Women's Group in General Council 173-4, 184, 186, 190-1, 205
transference of workers 231, 235
Transport and General Workers' Union 199, 204, 206, 207, 232, 237, 240, 250, 264, 279, 289-90
Transport Workers, Nat. Fed. of 132, 168
Treasury Agreement 148
Triple Alliance 168
Truck Act, 1896 81, 86
Tuckwell, Gertrude 70, 115, 118, 129, 131, 157, 168, 172, 173-5, 214-15
Turner, Ben 140, 168, 188, 199
Turner, John 114
Typographical Assocn. 61
Typographical Society 62
typographical societies 89

Unemployed Workers' Committees 180-1
Unemployment Insurance 180, 183-5, 195, 200, 202, 256
Upholstresses, London Soc. 70

vagabonds 10
Varley, Julia 124-5, 129, 135, 140, 141, 155-6, 175, 182, 184, 191, 199, 209, 210, 212, 240
Vaughan, Janet 248-9
Vehicle Builders, Nat. Un. of 249, 284-5
Vehicle Workers, United Soc. of 156
Vehicle Workers' Un., London and Provincial Licensed 157
Versailles Treaty 171, 252
Victoria, Queen 61, 84
Victoria Press 61
village unions 74

wages 5, 14, 15, 23, 32-3, 52, 92, 178-9, 236-9, 246, 280-3, 286-7

Wages Boards, Australia and New Zealand 120, 121
Wages Councils 232, 259, 281-2
Wages (Temporary) Regulation Act 167, 171
Walker, Helene 267
War Emergency Workers' Nat. Committee 144, 146, 147, 160
war injuries 238
war workers 145-7, 164-6, 235 ff
Ward, Irene 282
wars 27, 29, 30, 38, 144 ff, 235 ff
Watkins, J.T. 149
Weavers (cotton and synthetic fabrics) 258, 275
Weavers' Act, 1555 10
Weavers' Union, Bridgeton 103
Webb, Lily 201
Webb, Sidney and Beatrice 51, 120, 153-4, 169, 171
welfare, factory 59-60, 235-6, 239, 275
West of Scotland Power Loom Females' Soc. 33-4
Whewell, Miss M.A. 288
Whitley Committee 168
Whitley Council 229
Wigan Weavers' Assocn. 57, 140
Wild, Amy 210, 237
Wilkinson, Ellen 184-5, 189, 192, 208, 211-12, 223, 235
Williamson, Henry 88, 117
Williamson, Tom 223
Wilson, Harold 286-7
Wilson, Lizzie 117
Wilson, Mona 116, 117
Wolsey 213
Women and Young Persons Employment in Lead Processes Act 79
Women's Committee for Relief of Miners' Wives and Children 192-3
Women's Employment Committee 157, 162
Women's Industrial Council 118, 128
Women's Protective and Provident League 70-1, 75, 76; see also Irwin; Glasgow United Trades Council
women's suffrage 107-8, 134-5
Women's Suffrage Assocn. 67-8
Women's Trade Un. League 77, 78, 80, 83, 88, 91, 93, 101 117-19, 133, 144, 146, 157, 162, 173-5, 188-9, 191, 193, 203, 216, 230, 272
Women's Trade Union Review 78-80, 119-20
Women's Trades Councils 75, 76, 203
Woodworkers, Amal. Soc. of 257
Woolcombers, Amal. Soc. of 257
Woolcombers, Nat. Soc. of 97
woollen and worsted manufactures 10, 13-17, 51, 200, 263-4
Woollen Weavers Assocn., Dewsbury, Batley and Surrounding Districts Heavy 86-7, 92
Woolworths 211, 274
Workers' Union 141, 146, 155-6, 178, 199
Working Men's Club and Institute Union 67-8
Workmen's Compensation Acts 275
Worsted Small-ware Weavers' Assocn., Manchester 17

York bell-founders 5-6
Young, Arthur 39

Zugg, Mary 47-8

Set by Johel Printing Services Ltd, London
Printed in Great Britain by Cox & Wyman Ltd, London, Reading and Fakenham